GOVERNING GLOBAL TRADE

The G8 and Global Governance Series

Series Editor: John J. Kirton

The G8 and Global Governance Series explores the issues, the institutions, and the strategies of the participants in the G8 network of global governance, and other actors, processes, and challenges that shape global order in the twenty-first century. Many aspects of globalisation, once considered domestic, are now moving into the international arena, generating a need for broader and deeper international co-operation and demanding new centres of leadership to revitalise, reform, reinforce, and even replace the galaxy of multilateral institutions created in 1945. In response, the G8, composed of the world's major market democracies, including Russia and the European Union, is emerging as an effective source of global governance. *The G8 and Global Governance Series* focusses on the new issues at the centre of global governance, covering topics such as finance, investment, and trade, as well as transnational threats to human security and traditional and emerging political and security challenges. The series examines the often invisible network of G8, G7, and other institutions as they operate inside and outside established international systems to generate desired outcomes and create a new order. It analyses how individual G8 members and other international actors, including multinational firms, civil society organisations, and other international institutions, devise and implement strategies to achieve their preferred global order.

Governing Global Trade

International institutions in conflict and convergence

THEODORE H. COHN
Simon Fraser University, Canada

ASHGATE

Published by
Ashgate Publishing Limited
Gower House
Croft Road
Aldershot
Hampshire GU11 3HR
England

Ashgate Publishing Company
Suite 420, 101 Cherry Street
Burlington, VT 05401-4405 USA

Ashgate website: http://www.ashgate.com

British Library Cataloguing in Publication Data
Cohn, Theodore H., 1940-
  Governing global trade : international institutions in
  conflict and convergence. - (The G8 and global governance
  series)
  1.Group of Seven (Organization) 2.Group of Eight
  (Organization) 3.Organisation for Economic Co-operation and
  Development 4.Quadrilateral group 5.International trade
  I.Title
  382.9'1

Library of Congress Cataloging-in-Publication Data
Cohn, Theodore H., 1940-
  Governing global trade : international institutions in conflict and convergence /
  Theodore H. Cohn.
     p. cm. -- (The G8 and global governance series)
  Includes bibliographical references and index.
  ISBN 0-7546-1593-6
     1. International economic relations--History--20th century. 2. Organisation for
  Economic Co-operation and Development--History. 3. Group of Seven
  (Organization)--History. 4. Group of Eight (Organization)--History. 5. General
  Agreement on Tariffs and Trade (Organization)--History. 6. World Trade
  Organization--History. 7. Summit meetings--History--20th century. I. Title. II. Series.

HF1359 .C655 2002
382'.91--dc21   2002074547

ISBN 0 7546 1593 6

Printed and bound in Great Britain by MPG Books Ltd, Bodmin, Cornwall

Contents

List of Figures and Tables

Preface and Acknowledgements

This book is closely related to my long-term interests in international trade and in regime theory. Most studies of the global trade regime have focused on the General Agreement on Tariffs and Trade (GATT), and its successor the World Trade Organization (WTO) as the international organisations responsible for upholding the trade regime's principles, norms, and rules. However, to understand decision-making procedures of the global trade regime, it is not sufficient to limit one's study to the GATT/WTO. This book begins the process of examining the complexity of decision-making procedures in the global trade regime by focusing on the role of three developed country-led insitutions and their relationship to the GATT/WTO: the Group of Seven/Group of Eight (G7/G8), the Quadrilateral group (Quad), and the Organisation for Economic Co-operation and Development (OECD). Of these institutions, the Quadrilateral group of trade ministers from the United States, the European Union, Japan, and Canada has received the least amount of attention in the literature. This book devotes a smaller amount of space to developing countries and their institutions because they have been less influential in the global trade regime. However, Chapters 6 to 8 discuss the fact that developing countries have had a more important role in the global trade regime in recent years.

A major thesis of this book is that decision-making procedures in the global trade regime are pyramidal, with developed country-led and institutions near the top of the pyramid, and developing country-oriented institutions near the bottom. The idea of pyramidal structure is applied primarily to an examination of the United States and the European Union as the two largest trading entities, the G7/G8, the Quad, and the OECD. As this book discusses, the position of actors and institutions on the global trade regime pyramid is not static. Thus, three key questions are addressed: How and why have the United States, the EU, the G7/G8, the Quad, and the OECD become influential in the global trade regime, what is the nature of their influence, and how has their influence changed over time? The book also discusses the challenges developing countries and civil society groups have posed to the pyramidal structure of the global trade regime.

I am grateful for the comments, advice, and support of many individuals. First, I would like to thank John Kirton of the University of Toronto for asking

vii

me to write this book for the G8 and Global Governance Series. Initial discussions with John were extremely helpful in deciding on the organisation and content of the book. I also owe a great deal of thanks to Jonathan Fried, David Chatterson, and Randall Wilson in Canada's Department of Foreign Affairs and International Trade (DFAIT) for providing access to relevant documents, and helpful information and feedback. Another individual I owe special thanks to is Jerry Shannon, a former Canadian Deputy Minister of Trade, whose perspective on the issues was very helpful. I also am especially indebted to Peter Hajnal of the University of Toronto, and Heidi Ullrich of the London School of Economics and Political Science for providing useful information.

In addition, I would like to thank the following individuals (listed alphabetically) for their assistance: Nicholas Bayne, London School of Economics and Political Science; James Busumtwi-Sam, Simon Fraser University; Dorothy Dwoskin, Office of the U.S. Trade Representative; Joseph Guttentag, formerly with the U.S. Treasury; Jeffrey Hart, Indiana University; Gabrielle Marceau, World Trade Organization; Alex Moens, Simon Fraser University; Duane Van Beselaere, DFAIT; Gilbert Winham, Dalhousie University; and Robert Wolfe, Queen's University. I also want to thank the anonymous reviewers of my manuscript for their detailed comments that were extremely helpful in making revisions. Furthermore, I want to recognize the contribution that the late Harold K. Jacobson of the University of Michigan has made to my studies. The emphasis of this book on international institutions stems partly from the interest I developed in the subject years ago when Professor Jacobson was my Ph.D. supervisor.

I owe a great deal of thanks to Anita Mahoney for the careful and competent work she did in helping to prepare this book for publication. I would also like to thank Kirstin Howgate, Sarah Horsley, Amanda Richardson and others at Ashgate publishers for their careful attention to my manuscript. In addition, Madeline Koch at the University of Toronto provided valuable advice at several stages in producing the book. Two grants from Simon Fraser University were most helpful in financing this project: a small SSHRC grant and a publications grant.

I want to thank my wife Shirley for her limitless patience, advice, and encouragement. Finally, it gives me great pleasure to dedicate this book to my sons Daniel and Frank, who have helped me see beyond the Ivory Tower.

Theodore H. Cohn

Acronyms and Abbreviations

AASM	Associated African States and Madagascar
APEC	Asia Pacific Economic Cooperation
ASEAN	Association of Southeast Asian Nations
CAP	Common Agricultural Policy
CG.18	Consultative Group of Eighteen
CIEC	Conference on International Economic Cooperation
CSD	Consultative Subcommittee on Surplus Disposal
CSEs	consumer subsidy equivalents
CTA	Committee on Trade in Agriculture
CUSFTA	Canada-U.S. Free Trade Agreement
CVDs	countervailing duties
DAC	Development Assistance Committee
DAG	Development Assistance Group
DFAIT	Department of Foreign Affairs and International Trade
EC	European Community
ECSC	European Coal and Steel Community
EEC	European Economic Community
EFTA	European Free Trade Association
ERP	European Recovery Program
EU	European Union
FAO	Food and Agriculture Organization
FDI	foreign direct investment
FIRA	Foreign Investment Review Agency
FOGS	Functioning of the GATT System
FSU	former Soviet Union
G5	Group of Five
G7	Group of Seven
G8	Group of Eight
G9	Group of Nine
G10	Group of Ten
G48	Group of 48
G77	Group of 77
GATS	General Agreement on Trade in Services

GATT	General Agreement on Tariffs and Trade
GDP	gross domestic product
GMOs	genetically-modified organisms
GPA	Government Procurement Agreement
GSP	generalised system of preferences
ICITO	Interim Commission for the International Trade Organization
ILO	International Labour Organisation
IMF	International Monetary Fund
IPC	Integrated Program for Commodities
IR	international relations
ISI	import-substituting industrialization
ITA	Information Technology Agreement
ITC	International Trade Centre
ITO	International Trade Organization
KIEOs	keystone international economic organisations
MAI	Multilateral Agreement on Investment
MFA	Multifibre Agreement
MFN	most-favoured nation
MITI	Ministry of International Trade and Industry
MNC	multinational corporation
MTM	Ministerial Trade Mandate
MTN	multilateral trade negotiations
MTO	Multilateral Trade Organization
NAFTA	North American Free Trade Agreement
NEP	National Energy Program
NGO	non-governmental organisation
NIE	newly-industrializing economy
NIEO	New International Economic Order
NTB	non-tariff barrier
OECD	Organisation for Economic Co-operation and Development
OEEC	Organisation for European Economic Co-operation
OPEC	Organisation of Petroleum Exporting Countries
OTC	Organization for Trade Cooperation
PL 480	Public Law 480
PSEs	producer subsidy equivalents
Quad	Quadrilateral group
RTA	regional trade agreement
RTAA	Reciprocal Trade Agreements Act
S&D	special and differential

SOMs	senior officials' meetings
TRIMs	trade-related investment measures
TRIPs	trade-related intellectual property rights
UN	United Nations
UNCTAD	United Nations Conference on Trade and Development
UNEP	United Nations Environment Program
USTR	United States Trade Representative
WTO	World Trade Organization

To my sons Daniel and Frank

1 Introduction

A central characteristic of the postwar period has been the rapid expansion of international trade. Whereas real economic output increased by 3.7 percent per year on average from 1948 to 1997, trade grew at a much greater rate of about 6 percent per year during this period. From 1985 to 1997 the ratio of trade to gross domestic product (GDP) rose from 16.6 to 24.1 percent in developed countries, and from 22.8 to 38 percent in developing countries.[1] To manage this growing trade interdependence, the major economic powers gradually established a global trade regime. Regimes are institutional arrangements for managing problems and promoting stability and cooperation among interdependent states. Most commonly, regimes are defined as "principles, norms, rules, and decision-making procedures around which actors' expectations converge in a given area of international relations."[2] International organisations are "physical entities possessing offices, personnel, equipment, budgets, and so forth" that often provide a venue or setting in which international regimes can operate.[3]

In some sectoral areas, studies of an international regime may focus on a range of associated international organisations, or formal and informal institutions. For example, one study on the environment defines a world environmental regime as "a partially integrated collection of world-level organizations, understandings, and assumptions that specify the relationship of human society to nature."[4] However, in sectoral areas such as trade where there is a predominant international organisation, Robert Keohane maintains that in practice "organization and regime ... may seem almost coterminous."[5] Most international relations scholars have in fact described the General Agreement on Tariffs and Trade (GATT) from 1948 to 1994, and the World Trade Organization (WTO) since 1995, as being "virtually coterminous" with the global trade regime;[6] and some studies of global trade specifically refer to the "GATT/ WTO regime."[7] Nevertheless, as early as 1969 the trade law specialist John Jackson expressed an alternative view, arguing that global trade management involved a wide range of institutions in addition to the GATT:

> International regulation of international trade is ... an extraordinarily complex and muddled affair, involving a wide variety of organizations and institutions ... when

1

one considers GATT, it is necessary to relate it to the mosaic and ever-changing picture of other international institutions. In some cases the institutions complement each other in important ways ... In other cases the subject-matter attention of these institutions overlaps.[8]

Although the GATT/WTO has certainly been the key international organisation embedded in the global trade regime, this book builds upon Jackson's view of global trade governance. A major thesis of this book is that our understanding of the global trade regime will be greatly enhanced if we devote more attention to these "other" trade-related institutions and their relationship to the GATT/WTO. This study gives primary emphasis to three institutions that have had a significant impact on global trade relations: the *Group of Seven/Group of Eight (G7/G8)*, the *Quadrilateral Group (Quad)*, and the *Organisation for Economic Co-operation and Development (OECD)*. We devote a smaller amount of space to institutions representing developing country interests such as the *Group of 77 (G77)* and the *United Nations Conference on Trade and Development (UNCTAD)*, because they have been far less influential in the global trade regime. However, developing countries have had a more active and important role in the global trade regime in recent years, and the latter part of the book discusses the role of North-South coalitions such as the Cairns group in the GATT Uruguay Round.

Of the regional trade agreements (RTAs), this book devotes attention only to the European Union (EU), because over the years the European Commission has "established itself as the negotiator for the European Union ... on trade issues, but always operating under the watchful eyes of the member governments."[9] The EU has a special status among RTAs in the three institutions we focus on in this book: the G7/G8, the Quad, and the OECD. Most importantly, the members of the Quad are the trade ministers of the United States, the EU, Japan, and Canada. Furthermore, since 1978 the Presidents of the European Council and Commission have been regular participants in the G7/G8 summits (the relationship between the Commission and the Council in European external relations is disussed in Chapter 4). The European Commission is not a member of the OECD. However, Supplementary Protocol 1 of the OECD Convention indicates that the European Commission "shall take part in the work of that Organisation."[10] This protocol gives the EU more privileges than other international organisations, which are limited to having observer status in the OECD. In effect, "the Rules of Procedure, and the subsequent practices, give the Commission, which has its own Delegation in Paris, practically the same rights as a member country."[11] Thus, the European Commission is a member of various OECD committees and working groups such as the Development

Assistance Committee and the Working Party of the Trade Committee. The main privileges the European Commission is denied as a nonmember of the OECD are the right to vote and the right to participate in the formal adoption of Acts of the OECD (as a nonmember, the Commission also does not contribute to the general budget).

Although we refer to other institutions throughout the book, they are discussed only for illustrative purposes. Thus, this book systematically traces the changing role in the global trade regime only of the G7/G8, the Quad, and the OECD. This chapter explains why we focus primarily on these three institutions, and provides a general background discussion of the relationship of the GATT/WTO to other institutions in the global trade regime. Subsequent chapters examine the historical role of the G7/G8, the Quad, and the OECD in the post-World War II period.

The Role of the G7/G8, The Quad, and the OECD in the Global Trade Regime

Although regimes are usually defined in terms of principles, norms, rules, and decision-making procedures, most studies of international regimes in reality tend to focus only on the first three of these characteristics. Regime theorists have therefore directed their attention to the international organisation that has primary legal responsibility for upholding trade regime principles, norms, and rules: the GATT/WTO. Nevertheless, it is not sufficient to limit one's study to the GATT/WTO when examining the *decision-making procedures* of the global trade regime. Decision-making procedures are "prevailing practices for making and implementing collective choice,"[12] and collective choice in the global trade regime develops as a multi-layered process through discussion and negotiation in a wide array of formal and informal institutions.

It is important to direct more attention to decision-making procedures in the global trade regime, because these procedures can have a significant effect on the development and evolution of regime principles, norms and rules. For example, two basic trade regime principles are nondiscrimination (including most-favoured nation treatment and national treatment) and reciprocity. Although developed countries maintain that these principles are essential for creating "a level playing field," developing countries have argued that the nondiscrimination and reciprocity principles are biased in favour of the rich countries because they support "equal treatment of unequals." The developed countries have also been the main supporters of a trade liberalisation principle. Nevertheless, they have been most influential in deciding when exceptions should or should not be provided to this principle. As we discuss in Chapter 5, GATT Articles XI and XVI were designed to outlaw import quotas and export subsidies, but agriculture was initially treated as an exception to these regulations to conform with provisions in the U.S. farm program. When the European Community established its highly protectionist Common Agricultural Policy it became fully committed to these exceptions. Textiles and clothing have also been treated as an exception to the trade liberalisation principle, largely because the textiles sector in the South has presented a major threat to the textiles sector in the North. In 1974, the North successfully pressured the textiles-exporting developing countries to join in the Multifibre Agreement (MFA), which ironically was negotiated under GATT auspices. The MFA "introduced generally restrictive rules, as well as the principles of quotas and a selective safeguard mechanism."[13] Thus, decision-making procedures have ensured that the principles, norms, and rules (and exceptions to them) in the global trade regime largely reflect developed country interests and objectives. A "development principle" addressing the concerns and needs of developing countries gradually emerged in the GATT, but it was always subsidiary to other trade regime principles such as reciprocity and nondiscrimination.[14]

When the Final Act establishing the General Agreement on Tariffs and Trade came into effect in January 1948, 23 countries were *contracting parties* in the GATT. (This book uses the less accurate term GATT *members* for the sake of brevity.) Only 10 of the original 23 GATT members were developing countries, and they had little influence. Although 20 developing countries had joined the GATT by 1960, only 7 of them participated in the 1960-61 Dillon Round of GATT negotiations.[15] Until the early 1960s, the GATT therefore had the characteristics of a small club dominated by the developed countries. The GATT could readily perform most of the decision-making functions in the global trade regime during this early period, because the developed countries were the major traders. In the 1960s, however, developing countries joined the GATT in much larger numbers. As Table 2.1 (page 33) shows, 62 countries participated in the 1964-67 GATT Kennedy Round, which was a marked increase from the 26 countries participating in the previous Dillon Round. The growing membership of the GATT interfered with its small club-like atmosphere, and pressures therefore began to develop in the 1960s to establish smaller groups to facilitate consultations among the major developed country traders. Thus, one of the 3 main institutions discussed in this book, the OECD, was established in the 1960s. It was also in the 1960s that the G77 and UNCTAD were formed, highlighting the division between the North and the South.

As the GATT membership increased and became more diverse in the 1970s and 1980s, the major developed country traders sought additional smaller groupings to facilitate decision-making, both within and outside of the GATT. Within the GATT, a Consultative Group of Eighteen (CG.18) was formed on a temporary basis in 1975, and then made a permanent body in 1979; and other groups such as the "green room" sessions were also established. However, for reasons discussed later in this chapter, the developed countries felt that these groups within the GATT did not adequately facilitate decision-making on trade-related matters. In the 1970s the developed countries established the G7 outside of the GATT which deals with a wide range of issues including trade, and in the 1980s the developed countries established the Quad which focuses specifically on trade. Figure 1.1 shows that the decision-making procedures of the global trade regime are in many respects pyramidal, with developed country institutions near the top of the pyramid, and developing country institutions near the bottom. Thus, the G7/G8, the Quad, and the OECD have occupied important positions at the upper levels of the trade decision-making pyramid. Gilbert Winham has described the GATT Tokyo Round negotiations as a pyramidal process, in which

Figure 1.1 Pyramidal Structure of the Global Trade Regime

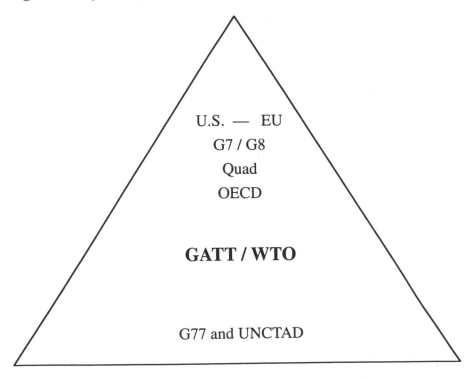

U.S. — EU

G7 / G8

Quad

OECD

GATT / WTO

G77 and UNCTAD

issues tended to be first negotiated between the United States and the EC [European Community]; and once a tentative trade-off was established the negotiation process was progressively expanded to include other countries. In this way co-operation between the United States and the EC served to direct the negotiation.[16]

Whereas Winham's description of a pyramidal structure refers to GATT/WTO negotiations, this book broadens the discussion of pyramidal structure to examine the relationship among several formal and informal institutions in the global trade regime. The G7/G8 and the Quad are placed above the OECD in the global trade regime pyramid because only the most economically important of the OECD members are included in these more select institutions. Furthermore, the G7/G8 which meets at the heads of government and state level is higher on the pyramid than the Quad which meets at the trade ministers level. As we will discuss, the United States was clearly the hegemonic actor in the global trade regime in the 1950s and 1960s; but its trade hegemony has declined since that time. Figure 1.1 shows that the European Union now occupies a place at the top of the pyramid along with the United States as the most prominent actors in the global trade regime.

The important point to note about the pyramid in Figure 1.1 is that it is *not* static. In tracing historically the role of the G7/G8, the Quad, and the OECD in the global trade regime we are particularly interested in addressing three questions throughout the book:

1. How and why have the G7/G8, the Quad, and the OECD become influential in the global trade regime?
2. What is the nature of their influence? (E.g., do these institutions have more influence over some aspects of global trade negotiations than others?)
3. How has their influence changed over time? (E.g., how have these institutions been affected by the growing influence of developing countries in the global trade regime?)

Other plurilateral institutions in addition to the G7/G8, the Quad, and the OECD of course have an important effect on decision-making in the global trade regime. (Plurilateral institutions are limited-membership institutions with more than two members.) It is therefore necessary to discuss why this book does not focus on these other institutions. Regional trade agreements (RTAs) have had a significant impact on the global trade regime from time the Rome Treaty establishing the European Economic Community came into effect in January 1958. The impact of RTAs increased considerably in the 1980s and 1990s with the formation of the Canada-U.S. Free Trade Agreement (CUSFTA),

Mercosur, and the North American Free Trade Agreement (NAFTA), and the deepening of integration in the European Union. Nevertheless, this book focuses on the governing of *global* trade, and the G7/G8, the Quad, and the OECD have been much more *directly* involved with global trade issues than the RTAs.

As discussed, the only RTA this book devotes attention to is the European Union, because the European commission has an important role in global trade negotiations, and in the G7/G8, the Quad, and the OECD. Thus, this study devotes far more attention to the EU's role in external trade negotiations and prenegotiations than to political and economic interactions within the EU. It is important to add a note about terminology regarding the EU. In 1958, three separate institutions existed: the European Coal and Steel Community (ECSC), Euratom, and the European Economic Community (EEC). (As we discuss in Chapter 2, the ECSC had been formed earlier, in 1952.) In July 1967, the separate administrations of these three bodies were merged and renamed the European Community (EC). In November 1993, the European Union (EU) subsumed – but did not replace – the EC when the Maastricht Treaty extending the Community from trade and economic matters to a much broader range of activities came into effect. In this book, we use the term "EC" when discussing events from 1958 to 1993, and the term "EU" for the period from November 1993 to the present.[17]

We also devote less attention to private groupings in this study, even though such groupings have had a significant role in the global trade regime. Regime analysis has generally been state-centric, and has underestimated the role of multinational corporations (MNCs), non-governmental organisations (NGOs), "epistemic communities" of experts such as scientists, and other private groups. In recent years, a growing body of literature has begun to appear on the role of non-state actors in international regimes.[18] Peter Haas, for example, has written on the critical role of NGOs and scientific organisations in global environmental regimes.[19] Private groupings have had an important role in many aspects of the global trade regime. For example, some MNCs pressured for the extension of trade regime principles, norms and rules to cover services trade, and along with the OECD these MNCs have helped to legitimise the idea that trade in services has many similarities with trade in goods. A major result of this altered perception of services was the approval of the General Agreement on Trade in Services (GATS) in the GATT Uruguay Round.[20] Although this book contains some discussion of private groupings such as the role of epistemic communities in legitimising the regulation of services and agricultural trade, and the role of NGO "civil society" groups in challenging trade regime principles and rules, a

more detailed study of private groupings and the global trade regime must await
another study.

The Role of Institutions in the Global Trade Regime

The influence of institutions other than the GATT/WTO in the global trade
regime stems from at least four major factors: the dominance of developed
countries in the North over developing countries in the South, the decline of
U.S. economic hegemony, the growing interaction of trade with other issues as
a result of globalisation, and the unique characteristics of the GATT/WTO as
an international organisation.

The first factor, the dominance of the North over the South, has contributed
to the pyramidal structure of institutions in the global economy and also in the
global trade regime. The size and diversity of the "keystone international
economic organisations" (KIEOs), the International Monetary Fund (IMF), the
World Bank, and the GATT/WTO has often hindered decision-making, because
they are striving to become universal-membership institutions.[21] Thus, the major
developed countries frequently confer among themselves in smaller like-minded
groups before seeking endorsement of their policies by the KIEOs. In the global
trade regime, several plurilateral institutions near the top of the pyramid have
facilitated developed country efforts to increase their influence and help set the
agenda for international trade negotiations. As discussed, the most important of
these institutions are the G7, the Quad, and the OECD. The economic powers
with the largest markets generally have the greatest influence in the global
trade regime, because market access is the primary goal of countries wishing to
export their goods and services. In 1999 the Quad members – the United States,
the EU, Japan, and Canada – accounted for 54.3 percent of global merchandise
imports. The United States and the EU were clearly the most important import
markets, accounting for 23.6 and 18.9 percent of global merchandise imports
in 1999. Japan and Canada ranked third and fourth, accounting for 6.9 and 4.9
percent of global merchandise imports. The Quad members are also the most
important exporters, although (unlike the case of imports) the EU rather than
the United States is the largest exporter. In 1999, the Quad accounted for 50.8
percent of global merchandise exports. The EU, the United States, Japan, and
Canada accounted for 18.9, 16.4, 9.9, and 5.6 percent, respectively, of global
merchandise exports.[22] In addition to their predominant share of merchandise
trade, the Quad members are also the largest traders in services, which have
become an increasingly important part of global trade flows. In 1997, the top

nine service traders included the United States, Japan, Canada, and six members of the EU (Germany, Italy, France, Britain, the Netherlands, and Belgium). These nine countries accounted for 54 percent of world imports and for 60 percent of world exports of services.[23] Thus, the dominance of important traders in the North is a major factor accounting for the influence of institutions other than the GATT/WTO in the global trade regime.

The second factor explaining the influence of institutions other than the GATT/WTO is the decline of U.S. economic hegemony. As U.S. hegemony has declined, the major industrial powers have established a variety of plurilateral institutions to provide collective management and resolve disputes – most notably among the United States, the EU, and Japan. The changing position of the United States as a global hegemon has been one of the most hotly debated issues in the international relations literature. Whereas some "declinists" argue that "one of the most important features of American hegemony was its brevity,"[24] "renewalists" counter that declinists underestimate the degree to which the United States has been able to preserve its influential position in the world.[25] Nevertheless, there is considerable evidence that U.S. hegemony has declined more in the economic than in the security sphere, and more in international trade than in many other economic areas. Since 1971 the United States has had chronic balance of trade deficits, and Judith Goldstein argues that "nowhere is America's hegemonic decline more evident than in changing trade patterns."[26] Although the United States as a postwar hegemonic power played an important role in creating or supplying an open liberal trade regime, Robert Keohane points out that it is necessary to look at "demand" as well as "supply" in explaining the maintenance of regimes. As U.S. economic hegemony has declined, the major developed countries that have benefited from the liberal trade regime have helped the United States maintain it through collective efforts and institutions.[27] As we discuss in this book, the OECD, G7, and Quad have performed important functions in upholding the liberal trade regime.

The third factor explaining the influence of institutions other than the GATT/WTO is the growing interaction of trade with other issues as a result of globalisation. For example, trade and investment have become increasingly interlinked in recent years, and a former WTO director-general has stated that "businesses now trade to invest and invest to trade – to the point where both activities are increasingly part of a single strategy to deliver products across borders."[28] Furthermore, "as the world economy becomes more globalized, the ubiquity of intertwined trade and financial issues ... tends to increase."[29] Inevitably the intertwining of issues contributes to closer linkages between the GATT/WTO and other institutions. For example, the international financial institutions – the IMF and World Bank – have become more important actors in the global trade regime as the interaction between trade and finance has intensified.

The founders of the IMF and World Bank at Bretton Woods in fact saw the close linkages between trade and finance (in relation to balance of payments matters) as early as the 1940s. Thus, the IMF *Articles of Agreement* state that one of the Fund's purposes is "to facilitate the expansion and balanced growth of international trade," and the World Bank *Articles of Agreement* state that the Bank will seek "to promote the long-range balanced growth of international trade."[30] The IMF and World Bank *Articles of Agreement* do not contain requirements for consultation with the GATT, because they were adopted before the GATT was established; and the GATT's informal nature precluded the development of formal institutional linkages. However, pressures for institutional linkages intensified as ties between trade and finance increased, and the ministers launching the Uruguay Round in 1986 instructed the negotiating group on the Functioning of the GATT System (FOGS) "to increase the contribution of the GATT to achieving greater coherence in global economic policy-making through strengthening its relationship with other international organizations responsible for monetary and financial matters."[31] Subsequently, the Marrakesh Agreement concluding the Uruguay Round explicitly called for WTO cooperation with the IMF and World Bank "with a view to achieving greater coherence in global economic policy-making."[32] WTO agreements with the IMF and World Bank were eventually signed in December 1996 and April 1997. The agreements have a number of provisions such as the requirement that the institutions consult with each other concerning possible inconsistencies between their policies.[33]

As is the case for trade and finance, the intertwining of trade and development issues has also induced the GATT/WTO to engage in a wide range of institutional linkages. For example, the United Nations Conference on Trade and Development (UNCTAD), as its name implies, plays a role in both the trade and development regimes. Although the GATT and UNCTAD were traditionally viewed as rival organisations with different perspectives on trade, their cooperation dates back to 1964 (the year UNCTAD was formed), when they established a joint venture – the International Trade Centre (ITC). The ITC provides developing countries with export promotion and marketing assistance as well as training and consulting services. Today the WTO cooperates more closely with the ITC and UNCTAD than was the case for its predecessor the GATT. The increase in trade-development linkages also provides further reasons for closer ties between the GATT/WTO and the World Bank. In his comments on the World Bank's development functions, an alternate Executive Director of the Bank has claimed that "no single organization around the world, including leading research centers and universities … has invested as much financial and human resources as the Bank has in measuring the costs of different forms of protection and the benefits of trade liberalization."[34] Recently, the November 2001 Doha Ministerial Declaration launching a new WTO round of multilateral trade negotiations announced the establishment of a work program to assist developing and least-developed countries with technical cooperation and capacity building as "core elements of the development dimension of the multilateral trading system."[35] This commitment will further solidify the linkages between the WTO and international development institutions.

The GATT/WTO has established linkages with a number of other international institutions such as the Food and Agriculture Organization (FAO), the International Labour Organisation (ILO), and the United Nations Environment Program (UNEP). The work of these institutions on trade-related issues is often complementary to the work of the GATT/WTO within the global trade regime. The interlinkages between trade and other issues has special relevance for two of the institutions we focus on in this book: the G7/G8 and the OECD. Because heads of state and government attend the G7/G8 summits, they consider it their responsibility to examine trade matters in the context of a wide range of related economic and political issues. For example, the July 1978 summit in Bonn "concluded the most elaborate set of interlocking commitments in economic policy, trade and energy attempted at any summit."[36] There are also numerous examples of the OECD's work in examining the linkages among issues, ranging from trade and agriculture to trade and the environment. Although the Quadrilateral group focuses more specifically on trade matters, subsequent chapters will show that even the Quad ministers have often examined the linkages between trade and other issues such as finance and development.

The fourth factor affecting the institutional framework in the global trade regime is the nature of the GATT/WTO as an international organisation. When the multilateral GATT/WTO has proved to be too large and unwieldy to deal with sensitive, complex issues, developed countries have increased their reliance on plurilateral institutions such as the OECD, G7, and Quad with smaller, more homogeneous memberships. We devote more detailed attention to the fourth factor here, because the unique characteristics of the GATT/WTO have had an important effect on the nature and degree of involvement of other institutions in the global trade regime.

The Nature of the GATT/WTO

Trade has been one of the most contentious issues in international economic relations, and this was particularly evident in the period between World Wars I and II. After the 1929 stock market crash, the U.S. Congress passed the 1930 Smoot-Hawley Tariff Act, which increased average U.S. *ad valorem* rates on dutiable imports to 52.8 percent, "the highest American tariffs in the twentieth century."[37] The Smoot-Hawley tariff had disastrous consequences as other countries rushed to retaliate with their own import restrictions, and world trade declined from $35 billion in 1929 to $12 billion in 1933. Although the 1934 U.S. Reciprocal Trade Agreements Act reversed some of the damage, protectionism continued to affect trade relations during the rest of the interwar period.[38] The United States and Britain wanted to ensure that the devastating effects of protectionism in the interwar period were not repeated, and they began to hold bilateral discussions in 1943 to lay the groundwork for postwar trade negotiations. In 1945 the U.S. State Department issued a document on trade and employment, that formed the basis for the Havana Charter negotiations to establish an International Trade Organization (ITO). While the Havana Charter talks were continuing, some of the participating governments began to hold separate negotiations to lower tariffs. At the conclusion of these tariff negotiations in October 1947, 23 countries signed the final act of the General Agreement on Tariffs and Trade (GATT). When 53 countries (including the 23 GATT signatories) signed the Havana Charter in 1948, it was assumed that the GATT would simply be folded into the planned ITO.

Most governments delayed ratifying the Havana Charter until the United States gave its final approval. In April 1949, President Harry S. Truman sent the Charter to Congress and requested a joint resolution from the Senate and the House of Representatives authorising American participation. (An international agreement with domestic legal force in the United States can be a treaty which is approved by a two-thirds majority vote of the Senate, or an Executive Agreement approved by both the Senate and the House of Representatives.[39]) However, the Congress was occupied with other major issues such as the North Atlantic Treaty and the Military Defense Assistance Program, and the Administration did not exert pressure for more rapid action on the ITO. It was not until April and May 1950 that the House Committee on Foreign Affairs held hearings on President Truman's request for Congressional approval. The committee did not submit a recommendation after its hearings, and the issue never reached the floor of the House of Representatives. In December 1950 the President withdrew the Charter from Congress, and in 1951 the U.S.

Secretary of State indicated that it would never be resubmitted to Congress. Without U.S. participation, there was no possibility that the ITO would be established.[40]

The reasons why the U.S. Congress did not approve the Havana Charter are complex and ironic, especially because the proposal to create an ITO had originated in the United States. In drafting the Charter, the trade negotiators faced the difficult task of reaching an "understanding on the proper balance between market rules and state intervention."[41] Although the negotiators developed a plan for trade liberalisation, they also offered concessions to a wide range of countries wanting to insulate themselves from the detrimental effects of freer trade. For example, the Charter permitted exceptions to trade liberalisation as a result of European concerns about their balance of payments problems, Australian concerns about unstable commodity prices, developing country efforts to promote their infant industries, and general efforts to promote full employment and social justice. However, in trying to satisfy everyone's demands, the negotiators satisfied neither free traders nor protectionists. International negotiation is a "two-level game" involving both domestic and foreign interests, and after U.S. officials negotiated the Havana Charter they then had to confront U.S. domestic interests.[42] Whereas protectionists feared that the ITO would threaten U.S. sovereignty and permit low-cost imports to undercut American producers, free traders felt that the numerous escape clauses and exceptions in the Charter would inhibit trade liberalisation. Influential members of the U.S. Congress who were subjected to these competing pressures found it difficult "to accept an agreement that made major concessions to the views of other countries and that could be construed as tying the hands of Congress in some areas of policy in which it had traditionally claimed primacy."[43] For example, Congressional leaders were concerned that the Charter would restrict future U.S. policies in such areas as trade preferences and countervailing duties. Presidents Franklin Roosevelt and Harry Truman failed to develop a domestic constituency that could counterbalance the numerous opponents of the Havana Charter, and in the end Congressional leaders ensured that the ITO would not be established.[44]

With the failure to establish the ITO, the GATT gradually became the main global trade organisation by default. Countries that signed the GATT were referred to as contracting parties rather than members, because the GATT was designed to be only a trade agreement. The U.S. President was able to approve the GATT by Executive Agreement as part of his constitutional powers to conduct foreign policy, but the GATT was never approved by the U.S. Congress. Thus, the GATT did not automatically have domestic legal force in the United States, even though it was binding on the United States under international law.[45] In some respects GATT's informal origins contributed to its adaptability, and it registered considerable success over the years in making binding decisions, reducing tariffs, and negotiating disciplines for nontariff measures. GATT's informality, however, also proved to be a source of weakness that became increasingly evident in the 1980s. For example, the GATT provided exemptions for sectors such as agriculture and textiles from some of its key provisions regulating trade, member states could too easily waive and circumvent GATT rules, and GATT mechanisms for settling trade disputes were inadequate. In the Uruguay Round, the negotiators therefore decided to replace the GATT with the WTO as the main global trade organisation. (The GATT has reverted to its original status as a treaty for trade in goods, now under the WTO.) In contrast to the GATT, the WTO is a formal, legally constituted international organisation like the IMF and the World Bank.

Despite the differences between the GATT and its successor organisation the WTO, they share certain characteristics that have encouraged the developed countries to turn to other institutions to achieve their objectives and facilitate governance in the global trade regime. These characteristics include the nature of the GATT/WTO policy-making bodies, the small size of the GATT/WTO budget and secretariat, and the GATT/WTO's legalistic approach to international trade.

The GATT/WTO Policy-making Bodies

The United Nations system in the postwar period was based on several key principles, including sovereign equality and universality. The democratic revolutions of the eighteenth and nineteenth centuries had advanced the principle that all men were created equal (women were normally not accorded equal rights), and subsequently this tenet was extended to states in the League of Nations and the United Nations.[46] Some exceptions could be found to sovereign equality in the United Nations, such as the right of the five permanent members of the Security Council (the United States, Britain, China, France, and Russia) to veto all substantive resolutions. Nevertheless, Article 2 of the UN Charter explicitly states that "the Organization is based on the principle of the sovereign equality of all its Members."[47]

Although the sovereign equality doctrine has had considerable appeal in theory, its practical relevance in a world of power politics has long been open to question. As early as 1815, four major powers (Great Britain, Prussia, Austria, and Russia) formed the Concert of Europe, and France was admitted as the fifth member in 1818. In its attempts to regulate the balance of power and prevent major conflicts among states, the Concert of Europe gave priority to the principle of great power diplomacy over sovereign equality. Thus, the sovereign equality principle often cannot be upheld in practice because it does not reflect the hierarchy of power in the international system. Another tenet endorsed by the United Nations that has raised serious questions is the principle of universality. The United Nations is a "universal membership institution" in which membership is open to all states.[48] However, some liberals maintain that the universality principle is problematic because it normally becomes more difficult for states to reach cooperative solutions as their numbers increase. As an organisation's membership increases, higher transaction and information costs interfere with the ability to identify common interests, and states tend to become "free riders" because it is difficult to identify and sanction defectors.[49]

The major industrial powers have dealt with their concerns about the sovereign equality and universality principles by giving themselves "minilateral" privileges within large multilateral institutions.[50] For example, the rules of two of the three KIEOs – the IMF and the World Bank – provide the major developed countries with formal minilateral prerogatives. The IMF and World Bank both have weighted voting in their policy-making bodies, in which the most economically powerful countries have the largest capital subscriptions and quotas, and the largest number of votes. In April 2001, for example, the Group of Five (G5) countries – the United States, Japan, Germany, France, and Britain – had 39.3 percent of the votes in the IMF Board of Governors.[51] The IMF and World Bank also have *Executive Boards* (or *Boards of Executive Directors*), which are select bodies of 24 members elected by their *Boards of Governors* every two years. As provided by the IMF and World Bank Articles of Agreement, the member countries with the largest number of votes (the G5 countries) can each appoint their own executive directors, whereas other countries must join together to elect directors based on the weighted voting system.[52] The IMF also has an *International Monetary and Financial Committee* of the Board of Governors (formerly the *Interim Committee*) composed of 24 IMF governors representing the same constituencies as the IMF Executive Board. This Committee, which meets twice a year, was formed in the 1970s to make policy recommendations at the highest political levels in a smaller forum than the annual meetings of the Board of Governors. Thus, the IMF and World Bank provide the major developed countries with ample opportunity to engage in minilateral cooperation through their executive boards and weighted voting systems.[53]

The major developed countries do not have the formal minilateral prerogatives in the GATT/WTO that they have in the IMF and World Bank. The GATT/WTO has nothing comparable to the smaller executive boards of the IMF and World Bank, because all GATT/WTO councils and committees are plenary bodies that are open to every member. The Havana Charter had included a provision for an executive board that was to be responsible for executing ITO policies, and was to consist of 18 ITO members including "the eight Members of chief economic importance."[54] When the ITO was not formed, however, the contracting parties "gave scant attention in the GATT articles to organizational structure, and the simple, very general rules for decision-making reflect this."[55] Thus, the GATT never established the executive board envisaged in the Havana Charter.

The closest the GATT came to having an executive board was the Consultative Group of Eighteen (CG.18), which was established on a temporary basis in 1975, and then made a permanent body in 1979. According to a former GATT director-general, the creation of the CG.18 resulted partly from "the considerable increase in the number of contracting parties."[56] As GATT membership increased, the CG.18 was established as a smaller representative group of 18 countries to facilitate discussion of trade issues (the CG.18's membership increased to 22 in 1985). However, the CG.18 was composed of senior officials from capitals that met only from two to four times a year. The CG.18 was purely consultative in nature, and did not normally deal with management issues. GATT members that were non-participants in the CG.18 were disturbed by its lack of transparency, because they were barred from the meetings and did not receive CG.18 documents. Thus, the CG.18 held its last meeting in 1987, just as the GATT Uruguay Round negotiations were beginning to take shape.[57]

Another departure from GATT/WTO practice of having only plenary bodies are the informal "green room" sessions, that have generally been limited to the GATT/WTO Director-General and the most important delegations in multilateral trade negotiations. The green room sessions were named after a small conference room adjacent to the Director-General's offices where they were initially held, but a convention developed to call these smaller meetings "green room" sessions wherever they were held. Participation in the green room sessions has varied by issue, and has generally increased over time. For example, the green room meetings during the GATT Tokyo Round usually involved less than 8 delegations, but meetings after the GATT Uruguay Round could have as many as 25 to 30 participants. Before the third WTO ministerial meeting in Seattle in late 1999, the larger WTO membership normally accepted the proposals developed in the green room sessions. However, the green room system broke down in the lead-up to the Seattle ministerial.[58] A number of developing countries resented the fact that they were excluded from critical green room sessions during the Autumn 1999 Informal Heads of Delegations meetings held in Geneva in preparation for the WTO Seattle ministerial. As a result, WTO Director-General Mike Moore "tried to move away from the Green Room, and thrash out issues in the General Council."[59]

Additional minilateral groupings such as the Invisible Committee, the Friends of the Chair, the Group of Eight, and the Group of Four have been formed to deal with trade issues, but they have been less prominent than the CG.18 and the green room sessions. For example, the Invisible Committee was an informal gathering of capital-based officials from about eleven key member states that offered policy advice on trade issues. Created at the initiative of a Deputy U.S. Trade Representative, the Invisible Committee was formed to develop a consensus on major issues in preparation for the first WTO ministerial conference in Singapore in December 1996. Despite the existence of smaller groups such as the CG.18, green room sessions, Invisible Committee, and Friends of the Chair, the GATT/WTO membership has never established formally constituted decision-making bodies comparable to the executive boards of the IMF and World Bank.

The GATT/WTO also differs from the IMF and World Bank in that it is a one-nation, one-vote organisation. The major developed countries could insist on weighted voting in the IMF and World Bank because of the large amounts of finance they provided through these organisations; but they had less basis for demanding weighted voting in a global trade organisation.[60] One could argue that the GATT/WTO voting system is of little importance, because almost all decisions are made by consensus. Furthermore, the GATT/WTO is a negotiating body even more than it is a regulatory body, and the negotiations are conducted in a manner that gives the developed countries predominant influence in the organisation. Expectations of reciprocity in GATT/WTO trade negotiations ensure that the major trading nations are the key actors, because they are the largest importing and exporting countries; that is, they are most able to provide and demand reciprocal advantages. If a country does not honour its reciprocity or other commitments, it is the major developed country traders that have the greatest capacity to retaliate. GATT/WTO negotiations are therefore often a pyramidal process, where agreements are "initiated by the major powers at the top and then gradually multilateralized through the inclusion of other parties in the discussions."[61] Furthermore, informal negotiations outside the formal procedures regularly occur among the major traders, and two GATT legal specialists have even argued that in the Tokyo Round "informal negotiations became the principal focus, to the point where the formal institutions had a very secondary role to play."[62]

Although consensus decision-making and negotiation decrease the centrality of voting in the GATT/WTO, "the legal structure of potential voting still has a great influence on any organization, no matter how hard the organization tries to avoid voting." Most importantly, negotiation occurs "in the context of the participants' knowledge of the likely outcome [of a vote] if the negotiation breaks down."[63] Thus, the atmosphere surrounding consensus decision-making is often different in the one-nation, one-vote GATT/WTO than it is in the weighted voting IMF and World Bank. Furthermore, consensus decision-making requires that no member "present at the meeting when the decision is taken, formally objects to the proposed decision."[64] The WTO had 144 members as of January 2002 with the admission of China and Taiwan, and Russia is expected to join in the not too distant future. Thus, it may become increasingly difficult to resolve issues in the WTO policy bodies solely by consensus decision-making.

Critics have argued that the WTO's one-nation, one-vote system is also not necessarily equitable in practice. Whereas the United States, Japan, Canada, and other countries have only one vote each in the WTO decision-making bodies, the EU has 15 votes in the WTO – one vote for each of its 15 members. Questions have been raised about the fairness of this arrangement, because the European Commission acts for the 15 member countries on global trade issues. However, the main concern of the developed countries has been with their prerogatives *vis-à-vis* the developing countries and transition economies. When the WTO replaced the GATT as the main global trade organisation, the United States expressed its concerns with the voting system by demanding changes in the amendment procedures "to ensure that major trading countries can prevent the WTO from instituting new obligations or amending existing rules that would undercut the negotiated results of prior trade rounds."[65] As a result, a three-fourths majority of WTO members is now required for interpretations of any of the agreements and for waivers from an obligation. Nevertheless, the possibility remains that the major trading nations could be outvoted in cases where WTO members could not reach a decision by consensus.[66]

The weighted voting system in the IMF and World Bank has been highly unpopular in some circles, and scholars and practitioners do not normally advocate the development of a weighted voting system in the WTO.[67] However, scholars and practitioners in the developed countries have put forth various proposals over the years to introduce a select executive body into GATT/WTO decision-making. For example, a 1975 Atlantic Council study recommended that developed countries conclude a supplementary trade liberalisation agreement among themselves with tighter rules than those of the GATT. The Atlantic Council suggested that either the GATT or the OECD should administer this new agreement. The traditional GATT framework would remain in force for developed country trade relations with the developing countries, because developing countries would initially not accept the obligations of the new agreement. The new agreement would be administered on a weighted-voting basis, and developing countries would be encouraged to join it as they industrialised.

A 1989 study sponsored by the Twentieth Century Fund similarly recommended that the OECD establish a Free Trade and Investment Area, that would be open to all countries that followed democratic principles, had market-oriented policies, and approximated OECD social welfare standards.[68] Furthermore, during the GATT Uruguay Round negotiations several developed countries called for the formation of an executive body directly within the GATT/WTO. The United States proposed the creation of a Management Board that would be similar to the IMF and World Bank executive boards, and Australia called for the formation of a permanent ministerial steering group patterned after the representative, official-level CG.18.[69]

Since the GATT Uruguay Round, some scholars have continued to propose that some type of executive body be formed within the WTO. For example, two fellows at the U.S. Institute for International Economics (Jeffrey J. Schott and Jayashree Watal) have argued that "a new, permanent management or steering group needs to be established to make WTO procedures more equitable and efficient."[70] The WTO would delegate to this steering group responsibility for establishing a consensus on major trade issues among the member countries. Unlike the green room sessions which have been formed largely on an *ad hoc* basis, Schott and Watal propose that participation in the steering group would be based on two objective criteria: the absolute value of foreign trade, ranked by country or common customs region; and global geographic representation, with at least two participants from each major region. These two criteria would ensure that all major traders, and all major geographic regions would be represented on the steering committee.

Despite the numerous proposals over the years for the establishment of a formal executive or steering committee within the GATT/WTO, to this point divisions among the membership has precluded the creation of such a group. Partly because of their failure to gain formal minilateral prerogatives in the GATT/WTO, the major developed countries have turned to smaller plurilateral institutions such as the G7, the Quad, and the OECD to facilitate their management of trade issues. The developed countries can often achieve their trade-related objectives more readily through these institutions because of their limited, more homogeneous memberships. For example, the OECD rather than the GATT eventually took responsibility for bridging the differences among developed countries on the provision of export credit, largely because the GATT/ WTO membership also includes net consumers of export credit. It would have been impossible to negotiate an agreement limiting the extension of export credit in the GATT/WTO, because the net consumers of credit would not have supported multilateral discipline limiting the softening of credit terms (the export credit issue is discussed later in this book).[71] As we will discuss, the OECD, the G7/G8, and the Quad have served as venues for resolving differences and forming a consensus among developed countries, helping to set the trade agenda, conducting initial studies and prenegotiation of sensitive trade issues, and facilitating GATT/WTO trade negotiations at critical junctures.

The GATT/WTO Budget and Secretariat

A striking characteristic of the GATT/WTO secretariat has been its small size, compared with the secretariats of other international organisations with comparable responsibilities. In 1995-96 professional staff members in the World Bank, IMF, and OECD secretariats numbered 5700, 2200, and 1700, respectively, whereas the WTO secretariat had only 510 professional staff members. Along with fewer staff members, the WTO also has a much smaller administrative budget. In 1995-96, the budgets of the World Bank, IMF, and OECD were 1375, 470, and 260 million dollars (U.S.) respectively, compared with a budget of only 55 million dollars for the WTO.[72]

The relatively small budget and staff of the GATT/WTO are partly the result of "the nebulous and uncertain legal status that GATT has had from its beginning."[73] Indeed, when the GATT was formed it was not formally authorised to establish its own secretariat. The Interim Commission for the International Trade Organisation (ICITO) had created a small staff to prepare for the ITO, and also to service the GATT's staff requirements until the ITO was created. When the ITO was not established as expected, the ICITO legislation served as the legal basis for establishing the GATT secretariat. The unusual origins of the GATT secretariat restricted its development, and limited its in-house capacity to conduct research. Despite these deficiencies, the major developed countries have been reluctant to increase the GATT/WTO's budget for staffing and research because of their dissatisfaction with the organisation's decision-making processes (discussed above). The GATT/WTO secretariat's budget is dependent on contributions by the members, and each member's contribution to the budget is determined by its share of world trade. Thus, the developed country traders are by far the largest contributors. Although the GATT Uruguay Round accords greatly expanded the responsibilities of the WTO, the developed countries have not agreed to provide adequate resources for administering the growing number of dispute settlement cases, servicing new trade negotiations, conducting trade policy reviews, and overseeing complex accession negotiations for new WTO members. Thus, the 2000 WTO budget of about $75 million had not grown much since 1995.[74]

Reliable factual investigations and reports are essential for the development of policies affecting trade, and "one can only speculate as to the contribution that a larger GATT secretariat could have made over the years in formulating ... necessary background studies."[75] In marked contrast to the GATT/WTO, organisations such as the OECD and World Bank have been able to draw on a considerable amount of resources for doing research and producing studies on international trade issues. The OECD as a general purpose organisation, for example, has research and investigatory capacities that have been essential to GATT/WTO negotiations in such areas as government procurement, agricultural trade, and trade in services. Thus, the developed countries often turn to institutions other than the GATT/WTO when studies on trade policy become necessary.

The GATT/WTO as a "Rules-bound" Organisation

The GATT/WTO's role as an organisation with binding rules and procedures is a third characteristic that has sometimes encouraged members to turn to other institutions. For example, the GATT/WTO has a difficult and complex amending procedure that has decreased flexibility in bringing about change. Since the GATT was originally a treaty, the amending procedure involved a treaty protocol process, which required that at least two-thirds of the members approve amendments. Even if two-thirds of the members accepted an amendment, those members voting against were not obligated to abide by it. Furthermore, some parts of the GATT required unanimous approval to amend. As membership in the GATT increased, it became virtually impossible to amend the General Agreement. Although the WTO in some respects has greater flexibility for changing trade rules than the GATT, it is also very difficult to make amendments to the WTO charter. The difficulty in amending is designed to protect national sovereignty. Nevertheless, the amending process in the WTO "could prove to be a problem almost as serious as it was in the GATT."[76]

This book will point to several institutions that GATT/WTO members have turned to for trade-related issues because they are less demanding and less rule-oriented than the GATT/WTO. For example. GATT Article XI prohibited quantitative restrictions on imports (or import quotas), and this prevented the organisation from adopting a flexible approach to the gradual removal of quantitative restrictions by Western European countries as they recovered from World War II. As we discuss in Chapter 2, the major trading nations tacitly agreed to overlook the fact that Western European countries were not adhering to GATT Article XI, and these countries gradually removed their quantitative restrictions in the more flexible and less legalistic Organisation for European Economic Co-operation (OEEC). The OECD which replaced the OEEC in the early 1960s has retained the OEEC's more flexible approach, and developed countries have often been willing to approve "gentlemen's agreements" in the OECD after refusing to agree to binding commitments on the same issues in the GATT/WTO.

Developing Country Reactions to the GATT/WTO Characteristics

It is important to point out that developing country views of the GATT/WTO's characteristics are quite different from the views of the developed countries. Indeed, developing countries have regularly complained about the GATT/WTO's lack of attention to their interests or concerns, and they have also looked to outside institutions in efforts to exert more influence on global trade issues. The Havana Charter that would have established the ITO was mainly devoted to promoting the trade interests of developed countries, and many developing countries considered the Charter provisions on development issues to be inadequate, unfair, and overly restrictive. Nevertheless, the Charter did give some recognition to developing country concerns, and only one of the thirty developing countries at the Havana conference – Argentina – failed to approve the Havana Charter.[77] Eight of the articles in the Charter dealt with development issues. These articles allowed developing countries with ITO consent to withdraw tariff concessions, and to use quantitative restrictions, subsidies, and preferential tariff arrangements. Furthermore, Chapter VI of the Havana Charter dealt with international commodity agreements, that were of particular importance to developing countries because of their dependence on commodity exports. Despite its shortcomings from a developing country perspective, Chapter VI legitimised "intergovernmental intervention into commodity markets to achieve greater stability and to address the perennial problem of excessive production."[78]

When the U.S. Congress failed to approve the Havana Charter, most of the Charter provisions on development were not incorporated in the GATT, and Chapter VI was omitted entirely. Indeed, "economic development as a positive trade policy remained one of the most glaring omissions in the GATT."[79]

Although the GATT gradually began to devote more attention to Third World trade issues, most developing countries did not believe that the organisation had departed significantly from its primary concern with trade among developed countries. As we discuss in subsequent chapters, developing country pressure (combined with pressure from the Soviet bloc) resulted in the convening of the first United Nations Conference on Trade and Development in Geneva in March 1964. The developing countries attending UNCTAD I met before the conference to itemise their demands, and this grouping became the Group of 77 (G77), which now consists of well over 100 developing countries. The UNCTAD, which was "the first institutional response in the economic sphere to the entry of the Third World on the international scene," became a permanent organ of the UN General Assembly in December 1964.[80] All UN members are members of UNCTAD, but the developing countries with their greater numbers have had the predominant role in setting the organisation's agenda and work program.

The developing countries hoped that UNCTAD would become a significant institution that would eventually supplant the GATT as the main global trade organisation. However, the UNCTAD has been far less influential than the developed country-dominated organisations. Earlier we discussed the fact that the professional staff numbers and administrative budget of the WTO are smaller than those of the World Bank, IMF and OECD; but the WTO has a *larger* budget and staff than UNCTAD.[81] Furthermore, Article III.5 of the WTO Charter calls upon the WTO to "cooperate, as appropriate, with the International Monetary Fund and with the International Bank for Reconstruction and Development [World Bank]," but does not mention UNCTAD even though it is a trade institution. Article V.1 of the WTO Charter states that the "General Council shall make appropriate arrangements for effective cooperation with other intergovernmental organizations that have responsibilities related to those of the WTO," and this article could be viewed as including UNCTAD. Nevertheless, there is no specific reference to UNCTAD in the WTO Charter.[82] The limited resources and influence of UNCTAD are a reflection of the developing countries' lesser economic power and the lack of unified interests in the Third World. Thus, UNCTAD's main role has not been in international trade management, but in serving as a pressure group for Third World trade and development interests.[83] The overall conclusion of most analysts is that

"UNCTAD's substantive initiatives have had, at best, only a marginal impact on the substance of North-South relations."[84]

Despite the developing countries' limited influence historically, it is important to note that their influence has increased in recent years as a result of their greater involvement in the global trade regime. The "Third World" has also been marked by considerable diversity in terms of level of economic, social and political development, and it has never been a fully unified group on trade issues. Later chapters in this book will point out that groups of developing and developed countries have had common interests on various issues, and that coalition behaviour between developed and developing countries was especially intense during the GATT Uruguay Round.

Is There Justification for the Pyramidal Structure of the Global Trade Regime?

Some analysts defend the central role of plurilateral developed country institutions such as the G7/G8, the Quad, and the OECD in trade decision-making, arguing that large organisations such as the GATT/WTO "must be led by a much smaller core group whose weight confers on them the responsibility of leadership."[85] Most developing countries excluded from these groups realise that without a degree of consensus between the United States and the EU today, there will be no significant multilateral trade agreements. Thus, Robert Putnam and Nicholas Bayne have argued that even those countries most sensitive to exclusion from the G7 generally admit that it is "better for those countries to meet than for them not to meet."[86] A second group of analysts is more critical of the central role played by plurilateral institutions such as the G7/G8, the Quad, and the OECD. Although "on paper the WTO agreement is a model of democracy," these analysts argue, "a major potential strain on the system … [arises] from the fact that this form does not reflect the underlying reality." In reality, "decisions are taken by a limited number of countries in closed groups, or … outside of the framework of the WTO altogether."[87] As we discuss throughout this book, developing countries are often dissatisfied with their exclusion from the inner circle of trade decision-making, and even developed countries such as Australia have expressed dissatisfaction with their exclusion from select groups such as the G7/G8 and the Quad. In recent years, "civil society" groups have added their voice to those calling for a more open decision-making process in the global trade regime. (As we discuss in Chapter 9, civil society criticisms have often been aimed at limiting global trade liberalisation, whereas most developing countries today recognise that an increase in their exports depends on the liberalisation of trade.)

This book takes a position somewhere between these two competing perspectives. On the one hand, we argue that smaller plurilateral institutions such as the G7/G8, the Quad, and the OECD perform an essential function in helping to provide guidance and overall management for the global trade regime. The simple reality is that without a degree of consensus among the major traders, it is impossible to have successful multilateral trade negotiations. On the other hand, we point out that it is important for these smaller plurilateral groups to respond and adapt to pressures for more open and inclusive decision-making procedures. Since the 1980s, for example, developing countries have become more involved in the global trade regime, for reasons we discuss in later chapters. Thus, the developing countries need to be better informed of the issues being discussed in the developed country plurilateral groups. Opening the decision-making process may also involve broadening the current membership of groupings such as the G7/G8, the Quad, and the OECD. However, there is always a "tradeoff between effectiveness and representation ... Those who call for larger representation must accept the inevitable consequence of a more laborious governance and lower quality output of international co-operation."[88]

Conclusion

Most international relations scholars discuss the GATT/WTO as being virtually coterminous with the global trade regime, because they focus on the regime's principles, norms and rules, and largely disregard decision-making procedures. This book contends that it is important to direct more attention to decision-making procedures, because they can have a significant effect on the development and evolution of the global trade regime's principles, norms and rules. Decision-making in the global trade regime is a multilayered process that occurs in a wide range of formal and informal institutions. Our understanding of the global trade regime will be greatly enhanced if we devote more attention to these institutions, and to their relationship with the GATT/WTO. Thus, this book systematically traces the changing role in the global trade regime of three developed country-led institutions that have had a significant effect on trade decision-making: the OECD, the G7/G8, and the Quad. As Figure 1.1 shows, these institutions are near the top of the trade decision-making pyramid, and the most important traders in these institutions are the United States and the European Union. We devote a smaller amount of space to less influential institutions representing developing country interests such as the G77 and UNCTAD (see Figure 1.1), and we discuss some other institutions throughout the book mainly for illustrative purposes.

Most importantly, this book rests on the assumption that the pyramid in Figure 1.1 is not static. In tracing historically the role of the OECD, G7/G8, and the Quad in the global trade regime this book addresses three central questions:

1. How and why have the OECD, G7/G8 and Quad become influential in the global trade regime?
2. What is the nature of their influence?
3. How has their influence changed over time?

In answering these three questions, we expect to reach some conclusions regarding the changing nature of pyramidal decision-making in the global trade regime.

This chapter has discussed four major factors that explain why GATT/WTO members sometimes turn to other institutions to deal with trade-related matters: the dominance of developed countries in the North over developing countries in the South, the decline of U.S. economic hegemony, the growing interaction of trade and other issues with the globalisation of the world economy, and the unique characteristics of the GATT/WTO as an international organisation.

The last factor mentioned is the most controversial because of the conflicting perceptions of developed and developing countries. From a developed country perspective, the lack of formal minilateral prerogatives such as an executive body in the GATT/WTO encourages the major traders to turn to plurilateral institutions such as the G7/G8, Quad, and OECD. Thus, one trade specialist maintains that the "major GATT/WTO trading countries" are often inclined to "take their business elsewhere, for example, to annual 'summit' meetings, small groups of trade ministers such as the 'quad group'... , certain regional arrangements, or other types of private meetings of trade ministers or major participants."[89] Another trade specialist argues that "member countries must be prepared to delegate responsibility for the management of WTO operations to a small steering committee of WTO members," and that "in the absence of WTO reforms, the United States and other major trading countries may well continue to resort to ad hoc, extra-legal processes like the Quad. Alternatively, the United States and the European Union could simply cut their own deal (as they did in the Uruguay Round on agriculture) and insist that others accept it."[90] In marked contrast, the UNCTAD Secretary-General Rubens Ricupero has argued from a developing country perspective that "unlike the IMF and the World Bank, the WTO is structured on the assumption that all members are equal, whereas the reality is otherwise." Many important trade policy decisions in Ricupero's view "are taken by a limited number of countries in closed groups or ... outside of the framework of the WTO altogether."[91] Developing country dissatisfaction with the GATT caused them to press for the formation of UNCTAD in 1964, but they have been disappointed with this organisation's lack of influence.

One issue that both developed and developing country members of the GATT/WTO agree on, is that the global trade regime is in fact composed of a wide range of formal and informal institutions. These institutions form a pyramid in the global trade regime, with the developed country-led institutions such as the G7/G8, the Quad, and the OECD near the apex. Among the members of the Quad, the United States and the EU are clearly the most important. It is to the historical role of these institutions from the 1940s to the present that we now turn.

Chapters 2 to 8 in this book trace the changes in the pyramidal structure of the global trade regime historically from the late 1940s to early 2002, with particular emphasis on the OECD, the G7/G8, and the Quad. Each chapter provides a brief overview of the changes in the pyramid (Figure 1.1), discusses the general developments in the GATT/WTO and the global trade regime, examines the role of the developed country-led plurilateral institutions, and discusses the response of the developing countries to the policies of the developed countries. This broader institutional analysis will hopefully provide a more complex and variegated view of the global trade regime than studies that limit their focus almost completely to the GATT/WTO.

Notes

1   World Trade Organization, *Annual Report – 1998* (Geneva: WTO, 1998), p. 5.
2   Stephen D. Krasner, "Structural Causes and Regime Consequences: Regimes as Intervening Variables," in Stephen D. Krasner, ed., *International Regimes* (Ithaca: Cornell University Press, 1983), p. 1.
3   Oran R. Young, "International Regimes: Toward a New Theory of Institutions," *World Politics* 39 (October 1986), p. 108. See also Carsten Otto, "'International Regimes' in the Asia-Pacific? The Case of APEC," in Jörn Dosch and Manfred Mols, eds., *International Relations in the Asia-Pacific: New Patterns of Power, Interest, and Cooperation* (New York: St. Martin's Press, 2000), pp. 45-46.
4   John W. Meyer, David John Frank, Ann Hironaka, Evan Schofer, and Nancy Brandon Tuma, "The Structuring of a World Environmental Regime, 1870-1990," *International Organization* 51-4 (Autumn 1997), pp. 623-651.

5   Robert O. Keohane, *International Institutions and State Power: Essays in International Relations Theory* (Boulder: Westview Press, 1989), p. 5.
6   Jock A. Finlayson and Mark W. Zacher, "The GATT and the Regulation of Trade Barriers: Regime Dynamic and Functions," in Krasner, ed., *International Regimes*, p. 274.
7   See, for example, Yoshi Kodama, *Asia Pacific Economic Integration in the GATT/WTO Regime* (The Hague: Kluwer Law International, 2000).
8   John H. Jackson, *World Trade and the Law of GATT* (Indianapolis: Bobbs-Merrill, 1969), p. 11.
9   Stephen Woolcock, "European Trade Policy: Global Pressures and Domestic Constraints," in Helen Wallace and William Wallace, eds., *Policy-Making in the European Union* (Oxford: Oxford University Press, 4th ed., 2000), p. 373. Woolcock discusses the fact that, even when the European Commission negotiates, it must receive a mandate from the Council of Ministers. See also John Peterson and Elizabeth Bomberg, *Decision-Making in the European Union* (London: Macmillan, 1999), ch. 4.
10   "Supplementary Protocol No. 1 to the Convention on the OECD," 14 December 1960.
11   Robert Wolfe, "The Making of Peace, 1993: The OECD in Canadian Economic Diplomacy," unpublished paper, October 1993, p. 80.
12   Krasner, "Structural Causes and Regime Consequences," p. 2.
13   Hugo Paemen and Alexandra Bensch, *From the GATT to the WTO: The European Community in the Uruguay Round* (Leuven: Leuven University Press, 1995), p. 40.
14   Finlayson and Zacher, "The GATT and the Regulation of Trade Barriers," p. 294.
15   Marc Williams, *Third World Cooperation: The Group of 77 in UNCTAD* (London: Pinter Publishers, 1991), p. 23.
16   Gilbert R. Winham, "The Prenegotiation Phase of the Uruguay Round," *International Journal* 44-2 (Spring 1989), pp. 289-290.
17   See E.P. Wellenstein, "Unity, Community, Union – What's in a Name?," *Common Market Law Review* 29-2 (1992), pp. 205-212; Desmond Dinan, *Ever Closer Union: An Introduction to European Integration* (Boulder: Lynne Rienner, second edition, 1999), p. 2.
18   See Virginia Haufler, "Crossing the Boundary between Public and Private: International Regimes and Non-State Actors," in Volker Rittberger with the assistance of Peter Mayer, ed., *Regime Theory and International Relations* (Oxford: Clarendon Press, 1995), pp. 94-111; Robert Wolfe, "Rendering unto Caesar: How Legal Pluralism and Regime Theory Help in Understanding 'Multiple Centres of Power'," in Gordon Smith and Daniel Wolfish, eds., *Who is Afraid of the State? Canada in a World of Multiple Centres of Power* (Toronto: University of Toronto Press, forthcoming).
19   On the role of scientific groups in environmental regimes, see Peter M. Haas, "Do Regimes Matter? Epistemic Communities and Mediterranean Pollution Control," *International Organization* 43-3 (Summer 1989), pp. 377-403; Peter M. Haas, "Introduction: Epistemic Communities and International Policy Coordination," *International Organization* 46-1 (Winter 1992), pp. 1-35.
20   See William J. Drake and Kalypso Nicolaïdis, "Ideas, Interests, and Institutionalization: 'Trade in Services' and the Uruguay Round," *International Organization* 46-1 (Winter 1992), pp. 37-100.
21   The term "keystone international economic organisations" is used in Harold Jacobson and Michel Oksenberg, *China's Participation in the IMF, the World Bank, and GATT: Toward a Global Economic Order* (Ann Arbor: University of Michigan Press, 1990).
22   World Trade Organization, "Developing Countries' Merchandise Exports in 1999 Expanded by 8.5%," Press Release/175, 6 April 2000, p. 19; Richard H. Steinberg, "Great Power

Management of the World Trading System: A Transatlantic Strategy for Liberal Multilateralism," *Law and Policy in International Business* 29-2 (1998), pp. 217-218.

23 Bernard M. Hoekman and Michel M. Kostecki, *The Political Economy of the World Trading System: The WTO and Beyond* (Oxford: Oxford University Press, 2nd edition, 2001), pp. 240-241.

24 Robert O. Keohane, *After Hegemony: Cooperation and Discord in the World Political Economy* (Princeton: Princeton University Press, 1984), p. 139.

25 For competing views on this issue, see Samuel Huntington, "The U.S. – Decline or Renewal?," *Foreign Affairs* 67-2 (Winter, 1988-89), pp. 76-96; Paul Kennedy, *The Rise and Fall of the Great Powers: Economic Change and Military Conflict from 1500 to 2000* (New York: Random House, 1987); David P. Calleo, *Beyond American Hegemony: The Future of the Western Alliance* (New York: Basic Books, 1987); Bruce Russett, "The Mysterious Case of Vanishing Hegemony: or, Is Mark Twain Really Dead?," *International Organization* 39-2 (Spring 1985), pp. 207-31; Susan Strange, "The Persistent Myth of Lost Hegemony," *International Organization* 41-4 (Autumn 1987), pp. 551-74; and Joseph S. Nye, Jr., *Bound to Lead: The Changing Nature of American Power* (New York: Basic Books, 1990).

26 Judith Goldstein, "Ideas Institutions, and American Trade Policy," *International Organization* 42-1 (Winter 1988), p. 179.

27 Robert O. Keohane, *After Hegemony: Cooperation and Discord in the World Political Economy* (Princeton: Princeton University Press, 1984); and Robert O. Keohane, "The Demand for International Regimes," in Stephen D. Krasner, ed., *International Regimes* (Ithaca: Cornell University Press, 1983), pp. 141-71.

28 Renato Ruggiero (WTO director-general), "Charting the Trade Routes of the Future: Towards a Borderless Economy," address delivered to the International Industrial Conference, San Francisco, 29 September 1997, *World Trade Organization Press Release*, Geneva, Press/ 77, p. 4.

29 Dukgeun Ahn, "Linkages between International Financial and Trade Institutions: IMF, World Bank and WTO," *Journal of World Trade* 34-4 (2000), p. 1.

30 *Articles of Agreement – International Monetary Fund* (Washington, D.C.: IMF, 1993), Article I.2; *Articles of Agreement – International Bank for Reconstruction and Development*, as amended effective February 16, 1989 (Washington, D.C.: IBRD, 1991), Article I.3.

31 "Punta del Este Ministerial Declaration," adopted 20 September 1986, Part 1.E.

32 "Marrakesh Agreement Establishing the World Trade Organization," Article III.5, in *The Results of the Uruguay Round of Multilateral Trade Negotiations – The Legal Texts* (Geneva: WTO, 1995).

33 For a detailed discussion of the WTO agreements with the IMF and World Bank, see Ahn, "Linkages between International Financial and Trade Institutions," pp. 13-16.

34 Julio J. Nogués, "Comment: The Linkages of the World Bank and the GATT/WTO," in Anne O. Krueger, ed., with Chonira Aturupane, *The WTO as an International Organization* (Chicago: University of Chicago Press, 1998), pp. 84-86. See also Hoekman and Kostecki, *The Political Economy of the World Trading System*, pp. 68-69.

35 World Trade Organization, Doha Ministerial Conference, "Ministerial Declaration," WT/ MIN(01)/DEC/W/1, 14 November 2001, paragraph 38.

36 Nicholas Bayne, *Hanging In There: The G7 and G8 Summit in Maturity and Renewal* (Aldershot: Ashgate, 2000), p. 7.

37 Robert A. Pastor, *Congress and the Politics of U.S. Foreign Economic Policy, 1929-1976* (Berkeley: University of California Press, 1980), p. 78.

38   Joseph M. Jones, Jr., *Tariff Retaliation: Repercussions of the Hawley-Smoot Bill* (Philadelphia: University of Pennsylvania Press, 1934); John W. Evans, *The Kennedy Round in American Trade Policy: The Twilight of the GATT?* (Cambridge, MA: Harvard University Press, 1971), pp. 5-7.

39   Patrick Low, *Trading Free: The GATT and U.S. Trade Policy* (New York: Twentieth Century Fund Press, 1993), pp. 43-44.

40   William Diebold, Jr., *The End of the I.T.O.*, Essays In International Finance no. 16 (Princeton: Princeton University, October 1952), pp. 6 and 24; Low, *Trading Free*, pp. 41-42. Studies favouring the ITO Charter at the time include Clair Wilcox, *A Charter for World Trade* (New York: Macmillan, 1949); and William Adams Brown, Jr., *The United States and the Restoration of World Trade: An Analysis and Appraisal of the ITO Charter and the General Agreement on Tariffs and Trade* (Washington, D.C.: Brookings Institution, 1950). A study highly critical of the Charter is Philip Cortney, *The Economic Munich: The I.T.O. Charter, Inflation or Liberty, The 1929 Lesson* (New York: Philosophical Library, 1949).

41   Jean-Christophe Graz, "The Political Economy of International Trade: The Relevance of the International Trade Organization Project," *Journal of International Relations and Development* 2-3 (September 1999), p. 290.

42   See Robert D. Putnam, "Diplomacy and Domestic Politics: The Logic of Two-Level Games," *International Organization* 42 (Summer 1988), pp. 427-60.

43   Raymond Vernon, "The U.S. Government at Bretton Woods and After," in Orin Kirshner, *The Bretton Woods – GATT System: Retrospect and Prospect after Fifty Years* (Armonk, NY: M.E. Sharpe, 1996), p. 60.

44   Susan Ariel Aaronson, *Trade and the American Dream: A Social History of Postwar Trade Policy* (Lexington: University Press of Kentucky, 1996), p. 132; Diebold, *The End of the I.T.O.*, pp. 11-24; Richard N. Gardner, *Sterling-Dollar Diplomacy in Current Perspective: The Origins and Prospects of Our International Economic Order* (New York: Columbia University Press, expanded ed., 1980), pp. 348-80.

45   Low, *Trading Free*, p. 45.

46   Stephen Zamora, "Voting in International Economic Organizations," *American Journal of International Law* 74-3 (July 1980), pp. 571-73.

47   *Charter of the United Nations*, Article 2.

48   Harold Jacobson, *Networks of Interdependence: International Organizations and the Global Political System* (New York: Alfred A. Knopf, 1979), p. 13.

49   Mancur Olson, *The Logic of Collective Action: Public Goods and the Theory of Groups* (Cambridge: Harvard University Press, 1965); Kenneth A. Oye, "Explaining Cooperation Under Anarchy: Hypotheses and Strategies," in Kenneth A. Oye, ed., *Cooperation Under Anarchy* (Princeton: Princeton University Press, 1986), pp. 18-20.

50   Miles Kahler, "Multilateralism with Small and Large Numbers," in John Gerard Ruggie, ed., *Multilateralism Matters: The Theory and Praxis of an Institutional Form* (New York: Columbia University Press, 1993), p. 296.

51   International Monetary Fund, *Annual Report 2001* (Washington, D.C.: IMF, 2001), p. 168.

52   In April 2001, Saudi Arabia, Russia, and China also had their own Executive Directors in the IMF. Unlike the G5 countries, however, these countries are not always *assured* of having their own Executive Directors. Indeed, Italy had more votes (70,805) than Saudi Arabia (70,105) in April 2001, and both Italy and Canada (63,942) had more votes than Russia (59,704). China (63,942) had the same number of votes as Canada. Italy and Canada both had Executive Directors in 2001, but they were elected by blocs of countries.

53   Margaret Garritsen de Vries, "Bretton Woods Fifty Years Later: A View from the International Monetary Fund," in Kirshner, ed., *The Bretton Woods-GATT System*, p. 135; International Monetary Fund, *Annual Report 2000* (Washington, D.C.: IMF, 2000), p. xiii.

54   *Havana Charter for the International Trade Organization*, Article 78.3.a. The eight seats for members of economic importance were to go to the United States, Britain, Canada, France, the Benelux customs union, India, China, and the Soviet Union if they joined the ITO. See Wilcox, *A Charter for World Trade*, pp. 154-55; Brown, *The United States and the Restoration of World Trade*, pp. 228-29.

55   Zamora, "Voting in International Economic Organizations," p. 579.

56   Olivier Long, *Law and Its Limitations in the GATT Multilateral Trade System* (Dordrecht: Martinus Nijhoff, 1985), p. 51.

57   Richard Blackhurst, "Reforming WTO Decision Making: Lessons from Singapore and Seattle," in Klaus Günter Deutsch and Bernhard Speyer, eds., *The World Trade Organization Millennium Round: Freer Trade in the Twenty-First Century* (London: Routledge, 2001), pp. 302-203; Richard Blackhurst, "The Capacity of the WTO to Fulfill Its Mandate," in Krueger, ed., *The WTO as an International Organization*, pp. 49-50.

58   Ernest H. Preeg, *Traders in a Brave New World: The Uruguay Round and the Future of the International Trading System* (Chicago: University of Chicago Press, 1995), p. 132; Hoekman and Kostecki, *The Political Economy of the World Trading System*, pp. 60-61; Jeffrey J. Schott and Jayashree Watal, "Decision Making in the WTO," Jeffrey J. Schott, ed., *The WTO After Seattle* (Washington, D.C.: Institute for International Economics, July 2000), pp. 285-286.

59   Anne Anderson, Ireland's trade negotiator, quoted in Elizabeth Olson, "Patching Up Morale at the World Trade Organization," *New York Times*, 31 October 2000, p. W1.

60   In the Havana Charter talks the United States in fact favoured a weighted voting procedure for the proposed ITO. However, the Europeans and Latin Americans obtained U.S. agreement to a one-nation, one-vote procedure in return for concessions they made to the United States. See John Odell and Barry Eichengreen, "The United States, the ITO, and the WTO: Exit Options, Agent Slack, and Presidential Leadership," in Krueger, ed., *The WTO as an International Organization*, p. 186.

61   Gilbert R. Winham, *International Trade and the Tokyo Round Negotiation* (Princeton, NJ: Princeton University Press, 1986), p. 376.

62   D.M. McRae and J.C. Thomas, "The GATT and Multilateral Treaty Making: The Tokyo Round," *American Journal of International Law* 77 (January 1983), p. 83.

63   John H. Jackson, *The World Trading System: Law and Policy of International Economic Relations* (Cambridge: MIT Press, 2nd edition, 1997), p. 69.

64   *Marrakesh Agreement Establishing the World Trade Organization*, Article IX.1, footnote 1.

65   Jeffrey J. Schott assisted by Johanna W. Buurman, *The Uruguay Round: An Assessment* (Washington, D.C.: Institute for International Economics, November 1994), pp. 138-139.

66   World Trade Organization, "Developing Countries' Merchandise Exports in 1999 Expanded by 8.5%," *Press Release/*175, 6 April 2000, p. 19.

67   Schott and Watal, "Decision Making in the WTO," p. 287.

68   See Atlantic Council of the United States, *GATT Plus – A Proposal for Trade Reform*, Report of the Special Advisory Panel to the Trade Committee of the Atlantic Council (New York: Praeger, 1975), pp.6-11 & 56-57; and Gary Clyde Hufbauer, "Background Paper," in *The Free Trade Debate*, Reports of the Twentieth Century Fund Task Force on the Future of American Trade Policy (New York: Priority Press, 1989), pp. 149-54.

69   Gilbert R. Winham, "The World Trade Organisation: Institution-Building in the Multilateral
     Trade System," *The World Economy* 21-3 (May 1998), p. 355; John Croome, *Reshaping the
     World Trading System: A History of the Uruguay Round* (Geneva: World Trade Organization,
     1995), p. 155.
70   Schott and Watal, "Decision Making in the WTO," p. 286.
71   John E. Ray, "The OECD 'Consensus' on Export Credits," *The World Economy* 9-3
     (September 1986), pp. 295-96.
72   David Henderson, "International Agencies and Cross-Border Liberalization: The WTO in
     Context," in Krueger, ed., *The WTO as an International Organization*, p. 102.
73   Jackson, *World Trade and the Law of GATT*, p. 150.
74   Jeffrey J. Schott, "The WTO after Seattle," in Schott, ed., *The WTO After Seattle*, pp. 10-11.
75   Jackson, *World Trade and the Law of GATT*, p. 150.
76   Jackson, *The World Trading System*, p. 343.
77   T.N. Srinivasan, *Developing Countries and the Multilateral Trading System: From the GATT
     to the Uruguay Round and the Future* (Boulder: Westview, 2000), p. 3.
78   Jock A. Finlayson and Mark W. Zacher, *Managing International Markets: Developing
     Countries and the Commodity Trade Regime* (New York: Columbia University Press, 1988),
     p. 30.
79   Abdulqawi Yusuf, *Legal Aspects of Trade Preferences for Developing States: A Study in the
     Influence of Development Needs on the Evolution of International Law* (The Hague: Martinus
     Nijhoff, 1982), p. 12.
80   Michael Zammit Cutajar, ed., *UNCTAD and the North-South Dialogue: The First Twenty
     Years* (Oxford: Permagon Press, 1985), p. vii.
81   Henderson, "International Agencies and Cross-Border Liberalization," p. 102.
82   "Marrakesh Agreement Establishing the World Trade Organization," Articles 3.5 and 5.1.
83   Marc Williams, *International Economic Organisations and the Third World* (New York:
     Harvester Wheatsheaf, 1994), p. 205.
84   Javed A. Ansari, *The Political Economy of International Economic Organization* (Boulder:
     Rienner, 1986), p. 296.
85   C. Fred Bergsten and C. Randall Henning, *Global Economic Leadership and the Group of
     Seven* (Washington, D.C.: Institute for International Economics, June 1996), p. 15.
86   Robert D. Putnam and Nicholas Bayne, *Hanging Together: Cooperation and Conflict in the
     Seven-Power Summits* (London: SAGE, revised edition, 1987), p. 149.
87   Rubens Ricupero, "Integration of Developing Countries into the Multilateral Trading
     System," in Jagdish Bhagwati and Mathias Hirsch, eds., *The Uruguay Round and Beyond:
     Essays in Honor of Arthur Dunkel* (Ann Arbor: University of Michigan Press, 1998), pp.
     33-34.
88   Michele Fratianni, Paolo Savona, and John J. Kirton, "Introduction, Summary, and
     Conclusions," in Michel Fratianni, Paolo Savona, and John J. Kirton, eds., *Governing Global
     Finance: New Challenges, G7 and IMF Contributions* (Aldershot: Ashgate, 2001), p. 5.
89   Jackson, *The World Trading System*, p. 64.
90   Schott assisted by Buurman, *The Uruguay Round: An Assessment,* p. 139.
91   Ricupero, "Integration of Developing Countries into the Multilateral Trading System," p.
     34.

2   The Origins and Early Period of the Postwar Trade Regime: 1947 to 1962

As discussed in Chapter 1, the origins of the GATT date back to October 1947, when 23 countries signed the final act of the General Agreement on Tariffs and Trade. In the 1947 to 1962 period, the GATT was a relatively small club-like organisation dominated by the developed countries. Thus, the major developed country traders could engage in decision-making in the GATT without having to contend with the problem of promoting cooperation with large numbers of countries, and without having to deal with significant opposition and demands from developing countries.[1] As Table 2.1 shows, only 26 countries participated in the 1960-61 Dillon Round of GATT negotiations. Although 20 developing countries had joined the GATT by 1960, only 7 of them participated in the Dillon Round.[2]

Table 2.1   The Rounds of GATT Negotiations

Name	Years	Countries Participating
Geneva	1947	23
Annecy	1949	13
Torquay	1951	38
Geneva	1956	26
Dillon	1960-61	26
Kennedy	1964-67	62
Tokyo	1973-79	102
Uruguay	1986-93	123

The 1947 to 1962 period predates the formation of the G7 and the Quad, and the OECD was established only at the very end of this period, in 1961.

Nevertheless, the pyramidal structure of institutions in the global trade regime with developed country-led institutions near the top of the pyramid was beginning to form as early as the late 1940s. This chapter discusses two plurilateral groupings established by developed countries during this early period, in which they could confer on their trade-related interests: the Organisation for European Economic Co-operation (OEEC) which was established in 1948, and the Food and Agriculture Organization's (FAO's) Consultative Subcommittee on Surplus Disposal (CSD) which was formed in 1954. Although the OEEC membership was limited to European countries, its successor organisation, the OECD, has a broader membership that includes all the developed countries. The CSD is a subcommittee of the FAO's Committee on Commodity Problems. Nevertheless, in its daily functions the CSD's responsibilities and preoccupations are very different from those of the FAO. Whereas the FAO is located in Rome and relies on substantial input from developing as well as developed countries, the CSD is located in Washington, D.C. and is dominated by the developed countries. This chapter also discusses the origins of the European Community, because it has become one of the two most important actors in the global trade regime. During this early period, the United States was clearly the hegemonic actor, and the EC did not yet occupy a place alongside the United States near the top of the global trade regime pyramid.

General Developments in the Postwar Trade Regime

The origins of the postwar trade regime stem back to the interwar period. After World War I, efforts to remove trade restrictions were largely unsuccessful as countries reacted to harsh economic conditions by increasing their tariffs. Tariffs were rising not only in European countries recovering from the war but also in the United States, which had emerged from the war as a net creditor nation and the world's largest industrial power. Despite the growing trade competitiveness of the United States, domestic U.S. groups seeking protectionist trade barriers benefited from the fact that the U.S. Constitution gives Congress the sole power to regulate commerce and impose tariffs. The members of Congress are far more susceptible than the President to protectionist pressures, because they do not have national constituencies.[3] Thus, after the 1929 stock market crash Congress passed the 1930 Smoot-Hawley Tariff Act, which increased average U.S. *ad valorem* rates on dutiable imports to 52.8 percent, "the highest American tariffs in the twentieth century."[4]

The Smoot-Hawley tariff had disastrous consequences as other countries rushed to retaliate with their own import restrictions, and world trade declined from $35 billion in 1929 to $12 billion in 1933.[5] In efforts to reverse this damage, the U.S. Congress passed the Reciprocal Trade Agreements Act (RTAA) in 1934. The RTAA permitted the Congress to insulate itself "from the direct one-sided pressure from producer interests" by delegating authority to the President to negotiate reciprocal tariff reductions with other countries of up to 50 percent.[6] Thus, the RTAA for the first time linked the setting of U.S. tariffs to international negotiation, and from 1934 to 1945 the United States negotiated 32 tariff-lowering agreements. The RTAA, however, authorised the President to conduct only bilateral tariff negotiations, and it became evident in the 1940s that multilateral negotiations were necessary to provide a firmer and broader basis for promoting trade liberalisation. Beginning in 1943, the United States took the primary initiative, often along with Britain, in discussions and conferences that eventually resulted in the creation of the GATT. Although it is a multilateral agreement, "almost all the clauses in GATT can be traced to one or another of the clauses contained in" the 1934 U.S. Reciprocal Trade Agreements Act.[7]

During the first decade of its existence, the GATT developed a series of *ad hoc* arrangements to deal with trade policy requirements while "waiting and hoping for the creation of permanent organizational structure."[8] In December 1950, however, the United States formally announced that it had suspended efforts to ratify the Havana Charter, under which an International Trade Organization would have replaced the GATT. The GATT contracting parties made another attempt to establish a formal trade organisation in 1955, when they prepared a charter for an Organization for Trade Cooperation (OTC). The OTC charter, like the planned ITO, called for the establishment of an executive board that would have included the major economic powers. According to its charter, the OTC was to contain three major organizational divisions: an assembly of all OTC members, an executive committee of elected members including the five members of chief economic importance, and a secretariat.[9]

Not surprisingly, the U.S. Congress which had not approved the ITO and had not even sanctioned the formation of the informal GATT, refused to endorse the creation of an OTC. By 1956 it was therefore evident that a formal trade organisation would not be established, and the contracting parties instead turned their attention to improving the GATT structure. Thus, the GATT gradually developed into a functioning, albeit informal, international organisation. As mentioned, the small GATT secretariat was "borrowed" from the Interim Commission for the planned ITO, and Geneva became the *de facto* location for the organisation. Heading the GATT secretariat was an Executive-Secretary, whose title was changed to Director-General in 1965. The member governments administering the General Agreement met at periodic gatherings called "Sessions of Contracting Parties." An Intersessional Committee met during the period between the Sessions which were held only once or twice a year, and in 1960 GATT members created a Council of Representatives to replace the Intersessional Committee. The Council of Representatives and the small secretariat essentially permitted the GATT to become a full-time international organisation.[10]

The principle GATT objectives from 1947 to the early 1960s were to lower tariff barriers, abolish import quotas, and begin applying rules to commercial policy measures. To achieve these objectives, the GATT became actively involved in organising multilateral trade negotiations and in settling trade disputes among the contracting parties. The GATT's initial efforts in dispute settlement were tentative and provisional, but it gradually developed procedures such as referring disputes to "working parties." Later, these working parties became "panels" of experts, and dispute settlement became a well-established function of the organisation. Most importantly, the GATT held its first five rounds of multilateral trade negotiations from 1947 to 1962 (see Table 2.1, page 33). These rounds dealt only with the reduction of tariffs, and the negotiating procedures were largely patterned after U.S. practices in the 1934 Reciprocal Trade Agreements Act. The procedures provided for selective product-by-product negotiations, in which each GATT member would submit a request list of items to other members from which it desired tariff concessions. Bargaining would then usually ensue in bilateral meetings, and the concessions each side granted would be extended to other GATT members in accordance with the unconditional most-favoured nation (MFN) principle. GATT members benefiting from MFN would be expected to grant equivalent benefits within a reasonable time period in accordance with the reciprocity principle.[11]

Although the developed countries could settle many of their disagreements and develop a consensus on issues within the GATT during this early period, they began to turn to smaller institutions and groupings for discussions of some particularly sensitive and complex issues. The discussion that follows examines the role of two of these groupings: the OEEC and the FAO's Consultative Subcommittee on Surplus Disposal. We also discuss the origins and early development of the European Community and the OECD.

The Organisation for European Economic Co-operation

As was the case with the GATT, the United States was the primary force behind the formation of the OEEC. The Western European economies were virtually bankrupt after World War II, and by 1947 there were fears that a lack of hard currency would force them to severely limit or even suspend imports. The European inability to pay for imports posed a serious threat to postwar economic prosperity and to American exports. To bolster Western Europe as a Cold War ally and contribute to its reconstruction, the United States launched the European Recovery Program (ERP) or Marshall Plan in 1947. In announcing the ERP, the U.S. Secretary of State George C. Marshall indicated that the United States would provide substantial amounts of assistance to European countries to aid in their postwar recovery. However, in providing this assistance the United States would require the Europeans to "put forth their maximum effort to help themselves" on a joint or collective basis. The United States "wanted partnership with the whole of Europe, not with its separate parts."[12] To coordinate their policies, the Western European countries initially established a Committee of European Economic Cooperation. However, there was a need for a more permanent body, and the Europeans created the OEEC in April 1948. The OEEC, which was designed to jointly allocate U.S. Marshall Plan aid, was originally composed of 16 non-communist European countries. West Germany joined the OEEC in 1949, and Spain joined in 1958. Although the OEEC membership was limited to European countries, the United States and Canada as contributors to the Marshall Plan were represented at OEEC meetings from the start; and they became associate members in 1952. As associate members the United States and Canada did not have formal voting powers in the OEEC, but they nevertheless had considerable influence.[13]

When the OEEC was established, it had no precisely formulated commitment to lower trade barriers. Faced with an American ultimatum, however, the OEEC members agreed to move toward liberalising intra-European trade. The worst obstacles to intra-European trade were quantitative restrictions on imports (or import quotas) rather than tariffs. Quantitative restrictions were a major problem in general, and in 1950 at least 20 of the 33 GATT members were imposing such restrictions to safeguard their monetary reserves. European countries in the postwar period were limiting imports to specified quantities or banning them completely for certain products as a result of their growing balance of payments deficits. A tacit division of labour developed between the GATT and the OEEC to deal with these postwar trade restrictions: Whereas GATT negotiations until the 1964-67 Kennedy Round focused exclusively on lowering tariffs, the OEEC was concerned primarily with removing quantitative restrictions. In 1950 the OEEC also established the European Payments Union (EPU), partly with U.S. funds. The EPU permitted the member countries to settle their accounts with each other on a multilateral basis, and this liberalisation of payments facilitated OEEC efforts to liberalise trade.[14]

The GATT and OEEC approaches to dealing with quantitative restrictions were quite different. As discussed in Chapter 1, GATT/WTO members sometimes turn to other institutions when they prefer to deal with trade issues in a less legalistic, rules-based venue – and the GATT's approach to quantitative restrictions was highly legalistic. Those who drafted the General Agreement considered quantitative restrictions to be far more damaging to trade than tariffs. Whereas producers can undercut a reasonable tariff and maintain their exports by increasing their efficiency, quantitative restrictions provide no rewards for efficiency. When countries place specified limits on the imports of a good, even the most efficient producers cannot circumvent those limits. In contrast to tariffs which the GATT sought to reduce through multilateral trade negotiations, GATT Article XI therefore called for the "General Elimination of Quantitative Restrictions." Articles XI and XII did permit exceptions to the ban on quantitative restrictions for agriculture and balance of payments deficits. The balance of payments exception proved to be a major problem for the Europeans. Although many European countries had serious payments deficits only with the United States, GATT Article XIII stipulated that countries imposing quantitative restrictions for balance of payments reasons had to apply them on a non-discriminatory basis to *all* foreigners.[15] Ironically, GATT's nondiscrimination requirement therefore resulted in a more widespread use of quantitative restrictions.

The GATT as a global organisation felt considerable pressure to insist on the nondiscrimination principle for the use of quantitative restrictions. In contrast, the OEEC which was limited to European countries could adopt a regional, discriminatory approach to dealing with quantitative restrictions. Furthermore, the OEEC did not declare quantitative restrictions illegal as the GATT had done, and it only pressured member countries to gradually reduce intra-European quantitative restrictions in accordance with a set formula. In pressuring members to alter their import controls, the OEEC depended primarily on persuasion. The techniques of persuasion included expert studies to estimate the probable impact of lower barriers on trade, lengthy discussions at the OEEC Permanent Council in Paris, and periodic council meetings at the ministerial level. The OEEC also relied on a new technique known as "confrontation," which required each country to explain its policies and programs to the other OEEC countries in response to a periodic review of its activities.[16]

The OEEC's less legalistic, more flexible approach permitted it to make more progress in negotiating the gradual removal of quantitative restrictions in Western Europe than the more rigid, rules-bound approach of the GATT. By October 1949, the OEEC countries had unilaterally removed quotas on about 30 percent of their private imports with each other (imports by governments and their agencies were not included). In November 1949, the OEEC Council (the organisation's highest decision-making body) decided that by 15 December 1949 member countries should remove quotas on 50 percent of their private imports with each other. Again, imports for the public sector were excluded. In 1950 the OEEC members accepted a Code of Liberalisation to promote greater equality in intra-European trade and also to plan for the further removal of quantitative restrictions. The liberalisation target was subsequently increased to 75 percent of private trade in 1951 and to 90 percent in 1955. By the time the OECD replaced the OEEC in 1961, 95 percent of private trade between OEEC countries was free of quantitative restrictions.[17]

Although some OEEC countries removed quantitative restrictions on goods from other weak currency countries that were not OEEC members, they discriminated against hard-currency countries, especially the United States. The United States as the global hegemon accepted this discrimination against its goods, because Cold War security was its foremost concern at the time. Following the American lead, the GATT tacitly accepted the discrimination in the OEEC's Code of Liberalisation even though it ran counter to GATT Article XIII. (Canada was less willing than the United States to accept this discrimination, and it protested as OEEC member countries gradually dismantled quantitative restrictions with each other but did not give equal treatment to Canada.[18]) The actual amount of liberalisation that the OEEC brought to European trade is debatable. As mentioned, the OEEC's liberalisation targets applied only to private trade, and some European countries engaged in a considerable amount of trade through government agencies. Nevertheless, "the fact cannot be denied that the OEEC contributed to a substantial relaxation of controls in intra-European trade in a period when members of the OEEC felt that there was little prospect of getting results in the GATT."[19] The OEEC's success in this area stemmed from its flexible, non-legalistic approach, and from its membership which was limited mainly to developed European countries.

Although the OEEC's Code of Liberalisation was somewhat successful in liberalising trade for industrial goods, its efforts to deal with restrictions in the highly sensitive area of agricultural trade encountered many more obstacles. In 1955 the OEEC therefore began a process of confrontation of national agricultural policies, which involved "the examination of each country's agricultural policy by all the rest, the sharing of experience, and the mutual exchange of suggestions and criticisms."[20] The goal of the confrontation process was to gradually develop agreed principles for governments to follow in their agricultural policy-making. The GATT by contrast focused on the application of binding international agreements, but it provided exceptions for agriculture under specified conditions. It is uncertain that the OEEC's process of policy confrontation and harmonisation was successful in resolving agricultural trade problems, and this approach to national agricultural policies was discontinued when the OECD replaced the OEEC in 1961.[21] As we will discuss, agricultural trade liberalisation also proved to be one of the most difficult (if not the most difficult) problems confronting the GATT.

In sum, the OEEC had a number of advantages over the GATT in fostering an exchange of views, developing techniques of persuasion, and engaging in a process of policy confrontation in highly sensitive areas of national policy related to trade. The OEEC's advantage *vis-à-vis* the GATT was that it was a plurilateral group of developed countries with common cultural and political ties that could take a more flexible and less legalistic approach to trade policy. Thus, the OEEC was one of the important early organisations contributing to the pyramidal structure of institutions that developed in the global trade regime. However, the OEEC's role in liberalising trade was limited to the removal of quantitative restrictions, and the issue of tariffs remained the preserve of the GATT. Ironically, the more successful the OEEC became in eliminating import quotas, the more tariffs became prominent as a remaining obstacle to intra-European trade. Low-tariff countries feared they would lose competitiveness by removing quantitative restrictions when other OEEC countries retained their high tariff barriers. Nevertheless, some OEEC members felt that tariffs should be dealt with only in a broader membership organisation, and the GATT remained the main forum for negotiating tariff reductions.[22]

After the OEEC had removed most quantitative restrictions on intra-European private trade, a series of changes contributed to the eventual demise of the OEEC as a viable organisation. First, the OEEC had realised many of its objectives such as ending the U.S. dollar shortage and restoring currency convertibility. The Western European countries no longer needed a recovery program, and as developed countries they had to begin to assume more responsibilities beyond their region for overall economic growth. Second, although the OEEC stimulated intra-European trade, in some respects its discriminatory approach frustrated GATT's efforts to promote *global* trade liberalisation. For example, OEEC members constantly pressured Belgium to limit its purchases from the dollar zone countries so it could purchase more from other European countries. Although the Americans had "accepted discrimination against themselves in the interest of European recovery," by the late 1950s they "wanted to revert to a more universal and nondiscriminatory arrangement."[23]

A third reason for the demise of the OEEC was the establishment of the European Economic Community by six Western European countries in 1958: Belgium, France, West Germany, Italy, Luxembourg, and the Netherlands. The EC was to be a common market with a common external tariff, and it produced a split among the non-communist European countries. Britain was not initially willing to join the EC because it feared a future "United States of Europe" and wanted to retain its economic and political linkages with the United States and the Commonwealth. Nevertheless, Britain was concerned about the exclusionary aspects of the EC. At an OEEC Council meeting in December 1958, the British tried to bring all 18 OEEC countries into a free trade area, but the meeting broke up in acrimony – particularly between the British and the French. The split widened in 1960 when seven non-EC countries under British leadership formed their own separate European Free Trade Association (EFTA). Both France and the United States opposed any new efforts to promote free trade between the six EC members and the seven EFTA members, for different reasons. The French feared that the EC's cohesion would be undermined if an OEEC-wide free trade area or an EC-EFTA free trade link was established. The United States was disturbed by its deteriorating balance of payments, and wanted to discourage any OEEC-wide free trade agreement that would discriminate against U.S. exports. Thus, the continued division between the EC and EFTA sealed the fate of the OEEC as a European institution, and it was phased out and replaced by the OECD in 1961.[24]

The Organisation for Economic Co-operation and Development

Although the Americans and Europeans eventually agreed that the OEEC should be phased out, they decided to create a new organisation to supersede it. A conference on adapting the OEEC to the new international environment was held in May 1960, and the result was the Convention of the Organisation for Economic Co-operation and Development that came into force in September 1961. Thus, the OECD became the first developed country-led institution near the top of the global trade regime pyramid (see Figure 1.1). Initially, the member countries of the OECD were the same as those of the OEEC with the addition of the United States and Canada. Other developed countries such as Finland,

Japan, Australia, and New Zealand joined in the 1960s and early 1970s, and today the OECD also includes a number of countries outside the industrial core group such as Turkey, Mexico, Hungary, Poland, the Czech Republic, South Korea, and the Slovak Republic. Nevertheless, the 30 members of the OECD today are mainly developed countries (see Table 3.1 for a list of the OECD countries and the years they joined the organisation).[25]

The major industrial powers decided to convert the OEEC into the OECD for a number of reasons. The OEEC had established effective procedures for intergovernmental consultation among developed countries, and a high quality secretariat able to prepare analytical reports, maintain comprehensive records, and promote understandings and agreements. Instead of totally discarding the organisation, plans were therefore developed to convert the OEEC machinery to new tasks. The greater mobility resulting from more rapid communications and transportation, combined with the progress toward freer trade and payments, demonstrated that Europeans, Americans, and Canadians could benefit from a new organisation with a membership extending beyond Europe. Thus, a consensus formed among the developed countries that the new organisation (the OECD) should no longer be limited to Europeans. There were early indications that the OECD would also extend beyond the Atlantic area, because the United States was already planning for the inclusion of Japan (Japan was admitted to the OECD in 1964).[26]

The EC, the United States, and Canada all perceived that the formation of a broader OECD extending beyond Europe was in their interests. From the perspective of the EC countries, it was best to include the United States and Canada in the new organisation because this would block the formation of an OEEC free trade area that could interfere with the development of the EC common market. From an American perspective, the OEEC had represented the asymmetrical donor-recipient relationship of the Marshall Plan, but Western Europe had experienced a remarkable economic recovery. Thus, "the Americans wanted a forum where they, the Europeans and other 'industrial democracies' could sit down together on equal terms."[27] Canada was also committed to the formation of the OECD in which it would be a full member, partly because of concerns about trade and other types of discrimination in Europe. Thus, Canada's Minister of Finance at the time argued that "trade policies are not made in isolation, but through inter-action. The commercial policies to be followed in Europe cannot fail to influence United States policies and both are of critical importance to Canada."[28]

Initially, it seemed that the OECD's most important functions would be in non-trade areas such as monitoring developed country aid-giving to developing countries. At the time the OECD was formed there was a growing awareness that the South required a substantial flow of resources from the North, and a major reason for forming the OECD from the United States perspective was to promote greater sharing of the aid burden. By 1960, the U.S. balance of payments deficit had increased to $3.7 billion, and foreign dollar holdings exceeded U.S. gold reserves for the first time.[29] Thus, the United States believed that the Europeans should be doing more to help provide assistance to the Third World. Even before the OECD was established, the OEEC had formed a Development Assistance Group in 1960 to monitor the extension of economic assistance to non-member developing countries. In 1961 this Group was incorporated in the OECD and renamed the Development Assistance Committee (DAC).

In contrast to the OECD's aid monitoring function, it seemed that the OECD would have an insignificant role in promoting international trade. Indeed, the OEEC's Code of Liberalisation was dropped when the OECD was formed, and the GATT took over responsibility for dealing with quantitative restrictions on trade for several reasons. First, by 1960 the OEEC had already been quite successful in reducing intra-European quantitative restrictions on trade, and the Code of Liberalisation no longer seemed to be necessary. Second, the United States and Canada opposed any extension of the Code of Liberalisation because they were concerned that it might encourage new forms of trade discrimination by the EC and EFTA. Instead of having a special trade code, the United States and Canada wanted the OECD to function in trade as it did in other areas, simply through a process of consultation. Third, the U.S. administration was reluctant to give the OECD competence in the trade area, because the Congress had failed to support the proposed ITO and OTC, and had also never even formally sanctioned the GATT. Although the Congress had gradually become accustomed to the GATT, there were concerns that it would oppose attempts to provide the new OECD with trade-related responsibilities. Finally, the United States and Canada were committed to a global approach to reducing trade barriers under the GATT rather than a plurilateral approach within a limited-membership organisation such as the OECD. Thus, they did not want the OECD's trade-related functions to detract in any way from the work of the GATT.[30]

Despite the initial efforts to give the OECD a low profile on trade matters, there were indications that its role in this area could become more important. Indeed, Article I of the 1960 OECD Convention states that one of the three main goals of the organisation is "to contribute to the expansion of world trade on a multilateral, non-discriminatory basis in accordance with international obligations."[31] Although the OECD was not designed to adopt GATT-like functions of establishing or administering trade rules, it was aptly suited to serve as a forum where developed countries could have frank discussions of each other's trade policies, and exchange views on specific trade problems. To perform these functions, the OECD established a Trade Committee of high-level officials along with working-level representatives to assist it, and the tasks assigned to the Trade Committee gradually increased to the point where the working-level representatives were almost permanently in session. Other OECD Committees, such as the Committee on Invisible Transactions, have also dealt with various aspects of commercial policy. Although the United States had initially been wary of giving the OECD trade responsibilities, it gradually reversed its policy and began to promote the OECD as a forum for discussing trade issues with increasing frequency. In view of the OECD's initial reluctance to deal with trade matters, a study published in 1967 concluded that the OECD's growing trade-related functions exceeded "the expectations of the organization's prime movers" more than in any other area. [32] The role of the OECD in the global trade regime is discussed in detail in subsequent chapters.

The FAO's Consultative Subcommittee on Surplus Disposal

The FAO's Consultative Subcommittee on Surplus Disposal (CSD), like the OEEC, demonstrated the propensity of developed countries to seek their own plurilateral groupings to deal with trade-related matters outside of the GATT as early as the 1940s and 1950s. As was the case for the OEEC, U.S. policies were a major factor explaining the establishment of the CSD. It is therefore important to discuss the role played by the United States in the CSD's creation.

As the global economic hegemon, the United States demonstrated its willingness to adopt a leadership role in the formation of international regimes. The United States was often willing to provide public goods to help create these regimes by accepting "what seemed like lopsided exchanges favoring other countries."[33] For example, this chapter has discussed the fact that the United States accepted and even promoted the formation of the OEEC and the European Community, despite its exclusion from these institutions. Nevertheless, "the United States continued to draw the line on agreements that seemed to tie its hands significantly in the choice of future policies."[34] As discussed, the U.S. Congress failed to ratify the Havana Charter partly because of feelings that a strong International Trade Organization would limit U.S. policy choices, and in 1955 the Congress refused to support the formation of an Organization for Trade Cooperation. The United States was also unwilling to significantly inhibit its policy choices in domestically sensitive issues such as agriculture. Thus, the

United States insisted on exceptions for agriculture in the General Agreement, and on some agricultural issues the United States opted for deliberations in groups such as the Food and Agriculture Organization that were less legalistic and demanding than the GATT.

The American propensity to opt for exemptionalism over liberalisation in agricultural trade was evident during the negotiation of the General Agreement. The GATT contained two agricultural exemptions that were included largely to conform with provisions in the U.S. farm program. GATT Article XVI prohibited export subsidies for manufactured goods, but an exception was provided for agricultural and other primary products. This exception was designed to accord with a 1935 amendment (Section 32) to the U.S. Agricultural Adjustment Act permitting the Department of Agriculture to use export subsidies. GATT Article XI called for the elimination of quantitative restrictions on imports, but permitted such restrictions for agriculture when they were needed to enforce government supply management measures. Article XI was patterned after Section 22 of the U.S. Agricultural Adjustment Act, that sanctioned the use of import quotas for commodities under price support programs.[35]

In additon to the GATT exceptions, some matters relating to agricultural trade were largely excluded from GATT determinations. At the end of the Korean War in 1953, the demand for foodgrains declined, but production in the major exporting countries was increasing to record levels. The problem was especially severe in the United States, where Congress approved the Agricultural Trade Development Assistance Act or Public Law 480 (PL 480) in 1954 to dispose of food surpluses through concessional transactions. Although PL 480 provided some developing countries with needed food aid, U.S. competitors feared that unregulated concessional sales would interfere with their commercial agricultural exports. At the 1954-55 GATT Review Session, Australia therefore proposed that a new article be added to the General Agreement calling for mandatory prior consultations and compulsory arbitration to protect competing exporters from concessional agricultural sales. The United States, however, was unwilling to accept a role for the GATT in this area. Instead, the United States agreed to have the less authoritative and demanding FAO monitor the effects of concessional transactions on commercial agricultural sales.[36]

In 1954, the major trading nations adopted the FAO Principles of Surplus Disposal, which are mainly concerned with the disposal of developed country agricultural surpluses.[37] The FAO Principles rely on the concept of "additionality" to ensure that surplus disposal programs do not interfere with normal trading patterns. According to this concept, agricultural products exported on concessional terms must be additional to – and therefore must not displace –

normal commercial exports. To monitor adherence to the FAO Principles, the FAO's Committee on Commodity Problems established a Consultative Subcommittee on Surplus Disposal (CSD). The CSD has monthly meetings in Washington, D.C., and its membership is open to all FAO members. However, only countries with a specific interest in the CSD's specialised activities have become members of the subcommittee.

The United States was more willing to accept CSD than GATT scrutiny of its surplus disposal policies for two major reasons. First, "the FAO's approach to food aid/commercial trade problems sharply departs from domestic legal models."[38] The CSD "is strictly limited to providing a forum for consultations and negotiations and to making recommendations which are not binding upon the governments concerned."[39] Governments are not required to modify their transactions in response to criticism, and the FAO Principles aim instead at voluntary acceptance of criticisms raised by other countries. The FAO's voluntary procedures in dealing with the surplus disposal issue form a marked contrast with the GATT/WTO's emphasis on binding, legal obligations. A second reason for U.S. acceptance of the CSD is that the developed country agricultural exporters are the dominant actors in the CSD. Although the CSD is a subcommittee of the FAO's Committee on Commodity problems, developing countries have far more influence at FAO headquarters in Rome than they have at CSD meetings in Washington, D.C. The CSD has been somewhat concerned with developing country needs, but it has always placed primary emphasis on the interests and objectives of the developed country agricultural exporters.[40] Thus, the CSD like the OEEC was an early indication of the propensity of developed countries to opt for minilateralism as a means of resolving their differences and reaching a consensus on sensitive trade policy issues.

The European Community

It is important to discuss the origins of the European Community, and the early American and British response, because the EC would eventually join the United States at the top of the global trade regime pyramid (see Figure 1.1).

In his 1947 speech announcing the European Recovery Program, U.S. Secretary of State George C. Marshall insisted only that the European recipients of American economic aid should engage in prior agreement and cooperation. However, many American policy-makers went further than Marshall and "hoped to link this aid to progress in European political unification both to meet a perceived Soviet threat and to resolve the general economic crisis."[41] France and some smaller Western European countries wanted the OEEC to assume these supranational powers and impose limits on the sovereignty of the member countries. Britain, by contrast, was reluctant to surrender national control over economic policy, and the OEEC was formed largely on British terms as a traditional intergovernmental organisation. In May 1950 the French Foreign Minister Robert Schuman announced a plan (developed by a senior French official Jean Monnet) to place French and German steel production under a Common High Authority, and this plan resulted in the establishment of the supranational European Coal and Steel Community (ECSC) in 1952. Since Britain refused to participate, the ECSC included only six member countries.

Although Britain had not joined the ECSC, it was invited to the Messina conference in 1955 where plans were being developed for the Rome Treaty. Britain sent only a low level servant to the preliminary talks, and it withdrew completely in November 1955. Instead of the proposed common market, the British called for a much broader free trade area composed of the OEEC countries. The British proposal, however aroused suspicions among the six ECSC members that Britain was simply trying to sabotage attempts to form a common market, and they proceeded to form the European Economic Community in 1958. Britain initially refused to join the EC because of concerns that membership would force it to subsume its national sovereignty to a supranational organisation, sacrifice its world role for a policy that focused mainly on one region, loosen its historically close ties with the United States, and weaken its political and economic linkages with the Commonwealth. As discussed, Britain opted instead to form the EFTA in 1960 with a group of smaller countries outside the EC: Austria, Denmark, Norway, Portugal, Sweden, and Switzerland. The EC, however, was producing more dynamic economic results than the EFTA, and the British economy was growing more slowly than the economies of the six EC members. As a result, the British government reversed direction and applied for EC membership in August 1961. This time French president Charles de Gaulle presented the major obstacle to British membership. De Gaulle vetoed British applications for EC membership on two occasions, in January 1963 and November 1967, and Britain did not join the EC until January 1973.[42]

In view of its Cold War security concerns, the United States as global hegemon "tolerated and in fact promoted, the creation of a preference area in Western Europe [the EC] which discriminated against American goods."[43] However, American policy toward Western Europe was an exception, since the United States generally opposed preferential agreements and any other type of discrimination that would interfere with an open multilateral trade regime at the end of World War II. American views in favour of multilateralism prevailed in the GATT, and it was no accident that Article I of the General Agreement was devoted to unconditional most-favoured-nation treatment. Nevertheless, GATT Article XXIV permitted an exception to MFN treatment for countries forming free trade areas and customs unions that discriminated against other GATT members. These regional trade agreements were permissible to the GATT if they were more trade-creating than trade-diverting, and covered substantially all trade among the member countries.[44]

Despite the political desirability of European integration in the American view, the United States "was fully determined to use all means at her disposal to soften the economic discrimination which accompanied the formation of the Common Market."[45] Furthermore, the U.S. "State Department began to receive objections from the Departments of Commerce and of Agriculture, which became aware, rather late in the day, of the economic side-effects of this politically desirable policy."[46] Beginning in 1950 the United States had a balance of payments deficit averaging about $1.5 billion per year, and in the late 1950s this deficit increased rapidly. Thus, the United States was concerned that the EC's common external tariff and Common Agricultural Policy would further restrict American exports. The United States wanted to negotiate with the newly formed EC before its customs union was fully developed, and the Under-Secretary of State C. Douglas Dillon proposed a new round of GATT negotiations at the Fall, 1958 GATT ministerial meeting. As a result, the fifth round of GATT negotiations – the Dillon Round – was held from 1960 to 1961.

The Dillon Round "was never destined for great accomplishment" because the U.S. Congress had not given the President sufficient negotiating authority, the product-by-product method of tariff reduction had become inadequate, and the EC member countries did not decide on the basic elements of their agricultural policy until shortly before the end of the negotiations.[47] In the view of some trade authorities "there is irrefutable evidence that limits on the [U.S.] President's authority restricted achievement" at the Dillon Round, "at least in the negotiation between the United States and the EEC."[48] At the beginning of the Dillon Round the EC offered an across-the-board reduction of 20 percent in industrial tariffs, but the United States and some other countries were not prepared to respond. In the U.S. case, Congressional limitations on the President's negotiating authority prevented him from agreeing to the EC offer. As a result, the Dillon Round continued the ponderous practice of product-by-product negotiations. Product-by-product negotiations were manageable in earlier GATT rounds, but they became less adequate as the number of GATT members and the variety of products traded increased. Despite its disappointing outcome, the

Dillon Round opened the way for a more successful Kennedy Round later in the 1960s. Almost immediately after the Dillon Round the United States began planning for a follow-up round in which the President would be granted authority to negotiate across-the-board or linear reductions in industrial tariffs.

The Dillon Round was the first GATT round in which the EC negotiated as a trading entity. Henceforth the United States and the EC would be the two most important trading entities, both in subsequent GATT negotiations, and in a range of plurilateral developed country institutions. Indeed, the GATT Kennedy, Tokyo, and Uruguay Rounds would not be concluded until the United States and the EC reached agreement on some of the most contentious issues.

The Early Role of Developing Countries

The developed countries were able to confer with each other in the small club-like atmosphere of the GATT during the 1947 to 1962 period, because developing countries were not active participants in the global trade regime. The limited involvement of the developing countries in the early postwar years stemmed from several factors, including their relatively small numbers (many were still colonial territories), their protectionist trade policies, and GATT's inattention to their development problems. Most developing countries in the 1950s adopted protectionist import-substituting industrialisation (ISI) policies, that were designed to replace industrial imports with domestic production. Raúl Prebisch, an Argentinian economist, was the most influential figure supporting ISI policies in the postwar period. (Hans Singer offered similar prescriptions to Prebisch favouring ISI.) Prebisch argued that structural inequality between the developed countries in the core and the developing countries in the periphery was a major characteristic of the capitalist world economy. As long as developing countries were dependent on exports of primary products, they could not achieve high economic growth rates. Prebisch therefore advised developing countries to pursue ISI policies to increase their production of manufactures.[49] Latin American developing countries in particular, influenced by Prebisch's arguments, adopted policies that emphasized industrial over agricultural development, production for the domestic market over production for export, and protection of local industry through import barriers. With this focus on inward-looking policies, most developing countries did not seek to actively participate in the GATT. Thus, the number of developing countries in the GATT increased from 10 in 1948 to only 20 in 1960, and only 7 developing countries participated in the 1960-61 Dillon Round.

As discussed in Chapter 1, the Havana Charter gave some recognition to developing country concerns, and eight of the articles in the Charter dealt with development issues. These articles allowed developing countries with ITO consent to withdraw tariff concessions, and to use quantitative restrictions, subsidies, and preferential tariff arrangements. Chapter VI of the Havana Charter dealt with international commodity agreements that were of particular importance to developing countries.[50] When the U.S. Congress failed to ratify the Havana Charter, most of the Charter provisions on development were not incorporated in the GATT, and Chapter VI was omitted entirely. Indeed, "economic development as a positive trade policy remained one of the most glaring omissions in the GATT."[51] The only major provision in the General Agreement dealing directly with Third World trade problems was GATT Article XVIII, which gave developing countries some flexibility in imposing import quotas to protect their infant industries and alleviate their balance-of-payments problems.[52] The developing countries insisted that GATT should be doing more to give them special and differential (S&D) treatment, but their influence in the GATT during the 1947 to 1962 period was extremely limited.

Although the developing countries have tried to adopt a unified position on trade issues, it is important to note that they have in fact often had divergent interests. One source of difference among developing countries in the 1947 to 1962 period that has persisted to the present was the establishment of EC trade linkages with its former colonies. When the EC was formed in 1958, France insisted that the trade preferences it was giving to its African Overseas Territories be continued. The French wanted to ensure that exports from its former colonies would have free access to the EC and that other EC members would eventually share the costs of providing economic assistance to its former colonies. Despite the opposition of some EC members, the French were adamant, and Part 4 of the Treaty of Rome provided for an extension of France's preferential arrangements under EC auspices. Initially, there were 18 developing countries with associate status, known as the Associated African States and Madagascar (AASM). Although Part 4 called for the gradual removal of tariffs between EC members and the associates, the associates could protect their infant industries and retain some tariffs for revenue purposes, and the EC was to provide financial aid to the associates through a European Development Fund.[53]

A number of countries in GATT argued that the EC was providing discriminatory trade preferences to its African associate members because the associate system did not constitute a genuine free trade area; that is, the African associates did not provide reciprocal free trade to EC members. As a result, the association agreements were in direct conflict with GATT's nondiscrimination principle.[54] The EC insisted, however, that the association agreements were fully coordinate with United Nations proposals that the North should promote economic and social development in the South. At a 1966 GATT working party examining the association agreements, for example, EC members expressed the view that in a free-trade area the developed countries should not require reciprocal advantages from the developing countries.[55] As discussed later in this book, the EU associate agreements with developing countries have been one of the continuing sources of division within the South on global trade issues.

Conclusion

From 1947 to 1962 the GATT was a relatively small club-like organisation dominated by the developed countries. The developed countries lacked the formal minilateral prerogatives in the GATT that they had in the IMF and World Bank, such as an executive board and weighted voting. Nevertheless, the developed countries dominated the rule-making and multilateral trade negotiations in the GATT, and the developing countries had little influence in the organisation. The developed countries could therefore engage in discussions to resolve their differences and develop a consensus on many issues within the confines of the GATT, and they did not feel a great need for plurilateral institutions for these purposes. Furthermore, the United States was clearly the global economic hegemon during this period, and collective management of the global trade regime had not yet become a major issue.

Despite the dominance of the United States as global hegemon and the developed countries' ability to set the multilateral trade agenda within the confines of the GATT, there were already signs of change in the pyramidal structure of the global trade regime during this early period. First, the European Economic Community was formed in 1958, and there were indications that it would become an important trading entity that would eventually challenge U.S. hegemony in the global trade regime. Second, the pyramidal structure of institutions in the global trade regime with developed country-led institutions near the top of the pyramid was beginning to form as early as the late 1940s. The 1947 to 1962 period predates the formation of the G7 and the Quad, and the OECD was established only at the end of this period, in 1961. However, this chapter discusses two plurilateral groupings established by developed countries: the OEEC which was formed in 1948, and the FAO's Consultative Subcommittee on Surplus Disposal which was formed in 1954.

As undisputed global economic hegemon in the 1940s and 1950s, the United States had the predominant role in the formation of the postwar global trade regime. The United States was the major force behind the formation of the GATT, and it strongly opposed preferential trade agreements that would interfere with open multilateral trade. Nevertheless, the United States viewed Western Europe as an exception, and encouraged European cooperation and even integration from the time it instituted the European Recovery Program in 1948. American leaders realised that European economic problems posed a serious threat to postwar economic prosperity and to U.S. exports, and they believed that Western European recovery was essential for the Cold War struggle with the Soviet Union. However, the U.S. economic position became less predominant as Western Europe and Japan recovered from the war, and U.S. government leaders began to view the EC increasingly as a potential competitor. Thus, the United States supported the GATT Dillon Round as a means of limiting EC restrictions on American exports, and the United States supported the shift from the OEEC to the OECD as a means of inducing Western Europe to adopt more outward-looking policies. It was increasingly evident that developing countries required a substantial transfer of financial resources, and the United States felt that the Europeans should share the responsibility of providing assistance. Implicit in the shift from the OEEC to the OECD "was the recognition that" the U.S.-European "relationship had changed and that the era of US economic predominance was drawing to a close."[56]

Institutional developments in the 1947 to 1962 period demonstrated the dominance of developed countries in the global trade regime. Although the FAO in Rome was a universal membership organisation, its Consultative Subcommittee on Surplus Disposal which was set up in Washington, D.C. to monitor the effects of surplus disposal on trade was dominated by developed countries. Both the OEEC and CSD provided the developed countries with a more flexible and less legalistic venue than the GATT for discussing and negotiating sensitive trade issues. For example, developed countries in the CSD have generally adhered to the FAO principles of surplus disposal mainly because of "the threat by others to employ the same grey area transactions that cause offence," and not because of "concern over 'exposure' in CSD."[57] Whereas European developed countries were able to agree on reductions on quantitative restrictions (or import quotas) in the OEEC, Western donors of development assistance found the CSD a useful forum for limiting the adverse effects of surplus disposal on commercial trade.

The developing countries had only a low level of participation in the global trade regime in the 1947 to 1962 period, because most of them were following inward-looking ISI policies. Furthermore, the GATT gave only limited attention to developing country needs and concerns during this period, and GATT Article XVIII was the only provision in the General Agreement that dealt directly with Third World trade problems. Although the developing countries tried to establish a unified front *vis-à-vis* the developed countries on trade issues, there were in fact a number of divisions in the Third World. This chapter outlined the divisions resulting from the association linkages of EC members with their former colonies.

In September 1961 the OEEC was replaced by OECD, the first of the developed country-led institutions we focus on in this book. Although it was initially uncertain as to whether the OECD would deal with trade issues, Chapter 3 shows that the OECD was already beginning to take on important trade-related functions in the 1960s. Chapter 3 also discusses the formation of the G77 and UNCTAD, and the growing presence of developing countries in the global trade regime.

Notes

1   The difficulties in promoting cooperation with large numbers was discussed in Chapter 1. See Mancur Olson, *The Logic of Collective Action: Public Goods and the Theory of Groups* (Cambridge: Harvard University Press, 1965); Kenneth A. Oye, "Explaining Cooperation Under Anarchy: Hypotheses and Strategies," in Kenneth A. Oye, ed., *Cooperation Under Anarchy* (Princeton: Princeton University Press, 1986), pp. 18-20.

2   Marc Williams, *Third World Cooperation: The Group of 77 in UNCTAD* (London: Pinter Publishers, 1991), p. 23.

3   See E.E. Schattschneider, *Politics, Pressures and the Tariff: A Study of Free Private Enterprise in Pressure Politics as Shown in the 1929-1930 Revision of the Tariff* (Hamden, CT: Archon Books, 1963).

4   Robert A. Pastor, *Congress and the Politics of U.S. Foreign Economic Policy, 1929-1976* (Berkeley: University of California Press, 1980), p. 78.

5   For a discussion of the effects of the U.S. 1930 tariff, see Joseph M. Jones, Jr., *Tariff Retaliation: Repercussions of the Hawley-Smoot Bill* (Philadelphia: University of Pennsylvania Press, 1934).

6   I.M. Destler, *American Trade Politics*, 2nd edition (Washington, D.C.: Institute for International Economics, June 1992), p. 14.

7   John H. Jackson, *World Trade and the Law of GATT* (Indianapolis: Bobbs-Merrill, 1969), p. 37.

8   Robert E. Hudec, *The GATT Legal System and World Trade Diplomacy* (New York: Praeger, 1975), p. 60.

9   Jackson, *World Trade and the Law of GATT*, p. 51.

10   Hudec, *The GATT Legal System and World Trade Diplomacy*, pp. 60-65; Kenneth W. Dam, *The GATT: Law and International Economic Organization* (Chicago: University of Chicago Press, 1970), pp. 335-350.

11   Jackson, *World Trade and the Law of GATT*, pp. 217-223.
12   Philip E. Jacob, Alexine L. Atherton, and Arthur M. Wallenstein, *The Dynamics of International Organization* (Homewook, ILL: Dorsey Press, revised ed., 1972), p. 336.
13   Clive Archer, *Organizing Western Europe* (London: Edward Arnold, 1990), pp. 35-36; Organisation for European Economic Co-operation, *A Decade of Co-operation: Achievements and Perspectives*, 9th Report of the OEEC (Paris: OEEC, April 1958); W. Randolph Burgess, "Problems of Managing in International Institutions," *California Management Review* 5-3 (Spring 1983), pp. 3-4; Robert Wolfe, "The Making of Peace, 1993: The OECD in Canadian Economic Diplomacy," unpublished paper, October 1993, p. 13.
14   Karin Kock, *International Trade Policy and the Gatt 1947-1967* (Stockholm: Almqvist & Wiksell, 1969), p. 141; Burgess, "Problems of Managing in International Institutions," p. 4.
15   General Agreement on Tariffs and Trade, *Text of the General Agreement* (GATT: Geneva, July 1986).
16   Burgess, "Problems of Managing in International Institutions," p. 4.
17   Michael Palmer and John Lambert, et al., *European Unity: A Survey of European Organisations* (London: George Allen & Unwin, 1968), pp. 100-102.
18   Frank Stone, *Canada, the GATT and the International Trade System* (Montreal: Institute for Research on Public Policy, 2nd edition, 1992), pp. 82-83.
19   Kock, *International Trade Policy and the Gatt 1947-1967*, p. 144.
20   T.K. Waley, "Western Trade in Agricultural Products," in Andrew Shonfield, ed., assisted by Hermia Oliver, *International Economic Relations of the Western World 1959-1971, Vol. 1: Politics and Trade* (London: Oxford University Press, 1976), p. 359.
21   Warley, "Western Trade in Agricultural Products," pp. 359-361.
22   Palmer and Lambert, et al., *European Unity*, p. 103.
23   Henry G. Aubrey, *Atlantic Economic Cooperation: The Case of the OECD* (New York: Praeger, 1967), p. 10.
24   Raymond Vernon, "Organizing for World Trade," *International Conciliation*, no. 505 (November 1955), pp. 172-175; Miriam Camps, *"First World" Relationships: The Role of the OECD* (Paris: Atlantic Institute for International Affairs and New York: Council on Foreign Relations, December 1975), p. 53; Wolfe, "The Making of Peace, 1993," pp. 14-15; Dam, *The GATT: Law and International Economic Organization*, pp. 148-161; Burgess, "Problems of Managing in International Institutions," p. 5.
25   On the transition from the OEEC to the OECD see Richard T. Griffiths, "'An Act of Creative Leadership': The End of the OEEC and the Birth of the OECD," in Richard T. Griffiths, ed., *Explorations in OEEC History* (Paris: OECD, 1997), pp. 235-256.
26   Camps, *"First World" Relationships*, pp. 10-11.
27   Nicholas Bayne, "Making Sense of Western Economic Policies: The Role of the OECD," *The World Today* 43-2 (February 1987), p. 27.
28   Donald Fleming, quoted in Wolfe, "The Making of Peace, 1993," p. 16.
29   On the U.S. balance of payments position in the 1950s and 1960s see Theodore H. Cohn, *Global Political Economy: Theory and Practice* (New York: Addison Wesley Longman, second ed., 2002, forthcoming), ch. 6.
30   Stone, *Canada, the GATT and the International Trade System*, pp. 83-84; Wolfe, "The Making of Peace, 1993," p. 41.
31   "Convention on the Organisation for Economic Co-operation and Development," Paris, 14 December 1960, Article 1.c.
32   Aubrey, *Atlantic Economic Cooperation*, p. 31.

33 Raymond Vernon, "The U.S. Government at Bretton Woods and After," in Orin Kirshner, ed., *The Bretton Woods-GATT System: Retrospect and Prospect After Fifty Years* (Armonk, NY: M.E. Sharpe, 1996), p. 61.

34 Vernon, "The U.S. Government at Bretton Woods and After," p. 61.

35 Despite the agricultural exception in Article X1, in 1955 the U.S. sought and received an unusually broad GATT waiver from its Article X1 obligations. See Theodore H. Cohn, "The Changing Role of the United States in the Global Agricultural Trade Regime," in William P. Avery, ed., *World Agriculture and the GATT* (Boulder: Lynne Rienner, 1993), pp. 20-24; General Agreement on Tariffs and Trade, *Text of the General Agreement* (Geneva: GATT, 1986).

36 Warley, "Western Trade in Agricultural Products," p. 350.

37 FAO, *FAO Principles of Surplus Disposal and Consultative Obligations of Member Nations*, 2nd edition (Rome: FAO, 1980).

38 Robert Bard, *Food Aid and International Agricultural Trade* (Lexington: D.C. Heath, 1972), p. 116.

39 Bard, *Food Aid and International Agricultural Trade*, p. 178.

40 For a detailed discussion of the FAO-CSD see Bard, *Food Aid and International Agricultural Trade*; and Theodore H. Cohn, *The International Politics of Agricultural Trade: Canadian-American Relations in a Global Agricultural Context* (Vancouver: University of British Columbia Press, 1990).

41 Charles Pentland, *International Theory and European Integration* (London: Faber and Faber, 1973), p. 52.

42 David M. Wood and Birol A. Yeşilada, *The Emerging European Union* (New York: Longman, 2nd ed., 2002), pp. 29-35; David Arter, *The Politics of European Integration in the Twentieth Century* (Aldershot, UK: Dartmouth, 1993), pp. 145-153; Derek W. Urwin, *The Community of Europe: A History of European Integration Since 1945* (London: Longman, 2nd ed., 1995), pp. 90-96.

43 Robert Gilpin, "The Politics of Transnational Economic Relations," in Robert O. Keohane and Joseph S. Nye, Jr., *Transnational Relations and World Politics* (Cambridge: Harvard University Press, 1972), pp. 61-62.

44 For a discussion of the GATT Article XXIV exception see Theodore H. Cohn, *Global Political Economy: Theory and Practice* (New York: Addison Wesley Longman, 2000), pp. 245-249.

45 Gerard Curzon, *Multilateral Commercial Diplomacy: The General Agreement on Tariffs and Trade and Its Impact on National Commercial Policies and Techniques* (London: Michael Joseph, 1965), p. 98.

46 Gerard and Victoria Curzon, "The Management of Trade Relations in the GATT," in Shonfield, ed., *International Economic Relations of the Western World*, p. 168.

47 Ernest H. Preeg, *Traders and Diplomats: An Analysis of the Kennedy Round of negotiations under the General Agreement on Tariffs and Trade* (Washington, D.C.: Brookings Institution, 1970), pp. 40-41.

48 John W. Evans, *The Kennedy Round in American Trade Policy: The Twilight of the GATT?*," (Cambridge: Harvard University Press, 1971), p. 16. See also Hudec, *The GATT Legal System and World Trade Diplomacy*, p. 199.

49 See Raúl Prebisch, *The Economic Development of Latin America and Its Principal Problems* (New York: United Nations Economic Commission for Latin America) 7-1 (February 1962), pp. 1-22 (first published in Spanish in May 1950); H.W. Singer, "The Distribution of Gains between Investing and Borrowing Countries," *American Economic Review* 40-2 (May 1950), pp. 473-485; Albert O. Hirschman, "The Political Economy of Import-Substituting

Industrialization in Latin America," *Ouarterly Journal of Economics* 82-1 (February 1968), pp. 1-32; Hollis Chenery, "The Structuralist Approach to Development Policy," *American Economic Review* 65-2 (May 1975), pp. 310-316.

50   Jock A. Finlayson and Mark W. Zacher, *Managing International Markets: Developing Countries and the Commodity Trade Regime* (New York: Columbia University Press, 1988), p. 30.

51   Abdulqawi Yusuf, *Legal Aspects of Trade Preferences for Developing States: A Study in the Influence of Development Needs on the Evolution of International Law* (The Hague: Martinus Nijhoff, 1982), p. 12.

52   On GATT Article XVIII, see Kenneth W. Dam, *The GATT: Law and International Economic Organization* (Chicago: University of Chicago Press, 1970), pp. 227-228; Robert E. Hudec, *Developing Countries in the GATT Legal System* (Aldershot, UK: Gower, for the Trade Policy Research Centre, 1987), pp. 23-24; and Evans, *The Kennedy Round in American Trade Policy*, pp. 113-115.

53   Enzo R. Grilli, *The European Community and the Developing Countries* (Cambridge: Cambridge University Press, 1993), pp. 7-8.

54   Gardner Patterson, *Discrimination in International Trade, The Policy Issues: 1945-1965* (Princeton, NJ: Princeton University Press, 1966), p. 234.

55   "European Economic Community – Association Agreements: Report of Working Party adopted on 4 April 1966," in General Agreement on Tariffs and Trade, *Basic Instruments and Selected Documents*, 14th supplement (Geneva: GATT, July 1966), pp. 105-106.

56   Camps, *"First World" Relationships*, p. 11.

57   Warley, "Western Trade in Agricultural Products," p. 358.

3   The OECD, the UNCTAD, and the GATT Kennedy Round: 1962 to 1972

In the 1962 to 1972 period, the GATT emerged from its small club-like atmosphere and gradually became a much larger and more diverse international organisation. Thus, the number of countries participating in GATT multilateral trade negotiations increased from 26 in the 1960-61 Dillon Round to 62 in the 1964-67 Kennedy Round. Whereas only 7 developing countries participated in the Dillon Round, 25 developing countries were recognised as participants in the Kennedy Round.[1] The developed countries therefore began to feel the need to establish institutions outside the GATT where they could conduct studies, resolve differences, and develop a consensus on important trade issues. It was in the 1960s that the OECD was formed and began to emerge as an important institution dealing with trade issues of particular interest to the North. When the OECD was established, the pyramidal structure of the global trade regime was beginning to take shape (see Figure 1.1, page 5). It was also in the 1960s that the G77 and UNCTAD were formed on the initiative of the developing countries, which highlighted the divisions between the North and the South. Despite the greater activism of developing countries and their increased membership in the GATT, their influence on trade issues continued to be limited. As discussed in Chapter 1, the UNCTAD never rivalled the GATT as the main global trade organisation, and it was relegated to the lower part of the trade regime pyramid (see Figure 1.1). Although 25 developing countries were recognised as participants in the Kennedy Round, relatively few of them "actually engaged in negotiations. Only nine of them, for example, negotiated with the United States."[2] Thus, the developed countries continued to dominate the GATT multilateral trade negotiations in the 1962 to 1972 period.

Among the developed countries, the European Community was clearly increasing its influence in the 1960s, but the United States continued to be the most important trader. The EC's growing influence was somewhat circumscribed by the fact that its membership remained at six countries during the 1962 to 1972 period, despite two attempts by Britain to become an EC member. In July

1961 Harold Macmillan's Conservative government abruptly reversed British policy and announced its intention to apply for admission into the EC. Several factors accounted for this change in policy: Britain was concerned that the economic rift between the two groups of Western European countries could result in major political divisions, the British-inspired EFTA had done little to counter the growing importance of the EC, Britain's economic performance was lagging behind the performance of the EC countries, and projections of the future indicated that Britain's trade with the Commonwealth would continue to decline.

Although the negotiations progressed only slowly, it seemed that a British agreement with the EC was possible by the end of 1962; but negotiations ended abruptly after French President Charles de Gaulle essentially vetoed Britain's entry into the EC in January 1963. The reasons for de Gaulle's drastic action included his suspicions about Britain's intentions, his concerns that Britain's participation would threaten France's influence in the EC and the Franco-German axis, his fears that Britain's entry would interfere with France's efforts to consolidate the EC's Common Agricultural Policy, and his concerns that Britain's entry would facilitate a greater role for the United States in Europe. In 1966 Britain began to discuss the possibilities that it would again apply for EC membership, but in November 1967 de Gaulle issued his second veto of this proposal. It became evident that British entry into the EC was impossible as long as de Gaulle was France's President, and Britain was not admitted to the EC until 1973.[3] Thus, although the EC's importance was growing steadily, its membership did not increase in the 1960s and the United States remained above the EC on the global trade regime pyramid.

Developments in the GATT: 1962 to 1972

Although the first five rounds of GATT negotiations from 1947 to 1961 registered some definite accomplishments, they were modest in nature. The GATT reduced tariffs, contributed along with the OEEC to the elimination of quotas on most non-agricultural products, and avoided serious political conflicts. The tensions of the Cold War generally did not impinge on GATT operations, because most Communist countries did not join the GATT, and the Western developed countries set the agenda and undertook most of the obligations of the global trade organisation.[4] However, the GATT faced some serious problems in the 1947 to 1961 period that raised questions about its effectiveness in the global trade regime. For example, the first five rounds of GATT negotiations failed to deal with agricultural trade restrictions and a wide array of non-tariff barriers. Changes in the international system also threatened to pose new political problems for the GATT. The creation of the European Economic Community in 1958 and the European Free Trade Association in 1960 highlighted the tensions between global and regional approaches to trade liberalisation; and developing countries that were joining the GATT in larger numbers were dissatisfied with the organisation's inattention to their special needs and concerns.

Tariff reductions in the second to fifth GATT rounds from 1949 to 1961 also did not even approach the reductions achieved in the first round – the 1947 Geneva Round. A number of factors accounted for the failure to achieve more substantial tariff reductions, including the limited objectives of the participants and the inadequate bargaining authority of U.S. negotiators. However, the method of negotiation was the most important factor hindering the achievement of more positive results. In the first five GATT rounds, tariff negotiations were conducted on a product-by-product (or item-by-item) basis. In numerous bilateral meetings, countries tabled "request" and "offer" lists with each other for tariff reductions, and negotiated reciprocal concessions. Each concession then had to be extended to all other GATT members on the basis of unconditional most-favoured-nation (MFN) treatment. This process was extremely complex, and it became more time-consuming as the number of GATT countries, and the volume and variety of traded goods increased. In the 1960-61 Dillon Round, the EC offered an across-the-board reduction of 20 percent in industrial tariffs, but the U.S. President lacked sufficient negotiating authority to respond. Thus, the product-by-product method of tariff negotiations continued in the Dillon Round. By this time the product-by-product negotiations were extremely cumbersome, because the six EC countries first had to agree on a common bargaining position for each product before negotiating with the other contracting parties.[5]

In contrast to the second to fifth GATT rounds, conditions were propitious for more rapid moves toward trade liberalisation in the Kennedy Round. In the U.S. Kennedy administration's view, a new GATT round was a necessary response to recessionary conditions, a growing U.S. balance of payments deficit, the trade diverting effects of the EC, and the Communist aid and trade offensive. The Kennedy administration was aware that it would require across-the-board negotiating authority, and the Congress agreed to pass the U.S. Trade Expansion Act which provided the Executive branch with authority to negotiate linear or across-the-board tariff reductions of up to 50 percent. The Kennedy administration also promised adjustment assistance to domestic firms and workers affected by the possible tariff reductions, and created the position of special representative for trade negotiations who would be directly responsible to the President. Other major trading powers agreed with the American view that a more ambitious GATT program was necessary, and a November 1961 GATT ministerial meeting was held in Geneva to prepare for the Kennedy Round.[6]

The 1961 GATT ministerial began a process of "prenegotiation" that culminated in the Kennedy Round. The main function of prenegotiation is "turning the problem into a manageable issue susceptible of a negotiated outcome."[7] Prenegotiations begin "when one or more parties considers negotiation as a policy option and communicates this intention to other parties," and they end "when the parties agree to formal negotiations or when one party abandons the consideration of negotiation as a policy option."[8] The ministers at the 1961 meeting agreed that developed countries should reduce their tariffs to developing country exports, that negotiating procedures should be established for agricultural products, and that a linear method of tariff reduction should be considered as an alternative to the traditional product-by-product method. As a further step in the prenegotiation process, another GATT ministerial meeting was held in early 1963. At this ministerial it was evident that the European Community had become a major player along with the United States. If the two largest trading entities "could agree, the negotiations would move forward; if they should fail to reach an accord, a serious and perhaps fatal crisis would undoubtedly follow."[9] At first there were serious U.S.-EC differences over agriculture and over the proposed linear approach to tariff cuts, and it seemed that the prenegotiations for a new round were near collapse. In late May 1963, however, the United States and the EC reached a compromise agreement that satisfied both sides, and the Kennedy Round was able to proceed. Although developing countries expressed frustration that the developed countries did not give sufficient attention to their concerns, they had only limited influence in affecting the course of the negotiations.

The Kennedy Round was longer than any previous GATT negotiation, with over four years elapsing from the initial ministerial agreement in May 1963 to the signing of the final agreement in June 1967. However, the Kennedy Round registered impressive progress in dealing with some of the major obstacles to multilateral trade liberalisation. Most importantly for tariff negotiations, the Kennedy Round changed from product-by-product reductions to linear reductions. By giving the President authority to negotiate tariff reductions of up to 50 percent in the 1962 Trade Expansion Act, the U.S. Congress provided a strong impetus to this change. Under the linear procedure, most developed countries agreed to offer an across-the-board cut in tariffs of 50 percent for nonprimary products. Although the linear approach was subject to exceptions and did not apply to agricultural goods, tariffs on industrial products were reduced on average by over 35 percent and substantial reductions were also made for agricultural products. Over $40 billion of trade was subject to some type of concession in the Kennedy Round, which was eight times higher than the concessions in the previous Dillon Round. In addition to the progress on tariffs, the Kennedy Round made the first serious – albeit limited – attempt to deal with some non-tariff barriers.[10]

The GATT decision-making process in the Kennedy Round reflected a new orientation of economic forces. The first GATT conference in 1947 had been dominated by the United States with strong support from Britain, and succeeding rounds were also subject to prevailing American influence. The 1960-61 Dillon Round, however, witnessed a new array of relationships that became much more evident during the Kennedy Round. In the view of some observers, the European Community emerged "as a unified and coequal bargaining force with the United States ... The Kennedy Round was the first major negotiation and agreement between two equal poles of economic power across the Atlantic."[11] Although the EC was probably not coequal with the United States during the 1960s, it had certainly become the most important bargaining power confronting the United States. Japan also assumed a larger role in the Kennedy Round than it had in earlier negotiations, and the discontent of developing countries was more apparent than previously.

In the 1962 to 1972 period two international organisations took on trade-related functions along with the GATT in the global trade regime. First, the OECD, which was formed in 1961, began to emerge as an important venue for developed country discussion, negotiation, and consensus-building on certain trade issues. Second, the UNCTAD was established in 1964 to represent developing country interests and express developing country frustrations with the GATT. This chapter devotes considerable space to the role of the OECD and the UNCTAD during the 1962 to 1972 period.

Organisation for Economic Co-operation and Development

The OECD has been involved in a wide variety of trade-related activities, and it is impossible to examine the full range of its activities in this book. Instead, this book focuses primarily on some of the OECD's most important trade-related activities during the period of study. This chapter and Chapter 4 discuss the OECD's role in the areas of export credit and government procurement, Chapters 5 and 6 examine the OECD's role in dealing with agricultural and services trade, and Chapters 7 and 8 focus on the OECD's role in promoting the GATT Uruguay Round negotiations and in attempting to negotiate a multilateral agreement on investment. Before examining specific issues, some general observations are offered regarding the OECD's role in the global trade regime.

The OECD as an Actor in the Global Trade Regime

The OECD is a plurilateral organisation composed primarily of Western developed states with similar values and economic goals. Initially, the member countries were the same as those of the OEEC, except that the United States and Canada were full rather than associate members. Although OECD membership gradually increased over the years, it was largely limited to the advanced capitalist states. A debate in the early 1990s resulted in a decision that the organisation should be open to some enlargement, and Table 3.1 shows that six countries outside the industrial core group have become OECD members since the 1990s: Mexico in 1994; the Czech Republic in 1995; Hungary, Poland, and South Korea in 1996; and the Slovak Republic in 2000. Other countries are also seeking membership in the organisation. Whereas some OECD countries are open to this enlargement, others warn that "transforming the OECD into a mini-United Nations could well jeopardize its ability to achieve high quality agreements among like-minded countries."[12]

Table 3.1   Members of the OECD (Years of Admission)

Australia (1971)	Luxembourg (1961)
Austria (1961)	Mexico (1994)
Belgium (1961)	Netherlands (1961)
Canada (1961)	New Zealand (1973)
Czech Republic (1995)	Norway (1961)
Denmark (1961)	Poland (1996)
Finland (1969)	Portugal (1961)
France (1961)	Slovak Republic (2000)
Germany (1961)	South Korea (1996)
Greece (1961)	Spain (1961)
Hungary (1996)	Sweden (1961)
Iceland (1961)	Switzerland (1961)
Ireland (1961)	Turkey (1961)
Italy (1961)	United Kingdom (1961)
Japan (1964)	United States (1961)

By promoting cooperation and coordination of their domestic policies, the OECD members seek to achieve common economic objectives. The OECD is particularly involved in areas of interdependence such as international trade and investment. Before assessing the OECD's role in the export credit and government procurement issues in the 1962 to 1972 period, it is necessary to discuss the organisation's general role in the global trade regime. It is often assumed that the OECD, unlike the GATT/WTO, does not engage in international trade negotiations. Negotiation may be defined as *"a process in which explicit proposals are put forward ostensibly for the purpose of reaching an agreement on an exchange or on the realization of a common interest where conflicting interests are present."*[13] The characteristic that distinguishes negotiation from tacit bargaining and other types of conflict resolution is the confrontation of explicit proposals. Whereas one outcome of negotiation may be an explicit agreement, negotiation may also result in "tacit understandings between the parties, a clarification of the points of disagreement, a reorientation of national objectives, new commitments to third parties ... and propaganda effects."[14] The OECD *does* in fact engage in trade negotiations and prenegotiations, as the term is defined here. OECD members have put forward explicit proposals regarding a number of trade issues on which states have had conflicting views. Subsequent discussion has sometimes resulted in an explicit agreement, a tacit understanding, a clarification of positions of OECD members, or a shift in national positions or objectives. The OECD also engages in many trade-related activities that do not involve negotiation. OECD committees often serve as fora for an exchange of views and information, the review of member policies, and an analysis of market trends; and the OECD conducts and publishes many analytical studies of trade issues that can be useful in subsequent negotiations.

Whereas some OECD negotiations relate to relatively simple issues such as whether or not to publish a report, others involve basic principles, norms and rules of the global trade regime. The OECD rather than the GATT/WTO has been the main negotiating forum for a small number of important trade-related issues such as export credits. However, the OECD has more commonly served as a venue for prenegotiation as a prelude to further negotiations in the GATT/ WTO. The OECD prenegotiation process typically involves three phases: defining issues and discussing how to handle them; providing detailed discussion and analysis, mainly on the basis of secretariat documents; and developing a common understanding or consensus that OECD members bring to subsequent GATT/WTO negotiations. OECD Council meetings at ministerial level have also served as fora to express the resolve of developed country ministers to successfully conduct or complete GATT/WTO negotiations.[15]

The OECD has been an appealing venue for promoting trade liberalisation for a number of reasons. First, the OECD's smaller, relatively homogeneous membership provides developed countries with an alternative to the much larger, heterogeneous GATT/WTO. Most OECD members have similar values, concerns, and levels of economic development, which makes it easier to reach a consensus on a number of trade-related issues. Second, the OECD is normally a forum for reaching non-binding agreements, and it is able to agree on constraints on state behaviour for some issues (often in sensitive areas that impinge on domestic policy) where countries are reluctant to bind themselves legally in the GATT/WTO. The OECD normally takes a consensus-building approach to international cooperation, with the goal of reaching a broad consensus on the principles, commitments, and actions required to attain particular objectives. Progress in reaching consensus depends on putting political pressure on countries to endorse the majority OECD view.

Finally, the OECD's long-term experience in promoting the harmonisation of domestic policies has given it a special role in dealing with trade issues. The involvement of domestic groups in international economic policy-making "varies among the different policy sectors, with trade-related matters frequently having the most significant level of [domestic] intrusion and impact."[16] The domestic component of trade policy became increasingly evident after GATT negotiators succeeded in lowering tariffs, and then directed their attention to the problem of non-tariff barriers (NTBs). Since most NTBs are "behind the border" measures that are closely linked with a country's domestic policies, the OECD has experience and expertise in dealing with them.[17] Although the OECD as a plurilateral organisation largely limited to developed countries has a number of advantages in trade-related negotiations, it is important to note that developing countries and other GATT/WTO countries that are not included in this select group have often been resentful. This resentment has sometimes limited the role of the OECD as a negotiating forum, particularly in recent years. A prime example was the strong negative reaction to OECD negotiations for a Multilateral Agreement on Investment (MAI) in the 1990s.

The OECD's trade-related functions have been so diverse, that it is impossible to examine all of them here. As discussed, this book focuses primarily on five trade-related issues in which the OECD has been closely involved. Chapters 3 and 4 (covering the period of the GATT Kennedy and Tokyo Rounds) examines the OECD's involvement in the issues of export credit and government procurement. Chapters 5 and 6 (covering the lead-up to, and the first part of the GATT Uruguay Round) discuss the OECD's involvement in the issues of services and agricultural trade. Chapter 7 provides some further discussion of the OECD's involvement in the Uruguay Round, and Chapter 8 discusses the OECD's unsuccessful attempt to negotiate an MAI in the post-Uruguay Round period. Export credit was one of the earliest trade-related areas of OECD negotiation, and in this area the OECD rather than the GATT/WTO has served as the main forum for negotiation. The OECD also devoted considerable attention to the government procurement issue in the 1960s and early 1970s, but in this case the GATT took over the government procurement issue during the Tokyo Round. Although the OECD was involved with the agricultural and services issues from the time of its formation, its major contribution in agricultural and services trade was in the prenegotiations leading up to the GATT Uruguay Round.

The OECD and Export Credit

Many factors have an influence on export competitiveness, including prices, exchange rates, quality, marketing, servicing, and taxes. In competition among developed states, export credit is particularly important for promoting expensive capital goods exports and exports to developing countries and transition economies. Export credit may be broadly defined as "an insurance, guarantee or financing arrangement which enables a foreign buyer of exported goods and/or services to defer payment over a period of time."[18] The payment deferral period for export credit may be short-term (less than two years), medium-term (two to five years), or long-term (over five years). "Official export credit" refers to deferred payment arrangements that are financed or underwritten by an exporter's government. Depending on the terms offered, official export credit may have the same effect as an export subsidy. Official support through export credit agencies may be provided in three forms: as financing support at commercial levels; as financing support at concessional levels (i.e., aid financing); and as export credit insurance, which "insures exports or guarantees creditors against commercial or political ... risks in international transactions."[19] "Pure cover" refers to export credit insurance or guarantees without any financing support.

Each OECD country has an export credit agency that "functions as a public or semipublic bank, borrowing from the treasury or public capital markets and using the funds to finance exports."[20] Among the OECD countries, the Group of 5 (the United States, Japan, Germany, Britain, and France) accounts for the largest share of officially-supported export credit. After World War II, developed states used export credits primarily to support sales to developing countries that lacked financial liquidity. Originally, the purpose of these sales was to provide aid to developing countries as well as to expand export markets. However, government-backed export credit agencies were also established to protect exporters from risks in foreign markets, and to assist in making export credit terms competitive with the terms offered by other governments. Increasingly, developed countries used export credit financing to support exports of heavy capital equipment and high technology products to other developed countries as well as to developing countries.[21] Without multilateral agreements, there was a danger that credit-supplying countries would engage in an export credit race through such means as lowering interest rates and lengthening repayment periods. The efforts of each developed country exporter to match other offers could threaten the advantages any exporting country hoped to gain from providing export credit. Whereas most export credit providers are in the OECD, the GATT/WTO also contains many developing countries and transition economies that are net consumers of export credit. The net consumers of credit would not be likely to support multilateral discipline that limits the softening of credit terms, because they benefit from the relaxation of credit conditions by the developed country exporters. As a result, the OECD rather than the GATT/WTO eventually became responsible for negotiating export credit agreements.

Efforts to promote international cooperation among export credit providers extend back to at least 1934, when a British government department and three private credit insurance companies in France, Italy and Spain agreed to form an organisation to coordinate their export credit insurance practices. The organisation's formal name has changed several times, but informally it has always been called the "Berne Union," and that name is used here.[22] The main purposes of the Berne Union are to develop sound principles of export credit insurance, and to maintain discipline over the credit terms offered in international trade. Although it was formed in 1934, the Berne Union became inactive during World War II and did not resume functioning until the late 1940s when the Union secretariat moved from Bern, Switzerland to London.[23]

By 1957 government agencies and private companies from a number of other countries had joined the Berne Union, but the Union found it was increasingly difficult to control competition among export credit providers for two major reasons. First, the Union was a non-governmental organisation of credit insurers that was trying to deal with expanding government involvement in the area. This became a more serious problem in the 1950s, when developed countries were increasing their sales of large capital goods items to developing countries. The size of the transactions and the financial status of the developing country buyers meant that many exports could only be sold on credit with longer terms. However, there were limits on how much credit the private sector could offer, and governments therefore increased their support for export credit in order to facilitate these sales. Most members of the Berne Union were not able to commit their governments on policy matters, and the rules were loosely written and had no binding legal force. A second reason for the Berne Union's ineffectiveness was that it dealt only with export credit guarantees of up to a maximum of five years. This limitation was not a major problem in the 1930s and 1940s, when governments normally offered export credit insurance for relatively short periods. In the 1950s, however, governments began to offer an increasing amount of export credit and credit guarantees for periods of longer than five years. These longer-term credit guarantees were not subject to the Berne Union's regulations.[24]

To fill the gap in international regulation resulting from the Berne Union's limitations, the Organisation for European Economic Co-operation adopted rules for export credit in 1955 and 1958 that committed OEEC member countries to abstain from artificial aid to exporters. The OECD did not initially become involved in the export credit issue when it replaced the OEEC in 1961, because the issue was transferred to a GATT working group on export subsidies. The working group categorized all export credit that resulted in a net loss of money to governments as export subsidies, which were prohibited under GATT Article XVI. However, major exporting countries considered the GATT ban on subsidized export credits to be unnecessarily strict, and GATT dispute resolution procedures operated too slowly to prevent export credit transactions.[25] Various developed country treasury ministries urged the OECD to become involved with the export credit issue, because its approach was less legalistic and more flexible than the GATT's. As a result, the OECD established a permanent high-level Group on Export Credits and Export Credit Guarantees (known as the "Export Credit Group") in November 1963. Composed of senior government officials, the Export Credit Group was open to all OECD member countries that had export credit agencies. The main objectives of the Export Credit Group were to reduce export credit competition, and to facilitate an exchange of information on credit issues. To fulfill these goals, the Export Credit Group's responsibilities included evaluating national policies, establishing common guidelines for export credits, and developing procedures for prior notification and consultation among members for individual transactions.

By 1970, concerns about the rising cost of export credit and the growing competition in this area prompted the OECD Export Credit Group to draft an agreement on prior consultation. However, the United States strongly opposed this agreement. American officials claimed that credit terms were simply one element of competition, that restrictions would be of limited effectiveness, and that the United States could not improve its balance of trade if it limited its export credit offerings. Because of the differences among countries, two agreements were negotiated in 1972. All OECD members participated in the first agreement, that simply permitted countries to request details on the credit terms other countries were prepared to offer for particular transactions. All OECD members except the United States, Japan, Australia, Greece, and Portugal participated in the second stronger agreement, that called for mandatory prior consultation by countries planning to offer export credit. The purpose of these agreements was to prevent cut-throat competition among export credit providers by increasing the transparency of each country's offerings.[26] Nevertheless, the failure of such major countries as the United States and Japan to commit themselves to the stronger agreement on mandatory prior consultation demonstrated the ineffectiveness of the two 1972 agreements. It was not until export credit competition increased substantially that all major OECD countries were willing to endorse a stronger OECD arrangement in the late 1970s. This issue is discussed in Chapter 4.

The OECD and Government Procurement

As the economic functions of the state expanded in developed countries, government procurement became an increasingly important factor in international markets. It is necessary to distinguish government procurement from state trading, which involves a more extensive role for the state. In state trading, "the government or its agent is involved in buying, selling and sometimes in manufacturing operations." Government procurement, by contrast, simply "involves the government or its agent acting as a consumer, procuring for its own consumption and not for commercial resale."[27] The 1947 General Agreement was largely silent on the issue of a country's responsibilities in the government procurement area. When a government purchased goods for its own use (and not for resale, as in the case of state trading), the GATT exempted it from the usual requirements of national treatment and most-favoured-nation treatment.[28] A major reason that countries resisted GATT discipline in the government procurement area related to national security. Indeed, discrimination in government procurement for national security reasons "is an inescapable fact of contemporary world politics."[29] GATT members also viewed government purchases as important instruments of national policy, and they insisted on the right to discriminate in favour of domestic goods in response to balance-of-payments problems. Furthermore, a strong feeling existed that governments should assist local industry whenever possible through their purchasing practices.

The GATT exemptions for government procurement were problematic, however, because a large share of the gross domestic product of most countries passes through public budgets. Thus, discrimination by government purchasing officials against foreign goods and services has been one of the most significant barriers to world trade. Governments imposed a wide range of formal and informal restrictions on their purchase of foreign goods in the 1950s and 1960s. In 1959, for example, the U.S. federal government awarded only 0.18 percent of the total value of its procurement contracts to foreign bidders; and in 1967 the French government concluded only 0.99 percent of its procurement contracts with foreign suppliers.[30] The impact of the GATT exemption for government procurement on the trading sectors of different states also varied enormously, because countries differ in the role they accord to the public sector. The exception on the basis of national security posed special problems, because "national security" could be used as a justification for almost any discriminatory action in government purchasing.

Many countries use formal or informal government procurement procedures that inhibit the purchase of foreign goods and services. However, the 1933 "Buy American Act" was the most well-known discriminatory procurement legislation, because its provisions were more explicit than those of most other countries, and because the United States is the largest single-country market for foreign goods. The U.S. Congress passed the Buy American Act during a period of heightened trade protectionism, which was partly a response to one of the greatest economic depressions in history. The Act required that goods the federal government purchased for use on federal territory had to be of domestic origin, and also had to be composed largely of domestic raw materials. Exceptions to this requirement were permitted if the cost of the domestic good was "unreasonable," domestic materials and products were unavailable in sufficient quantities, or a government agency head believed that domestic procurement was not in the national interest. To determine whether the domestic price of a good was unreasonable, an Executive Order specified the margins of preference to be granted when the prices of domestic and foreign goods were compared. Even bids by domestic producers were treated as foreign when foreign materials accounted for over 50 percent of the cost of all materials. Furthermore, government department heads could exceed the margins of the Buy American Act in favour of domestic producers if they decided it was in the national interest. Beginning in 1962, the U.S. Defense Department in fact greatly exceeded the Act's margins in response to the growing U.S. balance of payments deficit.[31]

When the United States enacted the Buy American Act in 1933 it was largely dormant and produced little reaction for twenty years. However, the Act began to attract considerable attention and resulted in a number of controversies as a result of the political and economic changes after World War II. The Act not only raised domestic concerns about the increased cost of government purchases, but it also seemed to conflict directly with the U.S. role as global economic hegemon in promoting trade liberalisation. Any OECD member country could refer a complaint to the organisation if it felt that another member's regulations were hindering its exports, and in 1962 Belgium and Britain registered a complaint with the OECD against the Buy American Act. The OECD Trade Committee responded by forming a working party to investigate the complaint. However, when the Trade Committee met in late 1964 to consider the working party's report, the United States managed to shift the Committee's attention from the Buy American Act to a general review of all OECD members' government procurement practices. It is interesting to note that studies of government procurement in fact pre-dated the OECD, since the OEEC had examined the government purchase of engineering products in 1959 to 1960. Nevertheless, the OECD broadened the investigation to examine all procurement of goods by central government authorities for government use.[32] As a result of this review, the OECD Secretariat published a report in 1966 which revealed that many countries permitted government departments to decide whether or not it was in the national interest to purchase foreign goods.[33] Almost all government departments admitted they lacked rules requiring invitations to foreign firms to submit bids. Some countries required tenders to be advertised for certain categories of government procurement, but usually with exceptions. Thus, most procurement officers had considerable opportunity to favour domestic over foreign producers.

As a result of its 1966 report, the OECD secretariat produced a brief draft text on guidelines for government procurement in 1967. The European Community was developing regional government procurement guidelines during this period, and there is evidence that the OECD and EC initiatives were somewhat complementary. In 1969 the United States submitted its own draft procurement guidelines text to the OECD, and the OECD then held discussions of the various draft guidelines. Following these discussions, the OECD produced a draft code in 1970 outlining procedures for liberalising government procurement. This draft code indicated that government purchasing practices should not discriminate against foreign products or suppliers, included provisions for monitoring the performance of signatory countries, described several approaches to dispute settlement, and specified conditions under which departures and exceptions to the procedures should be permitted.[34]

As was the case for export credits, the OECD rather than the GATT became actively involved in the discussions of government procurement because developed countries were far more interested than developing countries in reaching an agreement in this area. Realist writers and policy-makers extending back to Alexander Hamilton and Friedrich List have argued that government involvement in developing human capital and protecting infant industries is necessary for "late industrializers."[35] Thus, developing countries today believe that discriminatory government procurement is necessary to redress their structural cost disadvantages in producing industrial and higher-technology products, and to increase their domestic output of services and manufactures.[36] It has been possible for the OECD rather than the GATT/WTO to remain the primary venue for negotiating export credit agreements, because export credit is provided mainly by the OECD countries. The developed countries by contrast wanted the developing countries to participate in any government procurement agreement, and the OECD discussions were therefore designed to be prenegotiations which would eventually result in full negotiations in the GATT. Since the preparatory work in the OECD was not sufficiently advanced to warrant government procurement negotiations in the GATT Kennedy Round, OECD discussions of the draft code continued until the time of the Tokyo Round when the negotiations would shift to the GATT. The transition from the OECD to the GATT as a forum for government procurement negotiations is discussed in Chapter 4.

The Role of Developing Countries

Developing countries had only limited involvement in the global trade regime in the early postwar years, because of their relatively small numbers (many were still colonial territories), their protectionist trade policies, and GATT's inattention to their development problems. As discussed in Chapters 1 and 2, when the Havana Charter was not ratified, very few of its provisions regarding developing countries were incorporated into the GATT. Furthermore, most developing countries adopted protectionist import-substituting industrialization policies in the 1950s designed to replace industrial imports with domestic production, and their inward-looking ISI policies were not conducive to participation in the GATT.

By the 1960s, however, many developing countries following ISI were experiencing economic problems, including a slowdown in the growth of exports, dependence on intermediate imports for the production of industrial goods, and growing balance of payments deficits. Even Raúl Prebisch who had strongly supported ISI began to question the strategy, arguing that "the proliferation of industries of every kind in a closed market has deprived the Latin American countries of the advantages of specialization and economies of scale."[37] In the 1960s some developing countries therefore adopted a more outward-looking strategy demanding preferential treatment from the developed countries in promoting their exports, and the formation of the UNCTAD in 1964 was a key step in furthering this strategy. Prebisch, who was the first Secretary-General of UNCTAD, called for a new preferential program to encourage developing country exports as a replacement for the GATT's nondiscriminatory approach to trade liberalisation. If developing countries "were able to export more industrial goods under a preferential system," Prebisch wrote, "they could also import more, and this would enable them to relax the [import] substitution policy and make it more rational."[38] Key elements of this proposed program would include commodity agreements to provide developing countries with equitable prices for their primary products, compensatory finance for shortfalls in export revenues, and preferential treatment to encourage developing country industrial exports.

When the UNCTAD was established, many developing countries hoped it would replace the GATT. However, the UNCTAD has never posed a serious challenge to the GATT/WTO as the main global trade organisation, and it has therefore remained on the lower part of the trade regime pyramid (see Figure 1.1). Although the UNCTAD has conducted numerous studies on trade and has had an important role in some trade-related areas such as commodity agreements, its primary role in trade has been to serve as a pressure group for developing country interests. How successful the UNCTAD has been in directing the GATT/ WTO's attention to Third World trade interests is debatable. For example, GATT devoted significantly more attention to developing country problems in the 1960s than it had in the 1950s, and trade specialists have debated whether the UNCTAD had an important role in shifting the GATT's attention to the Third World. Two years after the UNCTAD was formed, in 1966, a new Part IV of the GATT on "Trade and Development" entered into force. In Part IV developed countries committed themselves to reduce and eliminate import barriers to products of export interest to developing countries, and indicated that they did "not expect reciprocity for commitments made by them [the developed countries] to reduce or remove tariffs and other barriers to the trade of less-developed contracting parties."[39]

Trade analysts and practitioners have disagreed on the degree to which the addition of Part IV to the GATT was a direct response to UNCTAD influence.

Kenneth Dam, for example, argued there was "little doubt" that the initiation of discussions leading to Part IV of the GATT "was a reaction to the preparations, already in progress, for the 1964 United Nations Conference on Trade and Development."[40] Although a number of GATT officials were willing to concede that UNCTAD might have accelerated GATT's development activities in the 1960s, they maintained that these activities were "merely the logical conclusion of earlier work within GATT" and "not really a function of UNCTAD's creation."[41] There is in fact considerable evidence that the GATT was becoming more involved with development issues even before UNCTAD was formed, and that UNCTAD's role was primarily to accelerate the process. Thus, as early as 1954, the GATT secretariat began to issue annual progress reports emphasising the widening gap between the trade expansion of developed and developing countries. In 1958 a panel of experts formed by the GATT Contracting Parties published a report (the Haberler Report on *Trends in International Trade*) indicating that many developing countries felt "the rules and conventions which are at present applied to commercial policy and international trade show a lack of balance unfavourable to their interest," and recommending a series of policy changes to address their grievances.[42] In response, the GATT launched a program to expand international trade that was aimed partly at increasing the export earnings of developing countries, and at the unilateral reduction of barriers to developing country exports with special emphasis on tropical products.[43] Thus, the introduction of GATT Part IV in 1966 could be viewed as the result of GATT's increasing attention to developing country needs and interests that predated the formation of UNCTAD.

In assessing UNCTAD's influence on GATT in the 1960s, it is also important to note that GATT's development-related activities in the 1960s were only of limited significance. Although GATT Part IV called on developed countries to reduce their barriers to developing country exports, it was a largely symbolic measure that was not legally binding. Indeed, developed states were actually raising their trade barriers in the 1960s for some products in which developing countries had a comparative advantage. A prime example was the case of textiles and clothing. To protect their domestic producers in the 1950s, some developed countries violated GATT Article XI which outlawed import quotas, and imposed "voluntary" restraints on textile and clothing imports from Japan, Hong Kong, India, and Pakistan. The developed countries then moved to legalize these restrictions through multilateral agreements. In 1961, a Short-Term Arrangement on Cotton Textiles was negotiated, and this was followed by a succession of Long-Term Arrangements and Multifibre Arrangements (MFAs). In marked contrast to GATT principles, these multilateral textile agreements endorsed developed country protectionism and restricted developing country exports in an area where the South had a comparative advantage.[44]

Although UNCTAD had only a limited amount of influence in the 1960s, in the early 1970s its influence increased to some extent. Unlike GATT Part IV which was largely symbolic, the developing countries received a concrete concession in 1971 when the GATT permitted developed countries to establish a generalised system of preferences (GSP) for developing country exports. It is important to note that the UNCTAD had a major role in bringing about acceptance of the GSP. The first GATT director-general had referred to nondiscrimination under the MFN principle as "the fundamental cornerstone" of the global trade organisation, and developing country demands for discriminatory one-way tariff preferences were therefore highly controversial.[45] Although the idea of granting preferential status to developing country exports first surfaced in the GATT, it was in UNCTAD that the preference scheme was debated and negotiated. In the early 1960s, the GATT held lengthy discussions in efforts to improve developing country export performance, but the developed states rejected a proposal that a GATT working party was considering on preferences for developing countries. A more acrimonious debate over preferences followed at UNCTAD I in 1964, and opposition from the United States and some other developed countries again prevented any action on the issue. American concerns that developing country preferences would violate the nondiscrimination principle and interfere with the GATT Kennedy Round were major factors in its opposition.[46]

Despite the failure of UNCTAD I to agree on a preference system for developing countries, the American position gradually softened. Several factors were responsible for this change, including U.S. opposition to the European Community's *selective* preferences for its developing country associate members, Latin American pressure on the United States for some sort of preferential scheme, and the failure of the GATT Kennedy Round to achieve large tariff reductions for manufactured goods of interest to developing country exporters. However, the UNCTAD also played a major role in altering attitudes and bridging the gap between countries on the issue of developing country preferences. Although divisions emerged among developing countries over which items should be included and excluded in a preference system, the G77 coalition in the UNCTAD helped to build a consensus among developing countries in favour of a preferential system. The UNCTAD secretariat leadership, especially Raúl Prebisch, played a central role in formulating developing country demands and unifying the position of developing country governments. The secretariat was particularly critical of the GATT commitment to equal treatment, arguing that it did not take account of the widely disparate bargaining positions of North and South. The secretariat also maintained that general preferences were a better alternative than regional EC or (proposed) U.S.-Latin American preferences, since these regional preference schemes would create a series of "satellite" relationships.[47]

After a consensus was finally reached on the GSP idea in principle, "the institutionalized group system of UNCTAD facilitated the achievement of concrete agreements on a series of functionally specific issues by means of an incremental and pragmatic pattern of bargaining in which ... conflicts of interest were brought into convergence."[48] Thus, in October 1970 UNCTAD members reached an agreement to give preferential developed country tariff treatment to developing country exports of manufactured and semi-manufactured goods. The GATT subsequently permitted developed countries to establish GSPs for developing countries through a ten-year renewable waiver from the MFN clause. However, one should not overestimate the degree to which the GSP has been a "success story" for developing countries. Although developing countries have received some benefit from the special preferences, the developed countries did not accept any legal obligation to provide them, and did not bind themselves to an internationally agreed GSP plan which the developing countries would have preferred. Instead, each developed country has established its own GSP plan, has often limited the amount of imports that could enter at lower duties, and has excluded sensitive products such as textiles from preferential status. In view of the complexities of the different GSP schemes, the more competitive developing countries such as the East Asian newly-industrialising economies (NIEs) benefited most from the GSP, and it offered very few benefits to poorer developing countries.

Although the developing countries in UNCTAD "presented a united front in their demands for preferences," it is important to note that "a fundamental conflict of interest among them persisted in private."[49] As discussed in Chapter 2, the EC's linkages with associate African states from the late 1950s created a division among developing countries in the South. This division persisted in the 1962 to 1972 period, because the EC renewed the association agreements in 1963 and 1969 in the *Yaoundé Conventions*, signed at Yaoundé, Cameroon. The associate African countries that benefited from preferential access to the EC market realised they would face increased export competition if EC preferences were extended to all developing countries through the GSP. Thus, the EC's associate African states had an ambivalent attitude toward the establishment of the GSP. Another source of division in the South that would persist in future years stemmed from differences in the size and stage of development of different developing countries. The smallest and least industrialised developing countries were aware that they would gain little from the GSP, because they would have to compete on equal terms with larger and more industrialised developing countries such as Brazil and India.[50]

In sum, the formation of the UNCTAD increased the visibility of developing countries in the global trade regime and provided them with an international organisation that supported their trade-related demands *vis-à-vis* the developed countries. However, the UNCTAD has never seriously challenged the GATT/WTO as the main global trade organisation, and it has instead served largely as a pressure group on behalf of developing country interests. Although, the UNCTAD's influence on trade issues in the 1960s was quite limited, in 1971 the GATT approved the GSP partly as a result of UNCTAD actions. Despite the appearance of a unified front among developing countries in the UNCTAD, there were in fact differences in their interests. Two major sources of difference stemmed from the associate status which only some developing countries had in the European Community, and the variations in size and stage of development among countries in the South.

Conclusion

The Kennedy Round from 1964 to 1967 was the most successful GATT round of negotiations since the Geneva Round in 1947. Most importantly, tariffs on industrial products were reduced on average by over 35 percent because of the shift from product-by-product to linear negotiations. The number of countries participating in GATT affairs grew dramatically from 34 in 1955 to 100 in 1973, largely as a result of the increased involvement of developing countries.[51] The growing number of Third World countries in the GATT, combined with the GATT's lack of an executive board, provided an impetus for developed countries to turn to the plurilateral OECD for research, discussion, prenegotiation, and negotiation of some trade issues. Developed country reliance on the OECD also stemmed from the relative decline of U.S. hegemony in international trade, with the EC becoming a more equal partner and Japan also increasing its influence. Beginning in 1971 the United States has had chronic balance of trade deficits, and Judith Goldstein has noted that "nowhere is America's hegemonic decline more evident than in changing trade patterns."[52]

As Figure 1.1 shows, the OECD has been an influential developed country-led institution on the global trade regime pyramid. This chapter has outlined two trade-related areas in which the OECD had a prominent role in the 1962 to

1972 period: export credits and government procurement. In the area of export credits, the OECD rather than the GATT has served as the primary forum for negotiations. OECD countries are the main suppliers of export credit, and there was concern that the net consumers of export credit in the GATT would not support multilateral discipline to limit the softening of credit terms. Ironically, GATT's legalistic approach resulted in a ban on subsidised export credit under GATT Article XVI which prohibits export subsidies. The ban, however, was unrealistic, and GATT dispute resolution procedures operated too slowly to prevent subsidised export credit transactions. The OECD with its flexible and less legalistic approach has served as a more practical forum for gradually establishing multilateral discipline on export credit terms.

Another trade-related area where the OECD became actively involved in the 1960s was government procurement, because the role of government as a consumer of goods and services was becoming an increasingly important factor in international markets. However, strong feelings existed that governments had a right to follow purchasing policies that would protect national security, alleviate balance of payments problems, and assist local industry. As was the case for export credit, the OECD with its less legalistic approach seemed to be a less threatening forum for beginning the government procurement as well as the export credit negotiations. The OECD was also the natural location for prenegotiations on government procurement, because the developing countries as "late industrialisers" want to preserve the right to redress their structural cost disadvantages and protect their infant industries through government involvement. Only after the OECD did preliminary work on government procurement would the issue be moved to the GATT for the Tokyo Round negotiations.

Among the members of the OECD, the United States and the EC countries (collectively) emerged as the most important actors in the GATT Kennedy Round. As a close observer of the Kennedy Round noted, if the United States and EC "could agree, the negotiations would move forward; if they should fail to reach an accord, a serious and perhaps fatal crisis would undoubtedly follow."[53] Nevertheless, the EC membership did not increase during the 1960s because of two French vetoes of British applications to join the Community, and the United States continued to remain above the EC on the global trade regime pyramid. It was not until the 1970s that the EC would become a trade regime actor on a par with the United States.

As more Third World states joined the GATT in the 1960s they became increasingly disturbed about the GATT's inattention to their concerns, and in 1964 they were successful in forming the United Nations Conference on Trade and Development. The developing countries never achieved their goal of having the UNCTAD replace the GATT as the main global trade organisation. Nevertheless, the UNCTAD has at times served as a reasonably effective pressure group on the GATT. During the 1962 to 1972 period, the UNCTAD may have accelerated the decision of GATT members to add a Part IV on Trade and Development to the General Agreement; and more importantly the UNCTAD played a role in pressuring the GATT to approve the GSP for developing countries. The creation of UNCTAD also had the ironic effect of increasing the importance of the OECD. After UNCTAD was formed, the developed countries felt the need to coordinate their positions in the OECD *vis-à-vis* the developing countries in the G77 and UNCTAD. Although UNCTAD pressure helped ensure that a "development principle" would be added to the global trade regime, development continues to be subsidiary to the liberalisation, nondiscrimination, reciprocity, and safeguard principles because the major trading nations were "willing to make only limited sacrifices to promote the trade interests of the developing countries."[54] As Figure 1.1 shows, the UNCTAD has remained well below the GATT/WTO and the OECD on the global trade regime pyramid.

Notes

1   John W. Evans, *The Kennedy Round in American Trade Policy: The Twilight of the GATT?* (Cambridge: Harvard University Press, 1971), p. 248.

2   Evans, *The Kennedy Round in American Trade Policy*, p. 253.

3   Derek W. Urwin, *The Community of Europe: A History of European Integration Since 1945* (London: Longman, 2nd ed., 1995), pp. 116-129; David Arter, *The Politics of European Integration in the Twentieth Century* (Aldershot, UK: Dartmouth, 1993), pp. 146-153.

4   China and Czechoslovakia were founding members of the GATT in 1948. However, the Chiang Kai-shek government, which had fled from the mainland to Taiwan, withdrew from the organisation in 1950 purportedly on behalf of China. Czechoslovakia was able to remain a GATT contracting party because of the informal nature of the organisation, but its membership was inactive for a number of years.

5   Robert E. Hudec, *The GATT Legal System and World Trade Diplomacy* (New York: Praeger, 1975), p. 199; Evans, *The Kennedy Round in American Trade Policy*, pp. 5-20; John H. Jackson, *The World Trading System: Law and Policy of International Economic Relations* (Cambridge: MIT Press, 2nd edition, 1997), pp. 143-144.

6   Ernest H. Preeg, *Traders and Diplomats: An Analysis of the Kennedy Round of Negotiations under the General Agreement on Tariffs and Trade* (Washington, D.C.: The Brookings Institution, 1970), pp. 39-56.

7   I. William Zartman, "Prenegotiation: Phases and Functions," *International Journal* 44-2 (Spring 1989), p. 246.

8   Janice Gross Stein, "Getting to the Table: Processes of International Prenegotiation," *International Journal* 44-2 (Spring 1989), p. 232.

9   Preeg, *Traders and Diplomats*, p. 5.
10 Jackson, *The World Trading System*, pp. 144-145; Preeg, *Traders and Diplomats*, pp. 12 & 24-25.
11 Preeg, *Traders and Diplomats*, p. 13.
12 Bernard Colas, "The OECD's Legal Influence in a Global Economy," *World Economic Affairs* 1-3 (Spring/Summer 1997), p. 67.
13 Fred Charles Iklé, *How Nations Negotiate* (New York: Harper and Row, 1964), pp. 3-4. Italics are in the original.
14 Iklé, *How Nations Negotiate*, p. 6.
15 David J. Blair, *Trade Negotiations in the OECD: Structures, Institutions and States* (London: Kegan Paul International, 1993), pp. 6-7; David Henderson, "International Agencies and Cross-Border Liberalization: the WTO in Context," in Anne O. Krueger with Chonira Aturupane, ed., *The WTO as an International Organization* (Chicago: University of Chicago Press, 1998), p. 127.
16 Stephen D. Cohen and Ronald I. Meltzer, *United States International Economic Policy in Action: Diversity of Decision Making* (New York: Praeger, 1982), p. 192.
17 Blair, *Trade Negotiations in the OECD*, pp. 8-9; Serge A. Devos, "Service Trade and the OECD," *Journal of Japanese Trade & Industry*, no. 4 (1984), p. 19.
18 OECD, *Export Credit Financing Systems in OECD Member and Non-Member Countries – 1999 Supplement* (Paris: OECD, 1999), p. 1.
19 Bruce Fitzgerald and Terry Monson, "Export Credit and Insurance for Export Promotion," *Finance and Development* 25-4 (December, 1988), p. 53.
20 Andrew M. Moravcsik, "Disciplining Trade Finance: The OECD Export Credit Arrangement," *International Organization* 43-1 (Winter 1989), p. 176.
21 Orit Frenkel and Claude G.B. Fontheim, "Export Credits: An International and Domestic Legal Analysis," *Law and Policy in International Business* 13-4 (1981), p. 1069.
22 The formal name of the organisation in 1934 was the Union of Insurers for the Control of International Credits, but its name was changed in 1957 to the Union of Insurers of International Credits, and in 1974 to the International Union of Credit and Investment Insurers. The International Union of Credit and Investment Insurers is still active today and currently has 47 members and observer members from a total of over 39 countries.
23 John L. Moore, Jr., "Export Credit Arrangements," in Seymour J. Rubin and Gary Clyde Hufbauer, eds., *Emerging Standards of International Trade and Investment: Multinational Codes and Corporate Conduct* (Totowa, NJ: Rowman & Allanheld, 1984), p. 139.
24 John M. Duff, Jr., "The Outlook for Official Export Credits," *Law and Policy in International Business* 13-4 (1981), p. 895; Joan Pearce, *Subsidized Export Credit* (London: The Royal Institute of International Affairs, 1980), pp. 42-43.
25 John E. Ray, "The OECD 'Consensus' on Export Credits," *The World Economy* 9-3 (September 1986), pp. 296-97; Blair, *Trade Negotiations in the OECD*, pp. 44-45.
26 Blair, *Trade Negotiations in the OECD*, pp. 46-47; Ray, "The OECD 'Consensus' on Export Credits," pp. 301-302; Pearce, *Subsidized Export Credit*, pp. 43-44; Moravcsik, "Disciplining Trade Finance," p. 180.
27 General Agreement on Tariffs and Trade, *The Tokyo Round of Multilateral Trade Negotiations*, Report by the Director-General of GATT (Geneva: GATT, April 1979), p. 75.
28 GATT, *Text of the General Agreement* (Geneva: GATT, July 1986), Articles 3.8(a) and 17.2; The Honourable Donald S. Macdonald, "The Multiltaeral Trade Negotiations – A Lawyer's Perspective," *Canadian Business Journal* 4 (1979-80), pp. 146-147.

29   Kenneth W. Dam, *The GATT: Law and International Economic Organization* (Chicago: University of Chicago Press, 1970), p. 201.

30   Dam, *The GATT: Law and International Economic Organization,* p. 199; J.H.J. Bourgeois, "The Tokyo Round Agreements on Technical Barriers and on Government Procurement in International and EEC Perspective," *Common Market Law Review* 19-1 (1982), p. 12.

31   Laurence A. Knapp, "The Buy American Act: A Review and Assessment," *Columbia Law Review* 61 (1961), pp. 430-462; Dam, *The GATT: Law and International Economic Organization,* pp. 199-205; William B. Kelly, Jr., Nontariff Barriers," in Bela Balassa, ed., *Studies in Trade Liberalization* (Baltimore: Johns Hopkins Press, 1967), pp. 278-284.

32   Morton Pomeranz, "Toward a New International Order in Government Procurement," *Law and Policy in International Business* 11 (1979), pp. 1270-1272.

33   Organisation for Economic Co-operation and Development, *Government Purchasing in Europe, North America and Japan: Regulations and Procedures* (Paris: OECD, 1966). Ten years later the OECD updated and expanded the report. See Organisation for Economic Co-operation and Development, *Government Purchasing: Regulations and Procedures of OECD Member Countries* (Paris: OECD, 1976).

34   Evans, *The Kennedy Round in American Trade Policy*, pp. 104-106; Gilbert R. Winham, *International Trade and the Tokyo Round Negotiation* (Princeton: Princeton University Press, 1986), pp. 139-140.

35   See Friedrich List, *The National System of Political Economy*, translated by Sampson S. Lloyd (London: Longmans, Green, 1916); Alexander Gerschenkron, *Economic Backwardness in Historical Perspective: A Book of Essays* (Cambridge: Harvard University Press, 1962).

36   Federico Trionfetti, "Discriminatory Public Procurement and International Trade," *World Economy* 23-1 (January 2000), pp. 70-72.

37   Raúl Prebisch, *Towards a Dynamic Development Policy for Latin America* (New York: United Nations, 1963), p. 71.

38   *Towards a New Trade Policy for Development*, Report by the Secretary-General of the United Nations Conference on Trade and Development (New York: United Nations, 1964), p. 34.

39   General Agreement on Tariffs and Trade, *Text of the General Agreement on Tariffs and Trade* (Geneva: GATT, July 1986), Part IV, Article XXXVI.8.

40   Dam, *The GATT: Law and International Economic Organization,* p. 237.

41   Robert S. Walters, "UNCTAD: Intervener Between Poor and Rich States," *Journal of World Trade Law* 7-5 (September/October 1973), pp. 527-554.

42   General Agreement on Tariffs and Trade, *Trends in International Trade*, Report by a Panel of Experts (Geneva: GATT, October 1958), p. 123.

43   Evans, *The Kennedy Round in American Trade Policy*, pp. 119-120.

44   Vinod K. Aggarwal, *Liberal Protectionism: The International Politics of Organized Textile Trade* (Berkeley: University of California Press, 1985).

45   Eric Wyndham-White, "Negotiations in Prospect," in C. Fred Bergsten, ed., *Toward a New World Trade Policy: The Maidenhead Papers* (Lexington, MA: Heath, 1975), p. 322.

46   Marc Williams, *International Economic Organisations and the Third World* (Hertfordshire: Harvester Wheatsheaf, 1994), p. 203; Anindya K. Bhattacharya, "The Influence of the International Secretariat: UNCTAD and Generalized Tariff Preferences," *International Organization* 30-1 (Winter 1976), pp. 77-78.

47 Bhattacharya, "The Influence of the International Secretariat," pp. 80-87; Kathryn C. Lavelle, "Ideas with a Context of Power: The African Group in an Evolving UNCTAD," *Journal of Modern African Studies* 39-1 (2001), pp. 35-36.
48 Bhattacharya, "The Influence of the International Secretariat," p. 90.
49 Evans, *The Kennedy Round in American Trade Policy*, p. 122.
50 Evans, *The Kennedy Round in American Trade Policy*, p. 122; David M. Wood and Birol A. Yeşilada, *The Emerging European Union* (New York: Longman, 2nd ed., 2002), p. 206.
51 Hudec, *The GATT Legal System and World Trade Diplomacy*, p. 208.
52 Judith Goldstein, "Ideas, Institutions, and American Trade Policy," *International Organization* 42-1 (Winter 1988), p. 179.
53 Preeg, *Traders and Diplomats*, p. 5.
54 Jock A. Finlayson and Mark W. Zacher, "The GATT and the Regulation of Trade Barriers: Regime Dynamics and Functions," in Stephen D. Krasner, ed., *International Regimes* (Ithaca: Cornell University Press, 1983), p. 294.

4 The Development of the G7 Summit Process and the GATT Tokyo Round: 1973 to 1979

The 1970s was a period marked by significant changes in the American, European, and Japanese positions in the global trade regime. Although the United States had a balance of trade surplus throughout the 1960s, its trade balance deteriorated by about $5 billion from 1964 to 1969. In 1971, the United States had a balance of trade deficit (of about $2 billion) for the first time in the twentieth century, and its trade deficit generally increased in subsequent years. On 15 August 1971, President Richard Nixon responded to the U.S. balance of trade and payments deficits by suspending the convertibility of the U.S. dollar into gold, and imposing a ten percent tariff surcharge on all dutiable imports. The U.S. position as global economic hegemon deteriorated further in January 1973, when Britain, Denmark, and Ireland became members of the European Community, making it the world's largest trading entity. Japan like the EC was a far more prominent trader by the 1970s. Whereas Japan had accounted for 3.6 percent of total world exports in 1960, it accounted for 6.6 percent of world exports by 1969. Thus, the EC and Japan were less willing to defer to American leadership on trade issues in the 1970s.[1]

The voluminous literature criticising hegemonic stability theory provides a warning against facile assumptions that U.S. trade hegemony in the 1950s to early 1960s was always conducive to trade liberalisation. In some sectors such as agriculture and textiles, the United States in fact contributed to trade protectionism.[2] Nevertheless, American hegemony in the early postwar years was *primarily* a force for trade liberalisation, because the United States provided public goods to promote economic reconstruction in Western Europe and Japan and an open international trade regime. In the 1970s, by contrast, U.S. leaders were "more concerned with specific national economic interests, making their behavior more similar to the behavior of policy makers in other states."[3] Thus, in the 1973 to 1979 period the EC began to occupy a place alongside the United States in the global trade regime pyramid (see Figure 1.1).

The relative decline of U.S. hegemony in the 1970s also contributed to moves by the most important developed countries to create new mechanisms for collective management of the global economy, and this is one of the reasons the G7 summits were established in the 1970s (see discussion later in this chapter). Although the G7 is a much more informal institution than the OECD, the two institutions are similar in that they both are concerned with a wide range of issues and policies; that is, trade is only one of their concerns. The G7 is placed higher than the OECD on the global trade regime pyramid, because its membership is limited to the most important advanced industrial states and its summit meetings are held at the heads of government and state level. Nevertheless, the range and scope of G7 government leaders' responsibilities are so great that they normally only become involved with trade policy issues when there is a need for intervention at the highest political level.

The membership of the GATT continued to grow dramatically during the 1970s, and Table 2.1 shows that the number of countries participating in multilateral trade negotiations increased from 62 in the 1964-67 Kennedy Round to 102 in the 1973-79 Tokyo Round. Thus, the developed countries continued to seek minilateral settings both within and outside the GATT where they could confer on trade issues. As discussed, two important plurilateral institutions outside the GATT dealing with trade issues in the 1970s were the G7 and the OECD. Within the GATT, the Consultative Group of Eighteen was established in 1975 as a smaller representative group of 18 countries to facilitate discussion of trade issues. However, the CG.18 was purely consultative in nature, and was composed of senior officials from capitals that met only two to four times a year. The CG.18 never had a role comparable with legally constituted minilateral groupings such as the Executive Boards within the IMF and the World Bank.[4]

In addition to the growing parity between the United States and the EC on trade issues, and the move towards more collective developed country leadership with the formation of the G7, a third change during the 1973 to 1979 period was the major challenge the developing countries posed to the pyramidal structure of the global trade regime. The success of the Organisation of Petroleum Exporting Countries (OPEC) in increasing oil prices in 1973-74 was a major factor encouraging the developing countries to issue calls for a New International Economic Order (NIEO) in the UN General Assembly in the 1970s.[5] To bring about the NIEO, the developing countries sought a wide range of concessions from the North relating to sovereignty over their natural resources, increased control over foreign investment, greater assistance for their debt and development problems, and greater influence in the international economic organizations. The developing countries also had specific trade-related demands such as increased prices for their commodity exports and improved access to developed country markets.[6] As we discuss, the efforts of the South in the 1970s to alter the hierarchy on the global trade regime pyramid were largely unsuccessful.

After outlining developments in the GATT, this chapter discusses the formation and early activities of the G7, the continuing role of the OECD in the areas of export credit and government procurement, and the role of developing countries during the 1973 to 1979 period.

Developments in the GATT: 1973 to 1979

In July 1971, a U.S. Commission on International Trade and Investment Policy (the "Williams Commission") appointed by President Richard M. Nixon called for a new round of GATT negotiations to liberalise trade. However, the Commission also recognised that the EC had "overtaken the United States as the most important trading unit," and it recommended that the United States "should more than in the past use its bargaining power in the defense of its economic interests."[7] The United States in the 1970s was in fact more inclined to adopt policies that circumvented GATT rules such as "voluntary" export restraints, and to take unilateral actions against "unfair" traders under Section 301 of the 1974 U.S. Trade Act. The EC for its part increased trade protectionism under its Common Agricultural Policy, and threatened the GATT's nondiscrimination principle by extending its area of preferential treatment to African and European associate states. The 1973-74 oil crisis posed yet another threat to trade liberalisation, when OPEC quadrupled oil prices and precipitated a steep recession in the OECD countries.

Despite the protectionist pressures stemming from U.S. hegemonic decline, states that benefited from the global trade regime had the incentive to continue liberalising trade through cooperative efforts. An open trade regime furnished "some of the sense of certainty and confidence that a hegemon formerly provided."[8] The degree to which U.S. hegemony declined, however, should not be overestimated, and the United States continued to have a great deal of influence in the GATT Tokyo Round. Indeed, some of the early initiatives leading to the Tokyo Round came from U.S. committees such as the 1971 Williams Commission that concluded negotiations were necessary to combat other countries' restrictions on U.S. exports. Among its recommendations, the Williams Commission report indicated that the new talks should deal with nontariff barriers, and that the key trading nations might adopt some "separate codes or understandings that apply initially only to the members particularly concerned, but are open to accession by other members."[9] It is interesting that the Tokyo Round in fact resulted in six NTB codes signed mainly by the OECD states.

As the largest trading entities, the United States and EC held informal discussions on contentious issues throughout the Tokyo Round to avoid the risk of a major confrontation, and U.S.-EC cooperation in fact directed the negotiation. When the United States and the EC did not cooperate, the negotiation became deadlocked because they had effective veto power. When the United States and the EC adopted a unified position, only the combined efforts of others had any chance of changing the outcome. For example, a U.S.-EC agreement on tariff reductions was reached outside of the Tokyo Round's formal institutional structure. The United States and the EC then presented this agreement to other Tokyo Round participants, and it was eventually accepted as an agreed formula for reducing tariffs. A bilateral consultation between the United States and the EC in Brussels in July 1977 (the Strauss-Haferkamp meeting) also was held at a time when the Tokyo Round was moving very slowly, and it provided an important impetus to the negotiations. Thus, the United States and the EC were near the top of the pyramid in the Tokyo Round negotiations.[10]

The first six rounds of GATT negotiations had produced a marked reduction in industrial tariffs, but the GATT had done little to deal with the formidable obstacles that NTBs were posing to freer trade. Although the Kennedy Round in the 1960s had resulted in several major breakthroughs such as the change from product-by-product to linear tariff negotiations, its progress in dealing with NTBs was very limited. An Anti-Dumping Code was one of the few Kennedy Round accomplishments in the NTB area, and the U.S. Congress refused to completely endorse the code. In September 1973 the ministers from 103 countries met in Japan to inaugurate the Tokyo Round, which was designed to deal with many of the trade issues that were unresolved after the Kennedy Round. When the Tokyo Round was concluded in 1979, the results were regarded as "the most comprehensive and far-reaching ... achieved in trade negotiations since the creation of the ... GATT in 1947."[11] The most important accomplishment of the Tokyo Round was the negotiation of a series of NTB codes dealing with customs valuation, import licensing, technical standards, government procurement, antidumping, and subsidies and countervailing duties. The results also included a major agreement to reduce tariffs, and some revisions of GATT articles of interest to developing countries.

The Tokyo Round's success in the NTB area resulted largely from the background work and prenegotiations on NTBs in the 1960s and early 1970s. Industrial and agricultural experts from GATT member countries had met repeatedly in Geneva to catalogue the various types of NTBs, and the GATT had already compiled voluminous documentation on existing NTBs by the time of the September 1973 Tokyo meeting.[12] Nevertheless, the NTB codes were discrete plurilateral agreements that only some GATT countries agreed to sign. Nonsignatories of a code did not assume its obligations, and also did not receive its benefits. Thus, the Tokyo Round's NTB codes were applied in accordance with conditional rather than unconditional MFN treatment. The codes were plurilateral agreements partly because of the nature of GATT as an international organisation. As discussed in Chapter 1, it was almost impossible to introduce amendments to the GATT because of difficulties posed by the amending process. Since many developing countries opposed the extension of GATT discipline to non-tariff measures, the only way to incorporate NTB rules was through plurilateral code agreements.[13] Thus, "the Tokyo Round was not particularly successful in achieving its stated goal of bringing developing countries into the trading system."[14] Another shortcoming of the Tokyo Round was that it strengthened the tendencies toward "differentiation" in the global trade regime. In some areas such as agriculture, development, and safeguards, the round reinforced "a discriminatory, government-dominated pattern of behavior" that did "little to increase trade."[15] Despite these shortcomings, the Tokyo Round's overall accomplishments in reducing tariffs and in confronting NTBs for the first time were a remarkable achievement in the view of the protectionist forces at work in the 1970s.

The Group of Seven

Directly below the United States and the EC in the trade regime pyramid was the Group of Seven economic summits, which were first held during the GATT Tokyo Round. The G7 is a highly exclusive club composed of the richest economies that meets once a year at the level of heads of state and government. The summit's agenda "has expanded well beyond its core concern with macroeconomic policy, trade and north-south relations, and its early interest in east-west economic and global energy issues" to "a host of microeconomic, environmental, transnational and political-security subjects."[16] Nevertheless, the summits have had a consistent concern with international trade, and one of the founders of the G7 summits – Helmut Schmidt – "saw the main rationale of the summits as deterring the leaders from protectionist policies."[17] The G7 is an informal institution that is not designed to be a forum for decision-making. Thus, the G7 political leaders rely on persuasion and exhortation rather than negotiation to resolve differences, reach a consensus, and bring about policy change on key political and economic issues.

Personal linkages among the heads of government and state have always been important to the G7 as an small, informal institution. As Robert Putnam and Nicholas Bayne relate, "many sherpas and summiteers note the utility of 'being able to pick up the phone' and talk to a well-placed friend in another capital."[18] In accordance with Prisoners' Dilemma, the personal iterative contacts among G7 leaders and the knowledge that they will be meeting again in a summit the following year contribute to habits of cooperation and less willingness to take unilateral actions that detract from a sense of mutual trust and confidence. Furthermore, the personal interactions help to educate the summit leaders, increasing their awareness of the complexity of issues, of the perceptions of others, and of the need for compromise. In trade, the G7 summit leaders "learn first-hand of the common pressures each of them is under from protectionist forces at home. So they ... take back to their respective capitals a better appreciation of the unpopular decisions each must make when special protection is sought by one group or another."[19] Nevertheless, the effect of personal contacts at the summits in limiting protectionism should not be overestimated, especially when weighed against domestic protectionist pressures confronting G7 leaders when they return home. Furthermore, close summit contacts do not necessarily result in cordial relationships, as the hostility between Jimmy Carter and Helmut Schmidt, and between Ronald Reagan and François Mitterand have demonstrated.[20]

The G7 summits began with six countries (the United States, Japan, Germany, France, Britain, and Italy) at a meeting in Rambouillet, France on 15-17 November 1975. (See Table 4.1.) Canada became the seventh member at the second G7 meeting in San Juan, Puerto Rico in 1976; and the EC was first represented in the summits in 1977. The EC (today the European Union) is represented by the president of the Commission, and also by the president of the Council of Ministers in years when a non-G7 European country holds that office.[21] In 1991 the G7 leaders invited the Russian President to meet with them at their summit in London, and Russia's involvement gradually increased with each successive G7 summit. Russia became a full member of the summit "on probation" at the 1997 Denver meeting, and since 1998 the G7 has become a Group of Eight (G8) with Russia participating.[22] Nevertheless, Russia is more involved in the summit's political and security discussions than the economic discussions, and the G7 continues to be the most important grouping for discussions of financial issues. Although the G8 now deals with international trade issues, Russia is not yet a member of the World Trade Organization and has only limited influence in the trade discussions. For example, the G7 leaders without Russia discussed trade on the first day of the Genoa summit on 20 July 2001 and pledged "to engage personally and jointly in the launch of a new ambitious Round of global trade negotiations."[23] Only at the end of the Genoa summit did the full complement of G8 leaders formally endorse the G7 call for launching a new WTO negotiating round.[24] This book refers to the G7 when discussing the period up to the 1997 Denver summit, and from 1997 it discusses the G7, G7/G8, or G8 depending on the issue.

Table 4.1   G7/G8 Annual Summit Meetings (1975-2001)

Location	Date
Rambouillet, France	15-17 November 1975
San Juan, Puerto Rico, U.S.	27-28 June 1976
London, UK (London I)	7-8 May 1977
Bonn, West Germany (Bonn I)	16-17 July 1978
Tokyo, Japan (Tokyo I)	28-29 June 1979
Venice, Italy (Venice I)	22-23 June 1980
Ottawa, Ontario, Canada	20-21 July 1981
Versailles, France	4-6 June 1982
Williamsburg, Virginia, U.S.	28-30 May 1983
London, UK (London II)	7-9 June 1984
Bonn, West Germany (Bonn II)	2-4 May 1985
Tokyo, Japan (Tokyo II)	4-6 May 1986
Venice, Italy (Venice II)	8-10 June 1987
Toronto, Ontario, Canada	19-21 June 1988
Paris, France	14-16 July 1989
Houston, Texas, U.S.	9-11 July 1990
London, UK (London III)	15-17 July 1991
Munich, Germany	6-8 July 1992
Tokyo, Japan (Tokyo III)	7-9 July 1993
Naples, Italy	8-10 July 1994
Halifax, Nova Scotia, Canada	15-17 June 1995
Lyon, France	27-29 June 1996
Denver, Colorado, U.S.	20-22 June 1997
Birmingham, UK	15-17 May 1998
Cologne, Germany	18-20 June 1999
Okinawa, Japan	21-23 July 2000
Genoa, Italy	20-22 July 2001

The decision to include some countries in the G7 and to exclude others has of course been a sensitive issue, for excluded developed as well as developing countries. The G7 has established various mechanisms in efforts to allay the dissatisfaction of excluded countries. Since 1976, for example, it has been customary to hold the OECD annual ministerial council meetings which include all the developed countries a few weeks before the G7 summits. The annual communiqué of the OECD ministerial "offers a reference model for preparation of the summit's economic declaration."[25] In the trade area, we later discuss the fact that the early summits repeatedly endorsed the OECD's Trade Declaration (the "Trade Pledge") of 1974 designed to combat protectionism. Shortly after a summit meeting, the Sherpa (or personal representative of the G7 leader) from the host country would also visit the OECD to report on the G7 meeting. This would give the non-participating developed countries a feeling that they were being involved in the summit process. To alleviate concerns of countries that are not OECD members, the summit communiqués have often linked the views of the G7 leaders with the work of the larger international organisations, the IMF, World Bank, and GATT/WTO.[26]

Despite these G7 efforts to make others feel included, there have been periodic tensions and differences of perspective between the G7 and the formal international organisations. For example, non-G7 OECD countries have sometimes indicated that the G7 summit leaders were not providing them with meaningful information about their proceedings. Furthermore, in the early 1980s the orthodox liberal policies of U.S. President Reagan and British Prime Minister Thatcher in the G7 diverged from the more interventionist policy preferences of the OECD. Table 4.1 contains a list of all the G7/G8 summit meetings. The summits are listed in groups of seven simply to indicate that the chair rotates among the seven members, and that a new cycle then begins (Russia has not yet chaired a summit meeting). Some writers identify summit cycles or periods differently, based on the changing nature of summit activities.[27]

The Reasons for Establishment of the G7 Summit Process

The G7 summits were established in the 1970s as a result of the emergence of serious economic problems, the increase in economic interdependence, the relative decline of American economic hegemony, the bureaucratisation of international relations, and the personal inclinations of some Western leaders.[28] First, serious economic problems developed in the 1970s stemming from the collapse of the Bretton Woods monetary regime, the 1973-74 oil crisis, and the 1974 recession that followed. The OECD, the IMF, and the informal meetings of finance ministers of the Group of Five (discussed later in this chapter) were "not suited to generating the political momentum the economic problems of the post oil-shock required. What was needed was a new series of consultations at the highest level."[29] Only the highest political leader in each of the major developed countries had the authority to make the commitments and decisions required to deal with the serious problems stemming from the monetary and oil crises.

A second reason for the G7 summits was the growth of economic interdependence in the 1950s and 1960s stemming from the rapid increase in trade, foreign investment, and capital flows. As interdependence increases it becomes more difficult to separate international from domestic politics, because international factors intrude "more deeply into domestic policy-making," and domestic policy-making is more likely to have significant international effects.[30] Thus, Richard Cooper wrote in the early 1970s that "the growth of interdependence of the world economy creates pressures for common policies, and hence for procedures whereby countries discuss and coordinate actions that hitherto were regarded as being of domestic concern exclusively."[31] Because international issues and events were having a growing impact on domestic policy, political leaders were no longer willing to leave the responsibility for coordinating their countries' economic policies to officials or even ministers. Thus, they became personally involved in G7 meetings at the highest political level. As heads of government and state, the G7 leaders were in the best position to reconcile the often competing demands of domestic and foreign policy.

A third reason for the G7 meetings related to the relative decline of American economic hegemony. In the early 1970s, U.S. hegemony was being challenged because of its growing balance of payments deficit and the imminent entry of Britain into the European Community. In response to the U.S. balance of payments problems, President Richard Nixon resorted to drastic actions on 15 August 1971 – suspending the convertibility of the U.S. dollar into gold, and imposing a ten percent tariff surcharge on all dutiable imports. Henry Kissinger, who was Nixon's national security adviser at the time, "recognized the limitations upon American power ... [and] could perceive that the world's balances were altering."[32] Kissinger was therefore concerned about the impact of the "Nixon shocks" on U.S. relations with Europe and Japan, and he wrote in his memoirs, "I recommended to Nixon that he intervene personally with the European heads of state. My original idea was a summit of the Western leaders."[33] However, France was not interested in such a summit, because it was concerned that Germany might side with the United States. After Britain, Denmark and Ireland joined the EC in 1973, the gross domestic products of the United States and EC were comparable, and the EC accounted for a much larger share of world trade than the United States. As was the case for the EC, Japan was experiencing rapid economic growth during this period. Thus, the United States was less willing and able to assume the sole responsibilities of leadership, and the Western European countries and Japan expected to play a greater role in global economic decision-making. By 1975, there was sufficient support for the idea that it was necessary to replace U.S. unilateral management of the global economy with collective management by the major economic powers, and the G7 was established.

A fourth reason for the G7 summits related to the increasing role of bureaucratic specialists in international relations, who contributed to a fragmented view of economic versus security affairs, and of the various economic areas such as finance, trade, and investment. As the growth of interdependence required more policy coordination among the major economic powers, it was necessary for each country to integrate and prioritise its wide range of policy-making activities. The increasing complexity "and interlocking nature of economic issues, as well as the political importance of what was at stake, called for direct dialogue between the leaders of the major nations."[34] Only the heads of government and state had the position and capacity to reassert political over bureaucratic authority, and to provide a more integrated view of the various components of foreign policy.

A fifth reason for the G7 summits stemmed from the personal inclinations and relationships of some Western leaders. Of particular importance was the close relationship between French President Valéry Giscard d'Estaing and German Chancellor Helmut Schmidt, who as finance ministers had participated with the finance ministers of the United States and Britain in informal meetings of the "Library Group" to deal with the crisis confronting the fixed exchange rate monetary regime in 1973. After Japan joined, the Library Group became the Group of Five (G5) finance ministers. Once they became government leaders, Giscard and Schmidt wanted to transfer the spirit and practice of the small, informal Library Group and G5 gatherings to meetings at the level of heads of state and government.[35] Despite the vision of Giscard and Schmidt for the summits, even at the first summit meeting in Rambouillet, France it was evident that the delegations would be larger than they envisioned. The summit meetings would also be prepared by the leaders' personal representatives who were later to be called "Sherpas." Thus the summits would essentially become quite different from what Giscard and Schmidt had envisioned. Having discussed the origins and nature of the G7 summits, this chapter examines the role of the G7 summits from 1975 to 1979.

The G7 Summits from 1975 to 1979

The first G7 summit at the Chateau de Rambouillet on 15-17 November 1975 was an unprecedented meeting. Indeed, "never before had presidents and prime ministers met multilaterally to discuss economic matters."[36] On monetary issues, for example, finance ministers and central bank officials had led the delegations from the time of the 1944 Bretton Woods conference to the 1971 Smithsonian meeting (that resulted in the devaluation of the U.S. dollar). Until the first G7 summit, the role of presidents and prime ministers had been limited to occasionally facilitating other gatherings such as the 1971 Smithsonian meeting. The G7/G8 summits have always dealt with a broad range of issues, and the Rambouillet summit addressed the issues of monetary relations, macroeconomic policy, trade, energy, East-West relations, and North-South relations. The most important issues discussed at Rambouillet dealt with macroeconomic policy, international monetary reform, and international trade. This was a period of monetary flux, because the Bretton Woods system of fixed (or pegged) exchange rates had essentially collapsed in 1973. An understanding designed to recognise the need for change in the global monetary regime (to a system of floating exchange rates), while also promoting a degree of monetary stability "was recognized as the main achievement of the Rambouillet summit."[37] Although the monetary understanding at Rambouillet was based on a prior agreement between the United States and France, summit support was essential to the subsequent completion of successful negotiations in the IMF.

On trade, the Rambouillet summit endorsed several objectives designed to preserve an open global trade regime and prevent a return to protectionism. Political leadership on this issue was necessary, because the volume of world trade declined by 5 percent in 1975 following the OPEC oil price increases and the ensuing recession in the developed states. The summiteers directed most of their attention to the slow pace of the GATT Tokyo Round negotiations, and to domestic protectionist pressures in countries such as Britain and Italy that had growing trade deficits and rising unemployment. Although the ministerial trade conference officially opening the Tokyo Round in September 1973 had announced the Ministers' intention "that the trade negotiations be concluded in 1975," a series of political and economic events had delayed progress in the negotiations.[38] Political obstacles included the EC's difficulty in forging a common negotiating position among its nine member countries until 1975, and the U.S. Senate's delay in approving trade negotiating authority for the President in the post-Watergate period. Economic obstacles included the 1973-74 oil crisis and the subsequent recession in the developed states. Thus, the G7 leaders at

Rambouillet expressed the desire to speed up the negotiations and bring them to a successful conclusion by a new deadline of 1977. The G7's forthright position on the Tokyo Round contributed to the resolution of a procedural impasse between the United States and the EC over agriculture, and demonstrated the role that the G7 would often try to play in prodding negotiations forward "at intervals by political decisions taken at a high level."[39] Nevertheless, Rambouillet also demonstrated that pledges by political leaders to complete trade negotiations can be difficult to implement when there are continuing divisions on substantive issues among the major trading powers. Despite the pledges at Rambouillet, the GATT Tokyo Round would drag on until April 1979.[40]

In addition to their actions on the Tokyo Round, the G7 leaders reaffirmed the principles of the Trade Pledge that the OECD Council of Ministers had adopted in May 1974. The Trade Pledge was a declaration signed by the OECD members in which they agreed to avoid new trade restrictions. As was the case for the G7's references to the GATT Tokyo Round, the G7 would reiterate its support for the OECD Trade Pledge in later summits. At the time of the Rambouillet summit, Britain's Prime Minister Harold Wilson was subject to considerable pressure to impose import restrictions in response to Britain's serious balance of trade problems. However, after Rambouillet the British government limited itself to imposing only selective controls on imports of certain textiles, clothing, and shoes. Some observers credited U.S. and EC pressures on the British to uphold the spirit of the Rambouillet communiqué with limiting the scope of restrictions the British imposed on trade.[41]

It was initially uncertain whether the summits would become annual events, but shortly after Rambouillet President Gerald Ford proposed that a second summit be held in San Juan, Puerto Rico. President Ford invited Canada to the 27-28 June 1976 Puerto Rico summit despite objections from France, and Canada then joined the other six countries as a full G7 member. The principal economic reason given for calling another summit was to avoid a new wave of inflation as a result of economic recovery that was proceeding faster than planned. A second reason for the summit related to concerns about the vulnerable condition of the Italian economy. However, another summit meeting did not seem to be necessary only seven months after Rambouillet, and the Puerto Rico meeting was "the shortest and least substantial of all the summits, lasting just over twenty-four hours."[42] On trade issues, the Puerto Rico summit communiqué endorsed the renewal of the OECD's Trade Pledge with its anti-protectionist commitment, and reaffirmed "the objective of completing the Multilateral Trade Negotiations by the end of 1977."[43] Despite these pledges, the GATT Tokyo Round proceeded very slowly in 1976, and the Puerto Rico summit did not provide much impetus to the negotiations.

The third G7 summit in London (London I) on 7-8 May 1977 was influenced by some major changes on the political scene in the United States and the EC. Most importantly, Jimmy Carter had become the new U.S. President, and he placed greater emphasis than his predecessors on careful preparations for the summits and on introducing a series of policy initiatives. In response to demands by smaller EC members, the EC was represented at the G7 summits for the first time in London after a compromise was reached with France at a European Council meeting. As is often the case in its external relations, the EC has dual representation at G7 summits, by the Presidents of the European Council and the European Commission. In the trade area where the EC commission has competence, "it has often played a role in encouraging the adoption of a common position by the European participants" at G7 meetings.[44]

The London I summit addressed a number of issues including macro-economic policy, trade, nuclear energy, and North-South relations. However, differences were evident among the participants on key issues such as the need for economic expansion of the stronger economies (Japan and Germany), and some critics charged that London I fell short on accomplishments. Major differences were also evident among the summiteers on trade policy, but some assessments of the London I summit in the trade area were remarkably positive. For example, one observer argued that "the major positive achievement of the London summit was a reaffirmation of the commitment of the Seven to a prompt and positive resolution of the Tokyo Round."[45] It is important to explain why this positive assessment was offered despite the differences among the London summiteers on trade.

Major differences of view among the G7 countries on the GATT Tokyo Round were evident in the preparations for the London I summit. Whereas the United States, Japan, and Germany wanted the summit to strongly condemn protectionism and recommit to a rapid completion of the Tokyo Round, Britain, France, and Italy had concerns about overly rapid trade liberalisation. Indeed, France referred to "organised trade" as an alternative to "free trade," because of its concerns regarding competition from the newly-industrialising economies in textiles, and from the United States in such industries as computers.[46] The divisions among the major traders continued to be evident at London I, and the summit declaration ("The Downing Street Declaration") reflected these conflicting views. On the one hand, the declaration expressed a joint G7 commitment strongly supported by the United States, Germany and Japan to "give a new impetus to the Tokyo Round of Multilateral Trade Negotiations" by making "substantive progress in key areas in 1977."[47] On the other hand, at the urgings of Britain and France the G7 qualified this commitment with a statement that the Tokyo Round "should not remove the right of individual countries under existing international agreements to avoid significant market disruption."[48] This qualification in effect recognised the right of countries to adopt some restrictive trade measures as an exemption from the OECD Trade Pledge.

Despite these mixed messages, the London "summit's endorsement of the Tokyo Round proved to be a useful prod to entrenched interests that had long stalled the negotiations."[49] The Democratic administration of Jimmy Carter gave a high priority to overcoming the obstacles to the Tokyo Round, and the appointment of Robert S. Strauss as U.S. Trade Representative (USTR) would prove to be an important turning point in the negotiations. The high-level commitment to the Tokyo Round at London I "gave Strauss a mandate, indeed an excuse, to work out the resolution of" problems "that had blocked negotiations through mid-1977."[50] Thus, Strauss held a series of meetings after the London I summit with leading political representatives of the EC, Japan, and Canada, in which important compromises on various trade issues were made.[51]

Two major items on the agenda of the 16-17 July 1978 Bonn I economic summit were macroeconomic policy and energy. Of particular importance was economic policy harmonisation, in which Germany agreed to stimulate its economy, and the United States agreed to reduce inflation and increase efforts to conserve oil. The Bonn summit was also responsible for a major breakthrough in the trade area, which in fact was achieved even before the summit convened. After the London summit had endorsed the Tokyo Round, the chief U.S. negotiator Robert Strauss pressured the other G7 members to set the Bonn I summit as the deadline for an agreement. Although it was impossible to reach a final agreement by the time of Bonn I, it "served as a review mechanism for the Tokyo Round that was crucial in setting an interim deadline for the work accomplished through mid-1978."[52] By publicly setting the interim deadline, the G7 increased pressure on governments to reach a final settlement. As the Bonn I summit meeting approached, Tokyo Round negotiators from the G7 and other countries agreed to a compromise formula for determining tariff reductions and made substantial progress in reducing tariffs and NTBs in specific sectors. Thus, the negotiators reached an agreement on a Framework of Understanding on the Tokyo Round on 13 July 1978 (only three days before Bonn I was to begin), in which most outstanding issues were resolved.[53]

The chief negotiators for the United States, the EC, and Japan were all present in Bonn, and at a special summit session on trade they "engaged in serious negotiations for mutually acceptable concessions in consultation with their leaders."[54] However, there were still outstanding issues to resolve after the Bonn I summit, and further discussions at the political level were necessary before the Tokyo Round could be concluded. Differences among the developed countries were eventually resolved when the United States offered to downgrade its demands of Europe in agriculture in return for a European agreement to a timetable for rapid completion of the round. However, it then became evident that the developed countries would have to contend with the dissatisfaction of developing countries. Although the Bonn I summit declaration indicated that the G7 would take "into account the needs of developing countries ... through special and differential treatment,"[55] the pyramidal process of negotiation that the G7 summits represented created major tensions with the developing countries that required resolution before the Tokyo Round could be completed. The developing countries were dissatisfied that they had no part in the Framework of Understanding on the Tokyo Round which the developed countries agreed to in the run-up to Bonn I. They also argued that the developed countries had not dealt with the Multifibre Arrangement for textiles and voluntary export restraints that were often aimed at the Third World. To counter these frictions, the developed countries had to give higher priority to developing country concerns when the Tokyo Round negotiations resumed after the Bonn I summit.[56]

On 12 April 1979, the GATT Tokyo Round was officially concluded. The G7 leaders at the 28-29 June 1979 summit in Tokyo (Tokyo I) that followed indicated that agreements reached in the GATT Tokyo Round were "an important achievement," and that they were committed to "early and faithful implementation" of the agreements.[57] Other than this statement, the G7 summit in Tokyo devoted little time to trade issues because it had to contend with several major crises. Indeed, the year 1979 began with the fall of the Shah of Iran, and OPEC decisions resulted in a second surge in oil prices on the eve of the Tokyo I summit. Originally, the G7 planned to devote the second day of Tokyo I to the discussion of monetary, trade, and other economic matters. The second oil crisis, however, changed these plans, and concerns with energy and related issues dominated the summit. The next three summits from 1980 to 1982 would also be strongly affected by the oil crisis and the extended recession that followed.[58]

In sum, from the time the G7 summits began in Rambouillet in 1975, they provided a stimulus to the Tokyo Round negotiations at the highest political level. However, the experience of the 1975 to 1979 period also demonstrated several shortcomings of the summits in dealing with multilateral trade negotiations. First, the G7 was often stymied by divisions among the major economic powers, and its role was limited to persuading and cajoling rather than negotiating. The G7 summiteers had to defer the proposed final deadline for the Tokyo Round on several occasions, because they had less influence during the period when many of the technical issues in the negotiations were still unresolved. It was only after the negotiations had proceeded to a final, breakthrough phase (as occurred before the 1978 Bonn I summit) that the G7 leaders could exert more influence. A second shortcoming stemmed from the fact that the G7 was already beginning to develop a more crowded agenda in which trade was only one of its concerns. At the crucial Bonn I summit, for example, trade had to compete with other major concerns such as macroeconomic policy and energy problems. A third shortcoming resulted from the fact that the G7 summits were devoted primarily to resolving differences and reaching a consensus among the major developed countries. Because the G7 did not adequately address the interests of developing countries, the deadline for conclusion of the Tokyo Round had to be deferred until more attention was given to developing country concerns.

Despite the shortcomings of the G7 in dealing with trade negotiations, the summits regularly encouraged actions to stem the rise of protectionism, and they had a significant influence on the multilateral trade negotiations in the latter stages of the Tokyo Round. Most importantly, the 1977 London I summit gave the U.S. Trade Representative the mandate he needed to pursue the negotiations more vigorously, and the 1978 Bonn I summit provided an interim deadline that served as a major impetus to concluding the round. In referring to the Bonn summit's impact on the GATT negotiators, a U.S. Under Secretary for Economic Affairs commented that "you can't judge summits just by what happens at the summit itself. Summit meetings also serve as an important focal point for other negotiations."[59] Although the GATT Tokyo Round was the main trade issue the G7 dealt with from 1975 to 1979, it was certainly not the only trade issue of concern to the G7 in this period. For example, the G5 (Britain, France, Germany, Japan, and the United States) and then the G7 summits also had an important role in fashioning an agreement on export credit, which was further developed and approved by the OECD in 1978. It is to the OECD, the next step in the trade regime pyramid in the 1970s, that we now turn.

Organisation for Economic Co-operation and Development

As was the case for the G7, the OECD played an important role in the 1970s in providing an impetus to the GATT Tokyo Round. The OECD was also involved with the export credit and government procurement issues in the 1970s as it had been in the 1960s (see Chapter 3). However, while the OECD continued to serve as the main forum for negotiation of export credit agreements, it largely transferred the government procurement issue to the GATT during the Tokyo Round.

The OECD and the GATT Tokyo Round

The OECD had a role in initiating and setting the agenda for the Tokyo Round negotiations, and it repeatedly encouraged the negotiators to overcome the obstacles to agreement and complete the round. In June 1971, the OECD Ministerial Council decided that a study should be done "of the opportunities for further progress towards the general objective of a greater liberalisation of international trade," and it asked the OECD Secretary-General to appoint a group of high-level experts to conduct the study.[60] The Secretary-General subsequently formed the High-Level Group on Trade and Related Problems (or the "Rey Group" named after the Group's Chair, Jean Rey). As discussed earlier in this chapter, it was in July 1971 that the U.S. Williams Commission issued its report calling for a new round of GATT negotiations to liberalise trade. The Williams Commission welcomed "the recent agreement to establish a high-level study group on trade problems in OECD as a step in this direction."[61]

In August 1972 the OECD's Rey Group issued a report entitled *Policy Perspectives for International Trade and Economic Relations*, in which it strongly supported a new round of GATT negotiations. The report argued that "a new effort to secure greater liberalisation, achieved through negotiation, is needed not only for the direct benefits it will bring but because without it the divisive forces of protectionism will grow stronger."[62] The Rey Group report clearly was one factor setting the stage for the launching of the Tokyo Round one year later. The OECD continued to be concerned about the forces of protectionism throughout the Tokyo Round, and on 30 May 1974 the OECD Ministerial Council adopted a Declaration on Trade (or Trade Pledge) "aimed at avoiding restrictions on trade ... which could lead to chain reactions and endanger the process of economic recovery."[63] The OECD renewed this Trade Pledge every year at its Ministerial Council meeting until the end of the Tokyo Round. When divisions among the major trading powers caused delays in the projected date for completing the Tokyo Round from 1975 to 1977, and then to 1979, the OECD as well as the G7 played a role in providing an impetus to the negotiations at higher political levels. The major trading countries were aware that the impasse at the Tokyo Round posed a threat to the global trade regime, and they used OECD meetings to profess their commitment to trade liberalisation. Thus, the OECD Ministers repeatedly "expressed their strong support for a successful outcome of the Multilateral Trade Negotiations."[64]

Export Credit

As discussed in Chapter 2, the United States resisted a stronger export credit agreement in the 1962 to 1972 period, claiming that easier credit terms were simply "an element of competition comparable to cheaper labour or higher productivity."[65] However, the 1973-74 oil shock raised the spectre that developed countries would respond to their growing balance of payments and unemployment problems with mercantilist policies. To promote their exports, developed countries began to extend export credits with subsidised interest rates and longer repayment periods, and export credit competition loomed as a major issue. Developed country governments resorted to these practices despite their awareness that export credit competition could have major economic costs, because of domestic political and economic pressures. Furthermore, it was necessary to recycle the large amount of funds that oil-exporting developing countries were depositing in OECD countries' commercial banks, and export credits became an important incentive to potential borrowers.

The United States was concerned that the growing competition for exports would lead to an export credit war, and it therefore rather abruptly altered its policies and assumed a leadership position in seeking an agreement on export finance. The renewed efforts to develop an export credit agreement began with the G5 and the G7, and only later would shift back to the OECD. The G5 finance ministers first explored the possibilities for an export credit agreement at the 1973 IMF Board of Governors annual meeting in Nairobi, Kenya, and discussions on the issue continued informally after the meeting. In 1974, the United States, Britain, France, Germany, Italy, and Japan – later joined by Canada (i.e., the G7 countries) agreed to establish a minimum interest rate of 7.5 percent for export credits with repayment terms of over five years. However, the scope of the agreement was very limited because the minimum interest rate applied only to officially supported credits on exports to signatories and some wealthy oil-producing states.[66] In 1975 the G7 countries tried to negotiate a more comprehensive accord covering most aspects of official export credit, but a divergence of views prevented them from accomplishing this goal. The Commission of the European Community in particular challenged these efforts to reach a comprehensive agreement. Although the EC Commission supported the idea of an agreement to control official export credit, it argued that the Commission rather than individual EC states should be negotiating such an accord because export credit was one element of the EC's common commercial policy.[67]

To understand the EC's position on negotiating export credit, a brief discussion of the EU decision-making system for trade issues is necessary. The European Commission gradually "established itself as the negotiator for the European Union ... on trade issues, but always operating under the watchful eyes of the member governments."[68] Although the European Commission acts for the EU in multilateral trade negotiations, the Council of Ministers (representing the member states) sets the objectives for the negotiations and has ultimate authority to adopt the results of the negotiations. Originally, GATT multilateral trade negotiations were essentially limited to negotiations to reduce tariffs on goods. As the GATT, and then the WTO agenda was progressively extended into new areas such as a wide array of non-tariff barriers, services, investment, and intellectual property, it was necessary to constantly redefine the European Commission's competence to deal with trade policy. Thus, over the years there has been a natural tension in trade policy between the Commission's prerogatives and those of the member states.

Shortly before the first G7 economic summit in 1975, the European Court of Justice determined that only the EC Commission had the competence to conclude an export credit agreement on behalf of EC countries. Nevertheless, the growing budgetary costs of subsidised export credit at low interest rates increased pressures on the G7 to stem the competition.[69] France therefore largely disregarded the European Court's ruling and maintained that the G7 countries should intensify their "efforts to achieve a prompt conclusion of the negotiations concerning export credits."[70] Building on work already done by the OECD, the G7 then established the first comprehensive agreement on export credits – the nonbinding "Consensus on Converging Export Credit Policies" of July 1976, which later came to be known as the "Gentlemen's Agreement." To circumvent the issue of the European Commission's competence, the 1976 Gentlemen's Agreement was not a signed accord. Instead, the G7 countries simply gave a verbal pledge to implement the agreement by unilateral policy declarations. The agreement established targets for the maximum duration, minimum down payments, and minimum interest rates for all export credits with a maturity of two or more years; and it provided very loose guidelines for notification and consultation in the case of "mixed credits." Mixed credits, which are also called "aid credits," often use a relatively small amount of aid to ease the financial terms for recipients. Although mixed credits on relatively soft terms with a large component of concessional aid may be a legitimate feature of bilateral aid programmes, mixed credits on relatively hard terms are commercially motivated.

Thus, mixed credits may circumvent guidelines on commercial credit, and may also divert scarce aid resources from the poorest countries to countries that already have access to export credit financing.[71]

At the June 1976 G7 economic summit in San Juan, Puerto Rico the summiteers welcomed "the adoption, by participating countries, of converging guidelines with regard to export credits," and recommended that countries outside the G7 also accept the guidelines "as soon as possible."[72] Several other European countries responded to the G7 recommendation by adopting the 1976 Gentlemen's Agreement. To prevent even more countries from responding, the EC Commission again brought the issue to the European Court of Justice, arguing that the EC countries had breached their obligations by acting individually. Eventually the Commission abandoned its Court action when the EC countries in the G7 recognised the Commission's competence to deal with the export credit issue. By the end of 1977, all members of the OECD Export Credit Group except Australia and New Zealand had joined the Gentlemen's Agreement. However, the agreement lacked the force of a single document because it was based on unilateral declarations by the participating countries. The G7 countries at the 1977 London I summit therefore proposed "that substantial further efforts be made this year to improve and extend the present consensus in this area."[73] Among the G7 countries, the United States assumed a dominant role in pushing for a stronger agreement.

In February 1978, the twenty participants in the Gentlemen's Agreement approved the "Arrangement on Guidelines for Officially Supported Export Credits" (henceforth, "the Arrangement"), which converted the unilateral declarations into a single document. Although all twenty countries formally participated in the discussions, the negotiations resulting in the 1978 Arrangement "were essentially between the United States and the larger EEC countries."[74] France had initially resisted a stronger agreement limiting export credit subsidies, but it backed down under strong pressure from the United States. Indeed, the 1978 Arrangement, and amendments strengthening it in 1983 and 1985, were possible

> because the United States threatened to use a unique power resource, grounded in the greater depth of North American capital markets, which permitted it to extend very long term loans. The French agreed to the Arrangement of 1978 in large part to restrict the use of such loans.[75]

The 1978 Arrangement was not formally an OECD agreement because it was not an act of the OECD Council, and the EC which was one of the signatories was not an OECD member. Nevertheless, the Arrangement was negotiated in the OECD, and the OECD Secretariat is responsible for servicing it. Furthermore, all 22 members of the OECD Export Credit Group accepted the 1978 Arrangement. Iceland and Turkey were the only OECD members that did not participate, because they lacked facilities for financing or guaranteeing export credit. The main objective of the Arrangement was to avoid an export credit contest among OECD countries by providing an institutional framework for orderly export credit competition. The Arrangement set minimum permissible interest rates, minimum required cash downpayments, and maximum repayment terms for officially supported export credits with a maturity of two years or longer; and it provided for limited exchanges of information on export credit practices. The Arrangement was negotiated in the OECD rather than the GATT primarily because it was in fact "a cartel designed to restrict political economic competition among credit agencies" in the OECD countries.[76] It is understandable that developing countries in the GATT/WTO would not be favourably inclined to such an agreement, because competition among credit agencies can provide recipient countries with better credit terms.[77]

Another reason why the Arrangement was negotiated in the OECD is that developed countries sometimes prefer to avoid the legalistic approach of the GATT/WTO when dealing with highly sensitive issues. As was the case for the OEEC's agreements on quantitative restrictions and the FAO-CSD's agreements on surplus disposal of agricultural products (see Chapter 2), the 1978 Arrangement on export credit is not a legally binding international treaty. In addition to the Arrangement's dependence on voluntary compliance, it has had a number of other shortcomings. Nevertheless, instead of replacing the 1978 Arrangement, the participants have gradually expanded its coverage for over twenty years.[78] The export credit issue is not discussed in later chapters in this book, because the revised 1978 Arrangement continues to be the main agreement for export credit negotiated among the OECD countries. To provide some understanding of the 1978 Arrangement's shortcomings, we provide a brief discussion here of the most significant revisions of the Arrangement.

A major problem with the 1978 Arrangement was that countries could contravene the guidelines for extending export credit, as long as they gave prior notice of their "derogations." In December 1982, OECD members added a "no-derogation engagement" under which participants agreed to abide by the main conditions of the Arrangement unless they were simply following the practices of other states. A second problem with the Arrangement was the difficulty in adjusting the minimum permissible interest rates for export credits. Although the allowable interest rates on export credits varied in accordance with the income level of the importing country, the minimum fixed rates could only be increased by unanimous agreement in the OECD, usually after protracted negotiations. In a world of rapidly changing *commercial* interest rates, the budgetary burden of subsidies for export credit at the minimum fixed rates varied considerably. In 1983, OECD members therefore adopted a system for automatically adjusting the minimum interest rates for export credits in response to changes in the commercial rates.[79]

In 1983, the focus of discussion shifted to a third problem – determining the proper relationship of export credits to development aid. Concessional loans (or soft loans) generally have lower interest rates, longer grace periods, and longer repayment periods than commercial loans (or hard loans). The "grant element" of a loan increases as the terms of repayment become more concessional. Concessional credits provided for development aid are often tied (like tied aid) to procurement of goods and services in the donor country. Whereas mixed credits with a large grant element are likely to be aid oriented, mixed credits with a small grant element may be designed to improve the competitive standing of the country through a basically commercial transaction. The question is how to separate tied aid from commercial financing so that commercial (as opposed to concessional) mixed credits cannot be tied to purchases in the financing country. The 1978 Arrangement tried to separate aid from commercial financing by requiring prior notification if a country provided mixed credits with a grant element of less than 15 percent; but it did not prohibit such transactions. In 1982 the participants strengthened the provisions by agreeing not to provide mixed credits with a grant element of less than 20 percent, and they raised this figure again to 25 percent in 1985. Nevertheless, there was still concern that competition in the use of mixed credits was distorting trade relationships and diverting aid flows from development objectives.[80]

The use of medium- and long-term official export credits in fact declined for much of the 1980s, largely because of the developing country debt crisis, which began with Mexico in 1982. Most debtor countries responded to their balance of payments problems by cutting back public sector investment programs, and this reduced the demand for imports financed through official export credits. Even when some developing countries tried to increase imports and seek new financing, export credit agencies were reluctant to extend new commitments because of concerns about their ability to service new debt. In the late 1980s, however, there was a dramatic reversal in the decline of export credits with the recovery of developing country demand for capital goods imports. A number of creditor governments also began to view export credits as an important means of supporting the transition economies, and they extended growing amounts of export credit to Eastern Europe and the former Soviet

Union. Thus, new export credit commitments almost tripled from $24 billion in 1988 to $70 billion in 1993.[81]

Mixed credits have continued to present a special problem. The OECD countries tried to resolve this issue by increasing the minimum permissible grant component in tied aid credits to 30 percent in 1987, and to 35 percent in 1988. Nevertheless, concerns that donor countries were shifting from soft to hard aid-giving led the 1989 OECD ministerial to call for continued efforts to strengthen "the multilateral disciplines on trade- and aid-distorting export credit subsidies."[82] The 1989 G7 summit in Paris similarly urged that the efforts to deal with trade and aid distorting credit subsidies "must be pursued actively and completed in the competent bodies of the OECD ... at the earliest possible date."[83] A significant step toward further reducing the use of mixed credits was the 1992 "Helsinki Package," which prohibits the use of mixed credits for commercially viable projects and for creditworthy developing countries that have commercial finance available. The United States strongly pressured for the Helsinki Package, and has been the key member ensuring that it is upheld. In addition to mixed credits, another problem has been that the 1978 Arrangement does not cover all areas of export credit. In 1994, participants agreed to begin work on export credits for agricultural products and other areas not covered by the Arrangement.[84]

Participants in the 1978 Arrangement have also contended with several issues related to the decision-making process. A major procedural question is whether the participants' group should be expanded to include non-OECD countries such as the NIEs (newly-industrialising economies) and larger developing countries. In the late 1970s, several developing countries including Brazil, India, and Mexico expressed an interest in joining the participants' group; and in the 1980s, concerns increased that the NIEs were rapidly establishing programs to provide export credits for their industrial exports. The growing use of export credit by some developing countries raised questions about expanding the membership in the OECD Arrangement. On the one hand, it would be easier to prevent the NIEs from undercutting OECD export credit terms by admitting them to the Arrangement. On the other hand, the NIEs continue to be important export credit *recipients*, and the OECD countries are reluctant "to have customers privy to their negotiations."[85] Although the participants' group has remained limited to OECD countries, OECD membership has gradually increased to include some NIEs and transition economies such as Mexico, South Korea, the Czech Republic, Hungary, and Poland (see Table 3.1).

Another decision-making question was whether the GATT multilateral trade negotiations should begin to deal with the export credit issue; but the participants decided to continue limiting export credit discussions to the OECD. The United States in particular argued that many GATT members would oppose reducing export credit subsidies because they were net credit consumers. Furthermore, as a less legalistic organisation than the GATT, the OECD was able to take a more flexible approach to export credits. The 1978 Arrangement among OECD members is a "Gentlemen's Agreement," which by definition is not legally binding, and does not have the status of international law. Enforcement of the 1978 Arrangement depends solely on the signatory governments, and the OECD secretariat acts only as a facilitator. The OECD's informal approach to export credit also permitted it to diverge from some of the trade principles normally associated with the GATT. Different subsidy limits were established for recipient countries depending on their level of economic development, with richer countries being subject to higher interest rates and shorter credit periods than poorer countries. This system runs counter to the GATT's most-favoured-nation (MFN) principle.[86]

Taking account of all the revisions in the 1978 Arrangement, it is important to assess the effectiveness of the OECD's export credit guidelines. Despite some lapses in compliance and continuing efforts to deal with mixed credits, the OECD guidelines have generally been helpful in preventing destructive competition among export credit providers. Although the OECD Secretariat could not directly resolve issues, it conducted background studies, proposed compromise solutions, and framed the issues in a manner that helped resolve differences. The export credit negotiations never broke down completely during periods of intense conflict, because they were conducted in permanent fora such as the OECD Export Credits Group and the Participants Group. Unlike *ad hoc* meetings, assurances that the Export Credits Group would always have another meeting kept the discussion channels open. As the export credit arrangement was gradually strengthened, participants began to place increasing value on it. Thus, by the late 1980s, none of the participants seemed to be willing to risk the collapse of the Arrangement.[87] Despite the commitment to the Arrangement, it has been repeatedly revised and expanded because "as surely as night follows day, export credit practices move one step ahead of the judge."[88] In efforts to test the margins of the Arrangement, participants always demonstrate creativity in inventing less transparent forms of competition that are more difficult to detect and evaluate. Despite these shortcomings, the 1978 OECD Arrangement has been reasonably effective in regulating export credit practices:

> The OECD Arrangement, as revised ... has successfully institutionalized trade finance within a strong international regulatory regime. The trade finance regime

has a broad scope, has remained dedicated to a consistent set of goals for over a decade, has adapted to a wide range of challenges, and enjoys compliance by its members.[89]

Government Procurement

The 1947 GATT had excluded government procurement from its national treatment and most-favoured-nation treatment provisions, and there was substantial discrimination in favour of domestic producers. As outlined in Chapter 3, OECD members sought to remedy this deficiency throughout the 1960s with discussions, background studies and the development of a 1970 draft code on government procurement. OECD discussions continued until mid-1976, when government procurement became a subject for negotiation in the GATT Tokyo Round. In July 1976, the Tokyo Round negotiators agreed to establish a subgroup on government procurement that held its first meeting in October of that year.

Several factors contributed to the pressure to incorporate the government procurement issue in the Tokyo Round. First, progress in OECD discussions had been slow, because European governments were reluctant to open the government procurement process to international competition. American and Canadian officials, by contrast, were committed to moving beyond the draft stage with a government procurement code, and they believed that moving the negotiations to the larger Tokyo Round setting would provide the needed impetus. Although some EC countries such as France strongly opposed the transfer to the GATT, the European Commission supported the move. The Commission believed it would gain more centralised control over the government procurement policies of EC member states if the negotiations shifted to the wider GATT forum. A second reason for the move of the government procurement discussions to the GATT was that all governments discriminate in favour of local producers when purchasing goods and services. Thus, the government procurement negotiations were considered too important to remain within the confines of the limited-membership OECD.[90] A number of countries were increasing the government sectors of their economies, and by the 1970s over 40 percent of the GDPs of some states was passing through government budgets. Thus, the GATT director-general's report on the Tokyo Round indicated that "in nearly all countries, developed and developing, the government is the largest single purchaser of goods."[91] A third factor in the move of the government procurement discussions was the position of developing countries, which were not participants in the OECD discussions. Some of the more advanced developing countries pressed for creation of the Tokyo Round subgroup, because they "believed that government procurement held out possibilities for the expansion of their trade and provided scope for special and differential treatment in their favour."[92] However, the less advanced developing countries were unenthusiastic about the government procurement negotiations.

Some developed countries "were of the view from the outset that government procurement practices were one of the most important obstacles to world trade and should be dealt with in the course of the Tokyo Round."[93] It was possible to involve all countries – including the developing countries – from the beginning of the Tokyo Round negotiations on government procurement, because the OECD had already developed a draft code and identified the main issues for negotiation. Indeed, "virtually all the problems that would have to be faced if an international procurement code was to be adopted, surfaced" in the OECD before 1976.[94] The OECD directly confronted many of the issues related to government procurement, and framed some of the remaining issues in such a manner that the GATT could resolve them in the final year of the Tokyo Round. Although the Tokyo Round negotiations resulted in substantial revisions in the OECD draft code, the OECD's "basic definitions and itemised breakdown of the tendering process were maintained in the final code."[95] The resolution of bilateral differences between the United States and the EC played a central role in the Tokyo Round negotiations on government procurement as they had in the OECD prenegotiations.

The "Agreement on Government Procurement" was one of the plurilateral non-tariff barrier codes resulting from the GATT Tokyo Round. The core provision of this code is found in Article II, which states that "all laws regulations, procedures and practices regarding government procurement covered by this Agreement" must give foreign suppliers treatment no less favourable than that given to domestic suppliers (i.e., national treatment).[96] Article II also calls for most-favoured nation treatment among foreign suppliers in government procurement. In addition, the code has transparency provisions (in Articles V and VI) designed to eliminate latent discrimination that may exist even without a formal system of preferences. To ensure that there is transparency, the code obligates signatories to publish all procurement laws and practices, advertise procurements, provide detailed tender documentation to permit informed bidding by interested suppliers, and give unsuccessful suppliers reasons for rejection of a tender. Finally, the code has dispute settlement procedures to address complaints that a government is not meeting the obligations of the procurement agreement.[97]

Although the Tokyo Round government procurement code was a substantial accomplishment, it also had some serious shortcomings. First, the code applied only to the procurement of goods, not services; second, the code did not apply to subfederal units such as U.S. states, Canadian provinces, or German länder, which often provide preferential treatment in government procurement; and third, the code applied only to governmental entities on a list appended to the agreement for each signatory (i.e., a number of government purchases were excluded). Furthermore, Article III of the code purported to give S&D treatment to developing countries, but there were no specific mandatory requirements that the developed countries accord such treatment. The most serious shortcoming of the government procurement code was that fewer GATT members signed it than any other Tokyo Round code. All but three of the signatories of the procurement code were developed states. The reluctance of governments to become signatories stems from the fact that "government procurement strikes to the heart of public spending prerogatives" that states wish to preserve, and this is especially true of developing countries as late industrialisers.[98]

In sum, discussions, prenegotiations, and the development of a draft agreement by the OECD in the 1960s to 1970s were a major contribution to the negotiation of the government procurement code in the GATT Tokyo Round. However, the OECD's involvement with the government procurement issue also demonstrates some of the organisation's shortcomings. In pressuring for a government procurement agreement the OECD was representing the interests of the developed countries. Despite a shift in negotiations from the OECD to the GATT, the Tokyo Round government procurement code had a limited membership that continued to consist mainly of developed countries. Export interests in the major trading nations considered public procurement markets to be "too big to be left beyond the reach of the multilateral trading system."[99] Nevertheless, the developed states were not sufficiently attuned to the importance late industrialisers such as today's developing countries often give to government involvement in promoting their economic development, and very few developing countries signed the government procurement code.

The Role of the Developing Countries

The decade of the 1970s was a period of increased North-South confrontation, in which the developing countries tried to alter the developed country-dominated regimes governing North-South relations by establishing a New International

Economic Order (NIEO). The developing countries were able to exert more influence in the 1970s because of the success of OPEC in drastically increasing oil prices. In 1974 the developing countries presented three documents to the UN General Assembly that outlined their negotiating agenda: the Declaration on the Establishment of a NIEO, the Programme of Action on the Establishment of a NIEO, and the Charter of Economic Rights and Duties of States. Although many features of this agenda were not new (i.e., UNCTAD had previously referred to many of the NIEO demands), the developing countries had more influence during a limited period in the 1970s and the developed countries were therefore more prepared to negotiate.[100]

Developing country demands for a NIEO were discussed not only in the UN, but also in the Conference on International Economic Cooperation (CIEC) or the "North-South Dialogue." The North-South dialogue began as a response to an October 1974 proposal by the French President Valéry Giscard d'Estaing to convene a conference on energy among the OPEC countries, the developed countries, and the non-oil developing countries. However, preparations for the conference reached an impasse because the developed countries led by the United States wanted the dialogue to focus only on energy problems, whereas the developing countries called for a much broader agenda. The March 1975 OPEC summit meeting supported the developing country position, indicating that the conference should include the broader issues of raw materials and development as well as energy. Because the developed countries felt the need to discuss energy issues with OPEC they were willing to compromise, and an agreement was reached to establish the CIEC. The CIEC was a 27-member conference, including 19 representatives from developing countries and 8 representatives from developed countries. Four commissions were established on energy, raw materials, development, and financial aid, to address the issues on the conference agenda.[101]

In the NIEO negotiations in the UN and CIEC, the developing countries sought greater sovereignty over their natural resources and economies, increased control over the level and nature of foreign investment, higher prices for their raw material and commodity exports, increased access to commercial markets of developed countries, lower costs for technology transfers, higher volumes of official development assistance, greater assistance in confronting their foreign debt problems, and increased decision-making power in the UN and the KIEOs. In regard to trade, the NIEO was mainly concerned with improving export markets for developing country producers, creating institutions that would favour the trade-related interests of the South, and providing S&D treatment for the South in international markets.[102]

One area that seemed especially promising for developing countries related to their demands to establish a special program to stabilise markets and increase prices for their commodity exports. At the Sixth Special Session of the UN General Assembly in April 1974 the G77 asked the UNCTAD Secretariat to develop a program to counter unstable earnings and declining terms of trade for developing country commodity exports. In 1976 the UNCTAD IV conference in Nairobi, Kenya responded to this request by passing a resolution to establish an *Integrated Program for Commodities (IPC)*. The IPC involved proposals to negotiate international commodity agreements for 18 commodities of export interest to developing countries. The two most important elements of the IPC were to be the creation of international buffer stocks and a "Common Fund," which would be used to acquire the stocks. To avoid excessive price fluctuations and ensure developing country producers of remunerative returns, the IPC would enlarge stockpiles of surplus commodities (those with declining prices), and sell stockpiles of scarce commodities (those subject to increasing prices). Some major developed countries opposed the IPC proposal on liberal-economic grounds because of its strong emphasis on market intervention to stabilise prices. Nevertheless, at the CIEC the developed countries agreed in principle to underwrite the cost of the Common Fund which would finance the buffer stocks for the IPC.

Despite the initial willingness of the North to confer with the South on their demands for a NIEO, the developed countries became less amenable to further talks with the South by the late 1970s for several reasons. First, there was increasing realisation that developing country producers of other commodities would not be able to emulate OPEC's success in limiting supply and increasing prices; and second, developed countries were recovering from their economic recession despite the OPEC price increases. In the 1980s the ability of developing countries to influence the developed states declined abruptly with the emergence of the Third World foreign debt crisis. Thus, it was evident that developing country efforts to increase their influence through demands for a NIEO would be unsuccessful. Although diplomatic activity on some of the issues continued for a number of years, "the NIEO itself lost ground during the second half of the 1970s, and was virtually eclipsed by the end of the 1980s."[103] In the longer term the South achieved little even in the IPC negotiations which had seemed to be particularly promising. Thus, authors of a 1988 study on developing countries and commodity trade concluded that "after decades of negotiations and the expenditure of significant human and financial resources by developing countries, the global commodity trade regime today remains remarkably similar to that during the immediate postwar years."[104]

At the same time as the South was confronting the North with demands for a NIEO in the UN, the South was negotiating with the North on trade issues for pragmatic reasons in the GATT Tokyo Round. In contrast to the Kennedy Round where the developing countries were very marginal to the negotiations, they were more actively involved in the Tokyo Round. As in the past, however, divisions among the developing countries reduced their effectiveness in the negotiations. On tariffs, for example, the Latin American states pressured for preferential tariff cuts for developing country goods; but African states feared that such general preferences would undercut the regional preferences they had through associate membership in the EC. The South did succeed in securing Tokyo Round adoption of the "enabling clause," which for the first time established preferential treatment for developing countries as a permanent legal feature of the global trade regime. The clause gave permanent legal authorisation for the GSP and for preferential trading agreements among developing countries. The North, however, insisted that the enabling clause include a "graduation clause," which states that those countries demonstrating notable progress in development would gradually dispense with their preferential treatment and "participate more fully in the framework of rights and obligations under the General Agreement."[105] The South only reluctantly agreed to inclusion of the graduation clause, and at UNCTAD V the G77 maintained that graduation would permit the North to discriminate among developing countries in a unilateral and arbitrary fashion.[106]

Despite the S&D treatment they received in the Tokyo Round, many developing countries were dissatisfied with the round. Indeed, the experience of developing countries in the GATT from the time of its formation was an exercise in frustration. Most of the "concessions" the North granted to the South such as the inclusion of Part IV on trade and development and the Tokyo Round enabling clause were largely rhetorical, and others such as the GSP were replete with qualifications. While the developed country concessions to developing countries were rather minor, they were reluctant to lower tariffs and remove NTBs for some products in which developing countries had a comparative advantage such as textiles and agricultural products. Clearly the developing country strategy of largely opting out of the GATT and demanding S&D treatment was not experiencing much success.

Developing country frustration was particularly evident near the end of the Tokyo Round when the major trading nations circulated a Framework of Understanding in the leadup to the 1978 Bonn G7 summit that contained the necessary elements for completing the round. The developing countries had played no part in drafting the Framework, and they pressured for a delay in concluding the round until they could convene an UNCTAD meeting scheduled for May 1979. However, the GATT director-general refused to accept this request and announced on 12 April 1979 that the Tokyo Round had ended.[107] Although the developing countries reluctantly accepted this decision, the UNCTAD secretariat charged that the Tokyo Round agreements "do little to help poor nations, and only serve to perpetuate a trading system that works more and more against them."[108] From the time the GATT was formed in the 1940s, developing countries had "remained bystanders in successive rounds of trade negotiations," and most developing countries refused to sign the Tokyo Round codes and to bind their tariffs.[109] In the 1980s, however, the foreign debt crisis and the failure of import substitution policies would induce the developing countries to become far more involved in the GATT Uruguay Round.

Conclusion

In August 1971, U.S. President Nixon suspended the convertibility of the U.S. dollar into gold, and in January 1973 Britain, Denmark, and Ireland joined the EC making it the world's largest trading entity. These two events signalled a significant change in the relative of influence of the United States and the EC, and in the 1973-79 GATT Tokyo Round the EC began to occupy a place alongside the United States in the global trade regime pyramid. The relative decline of U.S. economy hegemony was also one factor explaining the establishment of the G7 in the mid-1970s. In July 1971 a report by the U.S. Williams Commission emphasised the need for a new round of multilateral trade negotiations, but it also recognized that the European Community had "overtaken the United States as the most important trading unit."[110] Thus, the Williams Commission was aware of the need for more *collective* leadership, and it recommended that

> these negotiations should be launched at the highest political level through a joint initiative by the United States, Western Europe, Canada, and Japan. A high-level international steering committee should provide direction and thrust to the negotiations and monitor their progress.[111]

The G7 summits did not in fact begin until November 1975, over two years after the launching of the Tokyo Round. Although the main preoccupation of the G7 leaders was with monetary and financial matters, they also played an active role at the highest political level in pressuring governments to reach a settlement in the GATT Tokyo Round. Thus, the G7 came closest to fulfilling the role of the Williams Commission's "international steering committee."

Like most trade negotiations, the Tokyo Round operated at two levels – the technical and the political. Most of the work involved in the negotiation occurred at the technical level. The technical negotiations were highly detailed, and involved specific exchanges of concessions and the writing of agreements. However, the timetable for talks at the technical level was vague, and the political level was necessary to provide overall direction and pressure as to timing.[112] Government leaders in the G7 therefore discussed some of the most difficult problems that required intervention at a higher level, and set desired deadlines for completion of the negotiations. In the middle stage of the Tokyo Round the G7 had less influence over the negotiations, because unlike the negotiators and the technical experts, the G7 was not dealing in detail with the substance of the work to be accomplished. At this stage the G7's role was limited largely to persuading and cajoling, and it had to revise deadlines that proved to be unrealistic for completion of the Tokyo Round on several occasions. It was in the latter stage of the Tokyo Round when a breakthrough was possible that the G7 became far more influential. For example, the 1977 London I summit gave the U.S. Trade Representative the mandate he needed to pursue the negotiations more vigorously, and the 1978 Bonn I summit provided an interim deadline that served as a major impetus to the negotiations. Thus, the G7's influence was greatest when many of the technical aspects of the negotiation were resolved and the most difficult issues remaining required a stimulus at the highest political level.

Beneath the level of the G7 summits on the global trade regime pyramid, the OECD continued its important roles of fact-finding, prenegotiation, negotiation, and providing an impetus to the Tokyo Round negotiations. Compared with the G7, the OECD has been much closer to the technical level of negotiation, and the OECD's influence on trade issues was therefore more consistently felt before, during, and after the Tokyo Round. The OECD has also had a long-term involvement in developing expertise in specific trade-related issues, as this chapter and Chapter 3 have demonstrated with regard to export credit and government procurement. The efforts to develop an export credit agreement in the early 1970s in fact began with discussions in the G5 and G7, and the G7 representatives established the first comprehensive agreement on export credits – the Consensus on Converging Export Credit Policies – in July 1976. The G7 agreement provided a major stimulus for the approval of the 1978 Arrangement on Guidelines for Officially Supported Export Credits, which has been revised on numerous occasions but continues to be the primary instrument regulating export credit policies. Although the 1978 Arrangement is not formally an OECD agreement, the Arrangement was negotiated in the OECD and the OECD Secretariat is responsible for servicing it. The OECD rather than the GATT/WTO continues to be the main venue for negotiation and regulation of export credit, because most of the providers of export credit are OECD countries.

As was the case for export credit, the OECD countries began discussing government procurement in the 1960s. However, unlike export credit, the GATT took over the negotiation of government procurement issues in the Tokyo Round. Divisions among the OECD countries, the importance of government procurement in non-OECD countries, and the demands of developing countries were all factors contributing to the transfer of these negotiations to the GATT. The discussions, prenegotiations, and development of a draft agreement by the OECD in the 1960s and 1970s were a major contribution to the negotiation of a multilateral government procurement agreeement in the Tokyo Round. Nevertheless, the OECD countries (especially the United States and the EC) continued to dominate the negotiations, and almost all the signatories of the Tokyo Round agreement were developed states. Despite its important contributions to the negotiation of the government procurement agreement, the OECD's role also demonstrates some of its shortcomings as an organization. In pressuring for an agreement the OECD was representing the interests of the developed states, and was not sufficiently attuned to the needs and concerns of developing countries as late industrialisers. In the absence of sufficient safeguards, developing countries were simply unwilling to sign the Tokyo Round government procurement agreement.

The 1970s was a period when developing countries expressed growing dissatisfaction with the pyramidal structure of the global trade regime, and the marked success of OPEC in raising oil prices gave the South the opportunity to pressure for a NIEO. The North initially seem responsive (albeit reluctantly) to demands from the South, and it eventually agreed to establish the North-South Dialogue or CIEC. Nevertheless, the North gradually felt less urgency to meet the South's demands for change as developing countries were unable to demonstrate commodity power for products other than oil, and as the North recovered from recessionary conditions. Although the 1977 G7 summit in London was supposed to discuss the North's bargaining position for the concluding session of CIEC, "North-South questions did not rouse the passions of most of the summiteers, or touch their vital political interests."[113] In trade, for example, UNCTAD IV passed a resolution in 1976 to establish an Integrated Program for Commodities. Despite many years of effort on behalf of the IPC, it has been largely unsuccessful in improving the economic position of the South. The developing countries were also frustrated with the results of the GATT Tokyo Round, even though their quest for S&D treatment was enshrined in the "enabling clause." Like GATT Part IV, the enabling clause was largely symbolic, and even the GSP was replete with qualifications. S&D treatment had produced mixed results for developing countries, and in the view of liberal economists such treatment only marginalised them in the global trade regime. In the 1980s the foreign debt crisis would contribute to a major reconsideration by the South of its strategies *vis-à-vis* the North in the global trade regime.

Notes

1   Joan E. Twiggs, *The Tokyo Round of Multilateral Trade Negotiations: A Case Study in Building Domestic Support for Diplomacy* (Washington, D.C. and Lanham, MD: Institute for the Study of Diplomacy and University Press of America, 1987), pp. 3-6.

2   Theodore H. Cohn, "The Changing Role of the United States in the Global Agricultural Trade Regime," in William P. Avery, ed., *World Agriculture and the GATT* (Boulder, CO: Lynne Rienner Publishers, 1993), pp. 17-38.

3   Stephen D. Krasner, "The Tokyo Round: Particularistic Interests and Prospects for Stability in the Global Trading System," *International Studies Quarterly* 23-4 (December 1979), p. 491.

4   Richard Blackhurst, "Reforming WTO Decision Making: Lessons from Singapore and Seattle," in Klaus Günter Deutsch and Bernhard Speyer, eds., *The World Trade Organization Millennium Round: Freer Trade in the Twenty-First Century* (London: Routledge, 2001), pp. 302-203; Richard Blackhurst, "The Capacity of the WTO to Fulfill Its Mandate," in Krueger, ed., *The WTO as an International Organization*, pp. 49-50.

5   Developing country demands were contained in several documents submitted to the General Assembly in 1974: the *Declaration on the Establishment of a New International Economic Order (NIEO)*, the *Program of Action on the Establishment of a NIEO*, and the *Charter of Economic Rights and Duties of States*.

6   Jeffrey A. Hart, *The New International Economic Order: Conflict and Cooperation in North-South Economic Relations, 1974-77* (New York: St. Martin's Press, 1983), ch. 2.

7   *United States International Economic Policy in an Interdependent World*, Report to the President submitted by the Commission on International Trade and Investment Policy, July 1971 (Washington, D.C.: GPO, 1971), pp. 288 and 294.

8   Robert O. Keohane, *After Hegemony: Cooperation and Discord in the World Political Economy* (Princeton, NJ: Princeton University Press, 1984), p. 183. See also Duncan Snidal, "The Limits of Hegemonic Stability Theory," *International Organization* 39-4 (Autumn 1985), pp. 579-614.

9   *United States International Economic Policy in an Interdependent World*, p. 297.

10   Sidney Golt, *The GATT Negotiations 1973-1979: The Closing Stage*, (London: British-North American Committee, May 1978), p. 1; Gilbert R. Winham, "The Prenegotiation Phase of the Uruguay Round," *International Journal* 44-2 (Spring 1989), pp. 289-290;

D.M. McRae and J.C. Thomas, "The GATT and Multilateral Treaty Making: The Tokyo Round," *American Journal of International Law* 77 (1983), pp. 70-71.

11   Gilbert R. Winham, *International Trade and the Tokyo Round Negotiation* (Princeton: Princeton University Press, 1986), p. 16.

12   Ambassador Alan W. Wolff, "The Larger Political and Economic Role of the Tokyo Round," *Law and Policy in International Business* 12-1 (1980), pp. 1-2.

13   "MTN and the Legal Institutions of International Trade," Report Prepared at the Request of the Subcommittee on International Trade, U.S. Senate Committee on Finance (Washington, D.C.: U.S. Government Printing Office, June 1979), pp. 6-8.

14   Twiggs, *The Tokyo Round of Multilateral Trade Negotiations*, p. 77.

15   Krasner, "The Tokyo Round," p. 491.

16   John Kirton, "The Diplomacy of Concert: Canada, the G7 and the Halifax Summit," *Canadian Foreign Policy* 3-1 (Spring 1995), p. 66.

17   Nicholas Bayne, *Hanging In There: The G7 and G8 Summit in Maturity and Renewal* (Aldershot: Ashgate, 2000), p. 62.

18   Robert D. Putnam and Nicholas Bayne, *Hanging Together: Cooperation and Conflict in the Seven-Power Summits*, revised ed. (London: SAGE, 1987), pp. 256-257.

19   Anthony M. Solomon, "A Personal Evaluation," in George de Menil and Anthony M. Solomon, *Economic Summitry* (New York: Council on Foreign Relations, 1983), p. 44.

20   Putnam and Nicholas Bayne, *Hanging Together*, p. 257.

21   Peter I. Hajnal, *The G7/G8 System: Evolution, Role and Documentation* (Aldershot: Ashgate, 1999), p. 25.

22   Bayne, *Hanging In There*, pp. 116-118.

23   "Statement of the Group of Seven Leaders," Genoa, Italy, 20 July 2001, paragraph 6.

24   See "Communiqué of the G-8 Summit," Genoa, Italy, 22 July 2001, paragraph 10.

25   Hisashi Owada, "A Japanese Perspective on the Role and Future of the G-7," *International Spectator* 29-2 (April-June 1994), p. 111.

26   Putnam and Bayne, *Hanging Together*, p. 155.

27   Hajnal, *The G7/G8 System*, pp. 19-21; Bayne, *Hanging In There*, pp. 10-13 and 53-55.

28   Several of these reasons are discussed in Putnam and Bayne, *Hanging Together*, pp. 13-20, and in Bayne, *Hanging In There*, pp. 20-21.

29   George de Menil, "From Rambouillet to Versailles," in George de Menil and Anthony M. Solomon, *Economic Summitry* (New York: Council on Foreign Relations, 1983), p. 16.

30   Bayne, *Hanging in There*, p. 209.

31   Richard N. Cooper, "Economic Interdependence and Foreign Policy in the Seventies," *World Politics* 24 (January 1972), p. 179.

32   Paul Kennedy, *The Rise and Fall of the Great Powers: Economic Change and Military Conflict from 1500 to 2000* (New York: Random House, 1987), p. 408.

33   Henry Kissinger, *White House Years* (Boston: Little, Brown & Co., 1979), p. 958.

34   de Menil, "From Rambouillet to Versailles," pp. 16-17.

35   On the origins of the "Library Group" see Robert Putnam, "The Western Economic Summits: A Political Interpretation," in Cesare Merlini, ed., *Economic Summits and Western Decision-Making* (London: Croom Helm, 1984), pp. 53-56.

36   de Menil, "From Rambouillet to Versailles," p. 18.

37   Putnam and Bayne, *Hanging Together*, p. 40.

38   The "Tokyo Declaration" of GATT Ministers, adopted on September 14, 1973, point 11.

39   Andrew Shonfield, "Can The Western Economic System Stand the Strain?," *The World Today* 32-5 (May 1976), p. 172.

40   Guido Garavoglia, "From Rambouillet to Williamsburg: A Historical Assessment," in Merlini, ed., *Economic Summits and Western Decision-Making*, p. 8; Putnam and Bayne, *Hanging Together*, pp. 37-38. The G7 summit statements on trade are in "Declaration of Rambouillet, 17 November 1975, paragraphs 8 and 9.

41   de Menil, "From Rambouillet to Versailles," pp. 19-20.

42   Putnam and Bayne, *Hanging Together*, p. 43.

43   "Joint Declaration of the International Conference," San Juan, Puerto Rico, 28 June 1976.

44   Garavoglia, "From Rambouillet to Williamsburg," p. 14.

45   de Menil, "From Rambouillet to Versailles," p. 22.

46   Putnam and Bayne, *Hanging Together*, p. 67.

47   "Declaration: Downing Street Summit Conference," May 8, 1977.

48   "Appendix to Downing Street Summit Declaration."

49   Putnam and Bayne, *Hanging Together*, p. 72.

50   Winham, *International Trade and the Tokyo Round Negotiation*, p. 207.

51   Putnam and Bayne, *Hanging Together*, pp. 37-43 & 67-71; Garavoglia, "From Rambouillet to Williamsburg," pp. 15-16; Golt, *The GATT Negotiations 1973-1979*, pp. 5-6.

52   Winham, *International Trade and the Tokyo Round Negotiation*, p. 207.

53   de Menil, "From Rambouillet to Versailles," pp. 25-26.

54   Owada, "A Japanese Perspective on the Role and Future of the G-7," p. 98.

55   "Declaration: Bonn Summit," 17 July 1978, paragraph 17.

56   Putnam and Bayne, *Hanging Together*, pp. 82-86; Declaration from the Bonn Summit, 17 July 1978; Winham, *International Trade and the Tokyo Round Negotiation*, pp. 164-168.

57   Declaration from the Tokyo Summit, 29 June 1979, paragraph 6.

58   Putnam and Bayne, *Hanging Together*, pp. 110-118; Garavoglia, "From Rambouillet to Williamsburg," pp. 20-22.

59   Richard Cooper, quoted in de Menil, "From Rambouillet to Versailles," p. 26.

60   Organisation for Economic Co-operation and Development, *Policy Perspectives for International Trade and Economic Relations*, Report by the High Level Group on Trade and Related Problems to the Secretary-General of OECD (Paris: OECD, 1972), p. 9.

61   *United States International Economic Policy in an Interdependent World*, p. 10.

62   OECD, *Policy Perspectives for International Trade and Economic Relations*, p. 110. See also Twiggs, *The Tokyo Round of Multilateral Trade Negotiations*, pp. 14-15.

63   Meeting of the OECD Council at Ministerial Level in June 1976 – "Communiqué," paragraph 7.

64   Meeting of the OECD Council at Ministerial Level in June 1976 – "Communiqué," paragraph 8.

65   Quoted in Joan Pearce, *Subsidized Export Credit* (London: The Royal Institute of International Affairs, 1980), p. 43.

66   John M. Duff, Jr., "The Outlook for Official Export Credits," *Law and Policy in International Business* 13-4 (1981), p. 900.

67   Andrew M. Moravcsik, "Disciplining Trade Finance: The OECD Export Credit Arrangement," *International Organization* 43-1 (Winter 1989), p. 180; Pearce, *Subsidized Export Credit*, pp. 44-47.

68   Stephen Woolcock, "European Trade Policy: Global Pressures and Domestic Constraints," in Helen Wallace and William Wallace, eds., *Policy-Making in the European Union* (Oxford: Oxford University Press, 4th ed., 2000), p. 373. Woolcock discusses the fact that, even when the European Commission negotiates, it must receive a mandate from the Council of

Ministers. See also John Peterson and Elizabeth Bomberg, *Decision-Making in the European Union* (London: Macmillan, 1999), ch. 4.

69   Daniel F. Kohler and Peter H. Reuter, "Honor Among Nations: Enforcing the 'Gentlemen's Agreement' on Export Credits," RAND Note N-2536-USDP prepared for the Office of the Under Secretary of Defense for Policy, December 1986, p. 2.

70   "Declaration of Rambouillet," 17 November 1975.

71   The term mixed credits comes the French term crédit mixte, a system that France initially used for African developing countries which had previously been French colonies. John L. Moore, Jr., "Export Credit Arrangements," in Seymour J. Rubin and Gary Clyde Hufbauer, eds., *Emerging Standards of International Trade and Investment: Multinational Codes and Corporate Conduct* (Totowa, NJ: Rowman & Allanheld, 1984), p. 149; Michael G. Kuhn, Balazs Horvath, and Christopher J. Jarvis, *Officially Supported Export Credits: Recent Developments and Prospects* (Washington, D.C.: March 1995), p. 16; and David Stafford, "Wallén, Helsincki, Schaerer et al.: Some Major Achievements, Some Challenges to Meet," in Organisation for Economic Co-operation and Development, *The Export Credit Arrangement: Achievements and Challenges 1978-1998* (Paris: OECD, 1998), pp. 46-47.

72   "Joint Declaration of the International Conference," San Juan, Puerto Rico, 28 June 1976; David J. Blair, *Trade Negotiations in the OECD: Structures, Institutions and States* (London: Kegan Paul International, 1993), pp. 47-49. The 1976 Agreement did not apply to agricultural commodities, military equipment, and several sectors that had their own export credit agreements including aircraft, nuclear power plants, and ships.

73   "Declaration: Downing Street Summit Conference," 8 May 1977.

74   Pearce, *Subsidized Export Credit*, p. 47

75   Moravcsik, "Disciplining Trade Finance," p. 199.

76   Moravcsik, "Disciplining Trade Finance," p. 202.

77   John E. Ray, "The OECD 'Consensus' on Export Credits," *The World Economy* 9-3 (September 1986), pp. 298-305.

78   For a recent revision of the 1978 Arrangement, see "The Arrangement on Guidelines for Officially Supported Credits – 1998," in Organisation for Economic Co-operation and Development, *Export Credit Financing Systems in OECD Member and Non-Member Countries: 1999 Supplement* (Paris: OECD, 1999).

79   David M. Cheney, "The OECD Export Credits Agreement," *Finance and Development* 22-3 (September 1985), pp. 36-37.

80   John E. Ray, "The OECD 'Consensus' on Export Credits," *The World Economy* 9-3 (September 1986), pp. 305-308; Blair, *Trade Negotiations in the OECD*, pp. 51-53; Duff, Jr., "The Outlook for Official Export Credits," pp. 914-917.

81   Kuhn, Horvath, and Jarvis, *Officially Supported Export Credits*, pp. 1-7.

82   "Meeting of the OECD Council at Ministerial Level on 31 May to 1 June 1989 – Communiqué."

83   Paris Summit, "Economic Declaration," 16 July, 1989.

84   On the problems with agricultural export credit over the years, see Theodore H. Cohn, *The International Politics of Agricultural Trade: Canadian-American Relations in a Global Agricultural Context* (Vancouver: University of British Columbia Press, 1990), chapter 6. See also Kuhn, Horvath, and Jarvis, *Officially Supported Export Credits*, pp. 16 and 44; and Peter C. Evans and Kenneth A. Oye, "International Competition: Conflict and Cooperation in Government Export Financing," in Gary Clyde Hufbauer and Rita M. Rodriguez, eds., *The Ex-Im Bank in the 21st Century: A New Approach?* (Washington, D.C.: Institute of International Economics, Special Report 14, January 2001), pp. 117-118.

85   Kohler and Reuter, "Honor Among Nations," p. 26.
86   Moore, Jr., "Export Credit Arrangements," p. 156; Kohler and Reuter, "Honor Among Nations," pp. 2-3.
87   Blair, *Trade Negotiations in the OECD*, pp. 45-46, 57-59, and 79-84.
88   Evans and Oye, "International Competition: Conflict and Cooperation in Government Export Financing," p. 115.
89   Moravcsik, "Disciplining Trade Finance," p. 190.
90   Winham, *International Trade and the Tokyo Round Negotiation*, pp. 138 and 189-90; John H. Jackson, *The World Trading System: Law and Policy of International Economic Relations* (Cambridge: MIT Press, 2nd edition, 1997), p. 225.
91   General Agreement on Tariffs and Trade, *The Tokyo Round of Multilateral Trade Negotiations*, Report by the Director-General of GATT (Geneva: GATT, April 1979), p. 75.
92   General Agreement on Tariffs and Trade, *The Tokyo Round of Multilateral Trade Negotiations*, p. 77.
93   General Agreement on Tariffs and Trade, *The Tokyo Round of Multilateral Trade Negotiations*, p. 77.
94   Morton Pomeranz, "Toward a New International Order in Government Procurement," *Law and Policy in International Business* 11 (1979), p. 1276.
95   Winham, *International Trade and the Tokyo Round Negotiation*, p. 190.
96   "Agreement on Government Procurement," GATT Tokyo Round, Article II.1.
97   Joanne Fiaschetti, "Technical Analysis of the Government Procurement Agreement," *Law and Policy in International Business* 11 (1979), pp. 1345-1358.
98   Ernest H. Preeg, *Traders and Diplomats: An Analysis of the Kennedy Round of Negotiations under the General Agreement on Tariffs and Trade* (Washington, D.C.: Brookings Institution, 1970), p. 135. On the greater role of government in late industrialisers see Alexander Gerschenkron, *Economic Backwardness in Historical Perspective: A Book of Essays* (Cambridge: Harvard University Press, 1962).
99   Bernard Hoekman and Michel Kostecki, *The Political Economy of the World Trading System: From GATT to WTO* (Oxford: Oxford University Press, 2nd edition, 2001), pp. 378-379.
100 Jeffrey A. Hart, *The New International Economic Order: Conflict and Cooperation in North-South Economic Relations, 1974-77* (New York: St. Martin's Press, 1983), p. 30.
101 Jahangir Amuzegar, "A Requiem for the North-South Conference," *Foreign Affairs* 56-1 (October 1977), pp. 143-144.
102 Hart, *The New International Economic Order*, pp. 33-53; Jere R. Behrman, "Rethinking Global Negotiations: Trade," in Jagdish N. Bhagwati and John Gerard Ruggie, eds., *Power, Passions, and Purpose: Prospects for North-South Negotiations* (Cambridge: MIT Press, 1984), pp. 234-245.
103 Peter Marshall, "Whatever Happened to the NIEO?," *The Round Table* (July 1994), p. 331.
104 Jock A. Finlayson and Mark W. Zacher, *Managing International Markets: Developing Countries and the Commodity Trade Regime* (New York: Columbia University Press, 1988), pp. 288-289.
105 "Differential and More Favourable Treatment Reciprocity and Fuller Participation of Developing Countries," Decision of 28 November 1979, GATT document L/4903.
106 Paul Berthoud, "UNCTAD and the Emergence of International Development Law," in Cutajar, ed., *UNCTAD and the North-South Dialogue*, p. 83.
107 T.N. Srinivasan, *Developing Countries and the Multilateral Trading System: From the GATT to the Uruguay Round and the Future* (Boulder: Westview, 2000), pp. 26-27; Gerald M. Meier, "The Tokyo Round of Multilateral Trade Negotiations and the Developing Countries,"

Cornell International Law Journal 13-2 (Summer 1980), pp. 239-256; McRae and Thomas, "The GATT and Multilateral Treaty Making," p. 78.

108   Quoted in Ernest Preeg, *Traders in a Brave New World: The Uruguay Round and the Future of the International Trading System* (Chicago: University of Chicago Press, 1995), p. 24.

109   Anne O. Krueger, *Trade Policies and Developing Nations* (Washington, D.C.: Brookings Institution, 1995), p. 48.

110   *United States International Economic Policy in an Interdependent World*, p. 288.

111   *United States International Economic Policy in an Interdependent World*, p. 301.

112   Winham, *International Trade and the Tokyo Round Negotiation*, pp. 205-206.

113   Putnam and Bayne, *Hanging Together*, p. 68.

5   Uncertainty in the GATT and the Formation of the Quad: 1980 to 1986

One of the most significant developments in the global trade regime in the 1982 to 1986 period was the changing relationship between the North and the South. As discussed in Chapter 4, the developing countries posed a major challenge to the pyramidal structure of the global trade regime in the 1970s with their calls for a New International Economic Order. However, this challenge had largely dissipated by the late 1970s, because the South was unable to exercise commodity power for products other than oil, and the North regained its bargaining position as it recovered from recessionary conditions. Any further thoughts of a NIEO were quickly overshadowed by the Third World foreign debt crisis, which began in August 1982 when Mexico threatened to default on its loans.

As a result, the South shifted from challenging the pyramidal structure of the global trade regime in the 1970s to learning to adjust to the regime's principles, norms, and rules in the 1980s. As part of this adjustment, the developing countries began a gradual process of liberalising their economic policies and becoming more actively involved in the GATT (the reasons for this change are discussed in more detail later in this chapter). The developed countries welcomed and encouraged this change, because they had lost trade opportunities with the South over the years, and they viewed the developing countries as "the markets of the future."[1] As the South became more integrated in the global trade regime, it gradually began to gain more influence *within* the GATT. (This marked a contrast with Southern efforts in the 1970s to gain influence outside the GATT in their calls for a NIEO.) For example, this chapter discusses the fact that the South would only agree to the inclusion of services trade in the GATT Uruguay Round negotiations if the North would agree to the inclusion of textiles and clothing.

Another highly significant change in the 1980s was the creation of a new informal institution near the top of the global trade regime pyramid: the Quadrilateral group of trade ministers. The Quad, like the G7, was formed partly in response to the need for collective decision-making among the most important advanced industrial powers as U.S. economic hegemony continued to decline. Serious problems were also confronting the global trade regime in the 1980 to 1986 period (see discussion later in this chapter), and trade had to compete with many other issues in the wide-ranging agendas of the G7 and the OECD. The Quad by contrast was formed specifically to confer on trade issues and to help set the agenda for global trade negotiations. Furthermore the G7 heads of government and state were largely removed from the technical and policy-making aspects of global trade negotiations, and they would normally only address specific issues that were unresolved near the end of a trade negotiating round (as they did in the GATT Tokyo Round). The OECD also had limitations, because its relatively large membership prevented the most important traders from openly presenting their views on sensitive issues in a minilateral forum. The Quad provided the minilateral forum for the most important trade ministers, and was closer to the technical and policy-making aspects of multilateral trade negotiations (MTNs) than the G7. Thus, Figure 1.1 shows that the Quad is positioned between the G7/G8 and the OECD on the global trade regime pyramid.

Developments in the GATT: 1980 to 1986

The GATT Tokyo Round registered some important accomplishments, including the phased reduction of developed country tariffs on manufactured products by about one-third, and the negotiation of six codes to deal with non-tariff barriers. The NTB codes, however, permitted wide-ranging exceptions and were plurilateral with optional membership. As discussed, most developing countries decided not to join the NTB codes. Furthermore, the Tokyo Round did not confront a number of outstanding trade problems resulting from inadequate safeguard procedures, a weak GATT dispute settlement system, differences over subsidies, and the treatment of agriculture and textiles as exceptions to some important GATT regulations. As in the past the United States took the main initiative in supporting a new GATT round. However, the United States was no longer opposed to joining regional trade agreements, as he had been in earlier years when it was the undisputed global economic hegemon. In the 1980s, the Reagan administration began to follow a two-track policy aimed at exploring the possibilities of regional free trade in North America as well as supporting a new round of multilateral trade negotiations.

In 1971 the Williams Commission had welcomed the "agreement to establish a high-level study group on trade problems in OECD as a step" toward launching what came to be the GATT Tokyo Round;[2] and in the 1980s the U.S. strategy for another GATT round again began in the OECD. At the June 1981 OECD ministerial meeting, the new U.S. Trade Representative (USTR) William Brock called on the OECD to develop an action program to address longstanding problems such as agricultural subsidies and an unresolved safeguards code; and to deal with some new issues not covered by the GATT such as trade in services and trade-distorting investment measures. The 1981 OECD ministerial "agreed on the importance of action … to improve and to liberalise conditions of international trade," and "invited the [OECD] Secretary-General to begin as soon as possible to develop a programme of study within the Organisation, with a view to allowing the appropriate bodies to make a report on the issues by 1st May, 1982."[3]

The earliest moves toward forming an agenda for the new round were taken in the OECD rather than the GATT for two major reasons. First, the OECD ministers could agree to a joint work programme more easily, because the OECD (unlike the GATT) met regularly at ministerial level. Second, as discussed the GATT secretariat had limited resources, and was under strictures to limit most of its work to existing GATT commitments; it was therefore not inclined to engage in forward-looking policy analysis. The GATT would nevertheless have the central role in formal preparations for a new round, and the United States suggested that a GATT ministerial be held in 1982 to further develop a work program for new multilateral trade negotiations. Indeed, a U.S. delegate went directly from the June 1981 OECD ministerial to Geneva to confer with GATT officials, and the Consultative Group of 18 subsequently supported the idea of holding a GATT ministerial. The July 1981 G7 summit in Ottawa endorsed both the OECD work program on trade issues and the CG.18 proposal for a 1982 GATT ministerial. As a result, in November 1981 the GATT Council decided to convene its 1982 session at the ministerial level.[4]

GATT ministerial meetings were infrequent, and were usually associated with the beginning of a new round of multilateral trade negotiations. However, in 1981 many developing countries argued that the North's fulfillment of earlier commitments to reduce its trade barriers to Southern exports was a higher priority than launching a new GATT round. In outlining the purpose of the 1982 GATT ministerial, the CG.18 tried to satisfy both those developing countries that wanted existing GATT rules to be applied more vigorously, and those countries that wanted a new round of negotiations. Thus, the CG.18's guidelines provided the Preparatory Committee with little direction. The draft declaration and work program the Preparatory Committee subsequently sent to the 1982 GATT ministerial included a lengthy list of 25 to 30 separate items that involved unfinished business from the Tokyo Round as well as a number of new issues. The GATT ministerial also took place at a time of deep recession and growing tensions among the major trading powers. Differences between the United States and the EC over agriculture, the EC's impatience with Japan's import performance, the escalation of a number of bilateral disputes, and the threat of protectionist legislation in the U.S. Congress demonstrated the increasing strains on the multilateral trade regime.

The growing trade tensions combined with the incredibly large number of negotiating issues presented to the ministers contributed to a fractious and frustrating ministerial meeting. Although the ministers were able to avoid "an impasse that would have been interpreted as a collapse of the GATT, confidence in the multilateral trading system was shaken."[5] To avoid a breakdown of talks, countries had to compromise, and the 1982 GATT ministerial in fact produced a communiqué replete with compromise statements that frustrated virtually all the participants. Nevertheless, the ministers were able to agree on a common declaration and a work program that included seventeen mandates for action. Although the work program was somewhat of a "holding operation" designed to keep the global trade regime together, it stimulated exploratory work on issues that would become central to the Uruguay Round.[6] The GATT director-general Arthur Dunkel gave further stimulus to a new round by appointing a panel of non-governmental experts to report on current trade problems. In 1985 the panel issued the "Leutwiler Report," which referred to "the erosion of the trading rules" and called for a new GATT round "as soon as possible."[7] Despite the contributions of the CG.18 and the Leutwiler report, the GATT played a less important role in building support for a new round than the G7, the OECD, and the newly-formed Quadrilateral group (the Quad is discussed below). The discussion that follows examines the role of the G7, the Quad, the OECD, and the UNCTAD during the critical 1980 to 1986 period that ended with the launching of the GATT Uruguay Round.

The Group of Seven

A "striking property of Western summitry" from the time of the Rambouillet summit in 1975 was "its economic character."[8] Beginning in 1979, however, political issues became a more important part of the G7 summits for several reasons. First, Japan, Italy and Canada reacted strongly to their exclusion from a special summit held by the other four G7 members (the United States, Britain, France, and Germany) at Guadeloupe on 5-6 January 1979. This four-nation summit (which was not part of the G7 summit cycle) focused specifically on political issues such as arms control negotiations with the Soviet Union, missiles in Europe, and growing unrest in Iran. Japan, Italy, and Canada had a strong incentive to incorporate political discussions in the G7 economic summits, because "this would ensure that they would not be excluded from high-level political decisions in future."[9] Second, striking political events affecting Western security pushed political security issues to the forefront of the G7 summit agenda; most importantly, these events included the taking of American hostages in Iran in November 1979 and the Soviet invasion of Afghanistan in December 1979. After the events of 1979, the agenda of the G7 summits was formally broadened to include important political issues. Inevitably, this meant that trade would have to compete for attention with a wider array of issues on the G7 summit agenda.

In accordance with the shifting summit priorities the G7 leaders spent the first day of the 22-23 June 1980 Venice I summit discussing political matters, and on the second day they returned to the traditional economic subjects. The economic part of the Venice I summit was devoted largely to energy issues. Although the crisis atmosphere resulting from the 1979 OPEC oil price increases had receded somewhat, the summit discussions focused on decreasing energy dependence and on developing country financial problems as a result of the higher oil prices. As a result, there was little time remaining to discuss trade issues, and the Venice summit's failure to confront rising pressures for trade protectionism was disappointing. The G7 leaders in the Venice summit simply endorsed the positive outcome of the GATT Tokyo Round, and committed themselves to early and effective implementation of the Tokyo Round agreements.[10] They also expressed their determination "to avoid a harmful export credit race," and endorsed the OECD's work on export credit issues.[11]

By 1981 the energy issue was a less pressing concern, and the persistent economic recession brought the problem of trade protectionism to the attention of the G7. There were also serious tensions between Japan and the EC over trade in automobiles, and between the United States and the EC over East-West trade and the building of a trans-Siberian gas pipeline to Western Europe. Thus, the G7 leaders devoted more attention to trade issues at the 20-21 July 1981 Ottawa summit than they had at the 1979 and 1980 summits. In its 1981 summit communiqué the G7 pledged to "resist protectionist measures," and endorsed the Consultative Group of 18 proposal "that the GATT Contracting Parties convene a meeting at ministerial level during 1982."[12] The purpose of the 1982

GATT ministerial would be to limit protectionist pressures during the recession, and to develop a work program for a new round of multilateral trade negotiations. Most significantly, the United States, the EC, and Japan met on the margins of the 1981 Ottawa summit to discuss a proposal that their trade ministers should regularly hold informal trilateral meetings. The first meeting of the new *Quadrilateral group* of trade ministers or *Quad* would take place about six months later, and would also include Canada. Such a grouping was necessary because the G7 dealt with a broad range of economic and political issues, and could not possibly give international trade the attention it required at higher political levels. Unlike the G7 heads of government and state, the Quad trade ministers could focus specifically on the many unresolved disputes among major traders, and on the need to begin preparations for a new more ambitious round of multilateral trade negotiations. (See the discussion of the Quad later in this chapter.)[13]

In 1982, recession continued to affect the Western economies, and the value of the U.S. dollar was extremely high. Thus, differences over monetary policy between the U.S. Reagan administration and the Europeans was a top priority issue on the agenda of the 4-6 June 1982 G7 summit in Versailles. Although official discussions at Versailles focused mainly on economic matters, private discussions on urgent political matters relating to the Middle East and the Falkland islands were prevalent throughout the summit. One area of trade policy that received considerable attention related to East-West trade, because the U.S. administration was extremely hostile to Western European participation in the Siberian gas pipeline project. After Poland had declared martial law in December 1981, the United States had retaliated against the Soviet Union by imposing an embargo on materials produced by U.S. companies that were destined for use in constructing the pipeline. Discussions at the Versailles summit failed to resolve U.S.-EC differences on this issue, and after the summit the United States infuriated the Europeans by extending the pipeline sanctions to cover U.S. subsidiaries and licensees abroad. Despite the bitter conflict over this issue, some commentators maintain that the Versailles discussions formed the basis for a convergence of views on East-West trade in later G7 summits.[14]

The G7 leaders at Versailles also discussed Japanese-Western trade relations and the upcoming GATT ministerial. As was the case for East-West trade, the discussion of these issues was marred by disagreements. Japan's increasing exports to Western markets and its barriers to imports from the West were a major source tension between the EC and the United States. Whereas the Europeans wanted to confront Japan within the context of the summit, the United States preferred to deal with this issue bilaterally. The upcoming November

1982 GATT ministerial meeting also captured the interest of the summiteers. The United States and Germany wanted to reach a preliminary agreement on the priority issues for the ministerial, but transatlantic disputes over agricultural and steel trade increased tensions at the meeting. Furthermore, France questioned the emphasis the summit was giving to the GATT ministerial, and argued that the G7 should be giving priority to economic recovery over trade liberalisation.[15] The G7 leaders were able to agree on a general statement in the Versailles summit declaration that they would "participate fully in the forthcoming GATT Ministerial Conference."[16] Nevertheless, the persistent tensions and divisions on trade at Versailles should have served as a warning that the 1982 GATT ministerial would encounter serious problems. As discussed, the ministerial was a divisive and frustrating meeting, that at the time seemed to threaten the very existence of the GATT.

Despite the apparent failure of the 1982 GATT ministerial, it did help to establish a work program for agriculture, safeguards, trade in services, and other issues that would become central to the GATT Uruguay Round. Furthermore, some of the trade-related tensions at the Versailles G7 summit were alleviated by agreements later in the year. In October 1982 the EC Council of Ministers approved an accord to limit European steel exports to the United States, and one month later the United States decided to lift its sanctions on the supply of equipment for the Siberian gas pipeline. The G7 leaders therefore had some reason for optimism that they would have more success in dealing with trade issues at the 28-30 May 1983 Williamsburg summit. The United States had pressured for a new round of GATT negotiations since 1981, and it wanted the G7 to issue a joint call for a new round at the Williamsburg summit. Aside from Germany, however, the Europeans were skeptical about a new GATT round, and Japan was more preoccupied at the time with defending its own trade practices. Thus, the G7 leaders at Williamsburg would only agree to "continue consultations on proposals" for another round. In preparation for a possible new round of negotiations, the G7 pledged to "actively pursue the current work programs" in the GATT and OECD, "including trade in services and high-technology products."[17]

The overall prospects seemed good for a successful G7 summit in London (London II) on 7-9 June 1984, because the economic outlook was more positive than at previous summits, a conservative consensus led by Margaret Thatcher and Ronald Reagan was taking hold in the summit process, and the United States wanted to avoid a conflictual summit in a Presidential election year. Nevertheless, the London II summit was no more successful than the previous summits in reaching a firm consensus on a new round of multilateral trade negotiations. Although the 1983 Williamsburg summit declaration had expressed a commitment "to halt protectionism," pressures for protectionism had continued to increase.[18] A major problematic issue was the strong U.S. dollar and growing U.S. balance of trade deficit, which contributed to U.S. aggressive unilateralism in trade policy and to domestic protectionist pressures in a U.S. election year. The United States in fact had called for a new round of trade negotiations since 1981 as a means of addressing its trade problems, and Japan joined the United States at London II in pressuring for a 1985-86 target date for launching a new round. However, France and Italy were unwilling to support this idea because of concerns that the United States would attack the Common Agricultural Policy and other European trade practices.[19] Instead of a timetable for a new round, the London II summit leaders simply agreed "to consult partners in the GATT with a view to decisions at an early date on the possible objectives, arrangements and timing for a new negotiating round."[20]

As the exchange rate of the U.S. dollar rose and the U.S. current account deficit increased, protectionist pressures from American industries continued to intensify. The U.S. administration believed that a new GATT round would help combat this protectionism, and it was insistent that the 2-4 May 1985 G7 summit in Bonn (Bonn II) should decide on a date in 1986 for starting a new GATT round. In March 1985, the EC countries expressed a willingness to hold a new GATT round, but they were not prepared to agree on a precise date for launching the round. At the summit, the United States managed to gain the support of Britain, Germany and Japan for launching a new round in early 1986. However, France insisted on adhering to the March 1985 EC position that a date should not be set for launching the round, and Italy expressed some support for the French position. France was particularly opposed to the negotiation of the EC's protectionist Common Agricultural Policy, and President François Mitterand went so far as to briefly walk out of the Bonn II summit over this issue.[21] The Bonn summit economic declaration strongly endorsed "the agreement reached by the OECD Ministerial Council that a new GATT round should begin as soon as possible." However, in view of the dispute over agriculture the declaration hedged on the date for beginning the negotiations, adding that "most of us think this should be in 1986."[22] Robert Putnam and Nicholas Bayne argue that "this was the first time a summit had ended without a consensus, however fragile, on such a central issue."[23]

Despite this lack of consensus at the Bonn summit, international discussions relating to the trade negotiations had made considerable progress at the technical level, and in September 1985 the GATT Contracting Parties agreed to begin preparations for a new round of negotiations. It was also in September 1985 that the G5 finance ministers met at the Plaza Hotel in New York and agreed to coordinate their international economic policies to deal with the problem of the overvalued U.S. dollar. By the time of the 4-6 May 1986 G7 summit in Tokyo (Tokyo II), preparations for the new GATT round were well advanced. Thus, the G7 leaders in Tokyo indicated that they were "fully committed to the preparatory process in the GATT with a view to the early launching of the new round of multilateral trade negotiations," and that they would "work at the September ministerial meeting to make decisive progress in this direction." Advocating for the interests of the advanced industrial states, the G7 also asserted that the new round "should address the issues of trade in services and trade-related aspects of intellectual property rights and foreign direct investment." Due to the insistence of Canada and the United States, the 1986 summit marked the first time that a G7 summit communiqué referred to the contentious issue of agriculture.[24] The communiqué devoted considerable attention to the depressing effects of agricultural surpluses on trade, and pledged "to give full support to the work of the OECD in this field."[25]

The 1980 to 1986 G7 summits raised questions as to whether the summit process was becoming less important in international economic diplomacy, because the 1985 advances in international trade and monetary relations were made at lower-level meetings. There is no doubt that the G7 summits in the 1980 to 1986 period were marked by a wide divergence of views and considerable hostility over trade-related issues. Nevertheless, despite the tortuous process involved, there is evidence that the G7 summits made gradual progress in reaching a consensus on a new GATT round. In the 1983 Williamsburg summit, the European countries and Japan would not support the U.S. call for a target date for launching the round; in the 1984 London II summit, Japan was willing to join the United States in setting a target date; and in the 1985 Bonn II summit, Britain and Germany joined the United States and Japan in calling for a target date. Thus, the G7 was gradually reaching a consensus that the GATT Uruguay Round should begin in 1986. When the May 1986 G7 summit finally agreed to an early launching of the round, it was evident that the summiteers fully intended to play a role in setting the agenda for the round. Thus, they emphasised the importance of addressing issues of particular interest to the advanced industrial states, including trade in services, intellectual property, and foreign investment. It is also significant that the 1986 Tokyo II summit declaration marked the first time that the G7 was willing to address the problem of agricultural protectionism. Agricultural trade was an issue that threatened to block agreement on launching the GATT Uruguay Round, and would continue to be the most contentious issue throughout the round.

In sum, despite the tortuous path of the G7 summits, they played a role of some significance in delimiting trade protectionism and trade disputes, in gradually achieving a consensus on a new GATT round, and in helping to set the agenda for the new round.[26] Nevertheless, the G7 was unable to reach the necessary degree of consensus on a new round until sufficient progress was made in dealing with the negotiating issues at the technical and policy-making levels. The G7 also had a growing list of preoccupations in addition to trade, particularly after 1979 when political and security issues were included along with economic issues at the G7 summits. As the following section shows, the Quadrilateral Group of trade ministers was an important addition to the upper part of the global trade regime pyramid, because it focuses specifically on trade issues.

The Quadrilateral Group

The members of the Quadrilateral Group or Quad – the United States, the EU, Japan, and Canada – have been variously referred to as "the trouble-shooters of global commerce," and the "four largest shareholders" in the World Trade Organization.[27] The Quad's importance stems from the fact that its members account for a substantial share of world trade, and have been important advocates of trade liberalisation. Collectively, the Quad accounts for over 54 percent of global merchandise imports and for over 50 percent of merchandise exports. In addition, the Quad members are the largest traders in services, which have become an increasingly important part of global trade flows. In 1997, the top nine traders in services included the United States, Japan, Canada, and six members of the EU (Germany, Italy, France, Britain, the Netherlands, and Belgium). These nine countries accounted for 54 percent of world imports and for 60 percent of world exports of services.[28] Thus, the Quad has been a highly useful forum for dealing with conflicts among the major traders, and for providing leadership and strengthening cooperation in the global trade regime. Despite their differences, the four Quad members can normally reach a consensus on trade issues more easily than much larger institutions such as the GATT/ WTO and even the OECD. The Quad trade ministers can also devote more attention to global trade issues than the G7/G8 heads of state and government. Before discussing the role of the Quad in the 1982 to early 1986 period, it is necessary to provide some background on the formation of the Quad, and on the nature of the Quad as an informal institution.

The Formation of the Quad

In July 1981, the United States, the EC and Japan met on the margins of the G7 summit in Ottawa to discuss a proposal that their trade ministers should regularly hold informal trilateral meetings. There was some precedent for this proposal, because occasional restricted meetings had been held to develop agreements and manage major issues in the GATT Kennedy and Tokyo Rounds. These meetings were often but not always limited to the "Big 3" (the United States, the EC and Japan), or the "Big 4" with Canada included. As was the case for the G7, the proposal to establish a small grouping of powerful trade ministers represented a move toward collective decision-making in view of declining U.S. economic hegemony. Although the major traders wanted to pressure for full implementation of the GATT Tokyo Round and for consideration of a new round of multilateral trade negotiations, the proliferation of trade disputes among the United States, the EC, and Japan threatened to interfere with this process. Thus, a small informal institution was required to help manage decision-making in the global trade regime.

   G7 deliberations were clearly inadequate for addressing important trade issues, because the G7 met at the highest political level (the "sherpas" regularly met at a lower level as personal representatives of the G7 leaders). As heads of government and state, the G7 leaders had to deal with a growing list of political as well as economic issues, and various G7 ministerial groups therefore began to emerge in the 1980s. After the Quad was formed in 1981-82, the G7 finance ministers emerged publicly at the 1986 G7 summit in Tokyo, and in more recent years ministers dealing with the environment, employment, and other areas have also held periodic meetings. Thus, "there is an important distinction between the [G7] leaders' meeting and the activities that take place throughout the year at or below the ministerial level."[29] The Quad was the first of these G7 ministerial groups to be formed, because of the importance of trade and its lower ranking in the list of priorities of the G7 heads of state and government. Not only did the G7 leaders have an expanding agenda, and but they also normally gave priority to financial over trade matters in the economic sphere. Indeed, the finance ministries of the G7 countries have always been part of the inner circle involved in summit preparations. Although the trade ministries "provide papers on specific subjects," they "are rarely involved in broader discussions of summit strategy and tactics."[30] In the 1980s the G7 leaders also began to give higher priority to foreign policy and security issues, and both financial and trade matters were therefore often delegated to their respective ministers.[31]

A more immediate reason for the trilateral meeting of trade ministers on the margins of the 1981 Ottawa summit was the tension over U.S. and EC attempts to limit Japanese automobile exports. The Americans were concerned that a possible bilateral Japanese-EC agreement would divert more Japanese automobiles to the United States, and the Europeans had similar concerns about a possible Japanese-U.S. auto agreement. Although the EC-Japanese tensions over automobile trade was a topic of discussion at the 1981 G7 summit, there was no resolution of the problem. Indeed, "the European countries made repeated unsuccessful attempts to use the summits to put pressure on Japan to improve market access."[32] Thus, the EC and the United States believed that a smaller trilateral group of trade ministers would be better able to resolve such disputes among the major traders. Finally, the United States and the EC felt that trilateral meetings would help promote the shared interests of the Big 3 in trade liberalisation, and in discussing preparations for the November 1982 GATT ministerial.[33]

Whereas the EC and the United States supported the idea of trilateral meetings, Japan feared that the United States and the EC would use the meetings to jointly pressure for limits on Japanese exports. Nevertheless, there were divisions within the Japanese government on the general value of trilateral meetings, and Japan would have found it difficult to refuse to join such a group. Canadian officials were also concerned about the trilateral proposal, because Canada was not initially invited to join the select group. Although Canada had been excluded from the first G7 summit in Rambouillet in 1975, a U.S. invitation to attend the second summit in Puerto Rico had established Canada's membership in the G7 despite France's objections. However, the United States was less sympathetic to the idea of including Canada in a select group of trade ministers in the early 1980s because of serious bilateral tensions during this period. The U.S. response to Canada's National Energy Program (NEP) and the planned expansion of Canada's Foreign Investment Review Agency (FIRA) indicated that in 1981 "the Canadian-American relationship had undergone a severe crisis and shifted onto a new and treacherous path."[34]

When the United States, the EC and Japan met at the 1981 G7 summit, they were not in fact able to reach a final agreement to hold regular meetings among their trade ministers. The European summit participants also did not want the G7 to issue a public statement about the proposed group until the EC as a whole had endorsed the idea.[35] Thus, the proposal to establish the trilateral trade meetings was not mentioned in the communiqué at the end of the G7 Ottawa summit. The *New York Times* and several other newspapers, however, did publish articles on the proposal.[36] Further discussions were held after the 1981 summit, and during this period Canada engaged in a considerable amount of lobbying to be included in the meetings. Canada's efforts were eventually successful, and the U.S. Trade Representative, William Brock, invited the Canadian as well as the EC and Japanese trade ministers to what became the first Quad ministerial meeting in Key Biscayne, Florida on 15-16 January 1982 (see Table 5.1). Before discussing the role of the Quad from 1982 to the launching of the GATT Uruguay Round, it is important to examine the nature of the Quad as an informal institution.

The Quad as an Informal Institution

The Quad is an informal institution in which the trade ministers of the United States, the EU, Japan, and Canada can exchange views and exert leadership in the global trade regime. Discussions at the Quad ministerials have focused on resolving trade conflicts, managing international trade problems, promoting trade liberalisation, and strengthening the multilateral trade regime. The Quad ministers of course have devoted most of their attention to issues of interest to the developed countries such as trade in services, intellectual property, agriculture, investment, and safeguards. Trade irritants in sensitive sectoral areas such as agriculture, automobiles, steel, and textiles are also discussed. Furthermore, the Quad has had an important role in dealing with trade issues that are discussed at the G7 summits, the OECD ministerials, the UNCTAD conferences, and the GATT ministerials. As a former Canadian Trade Minister (John Crosbie) has explained, the Quad provides the opportunity for frank and informal discussion and the exchange of ideas rather than for decision making:

> [The Quad] is not a meeting to make decisions nor to negotiate. It's a meeting in which the four trade ministers can communicate together and exchange views and ideas. So what's achieved is a better understanding of just exactly where we are in the [GATT Uruguay] round, what are the remaining obstacles to be overcome, what are the problems that need to be dealt with to give the political direction to our officials who are here from Geneva and from our own capitals as to what we want them to do; within what time frames we want them to complete negotiations or to get a text in various areas.[37]

Quad ministerials are held on an *ad hoc* basis. The timing of the meetings is flexible, and they have generally been scheduled about two times a year when there is a consensus that a meeting would be useful. Quad ministerials have become less frequent in recent years, and a regular Quad ministerial was not held for three years after the 33rd ministerial in Tokyo in May 1999 (see Table 5.1). However, Quad members met at the official level during this three-

Table 5.1   Quadrilateral Meetings of Trade Ministers

	Location	Dates
1	Key Biscayne, Florida, U.S.	15-16 January 1982
2	Chateau d'Esclimont, France	12-13 May 1982
3	Tokyo, Japan	11 February 1983
4	Brussels, Belgium	29 April 1983
5	London, UK	16-17 July 1983
6	Ottawa, Ontario, Canada	26-27 September 1983
7	Islamorada, Florida, U.S.	2-4 February 1984
8	Erbach Im Reingau, Germany	28-30 June 1984
9	Kyoto, Japan	9-11 February 1985
10	Oba, Ontario, Canada	11-14 July 1985
11	San Diego, California, U.S.	16-19 January 1986
12	Sintra, Portugal	4-7 September 1986
13	Kashikojima, Japan	24-26 April 1987
14	Quadra Island, B.C., Canada	15-17 April 1988
15	Brainerd, Minnesota, U.S.	22-24 June 1988
16	The Hague, Netherlands	2-4 June 1989
17	Hakonemachi, Japan	12-14 November 1989
18	Napa, California, U.S.	2-4 May 1990
19	St. John's, Newfoundland, Canada	11-13 October 1990
20	Angers, France	12-14 September 1991
21	Fukushima, Japan	24-26 April 1992
22	Cambridge, Ontario, Canada	16-18 October 1992
23	Toronto, Ontario, Canada	12-14 May 1993
24	Tokyo, Japan	23-24 June 1993
25	Los Angeles, California, U.S.	9-11 September 1994
26	Whistler, B.C., Canada	3-5 May 1995
27	Ripley Castle, Yorkshire, UK	20-21 October 1995
28	Kobe, Japan	19-21 April 1996
29	Seattle, Washington, U.S.	26-28 September 1996
30	Toronto, Ontario, Canada	30 April - 2 May 1997
31	No meeting was held*	
32	Versailles, France	29-30 April 1998
33	Tokyo, Japan	11-12 May 1999

*See discussion in text.

year period. The location of the ministerials rotates among the four Quad members. Although the discussion of bilateral problems is discouraged during regular Quad ministerial sessions, bilateral discussions on the margins of the meetings have in fact been a central characteristic of the Quads. Bilateral interactions and the development of personal relationships among ministers and officials have been a major factor in preventing the escalation of trade disputes. Unlike the G7 summits, the European Commission represents the major European trading nations in the Quad because of its overall responsibility for trade policy. Some major European traders – especially France – have sometimes resented the fact that they do not participate directly in Quad discussions. The European Commission has opposed any effort to formalise the Quad ministerial meetings, because it is conscious of EU member state concerns. Some countries such as Australia that are excluded from the Quad have also viewed the Quad meetings with suspicion. These outsiders have expressed concerns that the major traders may use the Quad to arrange special agreements and understandings, and that plurilateral groups such as the Quad could in the long term weaken the multilateral GATT/WTO. (As discussed in Chapter 6, Australia is included in "Quint" meetings with the four Quad members that deal specifically with agriculture.)

Although the Quad has continued to function as an informal institution, the nature of its ministerials have changed somewhat over time. Early meetings of the Quad usually brought together the four trade ministers in small, informal discussions that permitted them to develop personal relationships and exchange ideas in a relatively private forum. The Quad ministers placed a high value on the spontaneous exchange of views, and initially they did not establish a formal agenda for the meetings. However, the agenda for Quad ministerials gradually became more formalised, and Quad ministerials became larger events that were of greater interest to the media. For example, over 150 delegates including support staff attended the 26th Quad ministerial in Whistler, British Columbia, on 3-5 May 1995. Japan had by far the largest delegation with over ninety members, whereas the EU had a delegation of less than ten members. The Japanese have requested larger delegations for Quad meetings to deal with ministerial rivalries and to provide expertise and input on issues that the Ministry of International Trade and Industry (MITI) does not include in its mandate. Nevertheless, the larger meetings have detracted from the informal nature of the Quad, and imposed limitations on the ability of ministers to freely exchange views and develop personal relationships. One way in which the trade ministers have dealt with the larger Quad gatherings is to set aside time for ministers-only meetings. For example, at the 1995 Whistler Quad the organisers set up a ministers-only dinner for the first day, and a one hour ministers-only meeting on the last day.[38]

In addition to Quad ministerials that have normally been held about two times a year, there are also Quad senior officials' meetings (SOMs). The SOMs are held to discuss ongoing work within the Quad process, and to prepare for the next Quad ministerial. The discussions and ideas generated in the SOMs provide the trade ministers with useful background material, which permits them to use their time more effectively in Quad ministerials. For example, the 25th Quad ministerial in Los Angeles in September 1994 called on Quad senior officials to discuss and prepare papers on a number of issues. It was particularly important to hold SOMs at this time to help develop ideas for a new trade agenda and new trade negotiations after the completion of the GATT Uruguay Round and the creation of the WTO. Thus, senior officials in the Quad met on 8-9 December 1994 on the margins of the WTO Implementation Conference in Geneva, and on 30-31 March 1995 in Ottawa in a "stand-alone" meeting. The work by the Quad senior officials in Geneva and Ottawa provided important background for the 26th Quad ministerial in Whistler, British Columbia in May 1995, and for the G7 summit in Halifax, Nova Scotia in June 1995.[39]

The Role of the Quad from 1982 to the Launching of the GATT Uruguay Round

The first Quad ministerial in Key Biscayne, Florida on 15-16 January 1982 was marked by its informality and lack of an explicit agenda. (See Table 5.1 for a complete list of the Quad ministerials.) The purpose of the meeting was to continue close consultations on trade matters, and not to conduct negotiations. The Quad ministers expressed concerns about increased protectionism in response to difficult economic conditions in the early 1980s, and they pledged to combat the mounting protectionist pressures. The ministers also agreed to pressure the newly-industrialising economies to sign the Tokyo Round non-tariff barrier codes, and to encourage the developing countries in general to participate more actively in the GATT. Since most developing countries strongly opposed discussing trade in services in the GATT, the Quad endorsed the preparatory work the OECD was doing in this area. However, the United States in particular insisted that services trade should eventually be subject to GATT principles, norms and rules. In addition to trade in services, specific issues under discussion at the first Quad ministerial included safeguards, agricultural export subsidies, and trade in steel and automobiles.

The second Quad ministerial was held in the Chateau d'Esclimont near Paris, France on 12-13 May 1982, immediately after the 1982 OECD ministerial.

Thus, the Quad discussions could build upon the exchange of views and decisions of the OECD ministers. The timing of the second Quad was also arranged to provide preparation for the June 1982 Versailles G7 summit and the November 1982 GATT ministerial. Trade in services continued to be a priority issue for the United States and other Quad members. Although the first and second ministerials were not intended to be policy coordination exercises, they were helpful in identifying Quad objectives and developing common approaches to specific issues as part of preparations for the GATT ministerial. Despite the intensive preparations in the Quad and elsewhere, the 1982 GATT ministerial almost resulted in a serious breakdown of cooperation in trade. As discussed, the ministers managed to salvage the situation by agreeing on a communiqué and a comprehensive work program for the GATT.

The third Quad ministerial was held on 11 February 1983 in Tokyo, Japan during a period of high unemployment in the developed countries, and a debt crisis that was requiring painful adjustment measures in a number of developing countries. The trade ministers viewed the third Quad as an important opportunity to discuss the negative outcome of the 1982 GATT ministerial, and to consider how trade issues should be addressed at the G7 Williamsburg summit scheduled for May, 1983. The Quad's general assessment of the 1982 GATT ministerial was that it was too large and unwieldy, had too long a preparatory period, provided no opportunity for frank discussion among ministers, and focused too extensively on technically complex issues. This assessment confirmed the view of the major traders that the Quad as a smaller grouping provided more opportunity than the GATT for open and informal discussions. The Quad ministers had to confront the fact that protectionist pressures were continuing to increase even after the 1982 GATT ministerial. Thus, the trade ministers discussed possible strategies to promote world economic recovery, revive trade liberalisation efforts, and give more impetus to the work program agreed to in the GATT ministerial.[40]

Subsequent Quad ministerials from 1983 to early 1986 continued to focus on efforts to decrease protectionism, accelerate the implementation of the Tokyo Round tariff concessions, and promote progress in the 1982 GATT ministerial work program. The four trade ministers also discussed their views on the best means for initiating a new round of multilateral trade negotiations. At the eighth Quad ministerial in Erbach, Germany on 28-30 June 1984, the ministers agreed that "the coming months should be used to continue ... preparations" for a new GATT round, and they had a "useful exchange of views on some of the likely items for negotiation in such a new round," including trade in services and agriculture.[41] At the tenth Quad ministerial in Oba, Ontario on 11-14 July 1985, the trade ministers recognised the need to build a consensus on a new GATT round among a broader range of countries, and they were particularly "conscious of the views which have been expressed by developing countries."[42] A number of Third World countries were concerned that a new round would include areas in which they were less competitive such as services and high technology, and would also increase pressures on them to accept the principles of graduation and reciprocity. The Quad members recognised the ongoing foreign debt problems of the South, but they warned the developing countries not to cut back their imports, and indicated that "the more advanced developing countries, particularly, must become more fully integrated into the world trading system."[43]

Although the Quad members generally agreed on multilateral matters such as the need for a new GATT round, bilateral differences sometimes created serious friction at the meetings. For example, Japan wanted to exclude agriculture, fisheries, and forest products from its commitment to accelerate tariff cuts; but Canada indicated that it would proceed with accelerated tariff cuts only if all Quad countries implemented them without exceptions for sensitive products. Although the United States and Canada jointly criticised the EC's reluctance to subject its Common Agricultural Policy to negotiation, Canada argued that the United States was imposing protectionist barriers against Canadian exports of hogs and softwood lumber. One of the most serious sources of friction was the strong U.S. reaction to its growing balance of trade deficit with Japan. For example, at the tenth Quad ministerial in Oba, Ontario the U.S. Trade Representative "warned that Congress was in no mood to tolerate Japan's huge and growing trade surplus with the United States."[44] The twelfth Quad ministerial in Sintra, Portugal on 4-7 September 1986 was the last Quad held before the GATT Punta del Este meeting launched the Uruguay Round. The Sintra ministerial focused on key outstanding differences among the Quad members, particularly their tactical and substantive differences regarding the majority draft for the proposed Punta del Este declaration. The differences among the Quad members at Sintra foreshadowed some of the disputes that would take place both at Punta del Este and during the Uruguay Round negotiations.

Despite the frictions among Quad members, the Quad ministerials resulted in some important accomplishments leading up to the launching of the GATT Uruguay Round in September 1986. By discussing their bilateral differences on the margins of the Quad meetings, the ministers were able to devote the main Quad sessions to the important multilateral issues. Thus, the Quads helped to develop a consensus and a common strategy among the major trading powers in preparation for the upcoming GATT negotiations; and they moved the debate forward on a range of issues such as trade in services, intellectual property, trade-related investment issues, and subsidies and countervailing duties. The Quad members also discussed measures to gain the approval of developing countries, because a group of developing countries led by Brazil and India was threatening to boycott a new GATT round if it included discussion of services and intellectual property. For example, ministers at the eleventh Quad in San Diego, California emphasised the importance of including areas that were of particular interest to developing countries such as agriculture and tropical products in the GATT negotiations.[45] Thus, the Quad ministerials had a critical role from 1980 to 1986 in delimiting divisions among the major traders, in coordinating their efforts in preparation for the GATT Uruguay Round, and in helping to set the negotiating agenda with an emphasis on services, intellectual property, and trade-related investment issues. Although the Quad could focus more consistently than the G7 on the multilateral negotiating agenda, the OECD was the developed country institution that dealt most intensely over the long term with specific issues such as services and agricultural trade. It is to the OECD that we now turn.

Organisation for Economic Co-operation and Development

At the beginning of this chapter we discussed the fact that the OECD played an important role in conducting background studies in preparation for the GATT Uruguay Round. Indeed, "the first step toward forming an agenda" for what was to become the Uruguay Round "was taken in the OECD, not the GATT."[46] The meetings of the OECD ministerial council also helped to build support for the Uruguay Round. Of particular note was the April 1985 OECD ministerial communiqué, which stated that

> Ministers reaffirmed their commitment to the open multilateral trading system and their determination to strengthen it by further liberalisation. A new round of trade negotiations in GATT would contribute significantly to achieving this objective. There was therefore agreement that such a round of negotiations should begin as soon as possible (some felt this should be in early 1986).[47]

The May 1985 G7 Bonn summit declaration strongly endorsed "the agreement reached by the OECD ministerial Council that a new GATT round should begin as soon as possible," and like the OECD the G7 added that "most of us think this should be in 1986."[48] However, the OECD's main contribution to the GATT Uruguay Round was not in its resolutions, but in its ambitious work program on specific issue areas that would be of importance in the round.

This chapter examines two issues that the OECD dealt with in the leadup to the Uruguay Round: agricultural and services trade. These issues were selected for several reasons. First, agriculture and services played a critical role in the Uruguay Round. Indeed, the authors of an important book on the GATT negotiations argue that "next to the reform of world trade in agriculture, the creation of a multilateral framework of rules to govern the trade in services constituted the Uruguay Round's main raison d'etre."[49] Second, the OECD had been concerned with services and agriculture from the time of its creation, and OECD background work and studies had a major impact on the negotiation of these issues in the Uruguay Round. Third, a study of agriculture and services demonstrates how the OECD has dealt with "older" trade issues such as agriculture that were exempt from some key GATT obligations, and also how the OECD has dealt with newer issues such as services trade.

Trade in Services

The OECD was concerned with the exchange of services from the time of its creation. In the 1960 Convention establishing the OECD, the member countries agreed to "pursue their efforts to reduce or abolish obstacles to the exchange of goods *and services* and current payments and maintain and extend the liberalisation of capital movements" (italics added).[50] The OECD also inherited two sets of rules from its predecessor the OEEC that affected services, but were not specifically directed at them: the "Code of Liberalisation of Current Invisible Operations" and the "Code of Liberalisation of Capital Movements." Most importantly, these two codes were not designed to regulate services *trade*, because "it was not until the 1970s that anyone thought of" services "as having the common property of being traded."[51] Although services transactions had crossed national borders for centuries, these transactions did not seem comparable with trade in goods because services could not be shipped and stored, and usually required the movement of service providers from one location to another. Thus, services were not considered to be within the purview of the GATT, and "fell under the auspices of institutions that gave preference to regulatory rather than market-based rules."[52]

William Drake and Kalypso Nicolaïdis point out that it was necessary to develop the "idea" that services like goods were a legitimate part of the global trade regime before the GATT could become involved in their regulation.[53] An epistemic community that played a major role in the development of OECD studies helped to alter the perception of services and thus to legitimise the regulation of services by the GATT. An "epistemic community" is commonly defined as "a network of professionals with recognized expertise and competence in a particular domain and an authoritative claim to policy-relevant knowledge within that domain or issue-area."[54] An epistemic community has shared causal and principled beliefs, shared ideas of validity, and a common policy project. As a result of the trade in services epistemic community, the OECD had a major role in promoting the transformation of ideas regarding services trade. As discussed in Chapter 4, a High-Level Group on Trade and Related Problems (the "Rey Group") was appointed in 1971 to examine opportunities for promoting trade liberalisation. The High-Level Group was an independent group of experts, but the OECD Secretary-General appointed the group and the OECD Council discussed its recommendations. The High-level Group's 1972 Rey report in fact coined the term "trade in services" and suggested more explicitly than ever before that services trade could be compared with merchandise trade:

> For some countries trade in services is at least as important as, and in some cases more important than, merchandise trade ... The Group has not made a detailed examination of questions concerning international trade in services. It considers however that, from the point of view of international economic relations, this sector poses problems similar in nature to those met within merchandise trade. Given that services are a sector which seems likely to expand rapidly in countries' economies, the main need is to avoid any tendencies to protectionism and to aim at achieving a more thorough liberalisation.[55]

The Rey report presented arguments for holding negotiations to liberalise trade in services, but it did not recommend that the GATT should be the first international institution to address the issue. Instead, the report looked to the OECD as the preferred forum, indicating that "action should be taken by the developed countries to ensure liberalisation and non-discrimination in the services sector."[56] Although the OECD was the preferred forum for the initial work on trade in services, the Rey report indicated that "as in the case of goods, consideration might be given to allowing developing countries a limited time to adapt themselves before undertaking the full commitments."[57] Thus, the implications of the Rey report were clear that after the OECD's preliminary work and prenegotiations, services trade negotiations should eventually be conducted in the GATT. The Trade Policy Research Institute in London which was examining services trade at the same time as the OECD High Level group also indicated that the OECD should do background studies on services trade before the GATT dealt with the issue:

For this approach, or any other, to succeed it would be necessary for a considerable degree of political will to be generated, perhaps initially through the OECD and thence through the GATT. That political will might be induced if the OECD was to initiate and maintain an inventory of constraints on invisible transactions. This would in any case be necessary in order to demonstrate the size of the problem and to provide a basis for inter-governmental discussions.[58]

Among the OECD countries, the United States was the strongest advocate of an agreement on trade in services. Influential business groups and multinational corporations such as American Express and Pan American Airways which were important service providers played a major role in pressuring the U.S. Administration and Congress to devote more attention to services trade. Furthermore, the United States regularly had balance of trade deficits beginning in 1971, and it sought to redress its growing trade and payments deficits by promoting trade liberalisation in areas where it was most competitive. The U.S. economy had become increasingly services-oriented, and the services sector in the 1970s accounted for about two-thirds of the U.S. GDP and provided employment for about 70 percent of American workers. Furthermore, the $23 billion U.S. surplus in the services sector in 1978 helped to offset the $34 billion deficit in merchandise trade. It is therefore not surprising that the U.S. Congress for the first time included services in Presidential authority for international trade negotiations in the 1974 U.S. Trade Act.[59] Section 102.g.3 of the Trade Act broadened the definition of "international trade" to include "trade in both goods and services," and Section 163.a.2 directed the President to report to the Congress on "the results of actions to obtain ... the removal of foreign practices which discriminate against United States service industries (including transportation and tourism)."[60]

American pressure to address the issue of services trade encountered resistance not only in the GATT, but also from some other developed countries in the OECD. The first significant U.S. effort to incorporate services trade in the GATT came during the Tokyo Round. It was impossible to have comprehensive negotiations on services trade in the Tokyo Round, because the Congress did not pass legislation formally authorising U.S. participation in the round until January 1975. The agreed agenda for the negotiations was onerous even without including trade in services, and the services issues were too complex to permit in-depth negotiations with so little preparation. Nevertheless, a White House Interagency Task Force on Services and the MTN "recommended that issues related to trade in services should be raised in the multilateral trade negotiations on a 'carefully selected' basis."[61] Following this strategy, the United States succeeded in inserting limited, indirect obligations on the treatment of services in the Tokyo Round NTB codes for government procurement, standards, and subsidies. Although the Tokyo Round failed to address most of the problems facing the services industries, the small gains in the NTB codes set a precedent for dealing with services in multilateral trade negotiations.[62]

After the GATT Tokyo Round, the United States was able to persuade the other OECD members to undertake a study of services trade for the purpose of identifying areas for future negotiation. Although a small number of studies had been written on services trade, business and government knowledge about trade in services was wholly inadequate. Other OECD members were initially uncertain that OECD studies were necessary, because "barriers to trade in services ... tend to be as invisible to the average person as trade in services itself, and this only compounds the skepticism that there is anything to talk about with respect to trade in services."[63] However, each phase of the debate in the OECD resulted in useful background studies on services trade, and foreshadowed the debates that would take place later in the preparations for services trade negotiations in the GATT. Several OECD committees engaged in a work program for trade in services. The OECD Trade Committee had the challenging task of developing a conceptual framework for trade in services, while other committees initiated a number of industry-specific studies.

Although most developed countries had decided by 1981 that the GATT should examine trade in services as a possible area for future multilateral negotiations, they were less willing than the United States to commit to negotiations in the near-term future. Most developing countries, by contrast, were strongly opposed to the discussion of services trade in the GATT. As a result, the November 1982 GATT ministerial could agree only to defer any decisions on the inclusion of services trade in future GATT negotiations. Over the next two years, the United States produced studies and exerted pressure for an acceptance of the idea that services trade was a legitimate subject for negotiation. The trade in services epistemic community had an important role in the development of these studies. During this period the major developed country traders became more supportive of the U.S. position, because they gradually accepted the idea that services trade liberalisation provided them with "an opportunity to conquer the markets of the future, those with promising growth potential."[64] Indeed, the annual growth rate for trade in services from 1970 to 1980 was about 19 percent, compared with only 5.4 percent for trade in goods.[65] At a November 1984 meeting of the GATT Contracting Parties, most OECD countries therefore dropped their objections to formalising GATT involvement with trade in services. However, two months before the GATT meeting, an UNCTAD secretariat document had warned that the "process of transnationalization of services operations includes serious risks for developing countries, one of these being the danger of their being allocated the 'bottom rung' of the intra-firm and international division of labour, as suppliers of relatively unskilled labour."[66] Thus, developing countries at the 1984 GATT meeting continued to strongly oppose an agreement to liberalise trade in services.

From 1984 to 1986 there was a gradual shifting of positions, as the major developed country traders became more uniformly in favour of including services trade in the upcoming GATT negotiations, and the developing countries by contrast became less unified in their opposition to the inclusion of services trade. Instead of outlining the reasons for these changes (they are examined in other studies of services trade), we refer here simply to the outcome for the GATT negotiations, and the role of the OECD during this period. At the September 1986 Punta del Este meeting, the decision was made to include services trade in the the Uruguay Round. In response to developing country demands, the Uruguay Round negotiations for trade in goods and trade in services were to be conducted separately. However, U.S. pressure resulted in an agreement that the Uruguay Round would be a "single undertaking," in which progress in the goods and services negotiations had to adhere to similar negotiating phases and deadlines.[67] The most important achievement of the OECD from 1982 to 1986 was the OECD Trade Committee's "development of a conceptual framework for service trade modeled on fundamental GATT principles such as national treatment."[68] In March 1987, the OECD published the results of this effort in a document entitled "Elements of a Conceptual Framework for Trade in Services."[69] Some of the conceptual framework's concepts and ideas had an influence on the course of the GATT Uruguay Round negotiations.

In summary, the OECD's involvement with services trade in the 1970s and 1980s demonstrated that it was a primary forum for developing and conveying new ideas. Building a consensus on the services trade issue among the developed countries required "research, analysis, and policy development – functions for which the OECD was ideally suited."[70] In conducting this analysis and research the OECD depended on assistance from the trade in services epistemic community. Of particular importance was the coining of the term "trade in services" by an OECD-appointed High Level Group in 1972, and the development of a conceptual framework for services trade by the OECD Trade Committee from 1982 to 1986. Thus, the OECD had a significant role in ensuring that services trade would be included as a major issue for negotiation in the GATT Uruguay Round.

Trade in Agriculture

As was the case with services, the OECD was a forum for discussing agricultural issues from the time it replaced the OEEC in 1961. In its early years, the OECD focused almost exclusively on domestic agricultural issues and largely ignored agricultural trade. The OECD's long-term familiarity with domestic agriculture provided important background for addressing the issue of agricultural trade, because "in no sector of the economy are domestic and international policies more closely related than in agriculture."[71] Nevertheless, major differences between the two largest agricultural traders – the United States and the European Community – prevented the OECD from dealing with agricultural trade problems for a number of years. It was not until 1972 that the OECD made a serious effort to develop recommendations for action on agricultural trade, and not until 1982 that it began a major study of agricultural trade issues in preparation for a new round of GATT negotiations. As was the case for services trade, the OECD helped to develop and convey new ideas for dealing with agricultural trade, often with the assistance of an epistemic community. Before discussing the OECD's activities in the agricultural trade area, it is necessary to provide some background on the GATT's role in agriculture from the 1940s to the end of the Tokyo Round.

Some analysts have pointed to inconsistencies in the U.S. commitment to trade liberalisation when it was the unquestioned hegemon after World War II, and there is no area where these inconsistencies were greater than in agriculture.[72] Thus, the GATT contained two major agricultural exemptions that were included largely to conform with provisions in the U.S. farm program. A 1935 amendment (Section 32) of the U.S. Agricultural Adjustment Act had permitted the Department of Agriculture to use export subsidies. Although GATT Article XVI prohibited export subsidies for manufactured goods, an exception was therefore provided for agricultural and other primary products. The only limitation on agricultural export subsidies was an ambiguous provision (in Article XVI.3) that they should not permit a country to gain "more than an equitable share of world export trade."[73] GATT Article XI called for the elimination of quantitative restrictions on imports (or import quotas), but permitted such restrictions for agriculture when they were needed to enforce domestic supply management policies. This article was patterned after Section 22 of the U.S. Agricultural Adjustment Act, which sanctioned the use of import quotas for commodities under price support programs. Unlike GATT Article XI, however, Section 22 permitted import restrictions even when there were no restraints on domestic production. As a result, in 1955 the United States sought and received an unusually broad waiver from its Article XI obligations which permitted it to impose import quotas for agricultural products even when it did not have domestic supply management programs.[74]

The early agricultural exceptions demonstrate a serious shortcoming of hegemonic stability theory. In positing that a hegemon contributes to open international economic regimes, the theory ignores both sectoral differences and domestic politics. The agricultural sector has been different because domestic political, social, and economic factors have a major impact on agricultural trade policy. In U.S. Congressional committee hearings on agricultural import quotas in 1952, executive branch officials argued that such quotas threatened to damage U.S. leadership and European economic recovery. The Congress, however, was focusing more narrowly on the plight of U.S. dairy farmers, and its protectionist approach carried the day because of Congressional authority over international trade.[75] Thus, in formulating agricultural trade policy, the United States often "found the pressures of special-interest groups ... so strong that it did not behave in a manner consistent with its hegemonic interests."[76]

Although the United States was an early contributor to agricultural protectionism, it became increasingly concerned about the financial cost of its agricultural programs and about the protectionist policies of others. Of greatest concern to the United States was the European Community, which introduced the main elements of its highly protectionist Common Agricultural Policy in the early 1960s. The CAP included high support prices for major crops, a variable levy system for imports, and the use of export subsidies (referred to as export refunds or restitutions) to deal with surplus production. In the 1960s the United States therefore became more committed to agricultural trade liberalisation, and President Lyndon Johnson stated in April 1964 that the United States would not enter into a GATT Kennedy Round agreement "unless progress is registered toward trade liberalisation on the products of our farms as well as our factories."[77] The EC, however, considered its CAP to be an integral part of the Community that was not negotiable. Since the United States and the EC were both committed to liberalising industrial trade in the Kennedy Round, they agreed to defer the difficult task of liberalising agricultural trade for the future. The failure to reach a significant agreement on agriculture was also an indication that U.S. hegemony had declined, and that the United States and the EC were far from reaching a consensus in this critical area:

> The Kennedy Round agricultural negotiations marked the shift in political power which had occurred in the postwar world. The United States had long dictated the course and form of international economic relationships. But in ... [the Kennedy

Round] it was defeated on ground of its own choosing. It was unable to prevent the European countries from persisting with, and indeed extending even whilst negotiations proceeded, a system and level of agricultural support of which it disapproved.[78]

In 1971 the United States had its first balance of trade deficit since 1893, and as its trade deficits increased in the 1970s, the United States began to pressure more aggressively for GATT negotiations in areas where it still had a comparative advantage. Agricultural trade was one of these areas. Between 1950 and 1975 U.S. farm output increased by 54 percent, but U.S. agricultural exports almost quadrupled. Exports accounted for 24 percent of U.S. farm cash receipts in the mid-1970s, up from only 10 percent in 1950.[79] Most importantly, agriculture was one of the few areas where the United States continued to have a positive trade balance, and its farm exports were viewed as one means of redressing unfavourable balances elsewhere. The United States was therefore determined that the Tokyo Round would be more successful than the Kennedy Round in applying GATT regulations to agriculture, and the U.S. Special Representative for Trade warned that in the Tokyo Round "progress in agriculture is the *sine qua non* of progress in normalising the international economic situation and improving our trade relations."[80] However, the EC insisted on a separate negotiation for agriculture, and the U.S.-EC agricultural differences resulted in a standoff that largely blocked further progress in the Tokyo Round from 1974 to 1977. After the election of President Jimmy Carter in November 1976 the United States was more conciliatory, and the deadlock was finally broken when the United States accepted the EC demand for separate agricultural negotiations. Thus, the results for agriculture in the Tokyo Round, as in the Kennedy Round, were disappointing.[81]

Many of the obstacles to agricultural trade liberalisation "stem from the operation of costly, but nonetheless durable, domestic farm support programs," and the OECD's long-term attention to domestic agricultural policies gave it the necessary background for dealing with agricultural trade issues.[82] The OECD countries accounted for only about 30 percent of world agricultural production in 1987, but their share of agricultural trade has been much greater. During the 1970s and 1980s, the OECD countries accounted for about 60 percent of world agricultural exports and for 67 percent of world agricultural imports. Nevertheless, significant OECD analysis of possible approaches to reducing agricultural protectionism did not really begin until the early 1980s.[83] The delay in OECD work on agricultural trade resulted from two major factors. First, unlike the case of export credits, the OECD was not the main international organisation for negotiations on agricultural trade. The most extensive agricultural trade negotiations occurred in the GATT, and in bilateral meetings, especially among the United States, the EC, Japan and Canada. Second, there was a notable lack of agreement among OECD countries regarding the extent to which international organisations should conduct negotiations in the agricultural trade area.

During the 1960s, discussion of agriculture in the OECD rarely ventured beyond domestic issues and was largely descriptive in nature. Nevertheless, the failure of the GATT Dunkel and Kennedy Rounds to bridge the gap between the United States and the EC on agricultural trade issues resulted in the OECD's first significant effort to develop recommendations for action on agricultural trade. The 1972 Report of the High Level Group on Trade and Related Problems, or the Rey report, devoted nine pages to agriculture, and pointed to the fact that "the agricultural sector has to a large extent remained on the fringe of the [GATT] liberalisation process that has been going on for the last 25 years."[84] Nevertheless, the High Level Group encountered the same problem as the GATT in reconciling divergent views, and the Rey report's summation on agriculture attested to the continuing divisions among developed countries:

> As was to be expected, it was the examination of agricultural problems which gave rise to the longest discussions within the Group ... this subject has been debated for years both within the Organisation and in other international bodies, without it having been possible so far to reconcile fully the divergent points of view held ... since all governments base the policies they pursue in this field not only on economic but also on social and political considerations the diverse situations with which they are confronted lead them to adopt widely different measures of protection with conflicting effects on international trade which are extremely difficult to reconcile.[85]

Two divergent approaches emerged in the Rey group's recommendations on agricultural trade. Some members of the group argued that only limited changes should be instituted, that would not alter "the essential principles and mechanisms of the agricultural policies now in force." Other members, by contrast, believed that the proposals for change should constitute only "a first step in a more far-reaching programme" leading to agricultural policy reforms that were much more market-oriented.[86] The United States was the principal supporter of the second approach, and it was dissatisfied with the cautious nature of the Rey report's comments on agriculture. Although, the U.S. Trade Representative agreed to sign the report, he insisted that his dissenting comments be included. The USTR strongly criticised what he viewed as the report's assumption "that agriculture is fundamentally different from industry, and that we not only can but must wait many more years before barriers and distortions to agricultural trade can be dealt with in any fundamental way."[87] The two divergent approaches prevented the Rey report from presenting a coherent set of principles for agricultural trade, but the report was nevertheless a first step in attempts to establish such principles.

In view of the divergent positions expressed in the Rey report, the OECD continued to give agricultural trade issues "relatively little direct attention during much of the 1970s in comparison with the countless studies on domestic agricultural issues."[88] By 1978, however, it was evident that the GATT Tokyo Round would not achieve the breakthrough the United States sought in agriculture, and the U.S. Under Secretary of Agriculture Dale Hathaway maintained that the OECD should become more involved with agricultural trade issues.[89] As the Tokyo Round was ending, the June 1979 OECD ministerial agreed to begin the OECD's first comprehensive study of agricultural trade problems.[90] Thus, a Joint Working Party of the OECD Committee for Agriculture and the OECD Trade Committee conducted a three-year study that examined the relationship between agricultural trade, domestic agricultural policies and the general economy. In 1982, the Working Party issued its final report, entitled *Problems of Agricultural Trade.*[91]

As was the case for services trade, the OECD work on agricultural trade from 1979 to 1982 had an important role (with the help of an agricultural epistemic community) in altering perceptions in preparation for GATT negotiations in agriculture. First, the OECD sought to demonstrate that domestic agricultural policies presented serious problems for the OECD countries. For example, OECD studies showed that domestic agricultural support wasted resources, impaired competitiveness in manufacturing, and sometimes reduced total employment and discouraged the development of efficient agriculture.[92] Second, the OECD sought to demonstrate that government-supported domestic agricultural policies had highly detrimental effects on international agricultural trade. For example, the May 1982 OECD ministerial formally recognised for the first time that "agricultural trade is affected by general economic developments and by domestic agricultural policies pursued by all countries which do not always take into account their international consequences."[93] Third, following upon the first two findings (that agricultural policies had negative domestic and international effects) the OECD drew the key conclusion that domestic agricultural policies were a legitimate subject of international trade negotiations. Thus, the 1982 OECD report on *Problems of Agricultural Trade* clearly indicated that agricultural trade had to be integrated "more fully with the open multilateral trading system to which all OECD countries subscribe."[94]

Having established the importance of GATT negotiations on agricultural trade, the OECD then identified three areas that required further study in preparation for the negotiations: national policies that have a significant impact on agricultural trade, strategies for a gradual reduction of agricultural protection, and the best methods to improve the functioning of international agricultural markets. To examine these three areas, the OECD's Trade and Agriculture Committees jointly initiated a Ministerial Trade Mandate (MTM) study in 1982.[95] The OECD's MTM study, which required over four years to complete, analysed the impact of all forms of agricultural assistance on production and trade protectionism, and discussed a range of assistance reduction scenarios. A number of country studies were also conducted under the MTM rubric to examine the effects of various support policies on agricultural trade. The country studies employed the concepts of "producer subsidy equivalents" (PSEs) and "consumer subsidy equivalents" (CSEs) in attempts to measure the overall subsidies provided to agriculture through a wide array of farm policies. Heidi Ullrich has noted that "key new analytical tools, such as the PSEs and CSEs, were developed by members of a pro-reform agricultural epistemic community operating within the OECD and the policy environments of the US and EC."[96] As Chapter 6 will discuss, the OECD's MTM study provided essential background information for the GATT Uruguay Round negotiations in agriculture.

It is important to note that in parallel with the OECD's MTM study, the GATT was involved in its own preparations for agricultural trade negotiations. Preparations for the Uruguay Round began at the 1982 GATT ministerial, and the GATT Committee on Trade in Agriculture (CTA) met throughout 1983 and 1984 to engage in detailed preparatory work on agriculture. Indeed, "for agriculture, more than for any other issue except perhaps services, the foundations of the Uruguay Round were laid by the work programme launched by ministers in 1982."[97] Chaired by a senior Dutch trade official Aart de Zeeuw, the CTA spent two years examining all the factors that influence trade, market access, competition, and supply and demand for agricultural products. In November 1984, this work resulted in a series of CTA recommendations on how to approach the task of agricultural reform. In 1985 and the first half of 1986, the CTA developed what was in effect a blueprint for negotiations, including specific proposals on how to implement its 1984 recommendations. Thus, by the time of the Punta del Este ministerial launching the Uruguay Round, the OECD and GATT studies had yielded detailed knowledge about agricultural policies that would be useful in the upcoming negotiations.[98]

Despite the OECD and GATT studies and prenegotiations in the 1980s, it was not a foregone conclusion that meaningful agricultural trade negotiations would take place in the Uruguay Round. Indeed, President François Mitterand briefly walked out of the 1985 G7 Bonn II summit because of France's unwillingness to agree to agricultural negotiations. Although the summit economic declaration made no reference to agriculture, it vaguely referred to this disagreement by stating that "we strongly endorse the agreement reached by the OECD Ministerial council that a new GATT round should begin as soon as possible. *Most of us* think that this should be in 1986" (italics added).[99] Furthermore, in May 1987 the OECD ministerial council approved the publication of the OECD's MTM study, *National Policies and Agricultural Trade*, only over the objections of France and Japan.[100] As we discuss in Chapter 6, OECD and GATT studies have played an important role in GATT/WTO agricultural trade negotiations during and after the Uruguay Round. Nevertheless, the wide divisions among OECD countries on agricultural trade have also resulted in persistent divisions in this area in the GATT/WTO.

The Role of the Developing Countries

For much of the postwar period, developing countries had adopted two strategies toward international trade negotiations that were somewhat contradictory. First, they had sought and received some special and differential treatment in the global trade regime. Their demand for S&D treatment was reinforced by the formation of UNCTAD in 1964, and culminated in developing country calls for a NIEO in the 1970s. Second, developing countries were largely passive participants (and some were non-participants) in the GATT multilateral trade negotiations. Although developing countries were more involved in the GATT Tokyo Round than the Kennedy Round, their efforts in the Tokyo Round were devoted primarily to legally enshrining their S&D treatment in the enabling clause of the GATT.[101] In view of their traditional attitude toward the GATT, it is not surprising that many developing countries were initially either ambivalent or opposed to a new round of GATT negotiations in the 1980s. Although the United States wanted the 1982 GATT ministerial to be the first step toward a new round, a group of developing countries led by Brazil and India indicated that they were not prepared to negotiate issues such as services trade with the developed countries. The developing countries also argued that developed countries had not fulfilled their earlier obligations with regard to trade in textiles and agriculture, and that further liberalisation should occur in these areas before there was a new GATT round.

However, the Third World foreign debt crisis which began in August 1982 when Mexico threatened to default on its loans caused the developing countries to soften their demands for S&D treatment, and to become more actively involved in the GATT. Several factors accounted for this change. First, the foreign debt crisis demonstrated that the inward-looking trade policies of many developing countries had been detrimental to their economic welfare. The debt crisis had a far more devastating effect on Latin American than on East Asian developing countries. Exports provide a critical source of foreign exchange for servicing a country's debt, and the East Asian developing countries which had been following export-led growth policies were able to rely partly on exports to help finance their debt. (Japan was also increasing its investments in East Asia at the time, which helped to alleviate East Asian debt problems.) The Latin American developing countries by contrast were far less successful in maintaining their exports, because they had been following inward-looking import substitution policies. Thus, the foreign debt crisis caused developing countries to shift toward more outward-looking export-oriented policies, and to recognise the importance of GATT negotiations in promoting their exports.

A second reason for the developing countries new interest in the GATT was that their strategy of seeking S&D treatment had resulted in disappointment. Although developing countries had received S&D treatment through Part IV of the GATT, the generalised system of preferences, and the Enabling Clause, these new GATT provisions provided them with only limited benefits. Even the GSP which was the most concrete benefit had major limitations. For example, each developed country could decide for itself what to include (and exclude) in its GSP, and the benefits of the GSP were largely concentrated in a small number of middle- to higher-income developing countries that least required S&D treatment. In 1986, the year the Uruguay Round was launched, 50 percent of the GSP benefits went to only four NIEs: Brazil, Hong Kong, Korea, and Taiwan.[102] A third factor explaining the shift in Third World policies related to developing country susceptibility to increased pressure from the developed countries. In response to the debt crisis, the developed countries were willing to reschedule their outstanding loans to developing countries, and the IMF and World Bank provided the indebted developing countries with structural adjustment loans. However, the IMF and World Bank placed conditions on these loans that required the recipients to decrease government spending, and to adopt privatisation and trade liberalisation policies. In response to this developed country pressure, most developing countries liberalised their trade policies.

The changes in position and attitudes of developing countries in the 1980 to 1986 period were mirrored by similar changes in the UNCTAD, which holds conferences every four years to provide direction to the secretariat's work project. In the four years from the 1979 UNCTAD V conference in Manila to the 1983 UNCTAD VI conference in Belgrade, the economic position of the South had deteriorated. Indeed, many developing countries were experiencing near crisis conditions with lower commodity prices, rising debts, and falling growth rates. Latin American, Asian, and African developing countries were also following divergent strategies to deal with the 1980s foreign debt crisis, and this tended to exacerbate their differences. Tensions among developing countries in different regional blocs "could no longer be papered over with rhetorical allegiance to dependency ideology or a 'common enemy' in the West."[103] Compared with their demands in the 1970s, the developing countries were more prepared to compromise at UNCTAD VI in 1983. Although the UNCTAD VI position was somewhat less confrontational than in previous years, the United States argued that it was still too one-sided and ideological. In 1984 the Western countries, led by the U.S. Reagan administration, established a "reflection group" to reconsider their view of UNCTAD. A series of green papers followed that strongly criticised the UNCTAD Secretary-General, Gamani Corea, for appointing too many executives who were more committed to North-South confrontation than to trade liberalisation. As a result, the UNCTAD Secretaries-General appointed after Gamani Corea were pragmatic negotiators who removed several of the organisation's more anti-Western executives from high-profile positions. Thus, UNCTAD began to take a more conciliatory position and was prepared to help the South develop a reasoned response to the GATT Uruguay Round.[104]

As the South became more integrated in the global trade regime, it gradually began to gain more influence *within* the GATT. (This marked a contrast with Southern efforts in the 1970s to gain influence outside the GATT in their calls for a NIEO.) Thus, the South refused to support the launching of the GATT Uruguay Round unless some of its key demands were met. Most importantly, the South demanded that textiles and clothing trade be a major issue for negotiation in the Uruguay Round before they would agree to the North's demand that services trade be included in the round. In GATT sessions from 1982 to 1986 the South continued to resist Northern pressures to agree to a new round until their demands regarding textiles and clothing trade were met. In the end, Hugo Paemen and Alexandra Bensch maintain that "the trade off was clear" between services and textiles at the Punta del Este meeting launching the Uruguay Round.[105] In accordance with developed country demands, the Punta del Este ministerial declaration stated that "negotiations in this area shall aim to establish a multilateral framework of principles and rules for trade in services." In accordance with developing country demands, the declaration stated that "negotiations in the area of textiles and clothing shall aim to formulate modalities that would permit the eventual integration of this sector into GATT on the basis of strengthened GATT rules and disciplines."[106] As a result, developing country resistance to a new round of GATT negotiations "gradually crumbled, and in the end the main surprise was that the resistance had been as effective and long-standing as it turned out to be."[107]

In sum, a combination of Northern pressure and Southern perception of self interest caused developing country attitudes to shift in the 1980s toward greater support for trade liberalisation and for a new round of GATT negotiations. In contrast to the Kennedy and Tokyo Rounds, developing countries became much more involved in the discussions that led to the Uruguay Round. Thirty-nine additional developing countries joined the GATT from 1982 to 1994 (the year before the WTO was formed), which was an indication of the importance they attached to the Uruguay Round.[108] As a result of their more active involvement in the global trade regime, the South gradually began to gain more influence in the GATT. Although Canada, the EU, and Uruguay all offered to host the meeting to launch the new GATT round, the Preparatory Committee selected Uruguay as a show of support for developing country participation. In view of the failure of developing countries to achieve their trade-related objectives by joining together in the G77, some observers argued that developing countries would experience more success in the Uruguay Round only if they joined in coalitions with developed countries. For example, John W. Sewell and I. William Zartman wrote in 1984:

> The South sees its interests furthered by solidarity, but this very solidarity stymies compromise (which is at the heart of any negotiation) ... perhaps the most important single innovation needed in North-South relations is ways and means to develop coalitions between Northern and Southern countries on various specific issues without undermining the unity of the Third World.[109]

As we discuss in Chapter 6, the developing countries did in fact form a series of coalitions with developed countries in the GATT Uruguay Round.

Conclusion

One of the striking events during the 1980 to 1986 period was the November 1982 GATT ministerial meeting, which came close to a serious breakdown and produced an acute crisis for the global trade organisation. At the time of the crisis, influential individuals in many GATT countries were referring to the possible abandonment of the GATT, and "recommending that their countries should instead act alone or in company with a few like-minded others ... to bring about the trade policy aims they sought."[110] Ironically, a work program emerged out of the 1982 crisis that eventually resulted in the most ambitious negotiating round in GATT history, the Uruguay Round.

The 1980 to 1986 period was also striking because of the creation of a new informal institution near the top of the global trade regime pyramid: the Quadrilateral Group of trade ministers or "Quad." The origins of the Quad can be traced to the margins of the July, 1981 G7 summit in Ottawa, when the United States, the EC, and Japan met to discuss a proposal that their trade ministers should regularly hold informal trilateral meetings. Joined later by Canada, the Quad held its first ministerial in January 1982, and continued to hold meetings about twice a year thereafter. In contrast to the heads of government and state in the G7 who are often preoccupied with political-security and monetary-financial matters, the Quad trade ministers focus exclusively on trade matters. In contrast to the OECD which has a much larger membership, the Quad is a small, informal grouping that permits the most important traders to engage in candid discussions to resolve their differences and form a consensus on key trade issues. Thus, the Quad has filled an important gap in the global trade regime pyramid. As was the case for the G7, the formation of the Quad marked a move toward collective decision-making in view of declining U.S. economic hegemony; and the growing pressure for protectionism in the 1980s was an important factor explaining the timing of the Quad's formation. Despite bilateral frictions, the Quad ministerials helped to develop a consensus on strategy among the major trading powers for the upcoming GATT negotiations; and the Quad also moved the debate forward on a range of issues of interest to the developed countries such as trade in services and intellectual property. To gain approval from the developing countries, the Quad discussed the inclusion of areas such as agriculture and textiles in the upcoming negotiations.

Although American economic hegemony had declined somewhat, especially in the trade area, the United States continued to play a critical role near the top of the global trade regime pyramid in pressuring others to move toward a new round of GATT negotiations. Indeed, "had it not been for the tenacity of the

Americans, the negotiations would never have taken place."[111] The United States was also the most important actor in the 1980 to 1986 period pushing for a broadening of the negotiations to include such issues as services, intellectual property, investment, and agriculture. Moreso than in the past, however, American pressure to broaden the negotiating agenda stemmed from U.S. weakness as well as strength. Although the United States had the strength to exert pressure on others to move the prenegotiations forward, its choice of issues for inclusion such as services and agriculture stemmed largely from efforts to alleviate its growing balance of trade and payments deficit. In view of its trade deficit, the United States pressed aggressively for trade negotiations in areas where it still had a comparative advantage.

The 12-member European Community of 1986, with its 340 million people, was the largest trading power in the world. Thus, it occupied the top of the global trade regime pyramid along with the United States. However, like the United States, the EC demonstrated some significant weaknesses. Although the European Commission is an independent body with the power to initiate and execute decisions, its proposals must first be approved by the Council of Ministers. In trade and agricultural policies the Commission can only act when it receives the support of the majority of member states. Because states naturally look after their own national interests, in EC "trade policy, negotiations between the Member states can sometimes be far more gruelling than negotiations with third countries."[112] As a result, the EC could be justly accused of not acting more forthrightly in the leadup to the Uruguay Round negotiations. Despite differences among the major developed countries, they generally agreed on the need for inclusion of new areas such as trade in services and intellectual property, and a major challenge was to gain acceptance from the developing countries. As discussed, the developing countries were far more conciliatory in the 1980s than they had been in the 1970s, and the conditions were therefore met for the launching of the Uruguay Round.

In addition to the United States, the EC, and the Quad, the G7 and the OECD continued to occupy important positions near the top of the global trade regime pyramid in the 1980 to 1986 period. As for the G7 summits, they had a significant role in delimiting protectionism and trade disputes during the early 1980s when pressures for protectionism were increasing. The G7 summits also played an important role in garnering support at the highest political level for a new GATT round, and in helping to set the agenda for the new round. Nevertheless, the G7 was unable to reach the necessary degree of consensus on a new round until sufficient progress was made in dealing with the negotiating issues at the technical and policy-making levels. Compared to the G7, the OECD was much more involved in the technical and policy-making aspects of the negotiations.

As was the case for the Tokyo Round, the United States turned first to the OECD rather than the GATT in its efforts to garner support for what would be the Uruguay Round. This chapter has examined two important areas of the OECD's action programme in preparation for the new round: in services and agriculture. The Tokyo Round had not dealt with services trade partly because of lack of preparation time, but also because of divisions among the developed countries, and strong opposition from the developing countries. However, the OECD made two landmark contributions that gave an important impetus to services trade negotiations. First, the OECD played a critical role in developing the "idea" that services like goods were a legitimate part of the global trade regime. In 1972, the "Rey Group" appointed by the OECD Secretary-General coined the term "trade in services," and explicitly indicated that services trade could be compared with merchandise trade. Second, the OECD helped to develop a conceptual framework for trade in services comparable to the framework for trade in goods. Of particular note was the OECD's March 1987 publication of "Elements of a Conceptual Framework for Trade in Services," which had an important influence on the course of the Uruguay Round negotiations. These two contributions demonstrated the OECD's ability to introduce new ideas of particular interest to the developed countries as areas of negotiation in the GATT. In doing so, the OECD utilised the assistance of a trade in services epistemic community.

Agricultural trade was another highly contentious area in which the OECD was able to make a significant contribution, because of its long-term experience with examining domestic agricultural policies. As was the case for services trade, the OECD contributed to the "ideas" that domestic agricultural policies of developed countries were costly and ineffective, that domestic agricultural policies had a detrimental effect on agricultural trade, and that agricultural trade should be subject to multilateral trade negotiations. After legitimising the idea of agricultural trade negotiations, the OECD then helped to develop a conceptual framework for negotiating agricultural issues. For example, in the 1982 to 1987 period the OECD's Ministerial Trade Mandate study employed concepts such as producer subsidy equivalents and consumer subsidy equivalents as a means of measuring and comparing the subsidies that different GATT countries provided to agriculture. As was the case with services, an epistemic community helped the OECD provide the outlook and methods for making agricultural trade a negotiable issue in the GATT. Although epistemic communities may exist in isolation, they are ultimately "dependent on politicians and government decision-makers in order to become influential and be successful in bringing about the desired change in policy."[113]

As this chapter discusses, the relationship between the North and the South was undergoing significant changes in the 1980 to 1986 period. In the 1970s, the developing countries had tried to alter the pyramidal structure of the global trade regime with their calls for a NIEO. However, the foreign debt crisis had a significant effect on the position and perceptions of developing countries toward the global trade regime. As a result of the debt crisis, the North had greater leverage through IMF and World Bank structural adjustment loans in inducing the South to liberalise its trade policies, and the developing countries began to question the efficacy of their traditional policies of seeking S&D treatment and limiting their involvement in the GATT. Thus, the developing countries became more involved in preparations for the GATT Uruguay Round than in any previous round. As a result of the developing countries' growing involvement, their influence within the GATT gradually began to increase. Thus, the North was able to include negotiations on services trade in the Uruguay Round only after it agreed to Southern demands for negotiations on textiles and clothing.

Notes

1   Hugo Paemen and Alexandra Bensch, *From the GATT to the WTO: The European Community in the Uruguay Round* (Leuven: Leuven University Press, 1995), p. 19.
2   *United States International Economic Policy in an Interdependent World*, Report to the President submitted by the Commission on International Trade and Investment Policy, July 1971 (Washington, D.C.: GPO, 1971), p. 10.
3   "Meeting of the OECD Council at Ministerial Level in June 1981 – Communiqué," paragraph 15.
4   Ernest H. Preeg, *Traders in a Brave New World: The Uruguay Round and the Future of the International Trading System* (Chicago: University of Chicago Press, 1995), pp. 24-31; John Croome, *Reshaping the World Trading System: A History of the Uruguay Round* (Geneva: World Trade Organization, 1995), p. 12; "Declaration of the Ottawa Summit," 21 July 1981.
5   Patrick Low, *Trading Free: The GATT and U.S. Trade Policy* (New York: Twentieth Century Fund Press, 1993), p. 192.
6   For a detailed discussion of the 1982 GATT ministerial and work program, see Low, *Trading Free*, pp. 190-207.
7   *Trade Policies for a Better Future: Proposals for Action* (Geneva: GATT, March 1985), pp. 19 and 47; *Trade Policies for a Better Future: The 'Leutwiler Report', the GATT and the Uruguay Round* (Dordrecht: Martinus Nijhoff, 1987); Preeg, *Traders in a Brave New World*, pp. 33-36; Croome, *Reshaping the World Trading System*, pp. 12-17.

8   Jacques Pelkmans, "Collective Management and Economic Cooperation," in Cesare Merlini, ed., *Economic Summits and Western Decision-Making* (London: Croom Helm, 1984), p. 89.

9   Robert D. Putnam and Nicholas Bayne, *Hanging Together: Cooperation and Conflict in the Seven-Power Summits,* revised ed. (London: SAGE, 1987), p. 105. See also Peter I. Hajnal, *The G7/G8 System: Evolution, Role and Documentation* (Aldershot: Ashgate, 1999), pp. 13-15.

10 Guido Garavoglia, "From Rambouillet to Williamsburg: A Historical Assessment," in Merlini, ed., *Economic Summits and Western Decision-Making*, pp. 22-25; Putnam and Bayne, *Hanging Together*, pp. 118-126.

11 "Declaration of the Venice Summit," 23 June 1980, paragraphs 31 and 32.

12 "Declaration of the Ottawa Summit," 21 July 1981, paragraphs 24 and 25.

13 Putnam and Bayne, *Hanging Together*, pp. 126-132; Garavoglia, "From Rambouillet to Williamsburg," pp. 25-29.

14 See Putnam and Bayne, *Hanging Together*, pp. 139-140. For a more negative view of the Versailles discussion on East-West trade see Garavoglia, "From Rambouillet to Williamsburg," pp. 30-33.

15 Putnam and Bayne, *Hanging Together*, p. 135.

16 "Declaration of the Seven Heads of State and Government and Representatives of the European Communities," Versailles, 6 June 1982.

17 "Williamsburg Declaration on Economic Recovery," 30 May 1983, paragraph 3.

18 "Williamsburg Declaration on Economic Recovery," 30 May 1983, paragraph 3.

19 Putnam and Bayne, *Hanging Together*, pp. 183-193.

20 "London Economic Declaration," 9 June 1984, paragraph 9.10.

21 Robert Wolfe, *Farm Wars: The Political Economy of Agriculture and the International Trade Regime* (London: Macmillan, 1998), p. 79.

22 "The Bonn Economic Declaration: Towards Sustained Growth and Higher Employment," 4 May 1985, paragraph 10.

23 Putnam and Bayne, *Hanging Together*, p. 203.

24 Wolfe, *Farm Wars*, p. 80; Susan Hainsworth, "Coming of Age: The European Community and the Economic Summit," University of Toronto G7/G8 website.

25 "Tokyo Economic Declaration," 6 May 1986, paragraph 12.

26 Putnam and Bayne, *Hanging Together*, pp. 196-223.

27 Imbert Mathee, "Trade Routes Lead to Summit Here: Actions of 'Quad' Watched Closely," *Seattle Post Intelligencer*, 23 September 1996, pp. A1 and A5.

28 World Trade Organization, "Developing Countries' Merchandise Exports in 1999 Expanded by 8.5%," Press Release/175, 6 April 2000, p. 19; Bernard M. Hoekman and Michel M. Kostecki, *The Political Economy of the World Trading System: The WTO and Beyond* (Oxford: Oxford University Press, 2nd edition, 2001), pp. 240-241.

29 William E. Whyman, "We Can't Go On Meeting Like This: Revitalizing the G-7 Process," *Washington Quarterly* 18-3 (Summer 1995), p. 142.

30 Putnam and Bayne, *Hanging Together*, p. 56. Putnam and Bayne refer to some exceptions where trade ministries have played a greater role.

31 Nicholas Bayne, *Hanging In There: The G7 and G8 Summit in Maturity and Renewal* (Aldershot: Ashgate, 2000), pp. 210-211.

32 Putnam and Bayne, *Hanging Together*, p. 165.

33   Clyde H. Farnsworth, "U.S., Japan, Europe Set Special Forum on Trade Tensions," *New York Times*, 12 August 1981, pp. A1 and D13; Bayne, *Hanging In There*, pp. 10-11; Gilbert R. Winham, *International Trade and the Tokyo Round Negotiation* (Princeton, NJ: Princeton University Press, 1986), p. 207.

34   Stephen Clarkson, *Canada and the Reagan Challenge: Crisis and Adjustment, 1981-85* (Toronto: James Lorimer & Co., 1985), p. 4.

35   Nicholas Bayne, "The G7 and Multilateral Trade Liberalisation: Past Performance, Future Challenges," in John J. Kirton and George M. von Furstenberg, eds., *New Directions in Global Economic Governance: Managing Globalisation in the Twenty-first Century* (Aldershot: Ashgate, 2001), p. 186.

36   On the trilateral meeting at the 1981 Ottawa Summit see Farnsworth, "U.S., Japan, Europe Set Special Forum on Trade Tensions," pp. A1 and D13.

37   Press conference with the Quad Ministers, St. John's, Newfoundland, 13 October 1990, p. 6.

38   Canada Department of External Affairs, "Minister Kelleher to Hold International Trade Talks in Canada," *Communiqué* no. 78, 10 June 1985; Jackie Hoffman, "Trade Talks 'of Substance' Set for Remote Fishing Lodge," *The Sault Star*, 26 February 1985.

39   Quadrilateral Senior Officials' Meeting, "Draft Annotated Program," Ottawa, Ontario, 30-31 March 1995, p. 1.

40   Minister Yamanaka's Opening Statement at Quadrilateral Meeting in Tokyo, Japan, 11 February 1983.

41   Final Press Statement by Vice President Wilhelm Haferkamp, Quadrilateral Meeting, Erbach, Germany, 28-30 June 1984.

42   Notes for a Press Statement by the Honourable James F. Kelleher, Canadian Minister for International Trade, 14 July 1985.

43   Final Press Statement by Vice President Wilhelm Haferkamp, Quadrilateral Meeting, Erbach, Germany, 28-30 June 1984.

44   Brian Milner, "Japan-U.S. Frictions a Likely Undercurrent at Quadrilateral Talks," *Globe and Mail*, 13 January 1986.

45   Bill Sing, "U.S., 3 Major Trading Partners Seek New Talks to Cut Barriers," *Los Angeles Times*, 19 January 1986; Bill Sing, "Putting the Bite Back into GATT Proving Difficult," *Los Angeles Times*, 20 January 1986.

46   Preeg, *Traders in a Brave New World*, p. 30.

47   Meeting of the OECD Council at Ministerial Level, *Communiqué*, April 1985, paragraph 11.

48   "The Bonn Economic Declaration: Towards Sustained Growth and Higher Employment," 4 May 1985, paragraph 10.

49   Paemen and Bensch, *From GATT to the WTO*, p. 83.

50   "Convention on the Organisation for Economic Co-operation and Development," Article 2.d.

51   William J. Drake and Kalypso Nicolaïdis, "Ideas, Interests and Institutionalization: 'Trade in Services' and the Uruguay Round," *International Organization* 46-1 (Winter 1992), p. 41.

52   Drake and Nicolaïdis, "Ideas, Interests and Institutionalization," p. 44.

53   Drake and Nicolaïdis, "Ideas, Interests and Institutionalization," pp. 41-53.

54   Peter M. Haas, "Introduction: Epistemic Communities and International Policy Coordination," *International Organization* 46-1 (Winter 1992), p. 3.

55   Organisation for Economic Co-operation and Development, *Policy Perspectives for International Trade and Economic Relations*, Report by the High Level Group on Trade and Related Problems to the Secretary-General of OECD (Paris: OECD, 1972, p. 77.

56   OECD, *Policy Perspectives for International Trade and Economic Relations*, p. 79.

57   OECD, *Policy Perspectives for International Trade and Economic Relations*, p. 79.

58   Brian Griffiths, *Invisible Barriers to Invisible Trade* (London: Macmillan, for the Trade Policy Research Centre, 1975), p. 109. See also Frank McFadzean, Chairman, *Towards an Open World Economy*, Report by an Advisory Group (London: Macmillan, for the Trade Policy Research Centre, 1972), pp. 21-24.

59   Geza Feketekuty, *International Trade in Services: An Overview and Blueprint for Negotiations* (Cambridge: Ballinger, 1988), pp. 299-309; Michael Cohen and Thomas Morante, "Elimination of Nontariff Barriers to Trade in Services: Recommmendation for Future Negotiations," *Law and Policy in International Business* 13-2 (1981), p. 496; Hugh Corbett, "Prospect of Negotiations on Barriers to International Trade in Services," *Pacific Community* (April 1977), p. 454.

60   U.S. Trade Act of 1974, as amended (Public Law 93-618) in U.S. Senate and House Committees on Foreign Affairs and Foreign Relations, *Legislation on Foreign Relations Through 1989*, volume 3 (Washington: U.S. Government Printing Office, 1990).

61   Feketekuty, *International Trade in Services*, p. 303.

62   Ronald K. Shelp, "Trade in Services," *Foreign Policy* no. 65 (Winter 1986), p. 71.

63   Feketekuty, *International Trade in Services*, p. 27.

64   Paemen and Alexandra Bensch, *From GATT to the WTO*, p. 83.

65   Anders Ahnlid, "Comparing GATT and GATS: Regime Creation under and after Hegemony," *Review of International Political Economy* 3-1 (Spring 1996), p. 71.

66   United Nations Conference on Trade and Development, *Services and the Development Process*, Study by the UNCTAD Secretariat (New York: United Nations, 1985), pp. 48-49.

67   Drake and Nicolaïdis, "Ideas, Interests and Institutionalization," pp. 68-69.

68   Shelp, "Trade in Services," p. 72.

69   OECD, "Elements of a Conceptual Framework for Trade in Services," Paris, March 1987.

70   Ronald Kent Shelp, *Beyond Industrialization: Ascendancy of the Global Service Economy* (New York: Praeger, 1981), p. 174.

71   Commission on International Trade and Investment, *United States International Economic Policy in an Interdependent World*, Report submitted to the President, Washington, D.C., July 1971, p. 164.

72   Susan Strange, "The Persistent Myth of Lost Hegemony," *International Organization* 41-4 (Autumn 1987), pp. 559-63; Isabelle Grunberg, "Exploring the 'Myth' of Hegemonic Stability," *International Organization* 44-4 (Autumn 1990), pp. 437-439.

73   General Agreement on Tariffs and Trade, *Text of the General Agreement* (Geneva: GATT, 1986).

74   Theodore H. Cohn, "The Changing Role of the United States in the Global Agricultural Trade Regime," in William P. Avery, ed., *World Agriculture and the GATT* (Boulder: Lynne Rienner, 1993), pp. 20-22.

75   Charles Lipson, "The Transformation of Trade: The Sources and Effects of Regime Change," in Stephen D. Krasner, eds., *International Regimes* (Ithaca: Cornell University Press, 1983), pp. 258-62; Robert E. Hudec, *The GATT Legal System and World Trade Diplomacy* (New York: Praeger, 1975), p. 172.

76   Peter F. Cowhey and Edward Long, "Testing Theories of Regime Change: Hegemonic Decline or Surplus Capacity?," *International Organization* 37-2 (Spring 1983), p. 161.

77   John A. Schnittker, "Reflections on Trade and Agriculture," in *Essays in Honour of Thorkil Kristensen* (Paris: OECD, 1970), p. 264.

78   T.K. Warley, "Western Trade in Agricultural Products," in Andrew Shonfield, ed., *International Economic Relations of the Western World 1959-1971* (London: Oxford University Press, 1976), p. 387.

79   James P. Houck, "U.S. Agricultural Trade and the Tokyo Round," *Law and Policy in International Business* 12-1 (1980), p. 268.

80   Quoted in Warley, "Western Trade in Agricultural Products," pp. 289-290.

81   Winham, *International Trade and the Tokyo Round Negotiation*, pp. 156-67; T.K. Warley, "Agriculture in the GATT: A Historical Perspective," in *Agriculture in the Uruguay Round of GATT Negotiations: Implications for Canada's and Ontario's Agrifood Systems* (Guelph, Ont.: University of Guelph, Department of Agricultural Economics and Business, 1989), pp. 8-13.

82   Robert L. Paarlberg, *Fixing Farm Trade: Policy Options for the United States* (Cambridge: Ballinger, 1988), p. 6.

83   Timothy E. Josling, Fred H. Sanderson, and T.K. Warley, "The Future of International Agricultural Relations: Issues in the GATT Negotiations," in Fred H. Sanderson, ed., *Agricultural Protectionism in the Industrialized World* (Washington, D.C.: Resources for the Future, 1990), p. 440; David J. Blair, *Trade Negotiations in the OECD: Structures, Institutions and States* (London: Kegan Paul International, 1993), pp. 109-110; Robert Wolfe, *Farm Wars: The Political Economy of Agriculture and the International Trade Regime* (London: Macmillan, 1998), p. 112.

84   OECD, *Policy Perspectives for International Trade and Economic Relations*, p. 68.

85   OECD, *Policy Perspectives for International Trade and Economic Relations*, p. 67.

86   OECD, *Policy Perspectives for International Trade and Economic Relations*, p. 70.

87   Commentary by Mr. W.D. Eberle, in OECD, *Policy Perspectives for International Trade and Economic Relations*, p. 115.

88   Blair, *Trade Negotiations in the OECD*, p. 115.

89   Blair, *Trade Negotiations in the OECD*, p. 153.

90   Meeting of the OECD Council at Ministerial Level in June 1979 – *Communiqué*, paragraph 21.

91   Organisation for Economic Co-operation and Development, *Problems of Agricultural Trade* (Paris: OECD, 1982).

92   "Reforming World Agricultural Trade," A Policy Statement by Twenty-nine Professionals from Seventeen Countries (Washington, D.C.: Institute for International Economics, and Canada: Institute for Research on Public Policy, May 1988), pp. 5-6.

93   Meeting of the OECD Council at Ministerial Level in May 1982 – *Communiqué*, paragraph 33.

94   OECD, *Problems of Agricultural Trade*, p. 132.

95   Blair, *Trade Negotiations in the OECD*, pp. 120-21; Josling, Sanderson, and Warley, "The Future of International Agricultural Trade Relations," pp. 440-441; T.K. Warley, "Issues Facing Agriculture in the GATT Negotiations," *Canadian Journal of Agricultural Economics* 35 (1987), pp. 516-518.

96   Heidi Ullrich, "The Impact of Policy Networks in the GATT Uruguay Round: The Case of the US-EC Agricultural Negotiations," unpublished Ph.D. thesis, London School of Economics, London, 2002, pp. 252-254.

97   Croome, *Reshaping the World Trading System*, p. 110.

98 Croome, *Reshaping the World Trading System*, pp. 110-111.
99 "The Bonn Economic Declaration: Towards Sustained Growth and Higher Employment," 4 May 1985, paragraph 10. See also Wolfe, *Farm Wars*, pp. 79-80.
100 Stefan Tangermann, T.E. Josling and Scott Pearson, "Multilateral Negotiations on Farm-Support Levels," *World Economy* 10-3 (September 1987), p. 279.
101 Miles Kahler and John Odell, "Developing Country Coalition-Building and International Trade Negotiations," in John Whalley, ed., *Developing Countries and the Global Trading System, vol. 1*: Thematic Studies from a Ford Foundation Project (Ann Arbor: University of Michigan Press, 1989), p. 149.
102 Paemen and Bensch, *From GATT to the WTO*, p. 20.
103 Kathryn C. Lavelle, "Ideas within a Context of Power: The African Group in an Evolving UNCTAD," *Journal of Modern African Studies* 39-1 (2001), p. 38.
104 Gwyneth Williams, *Third-World Political Organizations* (London: Macmillan, 2nd edition, 1987), pp. 44-49; Lavelle, "Ideas within a Context of Power," pp. 37-40.
105 Paemen and Bensch, *From GATT to the WTO*, p. 42.
106 Punta del Este Ministerial Declaration, adopted 20 September 1986, Part II and Part I.D.
107 Gilbert R. Winham, "The Prenegotiation Phase of the Uruguay Round," *International Journal* 45-2 (Spring 1989), p. 290. See also T.N. Srinivasan, *Developing Countries and the Multilateral Trading System: From the GATT to the Uruguay Round and the Future* (Boulder: Westview, 2000), pp. 28-30; John Whalley, "Recent Trade Liberalisation in the Developing World: What is Behind it and Where is it Headed?," in David Greenaway, Robert C. Hine, Anthony P. O'Brien, and Robert J. Thornton, eds., *Global Protectionism* (London: Macmillan, 1991), pp. 225-53; Anne O. Krueger, *Trade Policies and Developing Nations* (Washington, D.C.: Brookings Institution, 1995), pp. 48-50.
108 Hoekman and Kostecki, *The Political Economy of the World Trading System*, Annex 1, pp. 487-488.
109 John W. Sewell and I.William Zartman, "Global Negotiations: Path to the Future or Dead-End Street?," in Jagdish N. Bhagwati and John Gerard Ruggie, eds., *Power, Passions and Purpose: Prospects for North-South Negotiations* (Cambridge: MIT Press, 1984), p. 115.
110 Croome, *Reshaping the World Trading System*, p. 14.
111 Paemen and Bensch, p. 91.
112 Paemen and Bensch, p. 95.
113 Ullrich, "The Impact of Policy Networks in the GATT Uruguay Round," pp. 252-254.

6 From Punta del Este to the Brussels Ministerial: 1986 to 1990

The GATT Uruguay Round was originally supposed to be completed at the Brussels ministerial in December 1990, but persistent delays and divisions on key issues such as agriculture prevented the conclusion of the round as planned. This chapter examines the role of the G7, the Quad, and the OECD from the 1986 Punta del Este ministerial launching the Uruguay Round to the 1990 Brussels ministerial. The most significant change in the global trade regime pyramid during the first half of the Uruguay Round was some blurring of divisions between the North and the South. Although countries within the South (and within the North) have always had divergent interests on various issues, these differences became far more evident in the Uruguay Round as developing countries joined with developed countries in a number of coalition groups. For example, the Cairns Group of so-called "fair trading nations" in agriculture is discussed in this chapter and in Chapter 7. The Cairns Group is a coalition of middle and small power agricultural exporters, that some observers have described as a "third force" along with the United States and the EC in the GATT Uruguay Round agricultural negotiations.[1]

One should not overestimate the importance of the new alliances between developed and developing countries, because the G7, the Quad, and the OECD representing the North continued to remain near the top of the global trade regime pyramid and the United States and the EC continued to be the most important traders. Developing countries also were reluctant to identify themselves too closely with coalitions with developed countries, because the South continued to seek some special and differential treatment. Nevertheless, North-South coalition groups at the Uruguay Round marked the beginning of the South's greater involvement in GATT multilateral trade negotiations. Although a degree of consensus in the G7 and the Quad would continue to be *necessary*, it would no longer be *sufficient* for trade agreements to be concluded.[2] This change was beginning to become apparent as dissatisfied developing countries effectively slowed the Uruguay Round negotiations at ministerials in Montreal and Brussels (see discussion below).

Although the United States and the EC remained near the top of the global trade regime pyramid, they both showed a lack of leadership in the early stages of the Uruguay Round, and there were major differences between them – particularly on agriculture. The lack of effective U.S. and EC leadership during this period was a major factor contributing to the prolongation of the Uruguay Round. U.S. initiative and tenacity was primarily responsible for the launching of the Uruguay Round, and for the round's broad scope and forward-looking agenda. Nevertheless, in the early stages of the round the United States demonstrated less willingness and ability to lead in two major respects. First, the United States was less committed to nondiscrimination in trade, as Presidents Ronald Reagan and George Bush showed an interest in concluding regional free trade agreements in the Western hemisphere. Second, the United States resorted more often to unilateral actions outside the GATT such as threats of retaliation against alleged unfair trade actions, Section 301 cases, and increased demands for specific reciprocity (especially with Japan).

Despite the U.S. shortcomings, alternatives to U.S. leadership were not readily apparent because the EC and Japan had their own limitations. Proposals of the European Commission must be approved by the Council of Ministers, and the Commission normally cannot act unless the majority of member states support it. Thus, proposals designed to reflect the collective Community interest sometimes in effect become the "lowest common denominator." As we discuss in this chapter, the EC was unable to make specific offers in agriculture in the early stages of the Uruguay Round, and this put the Community on the defensive and angered other agricultural exporting countries. The EC was also preoccupied with deepening and broadening the integration process, which raised doubts about the degree of its commitment to the GATT. Although Japan's economic status had increased greatly in the 1980s, it was not prepared to assume a leadership role in trade, partly for cultural reasons. Furthermore, interministerial decision-making in Japan discouraged bold initiatives, and Japan was consistently on the defensive because of charges by the United States, the EC, and others that it was following mercantilist trade policies.[3]

In view of the persistent problems with agriculture in the Uruguay Round, a new informal institution called the *Quint* was established in 1989. The Quint includes the agricultural ministers of the four Quad members plus the agricultural minister from Australia. During the Uruguay Round the Quint met informally to discuss agricultural issues. Although no official negotiations occurred at these meetings, they provided a useful forum for presenting and developing new ideas. The Quint agricultural ministers, with officials, have continued to meet about once a year since the end of the Uruguay Round. Unlike the Quad, there has been no separate track of Quint officials meetings.[4] Despite the formation of the Quint, a lack of leadership from the United States, the EC, and Japan inevitably had a negative effect on the ability of the informal institutions – the G7, the Quad, and the Quint – to further the Uruguay Round negotiations in the 1986 to 1990 period. Thus, the Quad meetings "had been more prominent during the preparatory period leading up to Punta and would become most intense and productive only later, after the Brussels meeting."[5] As discussed, the OECD introduced new ideas and issues to the GATT, and conducted studies to further the GATT negotiations. However, like the G7, the Quad, and the Quint, the OECD could not bring about progress in the multilateral negotiations without sufficient leadership and commitment from the major traders. In sum, the early stages of the GATT Uruguay Round demonstrated that leadership by the major traders and developed country institutions near the top of the global trade regime pyramid is essential if global trade negotiations are to be successful.

Developments in the GATT: 1986 to 1990

On 14 September 1986, ministers from 96 countries began a week-long meeting at Punta del Este, Uruguay, which resulted in the launching of the GATT Uruguay Round. Progress in reaching a consensus before the Punta del Este ministerial was extremely slow, because there were major divisions among the participants. Two groups dominated the preparatory process: a Group of Nine (G9) middle-sized and smaller developed countries, including Australia, Canada, New Zealand, and the members of the European Free Trade Association (EFTA); and a Group of Ten (G10) developing countries headed by Brazil and India.[6] The G9 was fully committed to another round of GATT negotiations, and was alarmed by the polarisation that threatened to block a new round. The G10 by contrast had more negative views about a new GATT round, and was mainly concerned that the developed countries fulfill their earlier commitments to the developing countries. Although the United States, the EC, and Japan supported many of the G9's objectives, they adopted a low profile and did not openly associate themselves with either of these groups.[7]

Most developing countries were in the difficult position of choosing sides, and many of them were initially inclined to support the G10 bloc of developing countries. However, the G10 made the mistake of producing a draft text (which was mainly a Brazilian text) that was too oppositional for many of the other developing countries. The draft text not only rejected the idea of including new issues such as services, intellectual property, and investment in the negotiations, but also questioned whether a new round of GATT negotiations should even be held. The extreme position of the G10 "struck fear into a whole category of countries – all those who thought they had something to gain from the Uruguay Round."[8] As a result, a group of moderate developing countries began to confer with the G9, and 48 developed and developing countries eventually supported the G9 position. The new Group of 48 (G48) or "café au lait" group, chaired by Colombia and Switzerland, submitted the main draft ministerial text to the Punta del Este meeting, which called for an ambitious agenda to liberalise trade and broaden the GATT's mandate. Although the G10 argued that the North should fulfill previous commitments made to the South before negotiating new commitments, the G48's views prevailed and the Punta del Este meeting launched the most ambitious round ever to strengthen the global trade regime. The agenda included new areas favoured by the developed countries such as services, intellectual property, and investment; and areas of importance to developing countries such as textiles and clothing, and tropical and natural resource-based products.[9]

The role played by the G48 was an early indication that North-South coalitions would be far more important in the Uruguay Round than in previous GATT negotiations. The competing draft texts submitted to the Punta del Este ministerial were also an indication of the complexities and divisiveness that would mark the ambitious Uruguay Round.[10] At the time of the Punta del Este meeting, the ministers agreed that there should be a ministerial mid-term review conference half way through the Uruguay Round in 1988, and that the negotiations should conclude in 1990. However, the only negotiations that occurred during the first six months after Punta del Este were disputes over organisational issues. Although serious Uruguay Round negotiations did not begin until 1988, a mid-term ministerial review meeting of the Trade Negotiations Committee was nevertheless set for December, 1988 in Montreal. The hope was that this mid-term target would provide an incentive to accelerate the negotiations, offer ministers an opportunity to assess the Uruguay Round's progress, and provide a venue for implementing any early results (called an "early harvest") of the negotiations. Nevertheless, only six of the fifteen negotiating groups provided clear texts for approval in Montreal. Most texts simply demonstrated a diversity of interests, and the intention of participants to continue the negotiations. Particularly sensitive issues at Montreal included trade-related intellectual property rights, safeguards, textiles, and agriculture. Of these issues, the most contentious was agriculture.

The United States and the EC were the main protagonists in the agricultural trade disputes at Montreal. As discussed, the "Cairns Group" – which first met in Cairns, Australia in August 1986 – also had a significant role in the Uruguay Round agricultural negotiations. A major goal of the Cairns Group was to put an end to the U.S.-EC agricultural export subsidy "war," which was lowering world grain prices and threatening the revenues of smaller country agricultural exporters. Unlike the G7, the Quad, the OECD and the G77, which separate the North from the South, the founding members of the Cairns Group included fourteen developed and developing countries (and also one Eastern European country): Argentina, Australia, Brazil, Canada, Chile, Colombia, Fiji, Hungary, Indonesia, Malaysia, New Zealand, the Philippines, Thailand, and Uruguay. After the Uruguay Round, the Cairns Group continued as a coalition actively trying to exert influence on agricultural trade policy, and today it has eighteen member countries. (The Cairns Group and other North-South coalition groups are discussed later in this chapter.)

As discussed in Chapters 3 and 4, the United States had pressured the EC to decrease protectionism under its Common Agricultural Policy in the GATT Kennedy and Tokyo Rounds, but in the end the United States had settled for less in agriculture because of its desire to reach an agreement in other areas.[11] Agriculture again became a major issue in the Uruguay Round, with the United States issuing an ideologically-rigid "zero option" proposal to eliminate all agricultural subsidies that distort production or trade within ten years. The EC rejected the zero option proposal and was only willing to discuss limited, short-term measures. However, the United States, under pressure from various farm lobbies, continued to demand the zero-option at the Uruguay Round's Montreal ministerial midterm review. The Cairns Group sought a more realistic "early harvest" compromise solution that would produce some partial reforms, but the United States and the EC would not accept its plan.[12]

Although the United States was more adamant than it had been in earlier GATT rounds that agriculture be included, it was willing to join the EC in approving the results achieved in other areas at the Montreal midterm review, and in having their negotiators resume work on agriculture afterwards. However, eleven Latin American countries, led by Argentina and the other four Latin American Cairns Group members, threatened to bloc progress in 11 of the 15 areas of negotiation in the Uruguay Round if there was no progress in agriculture. This action served as a warning that the United States and the EC could no longer shape agricultural issues in the GATT to the same extent as they had in earlier years. Indeed, the Latin American walkout forced the GATT director-general to suspend the midterm review until an agreement was reached that would enable the agricultural negotiations to proceed. In April 1989 the Trade Negotiations Committee finally reached an agreement based on compromises by both the United States and the EC, and it was possible to resume the round with agriculture still a principle part of the negotiations.

Despite this agreement, the divisions on agriculture continued. The December 1990 Brussels ministerial was supposed to complete the Uruguay Round, but the EC remained intransigent on agriculture and there was a replay of the events in Montreal. Two Latin American members of the Cairns Group – Argentina and Brazil – refused to negotiate further, and the Brussels ministerial was suspended. Meetings did not resume until February 1991, when the EC finally agreed to make concessions on agriculture.[13] It was evident that the Uruguay Round negotiations were going to extend far beyond the initial deadline of 1990, and the planned completion date of the round had to be re-scheduled on several occasions. Thus, the Uruguay Round was far longer than any previous round of GATT negotiations. As a summary of important dates shows below, the Uruguay Round was a lengthy and tortuous process that was not completed until April 1994:

- *September 1986*: Punta del Este GATT ministerial launches the Uruguay Round with a four-year deadline for completion.
- *December 1988*: Montreal GATT ministerial midterm review produces some results, but continuing U.S.-EC differences over agriculture pose a major problem.
- *December 1990*: Brussels GATT ministerial fails to complete the Uruguay Round as planned, mainly because of the U.S.-EC deadlock over agriculture.
- *December 1991*: GATT director-general Arthur Dunkel produces a draft final act.
- *November 1992*: United States and EC reach the Blair House Accord, breaking the deadlock over agriculture.
- *December 1993*: Final Uruguay Round agreement reached in Geneva.
- *April 1994*: Ministers sign the final Uruguay Round agreement at Marrakesh, Morocco.

This chapter examines the role of the G7, the Quad, the OECD, and developing countries during the first four years of the Uruguay Round, from the Punta del Este GATT ministerial in September 1986 to the Brussels GATT ministerial in December 1990. The section on the developing countries discusses the important new role of North-South coalition groups in the Uruguay Round.

The Group of Seven

In view of their wide range of responsibilities, the G7 heads of government and state of course did not limit themselves to discussions of trade-related issues such as the GATT Uruguay Round. In the 1986 to 1990 period, the G7 addressed many other economic issues. For example, G7 summits discussed the issue of monetary policy coordination related to the Plaza and Louvre Agreements in 1985 and 1987, the summit leaders discussed structural measures to improve economic performance, and the 1988 Toronto summit agreed on a strategy of debt relief for low-income developing countries. The summits from 1986 to 1990 also had a full agenda to deal with on security issues. For example, the 1986 Tokyo II summit approved a declaration on terrorism, the 1987 Venice II summit leaders had a debate on political developments in the Soviet Union, the 1989 Paris summit took key decisions on helping Poland and Hungary, and the 1990 Houston summit encouraged the development of market economies in Central and Eastern Europe with the breakup of the Soviet bloc. Finally, the G7 summits dealt with a number of "newer" issues. Examples include the discussion of environmental issues at the 1989 Paris summit, and the discussion of illegal drug trafficking and addiction at the 1989 to 1991 summits.[14]

Despite the preoccupation of the summits with a wide range of economic and non-economic issues, the G7 leaders discussed trade at every summit from 1986 to 1990, and devoted considerable attention to the progress of the GATT Uruguay Round. Chapter 5 outlined the lengthy process of building a consensus in the G7 for setting a date for the next round. At the 4-6 May 1986 summit in Tokyo, the G7 members finally expressed their full commitment to launching the Uruguay Round at the upcoming Punta del Este meeting. Although the G7 members generally agreed that the Uruguay Round should deal with trade in services, intellectual property rights, and foreign investment, consensus on the agricultural trade issue was far more elusive. As a member of the Cairns Group, Canada argued that the U.S.-EC agricultural export subsidy war posed a serious threat to the global trade regime. Thus, Canada insisted that agriculture be included on the agenda of the Tokyo G7 summit, and the United States supported the Canadian position. The United States and Canada were able to overcome the European Commission's opposition to discussing agricultural trade subsidies at the summit, because two G7 European countries – Britain and West Germany – did not support the Commission's position on this issue.[15] Thus, the 1986 Tokyo II summit marked the first time a G7 summit had a spirited discussion of the agricultural trade issue, and mentioned agriculture in its communiqué. The 6 May 1986 Tokyo II summit declaration stated:

> We all recognise the importance of agriculture to the well-being of rural communities, but we are agreed that, when there are surpluses, action is needed to redirect policies and adjust structure of agricultural production in the light of world demand. We recognise the importance of understanding these issues and express our determination to give full support to the work of the OECD in this field.[16]

The leaders at the 8-10 June 1987 Venice II summit expressed concerns about rising protectionist pressures, and emphasised the positive role that the Uruguay Round could play in "achieving increased liberalisation of trade for the benefit of all countries."[17] Although they did not rule out the possibility that some agreements could be implemented at an earlier stage (an "early harvest"), the G7 leaders agreed that the outcome of the Uruguay Round should be treated as a "single undertaking"; i.e., that all countries must accept all parts of a final Uruguay Round agreement. The G7 supported the single undertaking idea to avoid a situation like the GATT Tokyo Round, where most developing countries chose not to sign the non-tariff barrier codes. As was the case with the 1986 Tokyo II summit, the Venice II summit also explicitly addressed the issue of agriculture. The G7 leaders endorsed the work of the OECD on agricultural trade, and also supported the May 1987 OECD ministerial communiqué which emphasised the need "to allow market signals to influence the orientation of agricultural production, by way of a progressive and concerted reduction of agricultural support."[18] Despite this agreement on the general issue of agricultural trade liberalisation, G7 members continued to have widely divergent positions on the specific commitments they were willing to make in agriculture.

Trade regionalism in Europe and North America loomed as a major issue at the 19-21 June 1988 G7 summit in Toronto. Thus, the non-European summit leaders called on the European Commission to provide assurances that the planned 1992 European internal market program would not become a "Fortress Europe," and Canada's Prime Minister Brian Mulroney who hosted the summit sought the G7's approval for the Canada-U.S. Free Trade Agreement (CUSFTA) which was still under consideration. Although the 1988 summit declaration welcomed the CUSFTA and the progress toward Europe 1992, it indicated that "these developments, together with other moves towards regional cooperation in which our countries are involved, should support the open, multilateral trading system and catalyse the liberalising impact of the Uruguay Round."[19] In regard to agriculture, the European G7 leaders felt that the EC had already made significant agricultural concessions with the approval of the "Delors package" of reforms in February 1988, and they were therefore not prepared to commit to further agricultural reform at the Toronto summit.[20] However, many countries considered the EC moves toward agricultural reform to be insufficient, and there were ominous signals regarding the conflict over agriculture at the Uruguay Round. Thus, the 1988 Toronto summit communiqué stated that "although significant progress was made in 1987 in tabling of major proposals, it is necessary to ensure that the Mid-Term Review in Montreal in December 1988 adds impetus to the negotiations" in agriculture.[21] Despite this summit declaration, the Montreal mid-term review as discussed was suspended in disarray because of the ongoing U.S.-EC conflict over agriculture.

The G7 leaders avoided conflict over trade imbalances, agriculture, and other trade-related issues at the 14-16 July 1989 G7 summit in Paris. As was the case with the 1988 Toronto summit, the Paris summit endorsed the CUSFTA and the EC's planned single market program, but cautioned that all such regional initiatives "should be trade-creating and complementary to the multilateral liberalization process."[22] Although the summit leaders discussed the Third World debt crisis in only general terms, they pledged to "help developing countries by opening the world trading system and by supporting their structural adjustment."[23] Finally, the G7 leaders warned against protectionism, and expressed their "full commitment to making further substantive progress in the Uruguay Round in order to complete it by the end of 1990."[24]

Beginning in 1990, many groups were looking to the G7 to give the necessary political impetus to the successful conclusion of the Uruguay Round. For example, an Eminent Persons Group composed of business and government officials from 12 countries called on the 9-11 July 1990 G7 summiteers in Houston, Texas to give their negotiators the "broad mandate required for a successful conclusion to the Uruguay Round";[25] and the International Chamber of Commerce representing trade associations and companies in 110 countries suggested that the G7 leaders convey firm instructions to their negotiators to make the necessary decisions for completion of the round.[26] The G7 leaders at Houston emphasised their "determination to take the difficult decisions necessary to achieve far-reaching, substantial results in all areas of the Uruguay Round" by the end of the year.[27] However, the Houston declaration also warned that an agreement on a framework for the agricultural negotiations "by the time of the July meeting of the Trade Negotiations Committee is critical to the successful completion of the Uruguay Round as a whole."[28] In efforts to complete the round, the leaders at the Houston summit agreed on a formula for conducting the agriculture negotiations. However, the formula proved to be too vague and ambiguous, and continued differences over agriculture forced an extension of the Uruguay Round negotiations into 1991.[29]

In summary, the G7 summit leaders made a serious attempt to pressure for completion of the GATT Uruguay Round by the end of 1990. However, the G7 as always had a number of other preoccupations ranging from monetary policy coordination to debt relief, terrorism, and political developments in the Soviet bloc that limited the amount of time it could devote to trade issues. The G7's performance on trade policy issues during the 1986 to 1990 period also demonstrated its limitations in exerting influence in the midst of multilateral trade negotiations. The G7's impact is normally greatest when it can muster the political will to launch a negotiation, help set the agenda for negotiations, and bring about the conclusion of a negotiating round. In the 1986 to 1990 period, however, the Uruguay Round negotiations were in the technical, policy-making phase. The G7 had special problems in exerting influence at this stage, because "the gap between the high-level strategic exchanges at the summit and the complex, detailed and technical discussions in Geneva often proved too wide to bridge."[30] Thus, it is not surprising that G7 declarations at the 1988 Toronto summit and the 1990 Houston summit were not effective in averting major conflicts at the Montreal mid-term review and the Brussels ministerial. Although the 1978 G7 Bonn I summit had provided an important impetus to the successful completion of the GATT Tokyo Round, the Uruguay Round had many more participants and a much wider range of complex issues to negotiate. Thus, it would be several more years before the G7 could exert influence in completing the Uruguay Round.

The Quadrilateral Group

The Quad of course devoted far more attention than the G7 to the GATT Uruguay Round and other trade issues during the 1986 to 1990 period. Thus, the following discussion of the Quad is divided into two periods related to the important GATT ministerials: from Punta del Este to the Montreal mid-term review, and from the Montreal mid-term review to the Brussels ministerial.

From Punta del Este to the Montreal Mid-Term Review

The first Quad meeting after the launching of the Uruguay Round at Punta del Este was the thirteenth Quad ministerial, held in Kashikojima, Japan on 24-26 April 1987. The meeting was marked by tensions over trade and current account imbalances, incompatible macroeconomic policies among the major trading nations, and allegations that Japan maintained its large trade surpluses through complex and non-transparent trade barriers. Although the thirteenth Quad resulted in few tangible accomplishments, it was somewhat successful in reducing tensions and building a resolve to take actions to liberalise global trade. Much of the discussion focused on the Uruguay Round, with emphasis on the importance of incorporating trade in services, trade related investment measures, and intellectual property rights into the GATT. Some Quad ministers also asserted that the Uruguay Round should address the deficiencies of the GATT as an international organisation. Of particular importance were proposals to have more regular ministerial participation in the GATT, and improved institutional arrangements for the GATT secretariat. One of the most contentious Uruguay Round issues at the thirteenth Quad was agricultural trade. Canada as the only Quad member of the Cairns Group argued strongly that agriculture should be given a higher priority, and be part of more rapid negotiations or an "early harvest" in the Uruguay Round. The United States supported the Canadian position, because it had been pressuring the EC and Japan to adopt less protectionist policies in agriculture. Although the EC agreed that agricultural trade had to be negotiated, it was not willing to support "early harvest" negotiations for agriculture in the Uruguay Round. Nevertheless, the April 1987 Quad resulted in a commitment to discuss the agricultural trade issue further at the OECD ministerial and G7 Venice II summit meetings in May and June, 1987.[31]

The fourteenth Quad ministerial was held on Quadra Island, British Columbia on 15-17 April 1988. The meeting was scheduled to exchange views on key negotiating issues before the OECD ministerial and Toronto Western Economic Summit meetings. The fourteenth Quad also provided a venue for discussing the Uruguay Round's progress in the lead-up to the December 1988 Montreal mid-term review. The ministers held detailed discussions on a range of subjects under negotiation, including market access, tropical products, agriculture, safeguards, subsidies and countervailing duties, functioning of the GATT system, dispute settlement, and the new issues of services, intellectual property, and investment.[32] Of particular concern was the slow pace of the Uruguay Round negotiations, and the contentiousness of some issues such as agricultural export subsidies. Indeed, the United States and the EC were engaged in an agricultural export subsidy war that was having a serious impact on other agricultural exporters.[33] Many of these exporters were Cairns Group members that did not have the financial resources to compete with the U.S. and EC subsidised sales. Thus, Canada as a member of the Cairns Group informed the other Quad members that there was an urgent need for early and substantial results on agriculture before the Montreal mid-term ministerial review. The United States also claimed to support an end to all agricultural subsidies by the year 2000, a position that the EC predictably would not accept. After the Quad meeting the U.S. Trade Representative Clayton Yeutter indicated that "we have a very major problem in agricultural trade."[34]

Although the EC was on the defensive at the Quadra Island Quad over agricultural export subsidies, it took an assertive position along with Canada and Japan in urging the United States to limit its use of countervailing duties (CVDs). The United States was unwilling to accept more discipline over the use of CVDs, and it preferred instead to pursue strong new discipline over subsidies – especially those relating to agriculture. Despite the divisions among ministers at the fourteenth Quad, there was progress in several key areas that improved prospects for positive results at the Montreal mid-term review. For example, the EC indicated that some of its agricultural policies were negotiable, and that it was committed to progressive and substantial reduction in agricultural support. The ministers decided to hold another Quad ministerial before the Montreal mid-term review scheduled for December 1988, because they viewed the Montreal meeting as a critical juncture in the Uruguay Round.

As a lead-in to the Montreal mid-term review, the fifteenth Quad ministerial in Brainerd, Minnesota on 22-24 June 1988 attempted to achieve a consensus on major Uruguay Round issues such as services, investment, dispute settlement, market access, safeguards, intellectual property, subsidies, the role of developing countries, and the functioning of the GATT system.[35] The Quad members had a shared interest in subjecting services, investment measures, and intellectual property to GATT discipline, and they agreed that it was necessary to convince developing countries that negotiated disciplines were in their interest. Furthermore, Quad ministers agreed on the need for a Trade Policy Review Mechanism to regularly review GATT members' trade policies, and on the need to increase ministerial involvement in the GATT through regular ministerial meetings. In addition, Quad ministers agreed on the importance of increasing the integration of developing countries into the global trade regime. The fifteenth Quad therefore helped to forge a consensus among the developed countries on a wide range of trade issues. Nevertheless, the Quad did not succeed in resolving the U.S.-EC dispute over agricultural export subsidies, and continuing differences between the United States and the EC resulted in suspension of the Montreal mid-term review.

From the Montreal Mid-Term Review to the Brussels Ministerial

The sixteenth and seventeenth Quad ministerials were held in the Hague, Netherlands on 2-4 June 1989, and in Hakonemachi, Japan on 12-14 November 1989. These Quads gave the trade ministers the opportunity to consider problems with the management of the GATT Uruguay Round after the Montreal mid-term review. A number of outstanding concerns were discussed, including the U.S. tendency to consider unilateral retaliation without GATT approval, the limited integration of developing countries in the global trade regime, and the impasse over agricultural trade and market access negotiations. Despite the problems with the Montreal mid-term review, the ministers at these Quad meetings continued their efforts to ensure that the Uruguay Round was entering its decisive final stage. The plan was that the round would be completed by the end of 1990 when the GATT would hold a concluding ministerial in Brussels.[36]

The eighteenth Quad ministerial in Napa, California on 2-4 May 1990 followed an informal ministerial on the Uruguay Round attended by 30 developed and developing countries in Mexico in April 1990 that conveyed "a sense of urgency and commitment to the successful final completion of the Uruguay Round."[37] The Trade Negotiations Committee had set July 1990 as the deadline to reach provisional agreements or negotiating texts in all areas of the negotiations. Thus, the eighteenth Quad explored the areas in which it was possible to reach provisional agreements, and the areas of major disagreement that would require further negotiations. Many developing countries felt they were being asked to make major concessions in services, investment, and intellectual property, and the Quad members devoted considerable attention "to what needs to be done to ensure that developing countries will see it in their interests to become full partners in the GATT trading system."[38]

The Quad ministers played a highly innovative role in 1989 and 1990 in discussing a possible change in status of GATT as an international organisation. An initiative to replace the informal GATT with a more formal World Trade Organization had begun in Quad discussions in late 1989. Although Canada and the EC supported the idea, the United States and Japan did not favour creating a powerful new international organisation for trade. In February 1990 the Italian trade minister voiced the first public support for a new organisation, and in April 1990 Canada's trade minister outlined a strategy that would lead to the establishment of a WTO to supersede the GATT. The broad substance of Canada's proposal was derived from a January 1990 study entitled *Restructuring of the GATT System* by the American legal scholar John Jackson.[39] The WTO proposed by Canada would be designed to "provide a new framework for the GATT," and to administer the new agreements in services, intellectual property, and investment.[40]

As in previous discussions, the strongest supporters of a new organisation to replace the GATT at the Napa Quad were the EC and Canada, and Canada wanted a reference to such an organisation to be included in the May 1990

OECD ministerial communiqué. Although Japan and the United States indicated they could support a new organisation in principle, they raised a number of pragmatic concerns. For example, the United States argued that it would be difficult to create a new trade organisation in the proposed timetable for the Uruguay Round, because discussion of a new organisation would take time away from substantive negotiations on critical issues such as agriculture. U.S. negotiators also believed that Congressional concerns over loss of sovereignty would be an issue in creation of a formal global trade organisation in the 1990s as it had been with the unsuccessful efforts to create the ITO in the 1940s and the OTC in the 1950s. If the U.S. Congress strongly opposed a proposal for a new global trade organisation, this could jeopardise U.S. support for the entire Uruguay Round. Finally, the United States was concerned that a more formal trade organisation would permanently establish one-nation, one-vote decision making. This voting system could lead to politicisation of the organisation when China and Russia became members.[41]

At the end of the Napa Quad, the USTR confirmed that "President Bush has made the successful completion of these talks by December of this year America's top trade priority," and the Quad ministers agreed that the upcoming May 1990 OECD ministerial and July 1990 G7 summit in Houston "should give a critical impetus" to the Uruguay Round negotiations.[42] The Quad ministers looked to these upcoming meetings as essential for dealing with issues that divided the developed countries, and for sending clear signals that the North was willing to address concerns of the South in key areas such as agriculture, textiles, resource products and safeguards.

The nineteenth Quad ministerial on 11-13 October 1990 in St. John's, Newfoundland was the last Quad before the Uruguay Round was scheduled to conclude at the GATT ministerial in Brussels. The host Canadian Trade Minister, John Crosbie, indicated that the Quad meeting was

> not designed to take decisions. That is the role for the established negotiating structure in Geneva under Arthur Dunkel, the director general of the GATT. However, it is our role and our responsibility to show leadership so that together with all our partners in the Geneva process we can bring the round to a successful conclusion within the agreed time frame.[43]

Despite Minister Crosbie's positive statement, there was by this time considerable alarm over the lack of progress in the GATT negotiations. Thus, the GATT director-general who does not normally participate in Quad sessions travelled to Newfoundland to address the ministers during the second day of the meeting. Arthur Dunkel viewed the Quad meeting as a key event in the final phase of the Uruguay Round, and hoped the ministers would leave the meeting with a clearer view of the outlines of the final agreement. He also cautioned the ministers that "the time is over when we blame each other."[44] Despite this warning, the United States, the EC, Japan, and Canada strongly criticised one another for failing to compromise on key negotiating issues. Athough Canada as the host country proposed to draft an agreement for each area of negotiation at the end of the Quad, this proposal was shelved due to EC objections and serious confrontation among the Quad members. Agriculture proved to be the most contentious subject, with the United States and the EC far apart on the issue of agricultural subsidies. The United States proposed that domestic and export subsidies to farmers be reduced by 75 and 90 percent, respectively, over the next ten years; but the EC was only willing to accept much smaller reductions. The United States and Canada also strongly criticised Japan for its unwillingness to open its market to rice imports.[45]

In response to the U.S. and Canadian criticisms, the EC Vice President Frans Andreissen complained that agriculture was receiving too much attention, and that the time devoted to other key issues such as market access, services, and intellectual property was insufficient. However, the USTR Carla Hills warned that "either the community of nations wants to rid itself of the very costly and destructive agricultural policies that we have put in place, or we will go out and war with one another over economics."[46] It was evident, therefore, that an Uruguay Round agreement would not be concluded without an agreement on agriculture. To dampen speculation about a possible delay in concluding the Uruguay Round, the Quad ministers pledged their resolve to complete the round by the December 1990 deadline. Questions nevertheless arose as to whether the trade talks were too ambitious and the divisions were too wide to bridge in the remaining time period. Thus, there were suggestions during the St. John's Quad that the Uruguay Round might be extended beyond 1990.[47] As discussed, the Brussels GATT ministerial did not conclude the Uruguay Round, and the round was eventually extended far beyond the initial proposed deadline.

The role of the Quad during the first phase of the Uruguay Round clearly demonstrated both its strengths and limitations. Despite the opportunity the Quad provided for the major traders to discuss issues in an informal and private setting, these Quad discussions did not result in successful GATT ministerials in Montreal and Brussels, and the Uruguay Round had to be extended. The Quad (like the G7) was unable to reach a consensus on agricultural trade, because the two main traders – the United States and the EC – remained far apart on this issue. The Quad also seemed to adhere to the proposed deadline for the Uruguay Round even after it had become unrealistic. For example, the ministers at the nineteenth Quad in October 1990 continued supporting the idea that the Uruguay Round could be completed at the December 1990 Brussels ministerial. Presumably the Quad sometimes adhered to unrealistic deadlines as a means of putting pressure on the negotiators. Although the Quad meetings did not result in a conclusion of the Uruguay Round by 1990, the ministers did engage in discussions to resolve their differences over a wide range of trade issues, and in this sense the Quads contributed to trade liberalisation. The Quad ministers also identified areas of the Uruguay Round in which they had common objectives such as services, intellectual property, and investment; and they agreed on the need for greater involvement of developing countries in the global trade regime. Furthermore, the Quad served as a venue in 1989 and 1990 period for innovative discussions on the need to establish a new global trade organisation. Although the Quad was initially split on this issue, with the EC and Canada more supportive of a new organisation than the United States and Japan, the eventual approval of the WTO in 1994 clearly owed something to the earlier Quad discussions of this issue.

Organisation for Economic Co-operation and Development

As in previous negotiations, the OECD Council meetings at ministerial level served as a forum for developed countries to pressure for the successful completion of the GATT Uruguay Round. The OECD ministerials are held shortly before the G7 summits, and the trade objectives outlined in the OECD and G7 communiqués are usually quite similar. For example, the May 1987 OECD ministerial reaffirmed that the outcome of the Uruguay Round negotiations "shall be treated as a single undertaking,"[48] and the May-June 1989 OECD ministerial reaffirmed the determination of the ministers "to press forward and complete the Uruguay Round negotiations in 1990."[49] As discussed in Chapter 5, the OECD's background work on agriculture and services was of considerable importance in the leadup to the Uruguay Round. This section provides a discussion of the OECD's involvement with agricultural and services trade after the Uruguay Round began in September 1986.

Trade in Agriculture

Despite the resistance to including agriculture and services in the Uruguay Round, the ministers at Punta del Este agreed that both sectoral areas would be part of the negotiations. Indeed, "next to the reform of world trade in agriculture, the creation of a multilateral framework of rules to govern the trade in services constituted the Uruguay Round's main raison d'etre."[50] The GATT negotiations on agriculture had two main objectives, because of the close linkage between domestic and international agricultural policies: to reshape the purposes and implementation of national agricultural policies, and to rewrite the rules regarding the conduct of agricultural trade. The OECD and GATT roles during the Uruguay Round were mutually reinforcing in this area, with the OECD providing analytical and political support for agreements that were ultimately forged in the GATT.[51]

Of critical importance to the agricultural negotiations was the final report of the OECD's Ministerial Trade Mandate study, *National Policies and Agricultural Trade*, that the OECD ministerial endorsed in May 1987.[52] As discussed in Chapter 5, the MTM study was initiated in 1982 and required over four years to complete. New Zealand first made the proposal for the MTM study, with strong support from the United States. The MTM study analysed the impact of all forms of agricultural assistance on production and trade protectionism, and examined a range of options for reducing assistance that contributed to protectionism. In addition to the main MTM study, a number of country studies were conducted to analyse and quantify the linkages between domestic agricultural policies and trade.

The OECD's MTM study was of considerable importance for several reasons. First, the study represented an acknowledgement at the political level that distortions in global agricultural trade result directly from national agricultural policies. Thus, the OECD study contributed to a consensus that trade-related domestic agricultural policies had to be subject to GATT regulation. Second, the study showed that all countries bore some responsibility for the interventions in national agricultural policy, and for the poor conditions in international agricultural markets. Third, the MTM study demonstrated that reducing agricultural protectionism would be beneficial for national and world income. Finally, the study showed that if all OECD countries reduced support and protection gradually and simultaneously, the resultant increases in market prices would alleviate adjustment pressures.[53]

One of the greatest obstacles to conducting agricultural trade negotiations was the lack of knowledge about the degree of agricultural protectionism and the effects of agricultural trade liberalisation. Relying on an agricultural epistemic community, the OECD's MTM study helped provide the GATT Uruguay Round with the "tools" of comparative measurement.[54] As discussed in Chapter 5, the MTM study began the process of estimating the level and composition of support to agriculture in the OECD member countries. As measures of comparison the OECD selected the concepts of producer subsidy equivalents and consumer subsidy equivalents. Australia had used the PSE and CSE indicators as early as 1965, and the Food and Agriculture Organization began to compute PSE and CSE figures for a small number of industrial states in the 1970s. However, the OECD's MTM study was much larger in scope. The PSE levels in the MTM study confirmed that agricultural protectionism was widespread among developed countries, and that the degree of protection had risen to unprecedented levels in the 1980s. After the OECD first made its PSE and CSE figures available in 1987, it then updated them annually and extended the study to include more countries. The PSE and CSE measures were later adapted to become the Aggregate Measurement of Support Indicator which provided the basis for the Uruguay Round agreement's discipline over domestic agricultural support policies. After systematic estimates of agricultural trade distortions across countries became available, it was possible to predict the effects of agricultural trade liberalisation with greater precision. Estimates by the OECD and others of the levels of agricultural protectionism, and of the benefits that would accrue from agricultural trade liberalisation, provided mechanisms and support for concluding an Uruguay Round agricultural agreement.[55]

As Robert Wolfe has noted, the "acceptance of new *ideas* about agricultural trade still had to be translated into concrete negotiating *objectives*," and the G7 summits, the OECD and Quad ministerials, and the GATT Committee on Agriculture served an important role in forging a political consensus on negotiating objectives in agriculture.[56] The May 1987 OECD ministerial played a central role in this regard, because it "agreed to a set of principles for the reform of agricultural policies and launched a process whereby progress towards the achievement of those principles would be monitored."[57] Thus, the USTR Clayton Yeutter described the agricultural portion of the 1987 OECD ministerial communiqué as "the most comprehensive statement on agricultural reform that a group of ministers has ever made."[58] The principles the OECD ministers endorsed for reforming agricultural policies included the following: First, they agreed to begin reform promptly with the long-term objective of permitting market signals to influence agricultural production, but they also recognised that food security and employment concerns had to be considered. Second, they recognised the need to lower guaranteed prices and other production incentives, and to impose quantitative production restrictions if necessary to prevent an increase in agricultural surpluses. Third, they sought to implement supply control measures in a manner that would minimise economic distortions and contribute to a better functioning of markets. Fourth, they agreed that direct income support was a better means of supporting farmers than farm price guarantees or other measures that were linked to production.[59] Finally, to increase the chances for success in the Uruguay Round, the ministers agreed that OECD governments should "refrain from actions which would worsen the negotiating climate." For example, governments should "avoid initiating actions which would result in stimulating production in surplus agricultural commodities and in isolating the domestic market further from international markets."[60]

It is important to note that the work of the GATT Committee on Trade in Agriculture (CTA) chaired by the Dutch trade official Aart de Zeeuw was complementary with the OECD's work in helping to define the negotiating objectives in agriculture in the 1986 to 1990 period. (On the role of de Zeeuw and the CTA before the launching of the Uruguay Round, see Chapter 5.) Most significantly, in June 1990 de Zeeuw put forward his own proposals for a framework agreement on agricultural reform in preparation for the December 1990 GATT ministerial in Brussels. De Zeeuw's framework agreement set out principles that would provide a basis for forming a consensus in every area of the agricultural trade negotiations. The July 1990 G7 summit in Houston "paid a rare tribute to the work of an unidentified civil servant [de Zeeuw]" by recommending that their negotiators use the de Zeeuw framework in coming to an agricultural agreement.[61] However, the OECD's background work, and the G7's endorsement of the de Zeeuw framework, were not enough to bridge the persistent U.S.-EC differences on agriculture at the December 1990 Brussels ministerial. Although the OECD and the GATT's CTA could introduce new ideas and propose negotiating objectives in agriculture, a final agreement on the issue would have to await political decisions by the United States and the EC at the highest political level.

Trade in Services

As discussed in Chapter 5, the OECD engaged in studies and prenegotiations of services trade in preparation for the GATT negotiations that would follow. Indeed, a High-Level Group appointed by the OECD Secretary-General released a report in 1972 (the Rey Report) that coined the term "trade in services" and suggested more explicitly than ever before that services trade could be compared with merchandise trade. In a 1981 book entitled *Beyond Industrialization*, Ronald Shelp argued that the OECD was the natural place to initiate discussions of services trade, because the developed countries had the most at stake in promoting trade in services. However, Shelp added that this is not to say that negotiations on services undertaken in the OECD necessarily must be ultimately limited to its membership. Instead, one can envision a process similar to the development of the GATT government procurement code. Laying the groundwork for that code originally began in the OECD, and it was transferred to GATT during the Tokyo Round. Something analogous could conceivably occur with at least some of the results of an OECD service exercise.[62]

True to Shelp's predictions, the services trade issue was transferred from the OECD to the GATT in the Uruguay Round just as the government procurement issue had been transferred from the OECD to the GATT during the Tokyo Round. The Punta del Este Declaration was divided into two sections, distinguishing between services trade negotiations on the one hand, and the rest of the negotiating agenda on the other. The developed countries had agreed to this separation to reassure developing countries that they would not be forced to open up their service sectors in exchange for receiving benefits on trade in goods. In practice this separation had little effect on the negotiations, because in the end there was a trading off among issues, including services. Furthermore, the Uruguay Round was a "single undertaking," in which progress in the goods and services negotiations had to adhere to similar negotiation phases and deadlines.[63]

After the Punta del Este ministerial, the OECD published a document entitled "Elements of a Conceptual Framework for Trade in Services" in March 1987.[64] The idea underlying this study was "that a relevant conceptual framework can contribute to strengthening international cooperation as well as the liberalisation and expansion of trade in services, just as a framework of concepts provided the basis for the trading system for goods."[65] Thus, the OECD study examined the basic concepts and principles that could provide the foundation for a trade regime for services. Some of the key principles the OECD study applied to services trade included market access, transparency, national treatment, and nondiscrimination. As was the case for the OECD's 1987 MTM study in agriculture, some of the concepts and ideas in the OECD's 1987 framework for services trade had an important influence on the course of the Uruguay Round. After the OECD Trade Committee reached a substantial consensus on the conceptual framework, they agreed to test the applicability of the framework to trade in individual service industries.[66]

In sum, the OECD background work on agriculture and services played a central role in inclusion of these areas in the GATT Uruguay Round, and in the course of negotiations. In both areas, the OECD relied on contributions from the epistemic communities. Of particular importance in services trade were the Rey Group's coining of the term "trade in services" in 1972, and the OECD's

1987 publication on the "Elements of a Conceptual Framework for Trade in Services." In agriculture, the OECD's 1987 MTM study and the 1987 OECD ministerial council contributed strongly to the "idea" that domestic agricultural policies had to be an integral part of the Uruguay Round agricultural trade negotiations. The MTM study also provided the negotiators with critical concepts and methods for measuring and comparing agricultural support in different countries, and for assessing the impact of agricultural trade liberalisation.

The Role of Developing Countries

The South adopted trade liberalisation strategies and became far more involved in the GATT Uruguay Round than in previous rounds because of the 1980s foreign debt crisis, and the failure of developing countries to gain the benefits they had expected from S&D treatment. The debt crisis was a major factor inducing developing countries to liberalise their trade policies, because it demonstrated that "decades of pursuing import substitution policies had failed to rejuvenate the economies of developing countries and put them on the path of sustainable growth and development."[67] As industries in these countries shifted to more export-oriented policies, the interest of developing countries in trade liberalisation increased. The conditions placed on IMF and World Bank structural adjustment loans provided a further inducement for developing country debtors to adopt orthodox liberal reforms such as deregulation, privatisation, and greater openness to trade and foreign investment.

A second factor explaining the LDC interest in the Uruguay Round related to the disappointment of developing countries with the benefits they had received from S&D treatment such as the GSP and the enabling clause. Because of this special treatment, the North viewed the developing countries as "free riders," and tended to marginalise them in trade negotiations. Ironically, the tariff preferences the South received through the GSP were eroding as tariffs on trade among the developed countries decreased with each round of GATT negotiations. In contrast to previous negotiations, developing countries were therefore more willing to engage in a reciprocal exchange of concessions and less inclined to demand S&D treatment. Thus, the South agreed to treat the Uruguay Round as a "single undertaking," in which they had to accept all of the agreements. The single undertaking was a marked contrast to the Tokyo Round's NTB codes, in which most developing countries did not participate.[68] The developing countries continued to receive S&D treatment in the Uruguay Round, but in contrast to previous rounds the single undertaking principle demonstrated that they were willing to accept "a dilution of special and differential treatment in exchange for better market access and strengthened rules."[69]

One indication of the changing Southern policies was the striking shift in the stance of UNCTAD. In contrast to the GATT Tokyo Round, "the UNCTAD secretariat supported the Uruguay Round negotiations from their inception" and attempted to carve out a role for itself in the negotiations.[70] For example, the UNCTAD secretariat maintained that it should be involved in the services trade negotiations because of its experience in dealing with insurance and shipping services. In adopting a more active role in the Uruguay Round, the UNCTAD secretariat was becoming less critical of the GATT and more supportive of the global trade regime. The change in UNCTAD stemmed not only from the shift of developing countries toward trade liberalisation, but also from the greater divergence of interests among developing countries. Divisions had always existed in the Third World, but they were more evident by the time of the Uruguay Round. For example, higher-income developing countries such as the East Asian NIEs and some OPEC countries had little in common with the poorest developing countries in sub-Saharan Africa and South Asia. Thus, "the Uruguay Round revealed a lack of purpose and an inability among developing countries to coalesce around common interests."[71]

Commentators on the Uruguay Round often discussed the position of "the Third World," but in most cases they were referring to the actions of Brazil and India and a few of their backers that did not give them consistent support. Thus, the G77 did not function as a bloc in the Uruguay Round, and a series of North-South coalitions were formed. A coalition in trade negotiations is any group of participants "who agree to act in concert to achieve a common end."[72] Some of the North-South coalitions in the Uruguay Round were informal in nature. For example, South Korea supported the EC and Japanese positions on agriculture, and sub-Saharan African countries sought to maintain their trade preferences as associate members of the EC against encroachments from Asia and Latin America. However, a number of more formal coalitions or alliances were also established. These coalitions were already evident at the 1986 Punta del Este ministerial meeting when a group of 48 developed and developing countries (the Swiss-Colombian or "café au lait" group) introduced the main draft negotiating text for the meeting. Another Uruguay Round coalition of some importance was the *De La Paix Group*, named after the Hôtel De La Paix in Geneva where it often met. The De La Paix Group was a coalition of small and middle-sized developed and developing countries that began to exert its influence early in the negotiations. Instead of focusing on a specific issue, the De La Paix Group had a general interest in a strong rules-based multilateral trade regime that would make a power-based system less justifiable. The De La Paix Group's efforts contributed to the launching of the Uruguay Round in 1986, and it played a role in negotiations on dispute settlement, antidumping, tariff and nontariff barriers, and the functioning of the GATT system.[73] As we discuss in Chapter 7, the De La Paix Group also pressured the major actors to successfully complete the Uruguay Round.

This section devotes attention to the most important of the North-South coalitions: the Cairns Group. As discussed, the Cairns Group is a coalition of agricultural exporters that first met in Cairns, Australia in August 1986. The Cairns Group added a powerful new voice to the Uruguay Round negotiations, ensuring that this time the GATT – and the EC, the United States, and Japan – would have to deal with agriculture. The founding members of the Cairns Group included 14 developed and developing countries (and also one Eastern European country): Argentina, Australia, Brazil, Canada, Chile, Colombia, Fiji, Hungary, Indonesia, Malaysia, New Zealand, the Philippines, Thailand, and Uruguay. The Cairns Group has continued as a coalition actively attempting to influence agricultural trade policy after the Uruguay Round, and today it has 18 members: Argentina, Australia, Bolivia, Brazil, Canada, Chile, Colombia, Costa Rica, Fiji, Guatemala, Indonesia, Malaysia, New Zealand, Paraguay, the Philippines, South Africa, Thailand, and Uruguay.

The Cairns Group is a heterogeneous collection of countries that has been able to function reasonably effectively because of the members' common position as middle power and small power agricultural exporters. Although the Cairns Group members had little influence individually, they were "collectively significant as producers of agricultural products, with more value added in agriculture than either the EC or the United States," and with more agricultural "exports than the EC and the United States combined."[74] The Cairns Group sought several major reforms, the two most important being to phase out agricultural export subsidies (and thus to end the U.S.-EC export subsidy war), and to decrease agricultural tariffs and convert all import quotas to tariffs which would be gradually reduced. The Cairns Group had some influence at Punta del Este in ensuring that agricultural trade would have a central place in the Uruguay Round negotiations. In the first half of the Uruguay Round from 1986 to 1990, the Cairns Group continued to ensure that agriculture would be a central part of the negotiating agenda, and it was also an important force for compromise between the United States and the EC.

As discussed, U.S. and EC intransigence at the Montreal mid-term review posed a major threat to the Uruguay Round. Whereas the United States insisted on a zero option proposal to eliminate all agricultural subsidies that distort production or trade within ten years, the EC rejected the zero option proposal and was only willing to discuss limited, short-term measures. As a result of this deadlock, 11 Latin American countries led by 5 members of the Cairns Group threatened to block progress in 11 of the 15 negotiating areas of the Uruguay Round, and the Montreal mid-term review had to be suspended. In taking this action, the Latin American Cairns Group members were signalling to the United States and the EC that they would not accept an Uruguay Round agreement without an agreement on agriculture. The Cairns Group also served as a force for compromise between the United States and the EC, which contributed to a softening of the positions of the two major actors. After the failure of the Montreal mid-term review, the Cairns Group submitted a proposal for progressive reductions in agricultural support that encouraged the United States to move away from its unrealistic zero option proposal. Despite its early role as a mediator between the United States and the EC, the Cairns Group had many common interests with the United States because they both had a comparative advantage in agriculture. Thus, as the U.S. position softened, it moved closer to the position of the Cairns Group. In response, the Cairns Groups shifted from its earlier role as a mediator to a position more supportive of the United States in the run up to the 1990 Brussels ministerial. At the Brussels ministerial, both the United States and the Cairns Group exerted pressure on the EC to accept an agreement to institute agricultural reform.[75]

Despite the Cairns Group's active role in the 1986 to 1990 period, divisions among the members detracted to some extent from the group's influence. For example, developing countries in the Cairns Group continued to be interested in S&D treatment, and they did not want to identify too closely with the developed country members of the group. The Cairns Group was also pressured by Third World food importers who feared that an end to agricultural export subsidies would increase their food import prices and have a negative effect on their balance of payments. Although a number of developing countries could suffer from an increase in agricultural prices, only five agricultural importers joined together in the Uruguay Round to formulate a common position on this issue: the W-74 group (named for the document number of their first submission), including Egypt, Jamaica, Mexico, Morocco, and Peru. One of these countries, Mexico, ultimately decided not to endorse the proposal. The W-74 group proposed that poorer developing countries should receive food aid or concessional food imports as compensation if the GATT Uruguay Round agreement resulted in a substantial increase in agricultural prices. Latin American members of the Cairns Group were concerned with maintaining some degree of G77 solidarity, and they assured the food importers that they would be consulted about the group's agricultural trade initiatives.[76] Even more serious than the North-South differences were the differences between Canada and other Cairns Group members. Although Canada strongly supported the Cairns Group objective of ending the U.S.-EC agricultural export subsidy war, Canada did not support the group's objective of "tariffication" or the conversion of all agricultural import quotas to tariffs. Canada had developed a supply management system with import quotas for dairy, eggs, and poultry products, and because Quebec was the largest dairy producer the Canadian government viewed this as a national unity issue.[77]

In sum, the Cairns Group had an important role in the 1986 to 1990 period in producing some compromise and in ensuring that agriculture would be a central part of the Uruguay Round. Nevertheless, an agreement on agriculture remained elusive at both the 1988 Montreal mid-term review and the 1990 Brussels ministerial. Divisions within the Cairns Group and persistent differences between the United States and the EC posed limits to the influence the Cairns Group could exert on the agricultural negotiations. As we discuss in Chapter 7, the Cairns Group was less influential after the Brussels ministerial, and the final stages of "the Uruguay Round proceeded at a pace only to the extent it was permitted by the U.S. and the EC negotiators."[78]

Conclusion

The ministers at the Punta del Este meeting launching the Uruguay Round in 1986 agreed to hold a ministerial mid-term review conference in 1988, and to conclude the negotiations in 1990. However, both the 1988 Montreal mid-term review and the 1990 Brussels ministerial ended in stalemate, and it was evident that the Uruguay Round would extend far longer. A major reason for the prolongation of the negotiations was the wide division between the United States and the EC on agriculture. Whereas the U.S. zero option proposal "was radical, that of the EC represented the opposite extreme," and the United States and the EC therefore did not provide the leadership needed in their positions at the top of the global trade regime pyramid.[79] The G7 leaders expressed strong support in the Toronto and Houston summit declarations for successful outcomes at the Montreal mid-term review and the Brussels ministerial. Nevertheless, the G7's ability to provide an impetus to the Uruguay Round during the 1986 to 1990 period was limited because it was preoccupied with a wide range of economic and political-security matters, it was removed from the detailed technical negotiations in Geneva, and it was confronted with a more complex array of actors and issues than was the case in the Tokyo Round.

The Quad performed some useful functions during the 1986 to 1990 period. The Quad ministers identified areas where they had common negotiating objectives such as services, intellectual property, and investment; agreed on actions to encourage greater involvement by developing countries in the Uruguay Round; had useful albeit inconclusive discussions regarding their differences over agriculture; and took initiatives such as discussing a proposal that a new global trade organisation should replace the GATT. The formation of the Quint in 1989 was designed to resolve the major differences on agricultural trade in an informal setting, and like the Quad it provided a useful forum for presenting and developing new ideas. However, as long as the two most important Quad and Quint members – the United States and the EC – were far apart on agriculture, the Quad and the Quint like the G7 had only limited influence in providing the impetus for the completion of the Uruguay Round.

The OECD's work on services and agricultural trade helped to ensure that these issues would be the subject of serious negotiation in the Uruguay Round. With the assistance of epistemic communities, the OECD contributed to the ideas that multilateral trade regulations for goods could be extended to services, and that domestic agricultural policies had to be an integral part of the Uruguay Round agricultural trade negotiations. The OECD also conducted background studies to develop a body of knowledge about the degree of agricultural protection and the effects of agricultural trade liberalisation, and to provide the Uruguay Round with the tools for comparative measurement. The OECD's work was complementary to the work of the Committee on Trade in Agriculture in preparing the GATT for the multilateral negotiations. Although the OECD could introduce new ideas, propose negotiating objectives, and provide the tools for negotiation, the U.S.-EC deadlock on agriculture in the 1986 to 1990 period demonstrated that a final agreement would have to await decisions at the highest political level.

As discussed, the more active involvement by developing countries and the formation of North-South coalitions distinguished the Uruguay Round from previous GATT negotiations. A combination of the foreign debt crisis, failed policies such as import substitution, and pressures from the IMF and World Bank accounted for the willingness of developing countries to liberalise their trade policies and form alliances with the developed countries. The developed and developing countries in these coalitions were middle and small powers that turned to collective action to achieve their objectives because of the limited influence they had individually. In this sense, the division between North and

South on the global trade regime pyramid became less well-defined. Whereas some of these coalitions such as the De La Paix group had more general objectives, the most important North-South coalition in the Uruguay Round was the Cairns Group which focused on a single issue. In previous negotiations in the Kennedy and Tokyo Rounds, the United States and the EC had agreed to defer the agricultural issue for future negotiations, but the U.S. position in the Uruguay Round was more militant than previously. The Cairns Group also would not permit the United States and the EC to delay dealing with the agriculture in the Uruguay Round. In addition to emphasising the importance of agriculture, the Cairns Group served as a mediator between the United States and the EC, which contributed to some softening of their extreme positions. After the United States moved closer to the Cairns Group's negotiating position, the Cairns Group was more supportive of U.S. pressure on the EC to liberalise its agricultural policies.

The Brussels ministerial was held over four years after the launching of the Uruguay Round, but there was still considerable uncertainty as to the outcome of the round. The G7, the Quad, and the OECD had helped to ensure that newer issues of interest to the developed countries such as services, intellectual property, and investment would be included in the negotiations. Although a number of developing countries were wary of including these newer areas, it was an older issue – agriculture – that presented the most difficulties. The deadlock over agriculture from 1986 to 1990 clearly demonstrated that a minimal degree of consensus between the United States and the EC at the top of the global trade regime pyramid was necessary if there was to be an Uruguay Round agreement. However, the position of Latin American Cairns Group members at the Montreal and Brussels ministerials also demonstrated that U.S.-EC agreement was no longer *sufficient* to ensure there would be an Uruguay Round agreement. Thus, the interdependent linkages between North and South on the global trade regime pyramid had increased.

Notes

1   Richard A. Higgott and Andrew Fenton Cooper, "Middle Power Leadership and Coalition Building: Australia, the Cairns Group, and the Uruguay Round of Trade Negotiations," *International Organization* 44-4 (Autumn 1990), p. 604.
2   Communication from an official at Canada's Department of Foreign Affairs and International Trade, 21 February 2002.
3   Hugo Paemen and Alexandra Bensch, *From the GATT to the WTO: The European Community in the Uruguay Round* (Leuven: Leuven University Press, 1995), pp. 93-98; Ernest H. Preeg,

Traders in a Brave New World: The Uruguay Round and the Future of the International Trading System (Chicago: University of Chicago Press, 1995), pp. 110-113.

4   Communication from official with Canada's Department of Foreign Affairs and International Trade, 2 April 2002; and comments from an anonymous external reviewer.

5   Preeg, *Traders in a Brave New World*, p. 111.

6   The EFTA members were Austria, Finland, Iceland, Norway, Sweden, and Switzerland. The G10 members were Argentina, Brazil, Cuba, Egypt, India, Nicaragua, Nigeria, Peru, Tanzania, and Yugoslavia.

7   Patrick Low, *Trading Free: The GATT and U.S. Trade Policy* (New York: Twentieth Century Fund, 1993), pp. 210-212.

8   Paemen and Bensch, *From the GATT to the WTO*, p. 45.

9   Gilbert R. Winham, "The Prenegotiation Phase of the Uruguay Round," *International Journal* 44-2 (Spring 1989), pp. 294-295; Preeg, *Traders in a Brave New World*, p. 3.

10   Three competing draft texts were submitted to the Punta del Este meeting, by the G48, the G10, and Argentina.

11   Theodore H. Cohn, "The Changing Role of the United States in the Global Agricultural Trade Regime," in William P. Avery, ed., *World Agriculture and the GATT* (Boulder: Lynne Rienner, 1993), pp. 24-29.

12   Robert L. Paarlberg, "Why Agriculture Blocked the Uruguay Round: Evolving Strategies in a Two-level Game," in Avery, ed., *World Agriculture and the GATT*, pp. 46-47.

13   Higgott and Cooper, "Middle Power Leadership and Coalition Building," pp. 589-632; Cohn, "The Changing Role of the United States in the Global Agricultural Trade Regime," pp. 29-34; John Croome, *Reshaping the World Trading System*, (Geneva: World Trade Organization, 1995), pp. 172-178 and 275-286; Preeg, *Traders in a Brave New World*, pp. 84-88.

14   Other books in the Ashgate G7/G8 series discuss these issues. For example, see Nicholas Bayne, *Hanging In There: The G7 and G8 Summit in Maturity and Renewal* (Aldershot: Ashgate, 2000), chs. 3 and 5.

15   Susan Hainsworth, "Coming of Age: The European Community and the Economic Summit," http://www.g7.utoronto.ca/g7/scholar/hainsworth1990/bispre.html.

16   "Tokyo Economic Declaration," 6 May 1986, paragraph 13.

17   "Venezia Economic Declaration," 10 June 1987, paragraph 13.

18   "Venezia Economic Declaration," 10 June 1987, paragraph 18. See also Robert Wolfe, *Farm Wars: The Political Economy of Agriculture and the International Trade Regime* (London: Macmillan, 1988), p. 80; Sylvia Ostry, Press Backgrounder, Kashikojima Japan, April 1987; "Meeting of the Council at Ministerial Level in May 1987, Communiqué," paragraphs 19-25.

19   "Toronto Summit Economic Declaration," 21 June 1988, paragraph 15.

20   Hainsworth, "Coming of Age."

21   "Toronto Summit Economic Declaration," 21 June 1988, paragraph 18.

22   "Paris Economic Declaration," 14-16 July 1989, paragraph 19.

23   "Paris Economic Declaration," 14-16 July 1989, paragraph 22.

24   "Paris Economic Declaration," 14-16 July 1989, paragraph 18.

25   Quoted in "International Group Urges G-7 Leaders to Add Boost to World Trade Talks," *Inside U.S. Trade*, Special Report, 15 June 1990, p. S-11.

26   "ICC Statement on Uruguay Round," in *Inside U.S. Trade*, Special Report, 22 June 1990, p. S-8.

27   G7 Summit, "Houston Economic Declaration," 11 July 1990, paragraph 19.

28   "Houston Economic Declaration," 9-11 July 1990, paragraph 23.

29 Bayne, *Hanging In There*, p. 62.
30 Bayne, *Hanging In There*, p. 62.
31 Chairman's Summary (Provisional Translation) at Kashikojima Quadrilateral Trade Ministers Meeting, 26 April 1987; Darryl Gibson, "Trade Ministers Agree to Grant Top Priority to Agricultural Problems," *Globe and Mail*, Toronto, 27 April 1987, p. B13; Sylvia Ostry, Press Backgrounder, Kashikojima, Japan.
32 Canada Department of External Affairs, "Minister Crosbie to Host the Quadrilateral Trade Ministers Meeting in April Point, B.C.," *News Release* no. 080, 14 April 1988; Notes for Opening Statement by Minister John Crosbie at Press Briefing, April 17, 1988, Pan Pacific Hotel, Vancouver.
33 On the U.S.-EC agricultural export subsidy contest see Theodore H. Cohn, *The International Politics of Agricultural Trade: Canadian-American Relations in a Global Agricultural Context* (Vancouver: University of British Columbia Press, 1990), pp. 82-90.
34 Brian Milner, "Trade Talks' Slow Pace Poses Worry to Ministers," *Globe and Mail*, Toronto, 18 April 1988, p. B1.
35 "Minister Crosbie to Attend the Quadrilateral Trade Ministers Meeting at Gull Lake, Minnesota," *Press Release*, 8 June 1988.
36 Canada Department of External Affairs, "Quadrilateral and International Trade Ministers Meeting – Media Backgrounder," 8 November 1989.
37 Canada Minister for International Trade, "International Trade Minister Crosbie to Pursue World Trade Initiatives at Quadrilateral Meeting," *News Release* no. 088, 1 May 1990.
38 Press Statement by the Honourable John Crosbie, Quadrilateral Meeting of Trade Ministers, Silverado, 4 May 1990.
39 John H. Jackson, *Restructuring the GATT System* (London: Royal Institute of International Affairs/Pinter, 1990).
40 Press Statement by the Honourable John Crosbie, Quadrilateral Meeting of Trade Ministers, Silverado, 4 May 1990.
41 Croome, *Reshaping the World Trading System*, pp. 271-274 & 358-361; Preeg, *Traders in a Brave New World*, pp. 113-114 & 124-126.
42 Statement by Ambassador Carla A. Hills Upon Conclusion of the 18th Quadrilateral Meeting of Trade Ministers, May 4, 1990, Napa, California.
43 Press Conference with the Quad Ministers, St. John's, Newfoundland, 13 October 1990.
44 "Quadrilateral Trade Meeting Fails to Carry Out Substantial Discussion," *Mainichi Shimbun* (translation from Japanese), 14 October 1990.
45 Kenichiro Ozeki, "U.S. Eyes Top Tariff of 50% on Rice, Other Farm Items," *The Daily Yomiuri*, 15 October 1990, p. 1; "Trade Partners End Meeting, Differ on Key Issues," *Japan Times*, 15 October 1990, p. 1. For a discussion explaining the wide differences of position between the U.S. and EC during this period see Robert L. Paarlberg, "Why Agriculture Blocked the Uruguay Round: Evolving Strategies in a Two-Level Game," in William P. Avery, ed., *World Agriculture and the GATT* (Boulder: Lynne Rienner, 1993), pp. 39-54.
46 Quoted in Kenichiro Ozeki and Yoshikuni Sugiyama, "Dunkel Urges Compromise to Spur Uruguay Round," *The Daily Yomiuri*, 13 October, p. 8.
47 "Big Four Traders Still Aim at December Wrapup," *Japan Times*, 14 October 1990, p. 1; Yuko Inoue, "Officials Won't Relent on Rice-Import Ban," *The Japan Economic Journal*, 20 October 1990, p. 5.
48 "Meeting of the OECD Council at Ministerial Level in May 1987 – Communiqué," paragraph 16.

49   "Meeting of the OECD Council at Ministerial Leave on 31 May to 1 June 1989 – Communiqué," paragraph 28.
50   Hugo Paemen and Alexandra Bensch, *From GATT to the WTO: The European Community in the Uruguay Round* (Belgium: Leuven University Press, 1995), p. 83.
51   T.K. Warley, "Issues Facing Agriculture in the GATT Negotiations," *Canadian Journal of Agricultural Economics* 35 (1987), p. 519.
52   See Organisation for Economic Co-operation and Development, *National Policies and Agricultural Trade* (Paris: OECD, 1987).
53   Warley, "Issues Facing Agriculture in the GATT Negotiations," pp. 519-520; Wolfe, *Farm Wars*, pp. 112-113.
54   See Heidi Ullrich, "The Impact of Policy Networks in the GATT Uruguay Round: The Case of the US-EC Agricultural Negotiations," unpublished Ph.D. thesis, London School of Economics, London, 2002.
55   Kym Anderson and Timothy Josling, "The Challenge to Economists of Multilateral Trade Negotiations on Agricultural Protection," *Food Research Institute Studies* 22-3 (1993), pp. 275-303; Organisation for Economic Cooperation and Development, "The OECD and Agricultural Trade Analysis: Recent History, Possible Future Directions," OECD Workshop on Emerging Trade Issues in Agriculture, COM/AGR/CA/TD/TC/WS(98)109, 16 October 1998; David J. Blair, *Trade Negotiations in the OECD: Structures, Institutions and States*, (London: Kegan Paul International, 1993), pp. 123-124.
56   Wolfe, *Farm Wars*, p. 113.
57   OECD, "The OECD and Agricultural Trade Analysis," paragraph 3.
58   Quoted in Robert L. Paarlberg, *Fixing Farm Trade: Policy Options for the United States* (Cambridge: Ballinger, 1988), p. 6.
59   Blair, *Trade Negotiations in the OECD*, pp. 124-125; Warley, "Issues Facing Agriculture in the GATT Negotiations," p. 518.
60   Meeting of the OECD Council at Ministerial Level in May 1987 – *Communiqué*, paragraph 23.
61   Croome, *Reshaping the World Trading System*, pp. 239-240. See also Preeg, *Traders in a Brave New World*, pp. 114-115.
62   Ronald Kent Shelp, *Beyond Industrialization: Ascendancy of the Global Service Economy* (New York: Praeger, 1981), p. 174.
63   William J. Drake and Kalypso Nicolaïdis, "Ideas, Interests and Institutionalization: 'Trade in Services' and the Uruguay Round," *International Organization* 46-1 (Winter 1992), pp. 68-69; Low, *Trading Free*, p. 213.
64   OECD, "Elements of a Conceptual Framework for Trade in Services," Paris, March 1987.
65   OECD, "Elements of a Conceptual Framework for Trade in Services," p. 3.
66   Geza Feketekuty, *International Trade in Services: An Overview and Blueprint for Negotiations* (Cambridge: Ballinger, 1988), p. 318.
67   Edwini Kwame Kessie, "Developing Countries and the World Trade Organization: What Has Changed?," *World Competition* 22-2 (1999), p. 95.
68   See Robert Wolfe, "Global Trade as a Single Undertaking: The Role of Ministers in the WTO," *International Journal* 51-4 (Autumn 1996), pp. 690-709.
69   Quoted in Mari Pangestu, " Special and Differential Treatment in the Millennium: Special for Whom and How Different?," *World Economy* 23-9 (September 2000), p. 1291. See also John Whalley, "Special and Differential Treatment in the Millennium Round," *World Economy* 22-8 (November 1999), pp. 1065-1093.

70   Kathryn C. Lavelle, "Ideas within a Context of Power: The African Group in an Evolving UNCTAD," *Journal of Modern African Studies* 39-1 (2001), p. 42.

71   Raymond F. Hopkins, "Developing Countries in the Uruguay Round: Bargaining under Uncertainty and Inequality," in William P. Avery, ed., *World Agriculture and the GATT* (Boulder: Lynne Rienner, 1993), p. 151.

72   Colleen Hamilton and John Whalley, "Coalitions in the Uruguay Round," *Weltwirtschaftliches Archiv* 125-3 (1989), p. 547.

73   The De La Paix group consisted mainly of Australia, Canada, Colombia, Hungary, Malaysia, New Zealand, Philippines, Singapore, South Korea, Sweden, Switzerland, Thailand, Uruguay, and Zaire. Hamilton and Whaley, "Coalitions in the Uruguay Round," p. 557; Higgott and Cooper, "Middle Power Leadership and Coalition Building," p. 591.

74   Rod Tyers, "The Cairns Group and the Uruguay Round of International Trade Negotiations," *Australian Economic Review* 93-101 (1993), p. 49.

75   Despite the closer ties between the United States and the Cairns Group, the Cairns Group criticised the 1990 U.S. Farm Bill for being inconsistent with the U.S. position in the GATT. See Tyers, "The Cairns Group and the Uruguay Round of International Trade Negotiations," p. 55.

76   Hopkins, "Developing Countries in the Uruguay Round," pp. 148-151; Kathryn C. Lavelle, "Ideas within a Context of Power: The African Group in an Evolving UNCTAD," *Journal of Modern African Studies* 39-1 (2001), pp. 42-43; Higgott and Cooper, "Middle Power Leadership and Coalition Building," p. 617.

77   Theodore H. Cohn, "Canada and the Ongoing Impasse over Agricultural Protectionism," in A. Claire Cutler and Mark W. Zacher, eds., *Canadian Foreign Policy and International Economic Regimes* (Vancouver: University of British Columbia Press, 1992), pp. 62-88; Andrew F. Cooper, Richard A. Higgott, and Kim Richard Nossal, *Relocating Middle Powers: Australia and Canada in a Changing World* (Vancouver: University of British Columbia Press, 1993), pp. 50-82; Andrew F. Cooper, *In Between Countries: Australia, Canada, and the Search for Order in Agricultural Trade* (Montreal: McGill-Queen's University Press, 1997), pp. 112-142.

78   John H. Jackson, *The World Trading System: Law and Policy of International Economic Relations* (Cambridge, MA: MIT Press, 2nd edition, 1997), p. 314; Cooper, Higgott, and Nossal, *Relocating Middle Powers*, p. 82.

79   Tyers, "The Cairns Group and the Uruguay Round of International Trade Negotiations," p. 55.

7   From the Brussels Ministerial to the End of the GATT Uruguay Round: 1991 to 1994

The GATT Uruguay Round was supposed to be completed at the December 1990 Brussels ministerial, but Chapter 6 discussed the fact that those near the top of the global trade regime pyramid did not provide the leadership necessary to conclude an agreement at Brussels. Developed country-led institutions such as the G7, the Quad, and the OECD were finding it difficult to influence the Uruguay Round negotiations for several reasons. First, many more key players participated in the Uruguay Round than in previous rounds, because of an enlarged more diverse GATT membership and more active participation by developing countries. Second, the Uruguay Round agenda was much broader than in previous rounds, and included sensitive issues such as agricultural and services trade that made a final agreement much more difficult. Third, and most importantly, the two largest trading entities – the United States and the EC – were still far apart on the issue of agriculture at the 1990 Brussels ministerial. Although the G7 and the Quad are important institutions, a U.S. administration official pointed out that "the bilateral efforts" between the United States and the EC "must fall into place for the process to move forward."[1]

As Hugo Paemen and Alexandra Bensch have noted:

> the U.S. and the European Community were, and still are, the biggest players on the world trade scene. Since they vie for first place, it is almost inevitable that when their objective interests put them on opposing sides, they should be the main participants in any dialogue to discuss the issues. This was certainly the case with agriculture.[2]

It was therefore evident that there would be no Uruguay Round agreement without a degree of consensus at the top of the global trade regime pyramid between the United States and the EC on agriculture. Despite the centrality of the United States and the EC, this chapter demonstrates that other actors also had important roles, and that the U.S. and EC roles evolved during the course of the Uruguay Round.

The United States had assumed a leading role during about 50 years of GATT negotiations, and its commitment and tenacity were essential to the launching of the Uruguay Round. Whereas the conceptual framework and diplomatic moves that led to Punta del Este came from the United States, the EC by contrast began the round with a more regional economic outlook. Furthermore, the EC's complex internal decision-making process often prevented the European Commission from taking strong international initiatives. As for Japan, it was reluctant to assert its leadership in the trade negotiations, and it continued to be defensive about access to its market. However, the U.S. leadership role weakened to some extent during the latter stages of the Uruguay Round. Growing U.S. protectionist pressures against some key provisions in the Dunkel draft agreement (discussed later in this chapter), and initial reluctance by the new U.S. President Bill Clinton to provide forceful direction for trade policy slowed the moves toward an Uruguay Round agreement. The EC Commissioner Leon Brittan by contrast began to adopt a more assertive role, and leadership in the latter stages of the Uruguay Round shifted to a more balanced position between the United States and the EC. Peter Sutherland, who replaced Arthur Dunkel as GATT director-general in July 1993, also contributed to a broader base of leadership in the final phase of the negotiations. Although Dunkel's contribution to the Uruguay Round had been important, Sutherland adopted "a more outspoken and pro-active public role for the GATT director-generalship."[3] In sum, as U.S. economic hegemony declined the EC began to share leadership with the United States in guiding the negotiations, and the GATT director-general also played a more assertive role.[4]

Although a degree of consensus between the United States and the EC was essential before the Uruguay Round could be concluded, the G7, the Quad, and the OECD had important roles in helping to limit protectionism and to keep the negotiations going in the interim. In addition, the G7 and the Quad provided small, informal settings in which the major developed country traders could resolve their differences, present and develop new ideas, and attempt to reach a consensus on important issues. The OECD also presented new ideas and conducted studies – often with the support of epistemic communities – designed to further the GATT negotiations. As we discuss in this chapter, the Quad provided a more concrete contribution when it helped to negotiate a market access agreement in July 1993 that had a critical role in the completion of the Uruguay Round.

As discussed in Chapter 6, the developing countries were more involved in the Uruguay Round than in previous rounds. The developing countries also joined in a number of North-South coalitions, and continued to engage in coalition behaviour in the latter stages of the Uruguay Round. Despite their more active involvement, the developing countries often felt excluded from the inner circle of discussions, prenegotiations, and negotiations. Thus, the developing countries protested that the Quad's July 1993 market access package was negotiated without their input and contained little of benefit to them. It was not until the discussions were "remultilateralised" – that is, moved from the G7 and the Quad back to the GATT – that the South was willing to approve a final Uruguay Round agreement.[5] After the agreement was reached, there was a feeling among many developing countries that they had lost more than they had gained from the negotiations. In sum, although developing country participation and influence in the GATT had increased, the South remained near the bottom of the global trade regime pyramid.

Developments in the GATT: 1991 to 1994

The major trading nations initially planned to complete the GATT Uruguay Round at the December 1990 Brussels ministerial. However, two Latin American members of the Cairns Group – Argentina and Brazil – refused to negotiate further at Brussels because of the EC's unwillingness to provide concessions on agriculture. Negotiations finally resumed in February 1991, when the EC agreed to consider changes in its agricultural policies. The EC's more flexible attitude resulted from internal as well as external pressures. Faced with continuing increases in the budgetary costs of the EC's Common Agricultural Policy, the member countries began to discuss CAP reform; and in May 1991 they agreed to decrease price supports – and thus relieve surpluses – for some agricultural commodities. Although EC members insisted there was no connection between the CAP reforms and the Uruguay Round negotiations, the two processes were certainly complementary.

Since the Uruguay Round was extending well beyond the initial deadline, one other issue had to be resolved before negotiations could resume after the Brussels ministerial – the imminent expiration of U.S "fast-track" authority in Spring 1991. The Omnibus U.S. Trade Act of 1988 provided the President with fast-track authority, which requires the U.S. Congress to vote yes or no on the implementing legislation for a trade agreement within 90 legislative days, without adding amendments to the agreement. This serves as a confidence-building measure with U.S. trading partners, who know that under fast-track the U.S. Congress cannot prolong ratification procedures for trade agreements, and cannot vote to amend agreements after they have been concluded. After a heated debate that focused more on fast-track authority for negotiation of a North American Free Trade Agreement than for the Uruguay Round agreement, a divided U.S. Congress approved a renewal of fast-track for two years until March 1993. This renewal provided essential added time for concluding the Uruguay Round.[6]

Despite the promising signs of some European movement on agriculture, an agricultural stalemate continued at the highest political level for another two years (see discussion of the G7 in this chapter). Nevertheless, negotiations on Uruguay Round issues other than agriculture were productive during 1991 and 1992. Professional trade negotiators were largely responsible for these gains, meeting in less formal settings in small and large groups, and in a more intensive negotiating process among Quad members. In Geneva, the GATT Director-General Arthur Dunkel and the secretariat began to play a more assertive role that would continue to increase throughout the Uruguay Round. Dunkel's favourite place to conduct informal negotiations was the "green room," a small conference room adjoining the director-general's office. Its size limited participation to about 30 people, including one delegate from each of the major countries with the European Commission representing the EC. The limited participation was contrary to GATT practice of having open plenary meetings, and smaller excluded countries sometimes complained. Nevertheless, participants informed others of the proceedings, and the green room meetings continued throughout the negotiation. In the latter stages of negotiation, the director-general held even more restricted dinner sessions.[7]

After five years of negotiation, Dunkel attempted to break the impasse by producing his own draft for a final agreement on 20 December 1991, the "Draft Final Act Embodying the Results of the Uruguay Round of Multilateral Trade Negotiations." The Dunkel draft "was a bold initiative to bridge the numerous substantive differences in the many sectors of negotiation and to present a balanced package agreement tilted in the direction of a maximum overall result."[8] However, early reactions from some quarters, especially the EC, indicated that some aspects of the Dunkel draft would not be accepted. Although agriculture was as usual the biggest problem, there were also other difficult areas of negotiation.[9] For example, there was a diversity of views on a draft agreement to establish a "Multilateral Trade Organization" (MTO). The issue of a new MTO (or WTO) had first been raised in a Quad meeting in 1989, but serious discussion of the issue only began after the Brussels ministerial. The United

States was not convinced that a new organisation was necessary, and it was concerned that the U.S. Congress would oppose the proposal; Japan was also not enthusiastic about the idea. Although the United States and Japan accepted the inclusion of an unfinished MTO agreement in an annex to Dunkel's Draft Final Act, the United States continued to oppose the creation of a new global trade organisation. It was not until near the end of the Uruguay Round that the United States accepted the idea of the WTO.[10]

Agricultural negotiations in Spring and Summer 1992 resulted in little progress, and the negotiations broke off shortly before the November 1992 U.S. election, in which Clinton became the new president. However, during the presidential transition period an agricultural trade crisis loomed between the United States and the EC over oilseeds, and efforts to avoid this crisis resulted in the 20 November 1992 Blair House Accord. The Blair House Accord was a comprehensive U.S.-EC agreement covering both the Uruguay Round agricultural issues and the oilseeds dispute. Although France expressed strong dissatisfaction with the Blair House Accord, it permitted U.S. and EC negotiators to turn to other outstanding issues in an attempt to reach an Uruguay Round agreement. In March 1993 a low point was reached when Dunkel indicated that the Uruguay Round could not be completed before the effective expiry of U.S. fast-track authority on 2 March 1993. Dunkel had accepted a final six-month extension of his term of office to help complete the round, but that would expire at mid-year. President Clinton responded to this crisis by asking Congress for another renewal of fast-track authority to 15 April 1994. Although the new authority was approved, the Uruguay Round negotiations would have to be completed by 15 December 1993 to provide the necessary 120-day consultation period with the U.S. Congress prior to formal signing.[11]

In July 1993 Peter Sutherland was appointed to replace Dunkel as GATT director-general, and this marked a shift in the negotiations. Despite Dunkel's major contributions, Sutherland was more outspoken and proactive, and he brought new enthusiasm to the Uruguay Round. On the day he took office, Sutherland accused the developed country leaders of moving too slowly, and he warned that the upcoming July 1993 G7 Tokyo III summit would have to provide a detailed communiqué for completing the round. Previous summits had done little for the negotiations, and the G7 leaders were under pressure from the rest of the world to produce a needed breakthrough in the round. The specific Uruguay Round objective the developed country leaders had set for the Tokyo III summit was a market access agreement on tariff cuts for industrial goods. Although the Quad trade ministers had met three times in May and June to develop the terms for a market access agreement, when the G7 leaders arrived in Tokyo an agreement had still not be achieved. However, a six-hour negotiating session produced an agreement that significantly increased market access commitments. The G7 summit participants endorsed the accord, and announced their determination to complete the Uruguay Round by the end of the year.

The G7 market access accord was a critical step forward for the Uruguay Round, and provided the political direction required to reactivate the stalled negotiations. Nevertheless, several obstacles remained that could still disrupt the negotiations, including problems with the developing countries, continued conflict between the United States and the EC, and the U.S. president's need to renew fast-track approval. Developing countries expressed annoyance that they had been excluded from discussions leading to the Quad's market access agreement, and they argued that the agreement did not take account of their interests. For example, the sectors the Quad had proposed for the greatest liberalisation excluded products that developing countries could produce most competitively. The Quad was successful in defusing this situation by emphasising that the market access package approved at the Tokyo III summit resulted only from discussions within the Quad, and that they now wanted to involve others in the negotiations.

The continuing problems between the United States and the EC posed a greater obstacle to concluding the negotiations. Although France had agreed in the Tokyo summit to move ahead on market access commitments for industrial goods, it continued to view the Blair House agricultural Accord as unacceptable. In September 1993 the United States indicated that it would not reopen the Blair House Accord, and the Cairns Group added its support to the U.S. position by threatening to walk out of the negotiations. In addition to the new U.S.-EC standoff on agriculture, the upcoming Congressional vote over NAFTA was of critical importance. If NAFTA was defeated, this would strengthen protectionist forces and would have a negative effect on the Uruguay Round. In November 1993, the U.S. Congress voted in favour of NAFTA, which bolstered Clinton and gave him more leverage *vis-à-vis* the EC in the Uruguay Round. It was also in November that the Maastricht Treaty came into effect creating the European Union.[12]

Despite the EU and U.S. rhetoric over agriculture, they were both eventually willing to compromise, and discussions in early December 1993 finally produced the breakthrough that would lead to the conclusion of the Uruguay Round. The United States made some significant concessions that altered the Blair House Accord to the advantage of the EU, and particularly French farmers. In return, the Europeans offered some significant market access commitments for U.S. agricultural exports. The United States and the EU also resolved other remaining differences over textiles, antidumping actions, and commercial aircraft and audiovisual services. The last major issue to be resolved was the agreement to replace the GATT with the WTO. Problems involving other GATT members of course posed obstacles to completion of the round, but the need for a consensus between the United States and EU was primary. Indeed, "the final bout of Euro-American arm-wrestling finally came to an end in the early hours of Tuesday, 14 December 1993," and one day later the GATT director-general declared that the Uruguay Round was completed.[13]

The Group of Seven

The problem of an overloaded G7 summit agenda increased during the 1991 to 1994 period as traditional economic concerns such as monetary and financial issues, trade, energy, and North-South relations were joined by a number of newer socio-economic issues. The G7 also had to devote considerable attention to political security issues such as the Gulf War that posed a threat to developed country oil supplies. Some of the most important newer issues on the G7 agenda included the dramatic changes in Eastern Europe and the former Soviet Union, and issues requiring global cooperation such as the problems of illegal drugs and environmental degradation. The introduction of these newer issues "while the old ones were still nominally on the agenda, weighed heavily upon the summit process."[14] The G7 finance ministers and Quad trade ministers therefore continued to assume much of the responsibility for economic policy coordination and international trade policy at the higher political levels. Nevertheless, two of the more traditional economic issues, international trade and foreign debt problems, continued to require G7 attention on a regular basis.

The 1991 Gulf War between Iraq and a U.S.-led coalition of states dominated the political agenda at the 15-17 July 1991 G7 summit in London (London III). Several issues that the summits had begun to discuss in 1989 such as the environment and illegal drugs were also addressed at the 1991 summit. In addition, 1991 was the first year that the summit leaders invited a Soviet president, Mikhail Gorbachev, to meet with them. (The meeting was held separately from the main proceedings.)[15] Despite the London summit's preoccupation with this diverse range of issues, the G7 leaders felt strong pressures to provide the political impetus for progress in the Uruguay Round. Some of these pressures came from a diverse range of business groups. For example, the president of the U.S. National Association of Manufacturers argued that the 1991 summit had to issue a strong statement urging the multilateral trade talks to move forward, or the talks could eventually fail.[16] As discussed, agriculture was the major issue blocking a completion of the Uruguay Round. Thus, the Cairns Group ministers meeting in Brazil in July 1991 expressed disappointment over the failure of the Brussels ministerial, and called on the G7 at their forthcoming summit "to exert leadership by facing squarely the political decisions necessary to fundamentally reform world agricultural production and trade."[17]

At the London III summit, the G7 leaders seemed to stake their credibility on a successful outcome of the Uruguay Round. The United States, Britain and Japan singled out the completion of the Uruguay Round as the highest economic priority.[18] President George Bush stated that the Uruguay Round was the most important issue of the summit and pressed for progress in bilateral and group meetings. British Prime Minister John Major as the summit host went even further and said he was prepared to call a special summit of the G7 leaders if it seemed that the trade talks would fail. Although individual countries would have to make some painful decisions, Major stated that the reward would be "a liberalisation of world trade, and a big step forward in the Uruguay Round."[19] The summit economic declaration contained the strongest G7 pledge to that point "to complete the Round before the end of 1991," and the summit leaders vowed to "remain personally involved in this process, ready to intervene with one another if differences can only be resolved at the highest level."[20]

Despite the strong statements of determination, the arrival of Soviet President Gorbachev for a post-summit meeting upstaged the discussion of the Uruguay Round, and the issue of Western aid to promote Soviet reforms dominated the discussion. Geneva negotiators were also skeptical that the G7 pledges would be fulfilled, and the GATT Director-General Arthur Dunkel indicated that it was vital to translate the commitments into "forthcoming and flexible negotiating positions."[21] Europe in fact was not prepared to respond to the London summit with specific commitments in agriculture, and the EC-U.S. divisions on this issue continued. Although the G7 leaders interacted frequently – both by telephone and in face-to-face meetings – in the latter months of 1991, these discussions did not bridge their differences, especially on agriculture. Thus, the Uruguay Round had to be extended again into 1992.[22]

In early 1992 chief negotiators for the major trading partners missed deadlines in the goods and services market access negotiations, and there were growing concerns about a breakdown of the Uruguay Round. Indeed, a senior GATT official reported that the trade talks were "totally blocked," because U.S.-EC disputes over agriculture were preventing progress in other areas.[23] International business groups and the Cairns Group expressed concerns that the round could fail and urged the G7 to take a more forceful position. For example, in April 1992 about 120 international business leaders wrote an open letter urging the world's political leaders to summon the will to conclude the talks; and in June 1992 the International Chamber of Commerce charged the G7 with a lack of leadership, and expressed frustration that a year and a half of declarations to support an early conclusion of the Uruguay Round had not achieved the desired results.[24] The communiqué of the June 1992 Cairns Group ministerial expressed "grave fears that the Round will fail unless a breakthrough on agriculture is achieved in coming weeks." Thus, the Cairns Group considered it essential "that G7 leaders demonstrate their will, their leadership and their joint responsibility to unblock the negotiations."[25]

Despite the pressures on the G7 to achieve a breakthrough in the Uruguay Round, the G7 summit in Munich, Germany on 6-8 July 1992 "was another summit where a congested agenda and too much ceremony frustrated the leaders."[26] Since the G7 summit in London a year earlier, communism had collapsed in the Soviet Union, which had broken up into 15 disparate states. Thus, the Munich summit had to address the issue of erupting military conflicts in Yugoslavia and Russia, and also had to confer on IMF loans to deal with Russia's foreign debt. Nevertheless, the main obstacles to revitalising the Uruguay Round at Munich were political, with the Europeans facing a difficult struggle to ratify the Maastricht Treaty on European Union after the referendum defeat in Denmark, and the United States in a presidential election year.

At the Munich summit, the EC indicated that it had already taken difficult decisions to reform the CAP, and France was unwilling to offer more concessions on agriculture. President François Mitterand had decided to hold a ratification vote on the Maastricht Treaty on 20 September 1992, and he did not want to give the anti-Europeans additional support in opposing further integration. Since France's farm lobby would oppose virtually any international agreement on agriculture, Mitterand indicated that no breakthrough in the world trade talks could be achieved before France held the referendum on Maastricht. Despite the French resistance to an agreement, the press speculated that Chancellor Helmut Kohl as the host of the Munich summit might launch an initiative to break the deadlock over agriculture. For example, the *Economist* wrote that

The sticking-point in the round remains the reluctance of the European Community, and of France in particular, to reshape a policy of helping farmers that is peculiarly disruptive of trade. This is not the round's only headache, nor is France its only villain. But, as things stand, the EC and France will take the blame if the Uruguay round fails. Mr. Kohl has both the motive and the clout to make sure that failure does not happen.[27]

However, Kohl was unwilling to take an assertive position to complete the Uruguay Round, largely because of the Franco-German partnership. Germany's powerful farm lobby was also a factor causing Kohl to exercise restraint. Instead of taking a leadership position, Kohl even attempted to exclude discussion of the Uruguay Round from the Munich summit agenda. The United States, however, pressed the agricultural issue, France reacted negatively, and an agricultural impasse at Munich seemed to end hopes for an Uruguay Round agreement in 1992. Although the 1992 G7 summit economic declaration stated that "we expect an [Uruguay Round] agreement can be reached before the end of 1992,"[28] the leaders at the previous two G7 summits had voiced the same expectation. In contrast to the 1987 to 1991 G7 summit declarations, the 1992 declaration did not even contain a separate section on international trade (discussion of the Uruguay Round was under a section entitled "World Economy"). Furthermore, the 1992 declaration did not contain the pledges found in the 1990 and 1991 declarations that the G7 leaders would intervene if necessary to bring about a successful conclusion to the Uruguay Round.[29]

After the French referendum on Maastricht, a renewal of negotiations between the United States and the EC finally resulted in the Blair House agreement on 20 November 1992. The Blair House Accord was a breakthrough that finally resolved some major U.S.-EC differences on domestic support, export subsidies, and market access for agriculture. Nevertheless, France opposed the accord and there was no assurance that the EC would give its final approval. Furthermore, agriculture was not the only issue delaying completion of the Uruguay Round. The U.S. President therefore had to request another renewal of fast-track authority to continue the negotiations into 1993. The Quad was attempting to develop an industrial goods and services market access package in time for the 1993 G7 summit in Tokyo (Tokyo III), and it would then be necessary to return to the problem of resolving the differences on agriculture. In the lead-up to the Tokyo summit, a wide range of business associations from the United States, Japan, Britain, and Canada urged the G7 to agree on a far-reaching market access package. The International Chamber of Commerce also indicated that the G7 in Tokyo had to repair the damage resulting from its weak statement on the Uruguay Round in the 1992 Munich summit declaration.[30] The Cairns Group expressed the strongest criticisms of the G7 in its June 1993 ministerial declaration:

> Each Summit has pledged to bring the [Uruguay] Round to a swift conclusion. Three years ago, at Houston the G7 leaders expressed their determination to take the difficult political decisions to do this. They resolved to achieve far-reaching substantial results across all sectors by the end of 1990. At the London Summit in

1991 the Leaders declared that the aim of all Contracting Parties should be to complete the Round by the year's end. They committed themselves to "remain personally involved in this process." Last year, at Munich the G7 "regretted the slow pace of negotiations" and expressed their "expectation that an agreement could be reached before the end of 1992." Sadly, none of these commitments have been realised. This year the world simply cannot afford another failure. The G7 should use the Tokyo Summit to provide leadership for the last, critical phase of the Uruguay Round negotiations.[31]

To avoid another embarrassing failure, the G7 asked the Quad trade ministers to reach an agreement on market access for industrial goods and services *before* the 6-9 July 1993 G7 summit in Tokyo. The Quad agreement was reached only hours before the G7 leaders gathered at the State Guesthouse in Tokyo (the Quad agreement is discussed in detail later in this chapter). The market access agreement gave important impetus to the Uruguay Round, and the Tokyo III summit had little to do on trade other than to outline the remaining issues (such as agriculture) that still required an agreement. In giving the Quad a deadline for reaching a market access agreement, the G7 demonstrated its ability to serve as a *catalyst* for moving multilateral trade negotiations forward in the final stages.[32] Thus, U.S. President Clinton made the following statement at Tokyo III about the market access agreement:

> While there are difficult negotiations ahead, today's agreement on manufactured goods breaks the logjam in the Uruguay Round. For years talks in that Round have languished. G-7 leaders have emerged from these summits pledging renewed commitment to complete the Round. Their pledges have gone unfulfilled. But this year, we have recaptured the momentum.[33]

Despite the impetus the market access accord gave to the Uruguay Round, the Tokyo III summit declaration cautioned that "there remain important issues to resolve," and the U.S. Trade Representative added that "no one should overstate what happened in Tokyo. It is not going to be easy to reach agreement by December 15."[34] The GATT did in fact oversee an agreement by the deadline, and in April 1994 over 100 governments signed the Uruguay Round agreement at Marrakesh. At the 1994 G7 summit in Naples, Italy, the G7 countries expressed their determination to "ratify the Uruguay Round Agreements and to establish the WTO by January 1st, 1995," and they called on other states to do the same.[35] The Naples summit rejected the Clinton Administration's so-called Open Markets 2000 proposal to agree on areas for new trade talks, because of concerns that the proposal would detract attention from ratification of the Uruguay Round. However, the G7 agreed that the Quad should consider future trade liberalisation, and it encouraged the "work under way in the OECD to study the interaction of international trade rules and competition policies."[36] In response to U.S. pressure, the G7 members also called for increased efforts to examine the new issues of employment and labour standards and their implications for trade; the labour standards issue was to become highly contentious for developing countries. It is important to note that the G7 at Naples took a major step toward becoming a G8. Although Russia had been a visitor to the 1991 to 1993 summits, it became a full member of the foreign policy discussions at Naples. Nevertheless, the G7 leaders would not yet agree to President Yeltsin's request that he be admitted to the economic discussions.[37]

In summary, 1991 to 1994 was a period of both frustration and accomplishment for the G7 in dealing with international trade. The Quad did much of the background work for the major traders, because the G7 had an overloaded agenda and the Quad trade ministers could focus their attention on the Uruguay Round. Furthermore, protracted differences and disputes among the G7 countries – particularly the U.S.-EC dispute over agriculture – prevented the summits from fulfilling pledges to complete the Uruguay Round in 1990, 1991, and 1992. While the trade negotiations were still in the technical and policy-making stages, the G7's influence inevitably was more limited. Nevertheless, the summits registered some accomplishments in trade during the 1990 to 1992 period. They helped limit protectionism and keep the trade negotiations going despite a recession, pressured for a stronger dispute settlement mechanism, and supported the idea of establishing a new WTO. Although the repeated rescheduling of deadlines had an adverse effect on the prestige of the G7 summits, re-setting these deadlines may have been the best way to pressure for eventual results. During the final stages of the Uruguay Round, the G7 was able to exert more influence at the highest political level, and its request that the Quad reach a market access agreement was crucial to completion of the round. The market access accord demonstrated the G7's ability to act as a catalyst in the Uruguay Round, just as the interim deadline established for the 1978 Bonn I summit had demonstrated the G7's ability to act as a catalyst for the Tokyo Round (see Chapter 4). Ultimately, the conclusion of the Uruguay Round in 1993 "restored the summit's morale" and also some of its prestige as a meeting place for the leading industrial states.[38]

The Quadrilateral Group

As discussed in Chapter 5, the Quad ministerials had a significant role in the preparatory period leading up to the Punta del Este meeting launching the Uruguay Round. The Quad also registered some accomplishments during the early phases of the Uruguay Round (see Chapter 6). Nevertheless, 1989 and 1990 were relatively quiescent years for the Quad, in which it demonstrated less collective leadership. After the disappointing 1990 GATT ministerial in Brussels, the Quad re-emerged as a prominent grouping. Quad ministerials – often supported by additional meetings at the senior officials level – became more numerous, and at times had a pivotal role in the successful completion of the Uruguay Round. Although the Quad's main function in the latter stages of the round was to produce mutual understanding among the major traders, the Quad meetings sometimes explored possible solutions to specific problems in the negotiations. On one occasion, the Quad served as a forum for negotiation of a key market access agreement in preparation for the 1993 Tokyo III summit.[39] This section traces the Quad's activities from 1991 to 1994.

From the Brussels Ministerial to the Quad/G7 Tokyo Agreement

Originally the Quad was going to have two ministerials in 1991, to discuss plans for implementing the results of the Uruguay Round and to help develop a post-MTN policy agenda. However, only one Quad ministerial was held in September 1991, because of the failure of the Brussels ministerial to complete the Uruguay Round. Several Quad meetings were held at the officials level in 1991. For example, the Quad MTN coordinators met on 26-27 May 1991 to provide an overview of problem areas remaining in the negotiations; and the coordinators met again on 28-29 August 1991 to discuss the final phase of the Uruguay Round and to help prepare for the twentieth Quad ministerial. The G7 leaders at their July 1991 London III summit had expressed a commitment to "complete the Round before the end of 1991,"[40] and the twentieth Quad ministerial in Angers, France on 12-14 September 1991 was concerned with "translating that commitment into action."[41] The G7 was aware that the negotiators in Geneva still had a considerable amount of work to do, and it singled out the issues of market access, agriculture, services, and intellectual property for urgent attention. To this list, the Quad added the investment negotiations. As part of an effort to accelerate the negotiations, the Quad ministers decided to keep the heads of their MTN delegations in Geneva on a semi-permanent basis.[42]

Although the Angers Quad focused primarily on accelerating the Uruguay Round, it also discussed trade issues that would require attention after the round. For example, the ministers agreed that the GATT should activate its working party on trade and the environment. As a result of this Quad consensus, the GATT Council decided in October 1991 to convene its Working Group on Environmental Measures and International Trade for the first time since it was established in 1971. The GATT Secretariat also published a report on trade and environment in February 1992. Despite the apparent new focus on the environment, the importance of this change should not be overestimated. A number of developing countries led by Brazil and India tried to prevent the GATT from convening its environmental working group in 1991, because they believed that the North would use the group to justify protectionism and to impose unreasonable environmental standards on the South. Thus, the environmental working group was given an extremely limited mandate.[43]

Plans to complete the Uruguay Round by the end of 1991 were again blocked by continuing differences over key issues such as agriculture. Thus, the status of the round dominated ministerial discussions at the twenty-first Quad in Fukushima, Japan on 24 to 26 April 1992. The timing of the Fukushima Quad was designed to permit an exchange of views on the progress of the negotiations before the May 1992 OECD ministerial and the July 1992 G7 summit. Whereas the Quad ministers focused most of their discussion on the general timing and process of the negotiations, their chief negotiators formulated a strategy to proceed with specific negotiating issues. However, the ministers could not avoid discussing key stumbling blocks such as agriculture. The Fukushima Quad failed to break the U.S.-EC impasse over agriculture, but the four ministers agreed to continue efforts to conclude the negotiations as soon as possible. Indeed, the ministers all expressed the desire to have key decisions made in regard to agriculture, services, and goods by the time of the July 1992 G7 summit in Munich. The ministers nevertheless conceded that the impasse over agriculture would hinder negotiations in other areas such as market access.

As was the case for the Angers Quad, the Fukushima Quad devoted some attention to issues that would be important after the Uruguay Round. For example, the Fukushima Quad discussed environmental issues such as the use of trade measures to protect the environment, the prevention of conflicts between international environmental agreements and the GATT, and the transfer of environmental technology and equipment through trade. The Fukushima Quad also discussed trade competitiveness and competition policies for the first time, because of pressure from the EC Competition Minister Sir Leon Brittan. Based on the EC's experience with competition law, Brittan called for the development of a multilateral framework for competition policy and for common rules to appraise mergers; and the EC Vice-Chair Frans Andriessen presented Brittan's ideas in the Quad ministerial. Other post-Uruguay Round issues discussed at the Fukushima Quad included the possible accession of China and Taiwan to the GATT, and the strategies for integrating the East European and former Soviet Union countries into the multilateral trade regime.[44]

Quad meetings below the ministerial level became more frequent at this time to facilitate the completion of the Uruguay Round and begin the process of post-MTN planning. For example, after the United States and the EC expressed a joint commitment to accelerate the talks on services and market access, the Quad's chief negotiators had an unscheduled meeting on 17-18 June 1992 in Geneva. The EC also used a 23 September 1992 meeting of the Quad's chief negotiators to propose that a permanent group be created after the Uruguay Round to deal with trade and environment issues.[45] The ministers at the next regular Quad ministerial, the twenty-second meeting on 16-18 October 1992 in Cambridge, Ontario, were confronted with the fact that the Uruguay Round had to be completed by the end of the year to give the U.S. Congress time to approve the agreement under fast-track authority. Thus, the ministers agreed to a plan of action aimed at completing the Uruguay Round by the end of 1992. Despite these efforts, the Uruguay Round was not completed in 1992 because of continuing U.S.-EC differences over agriculture, and North-South differences over market access, services, and government procurement.[46]

As discussed, in March 1993 the GATT director-general indicated that the Uruguay Round could not be completed before the expiration of U.S. fast-track authority. The U.S. Congress provided President Clinton with a further renewal of fast-track to 15 April 1994, but the Uruguay Round would have to be completed by 15 December 1993 to provide the necessary consultation period prior to formal signing. Thus, the major purpose of the twenty-third Quad ministerial in Toronto, Ontario on 12-14 May 1993 was to provide an impetus for completing the Uruguay Round by the new target date. More specifically, the Quad wanted to forge a consensus on trade in services and industrial market access before the July G7 summit in Tokyo. If the G7 countries could specify their commitments on services and industrial market access, they would then be able to pressure other key traders such as South Korea, Brazil, India, and the ASEAN (Association of Southeast Asian Nations) to improve their offers.[47]

The Toronto Quad did not succeed, however, in resolving the differences among the members on services and market access issues. For example, Japan was reluctant to increase its commitments on financial services, the United States was unwilling to improve its offer on maritime services, and the EC refused to improve its offer on audiovisual services. The Quad ministers therefore met on the margins of the June 1993 OECD ministerial in Paris, and agreed to have almost non-stop bilateral and quadrilateral meetings on goods and services market access leading up to the twenty-fourth Quad ministerial in Tokyo scheduled for 23-24 June 1993. These meetings were designed to reduce the differences among Quad members to a small number of key issues that the four trade ministers could resolve at the Tokyo Quad. Quad officials believed that the Tokyo Quad had to reach a consensus on industrial goods and services market access if the July G7 summit was to approve a basic package on these issues. The Quad recognised that "without some progress between the United States and EC, it would not be worthwhile to have these meetings with other major trading partners," because they were the two most important trading powers.[48]

Despite the high hopes for the Tokyo Quad, progress was limited because the United States, the EC, Japan, and Canada did not offer the concessions needed to produce a large market access package. Thus, the four trade ministers agreed to meet informally immediately before and during the July 1993 Tokyo III summit in attempts to finalise a market access report for the G7 leaders. The ministers held a marathon meeting that lasted from 9 p.m. on 6 July to 3 a.m. the next day. Then they had a second meeting that finally ended with an agreement on 7 July, just before the G7 leaders were scheduled to meet. The Quad market access agreement proposed the elimination or reduction of tariffs on 18 sectors of manufactured products, including some that were particularly sensitive. Two days later, the G7 summit leaders endorsed the Quad's "progress made towards a large market access package in goods and services as a major step to the immediate resumption of multilateral negotiations in Geneva."[49] In reality, the Quad's package agreement had both strengths and weaknesses. On the one hand, the Quad members demonstrated a willingness to accept larger tariff cuts and more specific commitments for goods liberalisation than expected. On the other hand, the package did not deal with disputed issues in agriculture and services, and developing countries complained that the eight products identified in the agreement for possible removal of trade barriers did not include their main export interests.[50] In response to the developing country concerns, the GATT director-general maintained that "a larger share of the responsibility for movement must lie with the major players," and he called on the Quad to offer concessions to developing countries in textiles and tropical products.[51]

From the Tokyo Agreement to the GATT Marrakesh Agreement

Despite the optimism stemming from the Tokyo market access accord, the United States and the EC had different interpretations of the agreement that had to be resolved before it could be expanded to include tariff cuts of interest to the developing countries. For example, the EC and the United States had different views of the provisions on "tariff peaks." EC tariffs were an average of the national tariffs of the original member states, and this averaging process had largely eliminated tariff peaks exceeding 15 percent. Although U.S. and Japanese tariffs were low on the average, unlike the EC they had a number of tariff peaks with higher duties to protect sensitive industries. The EC interpreted the Tokyo agreement as requiring the United States to cut most of its tariff peaks by 50 percent, but the United States interpreted the agreement as an objective to strive for rather than a firm commitment.[52] The EC Commissioner Brittan called for a Quad meeting as soon as possible to break the deadlock over these market access issues, and the GATT director-general supported this idea. However, the United States argued that a Quad meeting would not be useful until the EU provided a more substantial offer. Talks therefore continued on a bilateral basis, and in early December 1993 the United States and the EU finally agreed to a package of industrial tariff cuts. Whereas the EU made more concessions to the United States on industrial tariff cuts, the United States was willing to weaken the discipline on subsidised agricultural exports. The U.S.-EU accord made it possible to conclude a multilateral trade agreement by 15 December 1993, the effective deadline for notifying Congress under fast-track authority. Negotiations to improve the market access offers could continue even after the agreement, because U.S. fast-track authority would not expire until 15 April 1994.[53]

After President Clinton's notification to Congress, the United States put considerable pressure on Japan to expand its market access offer, particularly in view of its huge balance of trade deficit with Japan. The Japanese, however, refused to expand the market access offer they had submitted on 15 December 1993. Although the United States wanted to hold a Quad ministerial to exert collective pressure on Japan, the other Quad members were not enthusiastic. Instead, the Quad chief negotiators met in Geneva in January and February to resolve outstanding market access issues. The United States continued to exert pressure on Japan in these meetings, but in the end Japan offered no additional commitments. The Quad officials' meetings were more successful in encouraging developing countries to increase their market access offers during this period. Despite continued tensions over U.S.-Japanese relations, the planned role of the WTO, and the relationship between trade and environmental standards, the

GATT ministers assembled in Marrakesh, Morocco on 15 April 1994 to sign the Uruguay Round agreement. Over one hundred ministers signed the Final Act of the Uruguay Round, and made decisions to ensure that the WTO would begin operations on 1 January 1995.[54]

After the Marrakesh Agreement

The main issue at the first Quad ministerial after the Marrakesh Agreement – the twenty-fifth Quad on 9-11 September 1994 in Los Angeles, California – was the implementation of the Uruguay Round agreements.[55] Despite some anticipated problems, the EU, the United States, Japan, and Canada indicated that they all expected to enact implementing legislation in time for the scheduled 1 January 1995 entry into force of the WTO. The Quad also considered ratification of the Marrakesh agreement by Brazil, India, the ASEAN countries and other important developing countries to be essential for effective implementation of the WTO. However, some Quad members felt it was better not to name specific countries, because this might limit flexibility in determining what constituted the minimum requirement for approval of the WTO.

In addition to the implementation issue, the Los Angeles Quad provided the trade ministers with the first opportunity to engage in detailed discussion of plans for further trade liberalisation after Marrakesh. Quad ministers believed they had to consider further market opening initiatives to avoid losing the momentum built up from the Uruguay Round. If the ministers developed a proposal on market opening initiatives, they could present it to the 1995 G7 summit in Halifax. Some of the key areas Quad ministers identified for liberalisation after the Uruguay Round were standards, financial services, and investment. Although the Quad or OECD alone comprised the critical mass required for trade liberalisation in a small number of sectors, it was essential to involve additional countries in most sectors. Thus, post-Uruguay Round liberalisation depended not only on agreement in the Quad, but also on gaining acceptance by other key countries. The Quad ministers expressed differing views on the best venue for negotiating an investment agreement. The United States believed the OECD was the best forum for negotiation, because it could initially achieve a higher standard of obligations than the WTO; but the EU and Canada felt the WTO would be a better forum because developing countries were destinations for growing shares of foreign direct investment. Despite these differing views, the ministers agreed that parallel activity in the OECD and WTO could be useful, and that work on investment rules in the OECD would contribute to the subsequent success of WTO investment efforts. The Quad ministers also agreed that an OECD Multilateral Agreement on Investment should be kept open for non-OECD members if they were prepared to assume the obligations of the agreement.

The Los Angeles Quad also dealt with a number of institutional issues. First, the Quad suggested that there be coherence and perhaps some coordination of activity among the WTO, the IMF and the World Bank on trade-related issues. Second, the Quad ministers discussed issues that might arise in the transition from GATT to the WTO, and they agreed that Quad senior officials should continue discussions to increase understanding of the legal and practical problems involved. Third, the Quad discussed the issues of WTO transparency and WTO relations with non-governmental organisations. Although the ministers agreed that a large number of documents should be derestricted, they expressed differing views on whether NGOs should have greater access to WTO meetings and dispute settlement procedures.[56] Finally, the Quad discussed the contentious issue of selecting a WTO director-general. The United States argued that the first WTO director-general should be non-European, because all the GATT directors-general had been Europeans; and it supported the former Mexican President Carlos Salinas de Gortari for the position. Japan and most Asian countries supported the South Korean Minister of Trade, Industry and Energy Kim Chul-su, and the EU supported the former Italian trade minister Renato Ruggiero. The discussion of these candidates at the Los Angeles Quad ended in stalemate.[57]

In view of the many post-Marrakesh issues discussed in Los Angeles, the Quad ministers asked senior officials to prepare papers on a number of topics. Quad senior officials held meetings to carry out this work on 14-15 November and 8-9 December 1994 in Geneva, and on 30-31 March 1995 in Ottawa, Canada. In preparation for these meetings, Quad officials distributed discussion papers on agriculture, competition policy, investment, government procurement, market access, technical barriers to trade, standards and regulations, services, environment, and coordination of the WTO with other institutions. The senior officials' meetings examined a wide range of issues, including the transition from GATT to the WTO, the Dispute Settlement Appellate Body, WTO transparency and relations with NGOs, coherence between the WTO and other institutions, proposals for post-Uruguay Round trade liberalisation, and the accession of China to the WTO. These meetings were of particular importance, because the trade agenda in the immediate post-Uruguay Round period was relatively unshaped. Thus, the meetings helped to identify specific areas where the Quad and the G7 could provide the vision and direction needed to maintain the momentum of trade liberalisation. More specifically, the Quad senior officials' meetings laid the groundwork for the development of a trade package by the Quad and OECD ministerials in May 1995, and the G7 summit in June 1995.

Despite the contribution of Quad senior officials, it is important to note that differences emerged in their meetings. For example, U.S. and Canadian officials proposed an initiative to expand the tariff cuts negotiated in the Uruguay Round, but EU and Japanese officials were reluctant to endorse such a policy. The EU preferred to focus instead on implementing the Uruguay Round and the various regional trade agreements in Europe.[58] Differences on selection of the first WTO Director-General were also evident in the November 1994 meeting of Quad senior officials, with no obvious front-runner emerging. This particular issue was resolved on 21 March 1995 when the United States agreed to support the European candidate Renato Ruggiero in order to avoid a divisive vote on the issue. In return for U.S. support, the Europeans agreed to the U.S. demand that Ruggiero would serve only one four-year term as WTO Director-General, and that the next WTO head would be non-European.[59]

In sum, the Quad was extremely active from the Brussels ministerial to the immediate post-Uruguay Round period. Completing the Uruguay Round was a slow and tortuous process, and the Quad ministerial and senior officials' meetings were closely involved with the negotiations. The main function of the Quad was to contribute to understanding and cooperation among the major traders, but the Quad also sought solutions to specific negotiating problems. On one occasion, the Quad served as a forum for negotiation when it helped develop a market access package for industrial goods and services that was crucial to the completion of the Uruguay Round. After the Uruguay Round agreement was signed at Marrakesh, the Quad provided leadership in implementing the agreement, and in exploring trade issues for the post-Uruguay Round period. For example, the Quad took initiative in discussing trade-related issues involving the environment, investment, and competition policy. Although the Quad benefited from its small size and the importance of its members, divisions among its members sometimes interfered with the Quad's ability to reach a consensus on critical issues. The Quad's focus on developed country interests also sometimes antagonised developing countries that were excluded from the deliberations. Despite these shortcomings, the Quad had a significant role in helping to conclude the Uruguay Round, and in beginning the process of post-Uruguay Round planning.

Organisation for Economic Co-operation and Development

Previous chapters discussed three areas in which OECD background studies and prenegotiations were essential to eventual negotiations in the GATT: government procurement, services trade, and agricultural trade. This section briefly examines the outcome of these negotiations at the end of the GATT Uruguay Round, and assesses what the outcome indicates about OECD influence.

Chapters 3 and 4 discussed the fact that OECD discussions, background studies, and development of a draft code had a crucial role in leading to the negotiation of a Government Procurement Agreement (GPA) in the GATT Tokyo Round. Although the GPA was a substantial accomplishment, like the other Tokyo Round codes it was plurilateral with only a limited membership. Indeed, fewer GATT members signed the GPA than any other Tokyo Round code, and all but three of the signatories were developed countries. Clearly, the OECD countries had underestimated the degree to which developing countries as late industrialisers were committed to public spending prerogatives in efforts to promote their economic development.[60]

After the Tokyo Round GPA entered into force in 1981, there were two series of negotiations to improve the agreement. The first series from 1981 to 1986 resulted in a revised GPA that entered into force in 1988, and the second series from 1986 to 1994 resulted in a second revision to the GPA that became effective in 1996. The most important revisions to the GPA were made in the second series of negotiations conducted during (but separately from) the GATT Uruguay Round. These negotiations expanded the coverage and strengthened the enforcement provisions of the GPA; for example, the revised GPA applied to government procurement of services as well as goods, and extended coverage to subfederal units. However, the negotiations during the Uruguay Round were not successful in expanding the GPA membership, despite the efforts to address developing country concerns. Indeed, two NIEs that had signed the Tokyo Round GPA – Singapore and Hong Kong – refused to sign the new GPA.

The signatories of the latest version of the GPA include only Canada, the 15 members of the EU, Israel, Japan, Norway, South Korea, Switzerland, and the United States. Even some members of the OECD such as Australia, New Zealand, and Turkey (and more recent OECD members including Mexico, the Czech Republic, Poland, and the Slovak Republic) are not GPA signatories. Following the GATT Uruguay Round agreement, the updated GPA is one of only four remaining plurilateral agreements – along with the agreements on civil aircraft, beef and dairy products – that do not require the participation of all WTO signatories. These four areas were not affected by the Uruguay Round's single undertaking requirement, because they were not negotiated in the Uruguay Round.[61] In sum, the OECD background studies and prenegotiations were highly successful in getting government procurement on the GATT agenda, and in facilitating the negotiation of GPAs during the Tokyo and Uruguay Rounds. However, the OECD was not successful in inducing developing countries to join the agreements, and as a result the GPA continues to be an issue of concern primarily to the advanced industrial states.

As discussed in Chapters 5 and 6, the OECD coined the term "trade in services" and helped develop many of the conceptual ideas regarding services that facilitated the Uruguay Round's services trade negotiations. The WTO secretariat has described the General Agreement on Trade in Services resulting from the Uruguay Round as "perhaps the most important single development in the multilateral trading system since the GATT itself came into effect in 1948."[62] Nevertheless, the GATS has large sectoral exceptions, and some basic GATT principles such as national treatment are not automatic rights in the GATS. The limitations of the GATS stem from the fact that there were divisions among the OECD countries as well as between North and South in the Uruguay Round. The EU wanted the GATS to have "soft" obligations, with national treatment applying only to specific sectors; and some developing countries did not even support the idea of applying national treatment to services. Only the United States and some OECD and NIE small, open economies favoured a GATS with "hard" obligations similar to those of the GATT.

In the end, the EU-developing country preference for a soft agreement prevailed. GATS follows a "negative list approach" for MFN treatment; that is, MFN treatment is a general obligation, but members may list exemptions to this obligation for specific sectors in an annex to the agreement. GATS follows a far less demanding "positive list approach" for national treatment and market access; that is, a member is required to provide national treatment and market access only for those services it specifically lists in its services schedule. Many developing countries preferred this positive list approach, because they did not intend to make substantial commitments. Studies published in 1996 found that the average GATS commitment index for national treatment and market access for high-income countries (mainly the OECD countries) was 36.5 percent, whereas the commitment index for middle- and low-income countries was 10.7 percent. Although the variance in commitment was low among the OECD countries, it was very high among developing countries. One could attribute the limited nature of the GATS to the conceptual difficulties in applying economic principles such as comparative advantage to services trade, and to the relative newness of the area. As discussed, the liberalisation of trade in goods required 8 rounds of GATT negotiations over a 50-year period. Nevertheless, the OECD and North-South divisions also are a major factor explaining the limitations of the GATS.[63] According to liberal economists, "a significant expansion of the coverage of national treatment and market access commitments is needed to make the GATS more relevant."[64]

Agriculture was the third area we discussed in which OECD background work was of central importance prior to the GATT negotiations. The OECD continues to be actively involved in monitoring agriculture, because many agricultural trade issues are unresolved.[65] In contrast to government procurement and services trade, the North rather than the South has posed the main obstacles to agricultural trade liberalisation. Whereas many developing countries effectively tax agriculture and subsidise food consumption in urban areas, developed countries normally tax the urban areas to support agricultural production and incomes. Major developed country actors such as the EU and Japan subsidise their farm production, and even the United States which has aggressively pursued agricultural trade liberalisation provides substantial subsidies in this area. Agriculture was in fact "the central negotiating issue for the Uruguay Round, and to a large extent, the Uruguay Round proceeded at a pace only to the extent it was permitted by the U.S. and the EC negotiators who were locked in a very intense political struggle over the issues of agriculture."[66]

The Uruguay Round Agreement on Agriculture was a major breakthrough, because it applied "disciplines to practices that had never been subject to effective international restraints."[67] The agreement called for a reduction of agricultural export subsidies by 36 percent in value and 21 percent in volume, and for "tariffication," or the conversion of all agricultural NTBs to tariffs. Agricultural tariffs were then to be reduced by 36 percent on average over 6 years for developed countries, and by 24 percent for developing countries. Despite the groundbreaking nature of the Agreement on Agriculture, it had some serious limitations. Although the Uruguay Round constrained the use of agricultural export subsidies, most of the subsidies continued in reduced form. EU and U.S. agricultural export subsidies have continued to distort markets and interfere with agricultural exports from the Cairns Group countries. The Uruguay Round agreement resulted in tariffication, but some countries have substituted exceedingly high tariffs for their agricultural NTBs. Thus, agricultural markets continue to be "protected by tariffs considerably higher than those for almost all other goods."[68]

During the 1991 to 1994 period the OECD continued its custom of focusing on newer areas that the major traders believed should become major issues for multilateral trade negotiations. Two examples of these newer areas were competition policy, and the environment. For example, the OECD examined the trade and environment issue through its Joint Session of Trade and Environment Experts. The OECD's work program on the environment was oriented to five major areas: the effects of environmental policies on trade, the effects of trade policies on the environment, the increasing compatibility of environmental policies across countries, the applicability of the GATT and the OECD Guiding Principles to trade/environmental concerns, and developing country concerns about trade and the environment. The OECD also held detailed discussions on competition policy during this period, even though rules on competition policy never developed in the Uruguay Round.[69]

In sum, from the 1960s to the 1980s the OECD developed a reputation for generating new ideas and conducting background studies and prenegotiations in trade-related areas such as government procurement, services, and agriculture; and in the area of export credits the OECD became the main forum for negotiation. In the 1990s the OECD continued its practice of focusing on new ideas in its work on such areas as competition policy, and trade and the environment. One of the most important OECD contributions was its background work in areas that eventually became the subject of GATT negotiations. For example, the OECD (along with the Quad and the G7) registered some major accomplishments in inducing the GATT to include government procurement, services, and agriculture on its trade negotiations. These cases demonstrate, however, that there is a significant distance between the OECD group of 30 mainly developed countries where much of the background work has been done, and the WTO group of 144 developed, developing, and emerging countries where it is far more difficult to reach a consensus on signing and implementing agreements. Thus, agriculture and services were part of the "built-in agenda" for further negotiations after the Uruguay Round, because the agreements in these two areas were so incomplete. As discussed, the government procurement agreement is also incomplete, in the sense that almost all developing countries and some OECD countries have refused to sign it. The OECD experience indicates that a degree of management and agenda-setting by the developed countries is essential if many trade-related issues are to reach the negotiation stage in the GATT/WTO. Nevertheless, while developed country support is necessary for GATT/WTO negotiations in a range of areas, it is not sufficient to ensure that the negotiations will result in broad-ranging agreements. Increasingly, it is necessary to incorporate the views and concerns of developing and emerging countries.

The Role of Developing Countries

In Chapter 6, we discussed the fact that developing countries were more involved in the GATT Uruguay Round than in any previous round. Divisions were also more evident among the developing countries, and they engaged in more coalition behaviour with developed countries than ever before. These North-South coalitions were evident until the end of the Uruguay Round, and in some cases persisted after the round. One North-South coalition that persisted throughout the Uruguay Round was the De La Paix Group. The De La Paix Group had helped launch the Uruguay Round negotiations in 1986, and seven years later this group called on the major traders to show leadership in completing the round. At a low point in the negotiations when the round could not be completed without a second renewal of U.S. fast-track authority, the De La Paix Group moved to keep the negotiations going. Thus, the group sent letters on 11 March 1993 to U.S. President Clinton, the Presidents of the EC Council and Commission, and the Japanese Prime Minister urging them to resolve their differences. The group also called on the U.S. Congress to renew fast-track authority. The De La Paix Group's letters seemed to coincide with a slow improvement in relations among the major trading powers, and the U.S. Congress approved the renewal of fast-track authority.[70]

The most prominent example of a North-South coalition that continued throughout the Uruguay Round and afterwards is the Cairns Group. As discussed in Chapter 6, the Cairns Group had an important role in the first half of the Uruguay Round in ensuring that agriculture would be included in the negotiations, and in serving as a mediator between the extreme positions of the United States and the EC. In the later stages of the Uruguay Round after the 1990 Brussels ministerial the Cairns Group continued to send communiqués urging the major parties to settle their differences and conclude the round. Nevertheless, the Cairns Group had less influence after the Brussels ministerial as the agricultural negotiations came to depend on the outcome of bilateral bargaining between the United States and the EC, and to a lesser extent on bilateral bargaining between the United States and Japan.[71] Although the Cairns Group and to a lesser extent the De La Paix Group helped to stimulate negotiations and reach solutions, ultimately the final outcome of the Uruguay Round negotiations depended on those at the top of the global trade regime pyramid: the United States, the EU and the developed country institutions – the G7 and the Quad.

The crucial question for developing countries, of course, was whether or not they benefited from their greater involvement and coalition behaviour in the Uruguay Round. As discussed in Chapter 6, the Uruguay Round was a single-undertaking, in which the agreements would be binding on all members. The single-undertaking marked a significant change from the Tokyo Round, which permitted GATT members to opt out of joining the NTB codes. Although the single-undertaking weakened the concept of special and differential treatment for developing countries, they continued to have S&D treatment in the Uruguay Round agreement in different forms. Whereas S&D treatment before the Uruguay Round focused on preferential market access and special rights for developing countries, in the Uruguay Round agreement S&D treatment emphasised greater flexibility for developing countries in fulfilling their commitments, longer transition times for implementing agreements, and technical assistance from the advanced industrial states.[72]

In the Uruguay Round, the developing countries agreed to lower their industrial tariffs, accept fairly strong discipline in new areas such as intellectual property, and open up some of their services to trade with the developed countries. In return, the developed countries gave the developing countries assurances of increased and more secure market access for their exports, especially for agricultural products, and textiles and clothing. The new WTO also has a more effective dispute settlement system that developing countries have been using more frequently. Although the South gained some fairly significant benefits from the Uruguay Round, in the years after the conclusion of the round developing countries began to feel that they had gained less than they originally thought. This perception resulted "partly from the belated realisation that they had accepted fairly weak commitments in agriculture and textiles while making substantially stronger ones, especially in new areas such as intellectual property."[73] Developing countries were initially encouraged by the Uruguay Round Agreement on Textiles and Clothing, which provided a 10-year transition period of phasing out quantitative restrictions on imports. However, liberalisation was "back-loaded" toward the end of the ten-year period, and there are fears that the misuse of safeguards and other protectionist measures by developed country importers would prolong the restrictions on textiles trade. The developing countries were also dissatisfied with the lack of progress in dealing with agricultural trade protectionism, and countervailing and antidumping duties that the North often imposes on Southern exports. In addition, the developing countries maintained that they could not implement the Uruguay Round agreement within the allotted time period, and that developed countries were not providing sufficient technical assistance.[74] As Chapter 8 discusses, dissatisfaction of the developing countries with the results of the Uruguay Round was a major impediment to agreement on a new round of negotiations at the WTO ministerial meetings.

Conclusion

The Uruguay Round was by far the longest and most ambitious of the 8 rounds of GATT multilateral trade negotiations. Perhaps more than in any previous negotiation, a degree of consensus between the United States and the EU as the two largest traders was essential before the Uruguay Round could be completed. Thus, in the crucial final phase of the round, a U.S. administration official acknowledged that "the quad process is important but the bilateral efforts [between the United States and the EU] must fall into place for the process to move forward."[75] As U.S. trade hegemony declined, the EU became an actor on a par with the United States near the top of the global trade regime pyramid, and in the latter stages of the Uruguay Round the EU sometimes pressured more forcefully for a successful conclusion of the round than the United States. The GATT secretariat also supplemented U.S. leadership, and in the latter stages of the round the assertive role of Peter Sutherland as GATT director-general was of critical importance. Despite the centrality of the United States and the EU, the G7 and the Quad also had important roles in bringing about the completion of the round.

At each summit from 1990 to 1992 the G7 pledged to take actions to help conclude the Uruguay Round. However, continuing differences and disputes – especially the U.S.-EC divisions over agriculture – precluded the completion of the round until December 1993. Although the summits lost a good deal of credibility because of the repeated re-setting of deadlines, this re-scheduling may have helped to pressure for eventual results. During the latter stages of the Uruguay Round the G7 summits helped limit protectionism and keep the negotiations going despite a recession, pressured for a stronger dispute settlement mechanism, and supported the idea of establishing the WTO. Most importantly, G7 pressure on the Quad trade ministers resulted in the negotiation of a crucial market access agreement for goods and services in time for the July 1993 Tokyo III summit. This agreement had a crucial effect in reviving the Uruguay Round and permitting the negotiators to reach a final agreement. In exerting pressure for the market access accord, the G7 demonstrated its ability to act as a catalyst, and the completion of the Uruguay Round "restored the summit's morale."[76]

The main function of the Quad was to contribute to understanding and cooperation, and settle differences among the major traders. Quad ministers focused most of their efforts on the process and timing of the negotiations, and depended on their chief negotiators to formulate a strategy for specific negotiating issues. However, the Quad sometimes became more directly involved in seeking solutions to specific negotiating problems. Not surprisingly, Quad ministers and senior officials focussed on issues of particular interest to the North such as trade in services, industrial market access, and intellectual property. They were also concerned with issues that could block an Uruguay Round agreement such as agricultural trade. On one occasion the Quad served as a crucial forum for negotiation when it helped to develop a market access accord before and during the 1993 Tokyo G7 summit. After the Uruguay Round agreement was signed at Marrakesh, the Quad helped provide leadership in implementing the agreement, and in exploring post-Uruguay Round issues such as the environment, investment, competition policy, standards, financial services, and WTO relations with NGOs.

Some of the more specific accomplishments of the Uruguay Round owed a great deal to the background work and prenegotiations by the OECD. For example, the OECD's preliminary work on government procurement, services trade, and agricultural trade helped to put these issues on the agenda of the GATT negotiations. Although this was a major accomplishment, each of the agreements had shortcomings. The GPA was one of a small number of plurilateral agreements remaining at the end of the Uruguay Round, and all but three of the signatories were OECD states. The Uruguay Round services agreement was very uneven, because the national treatment and market access provisions followed a positive list approach in which countries agreed to liberalise only those services they included on their lists. The Uruguay Round agricultural agreement was also incomplete, because agricultural export subsidies were to be reduced rather than phased out, and some GATT/WTO members replaced their agricultural import quotas with exceedingly high tariffs. Thus, the OECD was more successful in helping to put items on the GATT negotiating agenda than in ensuring that the GATT's large and diverse membership would develop strong, effective agreements.

The OECD's shortcomings demonstrated that the developed countries could not achieve their objectives in specific agreements without support from important developing and emerging countries. Thus, the developing countries had a more important role in the Uruguay Round than in previous rounds. For reasons discussed, most developing countries increased their commitment to trade liberalisation and to active involvement in the Uruguay Round. Unlike previous rounds, the developing countries also joined in a number of North-South coalitions such as the Cairns Group. The Uruguay Round provided the

South with a number of benefits, but after the round many developing countries began to feel that they had lost more in the negotiation than they had gained. For example, the developing countries gained less than they had expected in agricultural and textiles trade. In Chapter 8 we discuss the dissatisfaction of developing countries and also of civil society with the decision-making process in the global trade regime, and the effects on the G7/G8, the Quad, and the OECD.

Notes

1   Quoted in "Uruguay Round Market Access Problem to Await Ministerial Decision," *Inside U.S. Trade*, 8 October 1993, p. S-4.

2   Hugo Paemen and Alexandra Bensch, *From the GATT to the WTO: The European Community in the Uruguay Round* (Leuven: Leuven University Press, 1995), pp. 170-171.

3   Ernest H. Preeg, *Traders in a Brave New World: The Uruguay Round and the Future of the International Trading System* (Chicago: University of Chicago Press, 1995), p. 159.

4   Preeg, *Traders in a Brave New World*, pp. 189-190.

5   Paemen and Bensch, *From the GATT to the WTO*, p. 233.

6   John Croome, *Reshaping the World Trading System*, (Geneva: World Trade Organization, 1995), pp. 287-291; Preeg, *Traders in a Brave New World*, pp. 127-131. For a detailed discussion of U.S. fast-track authority see Craig VanGrasstek, "Is the Fast Track Really Necessary?," *Journal of World Trade* 31-2 (April 1997), pp. 97-123.

7   Preeg, *Traders in a Brave New World*, pp. 131-132.

8   Preeg, *Traders in a Brave New World*, pp. 138-139.

9   On the EC reaction to the Dunkel draft see Paemen and Bensch, *From the GATT to the WTO*, pp. 202-203.

10   Croome, *Reshaping the World Trading System*, pp. 325-327.

11   Croome, *Reshaping the World Trading System*, pp. 344-345; Preeg, *Traders in a Brave New World*, pp. 143-158.

12   Preeg, *Traders in a Brave New World*, pp. 162-165.

13   Paemen and Bensch, *From the GATT to the WTO*, p. 247.

14   Nicholas Bayne, *Hanging In There: The G7 and G8 Summit in Maturity and Renewal* (Aldershot: Ashgate, 2000), p. 61.

15   Bayne, *Hanging In There*, pp. 59-71.

16   Joe Burey, "NAM Warns That Uruguay Round May Wither Away without Strong Push at Summit," *Inside U.S. Trade*, 12 July 1991, pp. 10-11.

17   Meeting of Cairns Group Ministers at Manaus, Brazil, 9 July 1991 – Communiqué, paragraph 2.

18   Rachel Johnson, "Top Priority for Completing Uruguay Round," *Financial Times*, 16 July 1991, p. 4.

19   Peter Norman, "G7 Leaders Pledge GATT Success," *Financial Times*, 18 July 1991, p. 22.

20   "Economic Declaration: Building World Partnership," G7 Summit, London, 15-17 July 1991, paragraph 10.

21   Dunkel quoted in Norman, "G7 Leaders Pledge GATT Success," p. 22.

22 Preeg, *Traders in a Brave New World*, pp. 131-132; Bayne, *Hanging In There*, pp. 62-63.
23 Robert Evans, "Talks on World Trade 'Blocked,' Source Says," *Financial Post*, 16 April 1992, p. 11.
24 Madeline Drohan, "Business Leaders Press for GATT Deal," *Globe and Mail*, 16 April 1992; "ICC Charges G-7 Lacks Leadership, Urges Quick Political Deal on GATT," *Inside U.S. Trade*, 26 June 1992, pp. 13-14.
25 Cairns Group Ministerial Meeting, Geneva, Switzerland, 28 June 1992, *Communiqué*.
26 Bayne, *Hanging In There*, p. 61.
27 "Mr GATT," *The Economist*, 15 February 1992, p. 17.
28 "Economic Declaration: Working Together for Growth and a Safer World," G7 Summit, Munich, 6-8 July 1992, paragraph 8.
29 Paemen and Bensch, *From GATT to the WTO*, pp. 211-213; Preeg, *Traders in a Brave New World*, pp. 138-43; Croome, *Reshaping the World Trading System*, pp. 330 and 338.
30 "Global Chamber Warns that Tokyo Is Last Chance for GATT Talks," *Inside U.S. Trade*, 25 June 1993, p. 7.
31 "Bangkok Declaration – Cairns Group," Cairns Group 12th Ministerial Meeting, Bangkok, Thailand, 26-27 June 1993.
32 "Full Speed Ahead on GATT," *Financial Times*, 8 July 1993.
33 Press Conference by the President, Hotel Okura, Tokyo, Japan, 8 July 1993.
34 G7 Summit Economic Declaration, "A Strengthened Commitment to Jobs and Growth," Tokyo, Japan, 6-9 July 1993, paragraph 7; "Kantor Cautious on GATT Progress Despite Breakthrough," *Inside U.S. Trade*, 16 July 1993, Special Report, p. 4.
35 G7 Summit Communiqué, Naples, Italy, 8-10 July 1994.
36 G7 Summit Communiqué, Naples, Italy, 8-10 July 1994.
37 Bayne, *Hanging In There*, pp. 116-117.
38 Bayne, *Hanging In There*, pp. 63-64.
39 Paemen and Bensch, *From the GATT to the WTO*, pp. 194-195; Preeg, *Traders in a Brave New World*, p. 111.
40 "Economic Declaration: Building World Partnership," London G7 summit, 15-17 July, 1991, paragraph 10.
41 Quotation from Canada's Minister for International Trade Michael Wilson in "Minister Wilson to Attend Quadrilateral Meeting in France Followed by Trade Mission to Iran," Minister of Industry Science and Technology and Minister for International Trade, *News Release* no. 195, 10 September 1991.
42 "Economic Declaration: Building World Partnership," paragraph 11; "Hills Says EC Insists on 'Scope and Direction' of Farm Plan Before Tackling GATT," *Inside U.S. Trade*, 27 September 1991, pp. 6-7.
43 Daniel C. Esty, *Greening the GATT: Trade, Environment, and the Future* (Washington, D.C.: Institute for International Economics, July 1994), pp. 63 and 181.
44 Jeffrey S. Thomas and Michael A. Meyer, *The New Rules of Global Trade: A Guide to the World Trade Organization* (Scarborough, ONT: Carswell, 1997), p. 344; Provisional Draft Agenda for the Next Quad Ministerial, February 1992; "Trade Ministers to Take Stock of Uruguay Round in Four Way Japan Meeting," *Inside U.S. Trade*, 24 April 1992, p. 20; "Hills Warns that GATT Talks in Jeopardy if Farm Deal is not Reached by July," *Inside U.S. Trade*, 1 May 1992, pp. 4-5.
45 "EC Proposes Environment-Trade Group in MTO to be Created in Uruguay Round," *Inside U.S. Trade*, 2 October 1992, p. 22.

46 "Quad Countries Agree on Timetable for GATT Deal if Farm Dispute is Resolved," *Inside U.S. Trade*, 23 October 1992, pp. 4-5.

47 Preeg, *Traders in a Brave New World*, p. 158; U.S. Officials Fail to Tip Hand on GATT Talks During Informal Quad Meeting," *Inside U.S. Trade*, 26 March 1993, pp. 1 & 10-11; "U.S., EC Press Japan on Financial Services; U.S. Hints at Maritime Commitments," *Inside U.S. Trade*, 21 May 1993, p. 16.

48 "U.S.-EC Ministers Hail Progress on GATT Talks While Negotiators See Little," *Inside U.S. Trade*, 4 June 1993, p. 14.

49 Communiqué of G7 Summit, Tokyo, Japan, 6-9 July 1993, paragraph 7.

50 "GATT Hails Trade Accord but Says Hurdles Remain," *Daily Yomiuri*, 8 July 1993, p. 13; "Trade Chiefs Agree on Tariff Cuts," *Japan Times*, 8 July 1993; Croome, *Reshaping the World Trading System*, p.348. The Quad market access agreement is found in Multilateral Trade Negotiations, the Uruguay Round, Trade Negotiations Committee, "Report on the Uruguay Round," MTN.TNC/W.113, 13 July 1993.

51 Quoted in "Sutherland Says Lack of Quad Concessions Blocks GATT Access Talks," *Inside U.S. Trade*, 1 October 1993, p. 6.

52 Paemen and Bensch, *From GATT to the WTO*, pp. 110-12.

53 "Clinton Meets GATT Notification Deadline; Tariff Talks Endure," *Inside U.S. Trade*, 17 December 1993, p. 1.

54 "The WTO is Born," *GATT Focus Newsletter* no. 107 Special Issue, May 1994, p. 1; Preeg, *Traders in a Brave New World*, pp. 178-180.

55 "MacLaren to Push for Uruguay Round Implementation at Quadrilateral Trade Ministers Meeting," *Government of Canada News Release* no. 171, 7 September 1994.

56 "Los Angeles to Host Quad Trade Meeting of World's Four Largest Economies," *News from the Office of the Mayor* Richard J. Riordan, 22 July 1994; Discussion Paper for 9-11 September 1994 Quadrilateral Ministerial Meeting, 17 August 1994; Quadrilateral Trade Ministers' Meeting Report, 9-11 September 1994, pp. 1-7.

57 Theodore H. Cohn, *Global Political Economy: Theory and Practice* (New York: Addison Wesley Longman, 2000), pp. 216-17; "U.S. Signals New Flexibility on GATT Financial Services Talks," *Inside U.S. Trade*, 16 September 1994, p. 4.

58 "Kantor Calls for New Zero-for-Zero Initiative among Quad Countries," *Inside U.S. Trade*, 7 April 1995, p. 3.

59 "Quad Countries See WTO Implementation on Schedule for January," *Inside U.S. Trade*, 18 November 1994, pp. 18-19; Nathaniel C. Nash, "U.S. Backed Candidate for Trade Post is Trailing," *New York Times*, 3 December 1994, p. 3; Madelaine Drohan, "Americans, Europeans at Odds Over Who Should Lead WTO," *Globe and Mail*, 15 March 1995, p. B6; David E. Sanger, "Yielding, U.S. Bows to Europe on Trade Chief," *New York Times*, 21 March 1995, p. C1.

60 On the role of government involvement in late industrialisers, see Friedrich List, *The National System of Political Economy*, translated by Sampson S. Lloyd (London: Longmans, Green, 1916); and Alexander Gerschenkron, *Economic Backwardness in Historical Perspective: A Book of Essays* (Cambridge: Harvard University Press, 1962).

61 Bernard M. Hoekman and Petros C. Mavroidis, "The WTO's Agreement on Government Procurement: Expanding Disciplines, Declining Membership?," in Sue Arrowsmith, ed., *Public Procurement Law Review 1995 – Volume 4* (London: Sweet & Maxwell, 1995), pp. 63-79; Federico Trionfetti, "Discriminatory Public Procurement and International Trade," *World Economy* 23-1 (January 2000), pp. 57-76; Croome, *Reshaping the World Trading*

System, pp. 92 and 326; Jeffrey J. Schott, assisted by Johanna W. Buurman, *The Uruguay Round: An Assessment* (Washington, D.C.: Institute for International Economics, November 1994), pp. 66-76.

62   WTO Secretariat, *Guide to the Uruguay Round Agreements* (The Hague: Kluwer Law International, 1999), p. 161.

63   André Sapir, "The General Agreement on Trade in Services: From 1994 to the Year 2000," *Journal of World Trade* 33-1 (1999), p. 58; Bernard Hoekman, "Assessing the General Agreement on Trade in Services," in Will Martin and L. Alan Winters, eds., *The Uruguay Round and the Developing Countries* (Cambridge: Cambridge University Press, 1996), pp. 88-124; John H. Jackson, *The World Trading System: Law and Policy of International Economic Relations* (Cambridge: MIT Press, 2nd edition, 1999), pp. 306-307; John Whalley and Colleen Hamilton, *The Trading System After the Uruguay Round* (Washington, D.C.: Institute for International Economics, July 1996), pp. 52-55.

64   Bernard M. Hoekman and Michel M. Kostecki, *The Political Economy of the World Trading System: The WTO and Beyond* (Oxford: Oxford University Press, 2nd edition, 2001), p. 272.

65   For example, see the annual editions of the OECD's *Agricultural Policies in OECD Countries: Monitoring and Evaluation*.

66   Jackson, *The World Trading System*, p. 314.

67   Randy Green, "The Uruguay Round Agreement on Agriculture," *Law and Policy in International Business* 31-3 (Spring 2000), p. 819.

68   Timothy Josling, "Agriculture and the Next WTO Round," in Jeffrey J. Schott, ed., *The WTO After Seattle* (Washington, D.C.: Institute for International Economics, July 2000), pp. 91-92.

69   Thomas and Meyer, *The New Rules of Global Trade*, p. 344.

70   Croome, *Reshaping the World Trading System*, pp. 344-45; Preeg, *Traders in a Brave New World*, p. 158.

71   Andrew F. Cooper, Richard A. Higgott, and Kim Richard Nossal, *Relocating Middle Powers: Australia and Canada in a Changing World Order* (Vancouver: University of British Columbia Press, 1993), p. 82.

72   John Whalley, "Special and Differential Treatment in the Millennium Round," *World Economy* 22 (November 1999), pp. 1065-1093; Mari Pangestu, "Special and Differential Treatment in the Millennium: Special for Whom and How Different?," *World Economy* 23-9 (September 2000), pp. 1285-1302.

73   Jayashree Watal, "Developing Countries' Interests in a 'Development Round'," in Schott, ed., *The WTO After Seattle*, p. 72.

74   Marcelo de Paiva Abreu, "Trade in Manufactures: The Outcome of the Uruguay Round and Developing Country Interests," in Martin and Winters, eds., *The Uruguay Round and the Developing Countries*, p. 72; Joseph E. Stiglitz, "Two Principles for the Next Round or, How to Bring Developing Countries in from the Cold," *World Economy* 23-4 (April 2000), pp. 437-454.

75   Quoted in "Uruguay Round Market Access Problem to Await Ministerial Decision," *Inside U.S. Trade*, 8 October 1993, p. S-4.

76   Bayne, *Hanging In There*, pp. 63-64.

8   The Post-Uruguay Round Period

As discussed in Chapter 7, the relative positions of the United States and the EU on the global trade regime pyramid changed somewhat during the GATT Uruguay Round. The United States had assumed a leading role during about 50 years of GATT negotiations, and the launching of the Uruguay Round owed a great deal to U.S. conceptual ideas and diplomatic behaviour. While the United States continued to exert leadership in the early stages of the Uruguay Round, the EU began the round with hesitation and a more regional economic outlook. However, U.S. protectionism increased, and U.S. leadership declined somewhat in the latter stages of the Uruguay Round. The round was successfully completed partly because the EU and the GATT secretary-general moved to fill this leadership gap by adopting more assertive roles. Thus, leadership in the latter stages of the Uruguay Round was more balanced between the United States and the EU. (In November 1993, the EU subsumed the EC when the Maastricht Treaty extending the Community from trade and economic matters to a much broader range of activities came into effect. This chapter uses the term "EU" throughout because most of the discussion relates to the period after November 1993.)

After the Uruguay Round, the trend toward a more assertive EU leadership role that was evident in the latter stages of the round continued. Indeed, a senior economist at Deutsche Bank Research maintains that

> After more than five decades of systemic leadership of the USA in world trade diplomacy, the European Union emerged as a rival contender in the late 1990s. More than any other trading entity, the EU tried to generate support for further multilateral trade liberalisation and rule making in a new round of trade talks under the auspices of the WTO. Former Trade Commissioner Sir Leon Brittan, in particular, deserves much credit for acting as a policy entrepreneur who moulded a host of unresolved technical and legal trade issues into a coherent EU policy position and a potential agenda for a new round of multilateral trade negotiations.[1]

In the post-Uruguay Round discussions, the United States shifted from its traditional position of favouring deeper integration, and instead wanted "to have a short negotiation, necessitating a limited agenda," and "to have concrete results in priority areas for US interests."[2] In other words, the United States wanted a new WTO round to be limited to the Uruguay Round's "built-in" agenda areas for future negotiation – agriculture and services – plus a few other areas. Several possible factors, which in some respects are partially conflicting, could explain the U.S. position. First, one could argue that after ten years of strong economic growth, the United States felt no urgent need to seek benefits from further trade liberalisation and to offer concessions to others necessary for launching a comprehensive new round. Despite U.S. prosperity, however, the late 1990s was a period of rapidly growing U.S. trade deficits. Indeed, the U.S. merchandise trade deficit increased from $74 billion in 1991 to $277 billion in 1999. The 1997 East Asian financial crisis, and growth differentials between the United States and its major trading parters, were major factors accounting for the increased U.S. deficits. The U.S. response to these trade deficits has been to seek trade liberalisation largely limited to areas where it has a comparative advantage such as agriculture and services rather than seeking a new more comprehensive WTO round.[3]

Another critical factor explaining the change in U.S. position relates to the substantial "domestication" of U.S. trade politics in recent years. Although domestic factors have also had a significant role in U.S. trade policy, domestic disputes have become more prominent since the ratifications of the NAFTA in 1993, and the GATT Uruguay Round agreement in 1994. Thus, "the fight over the implementation of the North American Free Trade Agreement dramatically changed the debate about and the politics of trade policy in the United States."[4] Environmentalists, labour unions, and other NGO civil society groups added greatly to the ranks of interest groups actively involved with trade policy. Whereas some of these groups opposed only certain types of trade liberalisation agreements, others began to oppose trade liberalisation in general as a symbol of the threat globalisation posed to national autonomy. The domestication of U.S. trade policy has interfered with the Congress's ability to promote trade liberalisation. Dividing lines have been drawn between Democrats and Republicans, with many Democrats favouring the inclusion of provisions on environment and labour in trade agreements, and with many Republicans opposing such provisions. The divided Congress has been unwilling to this point to renew the U.S. president's fast-track authority (more recently called "trade-promotion authority") which is necessary to conclude major trade agreements. The last Congressional grant of fast-track authority expired in 1994, and President Clinton was unable to renew this authority during his administration. In December 2001 the House of Representatives finally passed legislation to give President George W. Bush a renewal of fast-track authority. However, the strikingly narrow 215-214 House vote on the issue was highly contentious, and the Senate has not yet held its vote on fast-track renewal.[5] Although the U.S. executive has been able to negotiate with other types of authority, the lack of fast-track limits the offers it is able to make.

In the late 1990s the EU devoted considerable effort to encourage others to launch a comprehensive WTO round. One reason the EU favoured a comprehensive round was that it did not expect the scheduled negotiations on agriculture and services to provide it with sufficient benefits. The talks on agriculture could present political problems for the EU because of strong protectionist forces within the community, and sharp divisions on services trade were expected among the EU, the United States, and developing countries. By broadening the agenda, EU officials believed there would be more opportunities for a variety of cross-cutting agreements among sectors. Thus, a comprehensive round would make an agreement more politically acceptable in the EU. A more comprehensive agenda would also facilitate progress in the negotiations in general. As a former EU Ambassador to the United States has noted, "when you have to make trade-offs, it is easier to do so when you have more elements to an acceptable package of agreements than when you have only a few subjects."[6] Despite the EU's more proactive stance in favour of a new comprehensive round, the EU had neither the economic power nor the unity of purpose to substitute for U.S. leadership in the global trade regime. As discussed, the EU commission is often constrained by the need for approval of member states via the Council of Ministers, and this arrangement continues to limit the EU's ability to adopt an assertive leadership role. It was therefore evident that a degree of consensus was necessary between the United States and the EU if a new WTO round was to be possible.[7]

As long as the United States and the EU were far apart on the nature of a new round, the G7/G8, the Quad, and the OECD could not adopt an assertive position on holding a new round. This chapter examines the role these institutions played after the Uruguay Round in attempting to bridge the differences among the United States, the EU, and others sufficiently so that a new WTO round could be launched. In addition to the U.S.-EU differences, a wide divergence of views between the North and the South was an additional factor interfering with the launching of a new round. Divisions *within* the South that were evident during the Uruguay Round continued after the round, and some North-South coalitions such as the Cairns Group continued to blur the divisions between North and South on the global trade regime pyramid. Despite the divisions within the South, it is possible to generalise about the South's position in regard to some trade issues. For example, most developing countries were disillusioned with the results of the Uruguay Round, and were therefore reluctant to agree to launching a new WTO round.

In the Uruguay Round the South had agreed to significant commitments in services and intellectual property in exchange for Northern promises in regard to agriculture and textiles/clothing. However, the South gained less in agriculture and textiles/clothing than it had expected. Many developed countries replaced agricultural import quotas with high tariff rates, and although agricultural export subsidies were reduced, the United States and the EU in particular were still providing substantial subsidies to their agricultural sectors. The Agreement on Textiles and Clothing permitted developed countries to delay much of their market liberalisation until 2005, and U.S. and EU actions raised fears that they would replace the quotas on textiles/clothing imports with antidumping duties and other safeguard actions. Thus, the South was reminded by the longer-term outcome of the Uruguay Round that it remained near the bottom of the global trade regime pyramid. Before agreeing to a new WTO round, many developing countries argued that the North should first fulfill its commitments in agriculture and textiles/clothing from the Uruguay Round. The North had also promised technical assistance to assist the South in fulfilling its commitments in the Uruguay Round, but the amount of technical assistance actually provided was disappointing. If the South was to offer further concessions in a new round, the North would have to commit more seriously to providing technical assistance.[8]

The wide differences of view, particularly between the United States and the EU and between North and South, were the most important factors preventing the launching of a new MTN round at the third WTO ministerial in Seattle in November-December 1999. The protests of civil society groups caused some disruption and inconvenience, but this was not a major cause of the failure at Seattle. Despite the problems in Seattle, the WTO members (for reasons discussed in this chapter) agreed to launch a new round at the fourth ministerial in Doha, Qatar two years later. This chapter examines the role of the G7/G8, the Quad, the OECD, and the developing countries in the tortuous process from the end of the Uruguay Round to the launching of a new round at Doha. Before examining the role of these institutions, we provide some background on developments in the WTO.

Developments in the WTO

A major institutional accomplishment of the Uruguay Round was the replacement of the informal GATT with the formal WTO as the main global trade organisation. Although the WTO retains many of the characteristics of the GATT, it is much broader in scope. In addition to trade in goods (GATT), the WTO oversees trade in services (GATS), trade-related intellectual property rights (TRIPs), and trade-related investment measures (TRIMs). In comparison with the GATT, the WTO's dispute settlement system is stronger and more effective. The WTO has also established a Trade Policy Review Mechanism to examine the effect of members' trade policies on the global trade regime, and to improve adherence to trading rules through greater transparency. Country-specific reviews are conducted by the WTO on a rotating basis. Furthermore, the structure of the WTO provides more continuity in political leadership. Although the sessions of the GATT Contracting Parties occasionally met at ministerial level, the GATT ministerials were sporadic in nature and were normally held only to launch or conclude new rounds of trade negotiations (the 1982 GATT ministerial was an exception). In contrast, a Ministerial Conference composed of all WTO members is to meet at least once every 2 years. The Ministerial Conference is designed to improve communication and strengthen guidance of the WTO at the higher political levels. As the top decision-making body in the WTO, the Ministerial Conference has "the authority to take decisions on all matters under any of the Multilateral Trade Agreements."[9]

The first WTO ministerial in Singapore on 9-13 December 1996 dealt largely with defining a work program for the new global trade organisation, and it had many characteristics of a negotiating session. Agriculture and services were to be part of a built-in negotiating agenda after the Uruguay Round, because the members had agreed to negotiate trade barrier reductions in services and agriculture within 5 years of the WTO's creation. However, some members led by the EU argued that it was not sufficient to pursue the built-in agenda on services and agriculture. As discussed, the EU wanted to expand the agenda and have a new WTO round to increase the possibility for trade-offs among issues and strengthen the global trade regime.[10] Although the major traders had not yet formed a consensus to hold a new round, the Singapore ministerial began the process of deciding what should be on the WTO's negotiating agenda in addition to services and agriculture. Some developed countries wanted to put trade facilitation, government procurement, competition policy, and investment policy on the WTO agenda, and a small number of countries led by the United States and France also wanted to include labour standards. The South managed to prevent the Singapore ministerial from considering labour standards, but the ministerial agreed to create working groups to examine other issues of interest to the North such as government procurement, competition policy, and investment policy. In addition, a number of developed countries and East Asian NIEs expressed support for an agreement to expand world trade in information technology products. This proposal demonstrated the continuing divisions in the South, since most developing countries refused to support such an agreement.[11] After the Singapore ministerial, in March 1997, 40 WTO members concluded an Information Technology Agreement (see discussion later in this chapter).

The second WTO ministerial in Geneva on 18-20 May 1998 continued the process of deciding what should be included on the WTO negotiating agenda, and provided a mandate for a work program to prepare for launching a new round at the next ministerial conference in Seattle.[12] However, the third WTO ministerial in Seattle on 30 November to 3 December 1999 failed to launch the new round as planned. Several factors contributed to the failure at Seattle. Although anti-WTO civil society groups caused considerable disruption on the streets of Seattle, this was not a decisive factor contributing to the failure of the ministerial.[13] In the view of many analysts, the Seattle ministerial "failed because of the inability of the established players, principally the Quad group, to agree on an agenda between themselves."[14] By the time of the Seattle ministerial, the Quad members all wanted a new MTN, but they had strong disagreements over what issues should be negotiated. The EU backed by Japan wanted a more comprehensive round, while the United States wanted a more limited negotiation. Each Quad member also had its own specific preferences for negotiation. For example, the United States favoured deep cuts in agricultural subsidies, but it opposed efforts to reform antidumping rules (which the United States used most frequently). Europe and Japan by contrast opposed further agricultural reforms, but sought new talks on competition and investment policy; and Canada wanted special exemptions for its cultural industries. The sharp differences among the major traders prevented the Quad from helping to forge a consensus at Seattle.

Although divisiveness within the Quad was the major factor contributing to the failure of the Seattle ministerial, North-South differences were another factor explaining the failure. Developing countries argued that the developed countries should fulfill earlier promises in textiles and agriculture before they would consent to negotiations in services, investment, and competition policy. Furthermore, the developing countries wanted additional time to fulfill the commitments they had agreed to in the Uruguay Round, and they required more technical assistance from the developed countries if they were to agree to additional commitments in a new round. Thus, it was evident in Seattle that the North would have to increase it offers to the South if it wanted developing countries to join in a new round. Some analysts attribute the failure in Seattle to a third factor: the lack of U.S. leadership. For example, Henry Nau maintains that "although not solely at fault, the United States bears the major responsibility for the failure of the ministerial conference of the World Trade Organization ... in Seattle."[15] As discussed, debate over the NAFTA negotiations had contributed to the domestication of trade policy, and in some respects U.S. President Clinton "sacrificed trade leadership for domestic political reasons."[16] Most developing countries had a hostile reaction to Clinton's speech in Seattle supporting trade sanctions as a means of enforcing labour rights, and this did nothing to repair the North-South divisions at the ministerial.

Despite the divisions and lack of leadership in Seattle, the Quad members have become more dependent on trade and have considered a new WTO round to be in their interest. For example, trade accounted for almost 25 percent of U.S. GDP in 1999 compared with only 11 percent in 1970; and the EU is the largest trading region in the world. Both the United States and the EU would benefit from a decrease in developing country import barriers, and the best way to achieve this objective is through a new WTO round. After the failure in Seattle, the developed countries therefore planned to launch the new round at the fourth WTO ministerial in Doha, Qatar on 9-13 November 2001. A major factor in the decision to hold the meeting in Doha related to the ability to insulate the meeting from disruptive demonstrations of the type that had occurred in Seattle. In view of continued divisions, the delegates had to offer major compromises before launching a new round at Doha. For example, the EU accepted a stronger commitment to discuss phasing out farm export subsidies, the United States agreed to negotiations on the use of countervailing and antidumping duties, the North agreed to a (nonbinding) declaration that intellectual property rules should not prevent the South from gaining access to cheaper medicines for illnesses such as AIDs, and the South consented reluctantly to a commitment to future negotiations on foreign investment, competition, and environmental issues.[17]

Although the Doha agreement was a major achievement, there were indications that "this first step ... [was] in fact the smallest one."[18] Shortly after the Doha ministerial was concluded, the United States and India offered conflicting interpretations as to what exactly the delegates had agreed to in the final declaration.[19] The new "Doha Round," which began in January 2002 will deal with highly contentious topics such as agriculture and the environment, and must be completed within three years. As the Doha ministerial declaration states, "The negotiations to be pursued under the terms of this Declaration shall be concluded not later than 1 January 2005."[20] Thus, there is considerable uncertainty regarding the outcome of the new WTO round. What is certain is that more leadership will be necessary from the United States, the EU, and the developed country-led institutions if the Doha Round is to be a success. Another certainty is that the North will have to become more responsive to the concerns and demands of the South. The discussion that follows examines the role of the G7, the Quad, the OECD, and the developing countries in the post-Uruguay Round global trade regime.

Group of Seven/Group of Eight

Beginning in 1994, Russia was gradually integrated into the G7 summit process. The 1997 Denver summit marked the first time that Russia was included from the beginning of the summit proceedings, and the 1998 Birmingham summit was the first G8 summit. Although this chapter refers to the G8 as well as the G7, Russia is not yet a member of the WTO. Thus, the G7 with the participation of the EU in fact continues to hold most of the trade policy discussions at the annual summits.[21]

The G7 summits had a marked tendency to neglect international trade after the Uruguay Round, for several reasons. First, "the agenda of the G7 summit had become hopelessly overloaded. The original list of topics was expanded to cover a growing range of new ones."[22] The need to focus on crises of the day, and Russia's gradual integration into the summit process added further complications to the summit deliberations. Inevitably, international trade received less attention because of the summit leaders' overloaded agenda. A second reason for inattention to trade related to the transition from the GATT to the WTO. Unlike the GATT, the WTO has regular ministerial meetings. The G7 may have felt less pressure to become directly involved, because the WTO ministerials deal with trade issues at the higher political levels. A third reason for inattention to trade resulted from a notable lack of leadership by the two main actors, the United States and the EU. The U.S. President was seriously constrained by his inability to get a renewal of fast-track authority from Congress, and (as discussed) labour, environmental, and other groups were contributing to a domestication of U.S. trade policy. Although the EU began to pressure for a comprehensive MTN round, both the United States and the EU were reluctant to agree to negotiations in key areas such as antidumping duties (the United

States) and agriculture (the EU). The G7 review of international institutions from 1995 to 1997 provides a prime example of the summit's post-Uruguay Round neglect of international trade. Finance was the main topic of the institutional review at the Halifax 1995 summit, development was the main topic at Lyon 1996, and Africa and the environment were the main subjects at Denver 1997. International trade was not included in the institutional review, because of the recent conclusion of the Uruguay Round and creation of the WTO.[23] Another indication of the G7's inattention to trade was the decreased frequency of Quad ministerials (discussed later in this chapter).

As events unfolded in the late 1990s, it became evident that the G7's neglect of trade was a serious error. Political leadership by the heads of government and state was necessary to address differences among the major traders in intractable areas such as agriculture. Political leadership was also needed to respond to the growing dissatisfaction of developing countries and civil society groups with the global trade regime. WTO ministerials are simply too large, diverse, and unwieldy to take on the leadership mantle, and active G7 and Quad attention to preparations for WTO ministerials is essential if they are to succeed. Although "many factors combined to cause" the failure of the 1999 Seattle ministerial to launch a new round of trade negotiations, "the G7 Summit cannot escape its share of the responsibility."[24] Ironically, one possible benefit of the Seattle fiasco was that it increased the resolve of the G7 to launch a new round. Despite some reluctance, the United States and the EU began to demonstrate more flexibility toward negotiations in sensitive areas. The G7 leaders were not willing to commit to a new round in the first summit after Seattle (Okinawa 2000), but at the Genoa 2001 G7 summit the leaders "pledged to launch a new round of multilateral trade negotiations at the World Trade Organization (WTO) ministerial meeting in Doha, Qatar."[25] Although the Doha ministers agreed to launch a comprehensive WTO round, marked divisions on critical issues at Doha combined with recent experience indicate that political leadership from the G7 and the Quad is essential if the new round is to succeed. This section examines the role of G7/G8 summits in the post-Uruguay Round period.

From the Uruguay Round to the Singapore WTO Ministerial

The 15-17 June 1995 Halifax summit was the first G7 summit held after the establishment of the WTO. The crisis in Bosnia dominated political discussions at the Halifax summit and "even threatened to drive everything else off the summit agenda."[26] Canada had resolved to focus on international financial institutions in the economic discussions, and Mexico's December 1994 financial crisis ensured that financial issues would be the "centrepiece" of the economic agenda at Halifax.[27] Some discussion was devoted to trade issues, but the summit communiqué contained no new trade initiatives. U.S. President Clinton had referred to a possible new trade round at the 1994 summit, and Canada picked up on this idea at Halifax and called on other G7 members to pressure for new international trade talks. Canada also proposed that the G7 accelerate the tariff cuts negotiated in the Uruguay Round and add new sectors for tariff elimination. However, the G7 members had widely divergent views regarding the agenda for new negotiations, and nothing came of Canada's proposals.

Although the Halifax communiqué referred to work on labour and the environment, the G7 members could not agree on how strongly they should address these sensitive issues. Differences also emerged in the area of competition policy. Canada wanted the communiqué to encourage the development of global rules on competition policy, but the United States preferred much weaker language, and the final version only called for work on "the scope for multilateral action" on trade and competition policy. This vague language suited the United States, because it was concerned that a working group on competition policy focus on cartels and other private anticompetitive practices, but not on antidumping rules (the United States is the most frequent user of antidumping actions).[28] The only areas of genuine agreement at the Halifax summit related to the G7's resolve to "encourage work" on "technical standards, intellectual property and government procurement," and to give "immediate priority" to negotiation of an MAI in the OECD. The G7 also pledged to work with others "to create the basis for an ambitious first WTO Ministerial Meeting in Singapore in 1996."[29] On the margins of the Halifax summit, the United States and Japan engaged in intense bilateral exchanges over U.S. threats to levy high tariffs on Japanese luxury automobile imports. Thus, the Halifax summit did little to advance the multilateral trade agenda.

A terrorist attack on U.S. servicemen in Saudi Arabia shortly before the 27-29 June 1996 summit in Lyon, France ensured that a crisis would again dominate the G7 political discussions. The economic discussions at Lyon focused primarily on development and on reorganising the work of the UN secretariat. Thus, the Lyon summit, like Halifax, did not contain any major new trade initiatives. Much of the language on trade in the summit communiqué came from statements issued by the Quad and OECD ministerials. On some trade issues the Lyon summit expressed a fairly strong consensus. For example, the G7 expressed a commitment to "work for the success of the first ministerial conference of the WTO."[30] The communiqué also favoured an increase in "the number of countries subscribing to the Agreement on Government Procurement," and initiated an effort to standardise and simplify customs procedures as a means of facilitating trade. In most areas of trade policy, however, the summit communiqué was marked by vague statements indicating a lack of consensus among G7 members.

Although the G7 supported a broad agenda including a number of new issues for the WTO Singapore ministerial, the tentative language on these new issues demonstrated the divisions among G7 members, and between North and South. On investment, for example, the G7 communiqué gave "high priority to achieving" an MAI in the OECD, and also invited the Singapore ministerial to begin "an examination of trade and investment in the WTO and work towards a consensus which might include the possibility of negotiations." This careful wording reflected the divergence between the U.S. preference for limiting MAI negotiations to the OECD, and the EU preference for including developing countries. The G7 communiqué was even more vague in regard to labour standards (which developing countries strongly opposed), simply stating that "there is a will to address the question of the relationship between trade and internationally-recognized core labour standards." The communiqué was equally vague on competition policy, inviting the WTO ministerial to discuss "the interaction between trade and competition policy with a view to determining how to proceed." In sum, the Lyon summit helped to set a framework and provide some detail for the Singapore WTO ministerial, but the vagueness of its prescriptions demonstrated a division of views on a number of key issues.

From the Singapore WTO Ministerial to the Seattle WTO Ministerial

The 20-22 June 1997 Denver summit marked the first time that Russia was included from the beginning of the summit proceedings. Although Russia's involvement did not unduly affect the economic part of the Denver summit, it raised the possibility that future summits would devote more attention to political (and less to economic) issues. The economic portion of the Denver summit focused on assistance to Africa and a number of other issues ranging from the environment to infectious diseases.[31] Thus, the summiteers could devote only a limited amount of attention to trade. The Singapore WTO ministerial had provided a mandate for extending the WTO agenda to several new areas, but business and labour groups expressed widely divergent views as to which new areas the G7 should emphasise at the Denver summit. For example, the International Chamber of Commerce wanted the G7 to support the development of international rules for cross-border investment, competition policy, trade-distorting corruption, and customs modernisation. Labour unions such as the AFL-CIO by contrast felt that the G7 should endorse trade and investment agreements with well-defined and enforceable labour standards.[32] The Denver summit addressed some of these issues, renewing its "commitment to the observance of internationally recognized core labor standards," urging completion of the work to improve customs procedures, and supporting the "successful completion in 1998" of the OECD's MAI negotiations. Nevertheless, the summit did not endorse WTO negotiations on some sensitive issues such as agriculture and on some newer issues such as financial services and competition policy. As was the case for the 1995 and 1996 summits, there were no new trade initiatives at the Denver summit. One factor constraining the work at Denver and future summits was the U.S. administration's difficulties in getting a Congressional renewal of fast-track authority.[33]

Preparations for the 15-17 May 1998 summit in Birmingham, UK, emphasised a return to the more informal summits with lighter agendas of earlier years. Thus, the summit had a limited agenda of three major items: the East Asian financial crisis and the related issue of debt relief for poorer developing countries, employability and social inclusion, and drug trafficking and other forms of international crime.[34] Although the Birmingham summit was held immediately before the 18-20 May Geneva WTO ministerial, the G8 "did not address the need for new trade negotiations."[35] This silence on new trade talks stemmed from marked differences of view, with the EU and Japan supporting a more comprehensive Millennium Round, and the United States and Canada favouring more limited negotiations. Thus, the Birmingham communiqué simply reaffirmed the G8's support "for efforts to complete existing multilateral [trade] commitments, push forward the built-in agenda and tackle new areas in pursuing broad-based multilateral liberalisation." If there was to be a new Millennium Round, a more in-depth discussion of trade would be necessary in the 1999 G8 summit. Finally, a London-based civil society organisation with worldwide connections called "Jubilee 2000" formed a human chain of about 50,000 people around the convention centre for the Birmingham summit. The protestors believed an endorsement by the G7 would ensure that the IMF, World Bank, and Paris Club would upgrade assistance for the heavily-indebted poor countries.[36] Much larger civil society protests over trade issues would follow in the 1999 WTO Seattle ministerial.

The 18-20 June 1999 G8 summit in Cologne, Germany had a more crowded agenda than the Birmingham summit, focusing on debt relief for the poorest developing countries; crime and conflict prevention; and, employment, social protection, and education. In the trade area, the Cologne G8 communiqué called for "ambitious negotiations" in a new WTO round.[37] Nevertheless, the G8 leaders "did not pledge their personal commitment for a new round," and they "gave their trade ministers no shared political direction in the critical period before the [WTO] Seattle ministerial."[38] The G8 also did not specify which sectors should be included in the negotiations beyond the WTO's built-in agenda for agriculture and services. One possible explanation for this lack of direction is that the G8 did not want to appear to be setting the agenda for the WTO in view of growing sensitivities among developing countries and civil society groups. From this perspective, the G8 may have expected that a more detailed description of the new Millennium Round would be worked out at the Seattle WTO ministerial. However, a marked lack of consensus combined with some bitter trade disputes among the G8 were more important factors explaining the Cologne summit's lack of direction. The summit communiqué's general language in fact masked persistent differences within the G8 on the scope and nature of negotiations. For example, the Cologne summit called "on all nations to launch at the WTO Ministerial Conference in Seattle … a new round of broad-based and ambitious negotiations with the aim of achieving substantial and manageable results."[39] Whereas the reference to "substantial" results catered to EU and Japanese demands for comprehensive negotiations based on a "single undertaking," the reference to "manageable" results catered to U.S. demands for more limited negotiations with the possibility of concluding some aspects of the negotiations earlier (referred to as an "early harvest").

Serious U.S.-EU trade disputes at the Cologne summit also did not bode well for efforts to launch a new round. For example, European import barriers on food containing genetically-modified organisms (GMOs) were a major source of tension at Cologne. In May 1999, 65 members of the U.S. Congress had responded to pressure from agricultural producer and industry groups by urging the Clinton administration to put the GMO issue on the Cologne summit agenda. Some EU members, however, were determined to continue barring food imports with GMOs. Thus, the French President proposed that countries should be permitted to impose trade restrictions to protect their citizens when scientific information is uncertain or unavailable. The G8 rejected this proposal and indicated that it was "committed to a science-based, rules-based approach to addressing" trade and biotechnology issues. However, the G8 also invited the OECD to "undertake a study of the implications of biotechnology and other aspects of food safety," and to report back to the next G8 summit on ways to improve the WTO approach to these issues.[40]

As discussed, the Seattle WTO ministerial following the Cologne summit has been variously described as "a fiasco" and "a disaster." Indeed, the ministerial's failure "to launch a new round was unique in the history of the postwar global trading system," because "never before had countries come together to start a negotiation and failed to do so."[41] Although street protests and demonstrations disrupted the Seattle meeting, differences among the delegates were the main factor preventing agreement on launching a new round. The divisions in the G8, the Quad, and the OECD in their 1999 meetings carried over into the Seattle ministerial, and were magnified by the North-South differences.

From the Seattle WTO Ministerial to the Doha WTO Ministerial

Although G8 leadership in trade was essential after the failed WTO Seattle ministerial, it was not forthcoming at the 21-23 July 2000 summit in Okinawa, Japan. The Okinawa summit placed considerable emphasis on new areas related to information and communications technology; foreign debt and development; and a range of social areas involving aging, health, and cultural diversity. The trade discussions at Okinawa were inevitably affected by the civil society protests in Seattle. Questions arose as to whether high profile meetings such as G8 summits were the best venue for discussing trade liberalisation issues, and advances in technology offered alternative possibilities such as virtual conferencing. Developing country complaints about inattention to their concerns also raised questions as to whether it would be better to shift some of the G8 trade discussions to the more inclusive WTO process in Geneva. (Several developing country leaders met with some G8 members on the sidelines of the Okinawa summit.)[42]

However, protests and dissatisfaction of civil society groups and developing countries were certainly not the main reasons for the Okinawa summit's failure to provide leadership on trade. As was the case in Birmingham and Cologne, the main obstacles to leadership in Okinawa were the serious trade disputes and lack of consensus among G8 members. One indication of the disarray on trade was that 2000 was the first year the Quad failed to hold a single ministerial since 1982 (see Table 5.1). Between the failed Seattle WTO ministerial and the Okinawa summit, U.S. trade disputes with the EU and Japan thwarted efforts to revive discussions on launching a new round. U.S.-EU disputes related to the EU's failure to implement WTO dispute settlement decisions against it on bananas and beef, European aircraft production subsidies, and U.S. tax subsidies for American exporters. U.S.-Japanese disputes related to a growing U.S. trade deficit; differences over insurance, flat glass, and Japanese deregulation; and the upcoming expiration of the U.S.-Japanese automotive agreement.

As a result, the Okinawa summit's communiqué demonstrated a lack of direction on trade. The communiqué's statement that the G8 would "try together with other WTO members to launch ... a [new] round during the course of this year" created an air of uncertainty as to whether this would actually occur.[43] Although the communiqué stated that the G8 was "firmly committed to a new round of WTO trade negotiations with an ambitious, balanced and inclusive agenda," U.S. differences with the EU and Japan on the scope of negotiations had not been resolved. The communiqué recognised the need to address the concerns of developing countries, but offered them no new market access commitments. In sum, a lack of consensus on key trade issues, bilateral disputes, and multilateral constraints stemming from developing country and civil society dissatisfaction, prevented the Okinawa summit from providing the forceful leadership needed to launch a new WTO round.

Despite the continuing differences among the major traders, all the G7 leaders had reasons for wanting a WTO round. As a new organisation the WTO needed some successes to prove its value, and the failure to launch a new round could be severely damaging to the WTO. The two largest trading entities in particular had a strong interest in the ensuring the success of the WTO, because trade accounted for almost 25 percent of U.S. GDP in 1999 compared with only 11 percent in 1970, and the EU is the largest trading region in the world. Thus, the 20-22 July 2001 G8 summit in Genoa, Italy finally agreed "to support the launch of an ambitious new Round of multilateral trade negotiations with a balanced agenda."[44] Despite this breakthrough, the G8 communiqué had no separate section on trade and provided no details on what was meant by a "balanced agenda." In a meeting without Russia (who is not yet a WTO member), the G7 at Genoa provided more detail on the call for new negotiations. (The G7 leaders continue to hold a meeting at the summits, after which they release a statement on world economic conditions and joint policies.)

The G7 at Genoa pledged "to engage personally and jointly in the launch of a new ambitious Round of global trade negotiations at the Fourth WTO Ministerial Conference in Doha, Qatar" in November 2001.[45] The G7 leaders also identified some of the negotiating priorities, including WTO transparency and interaction with civil society; the development of more effective dispute settlement procedures; the admission of China; and developing country concerns regarding market access, implementation of the Uruguay Round, and capacity building.[46] Nevertheless, the G7 avoided specific commitments on contentious issues such as agriculture, anti-dumping duties, environmental and labour standards, and textiles. As discussed, an agreement on launching a new WTO round was achieved at Doha, Qatar only because the United States, the EU, and the developing countries offered some major concessions near the end of the ministerial.[47]

In summary, the G7/G8 had a marked tendency to avoid dealing with international trade issues after the Uruguay Round. Although the G7/G8's overloaded agenda was one factor explaining this inattention, sharp divisions among the major traders and a notable lack of leadership by the United States and the EU were also factors. Furthermore, in a period of growing dissatisfaction by developing countries and civil society groups, the G7/G8 did not want to appear to be dictating the agenda on contentious trade issues. Although many responsible NGOs were present at the G8 summit in Genoa, and some had consultations with G8 government leaders and ministers, a relatively small group engaged in violent protests.[48] A central factor in the decision to hold the fourth WTO ministerial in Doha was to avoid such disruptive demonstrations. The difficulty in reaching agreement on a new round at Doha, conflicting interpretations as to what exactly the delegates had agreed to in the final declaration, and the failure to fully confront some of the most contentious issues such as agriculture and anti-dumping actions provide forewarning that the G8 and the Quad must become more actively involved in providing leadership if the WTO round is eventually to succeed.

The Quadrilateral Group

The Quad continues to be important in the post-Uruguay Round period, because its members account for a substantial share of global trade and have had a major role in promoting trade liberalisation. The Quad's active participation is critical to the success of MTNs, because tariffs and NTBs of Quad members can "lead to welfare losses ... on a global scale."[49] Although the Quad of course does not take decisions on behalf of the WTO membership, it provides leadership in thought, in policy direction, and in providing political momentum for MTNs. Nevertheless, Quad ministerials have had lower visibility in recent years. Whereas Quad ministerials were normally held twice a year from 1982 to 1996, they were held only once a year from 1997 to 1999; and in 2000 and 2001 there were no regular ministerials.[50] It is important to note that Quad ministers have met informally on the margins of other organisational gatherings, and that Quad officials below the ministerial level continue to meet. Quad deputy ministers meet about once every two months, and lower level officials also discuss issues, positions, and strategies. Informal Quad discussions often occur on the margins of meetings of the OECD, the Asia Pacific Economic Cooperation (APEC) forum, and other organisations. Quad officials converse every second week, and sometimes as often as two times a week. There is in fact a Quad grouping of working level officials for almost every significant trade issue, agreement, and committee. Furthermore, there are regular meetings of Quad ambassadors and various officials in Geneva.[51] On occasion the officials' meetings can be of considerable importance. For example, a Quad implementation paper served as a basis of discussion in the lead-up to the launch of the WTO round at Doha.

Despite the numerous ongoing contacts among Quad members, the decreased visibility of Quad ministerials after the Singapore WTO ministerial in 1996 was a significant development that stemmed from several major changes. First, and most importantly, the Quad had serious disagreements over a wide range of issues. Although the ministers had disagreements from the time the Quad was formed, the failure of the G7/G8 after the Uruguay Round "to address contentious trade-related issues or to promote its vision of the multilateral trading system at the summit level caused discord among the Quad members."[52] Most significant were the major differences between the United States and the EU. It was evident that some of these differences could not be bridged at the Quad ministerials, and the major traders hoped the differences could be resolved at the GATT ministerials in Seattle and Doha. A second reason why Quad ministerials became less important was that personal relationships among Quad ministers were less close after the Uruguay Round (for example, between the USTR Charlene Barshefsky and the Acting EU Trade Commissioner Leon Brittan). Frequent changes in the Japanese trade ministers also interfered with personal relationships in the meetings. Third, although the Quad had been an important forum during the Uruguay Round, after the round the United States was more skeptical that the Quad could be effective and it often preferred to meet with other Quad members individually. On several occasions the United States refused to agree to suggestions that a Quad ministerial be held. U.S. skepticism about Quad ministerials was compounded by domestic political changes in the United States. For example, the United States was not in a position to meet at Quad ministerials for several months after George W. Bush became president, because of the lengthy period before Robert Zoellick was appointed and confirmed as U.S. Trade Representative.

A fourth reason for the Quad's lower visibility stemmed from the proliferation of other fora in which members could discuss trade issues in smaller groups. For example, the United States and the EU discussed bilateral and multilateral trade issues in their Transatlantic Business Dialogue, and the EU and Japan instituted a ministerial level exchange. Fifth, the WTO unlike the GATT had regular ministerial meetings, and the major trading powers may have felt there was less necessity for holding ministerials limited to the Quad. Sixth, developing countries argued that the Uruguay Round agreements should be fully implemented before new negotiations were held, and their hostility to developed country dominance of the mulilateral trade agenda may have contributed to a lower profile for the Quad ministerials. For example, Canada's membership in the Quad was one of the reasons Roy MacLaren of Canada was unsuccessful as a candidate for the new WTO director-general position. Some developing countries were reluctant to support a Quad member for the post, because they felt that the Quad already had an excessive amount of control over the global trade agenda.[53]

A senior WTO official has summarised the changing position of the Quad *vis-à-vis* other members of the WTO, stating:

> Agreement among the Quad is very important, but they are not the critical element that they used to be. Their exclusive position is over. They must now build a consensus (since there are many other participants).[54]

As one Canadian official has indicated, Quad agreement continues to be necessary for many important decisions in the WTO, but it is no longer sufficient for a WTO agreement.[55] The discussion that follows traces the changing role of the Quad in the post-Uruguay Round period.

From the Establishment of the WTO to the WTO Singapore Ministerial

The first Quad ministerial after the establishment of the WTO was the twenty-sixth Quad in Whistler, British Columbia on 3-5 May 1995. Bilateral side issues such as disputes over U.S.-EU banana trade, U.S.-Japanese auto trade, and Canadian-EU sugar and pasta trade were more prominent at the Whistler Quad, because a consensus had not yet developed on a new multilateral agenda after the Uruguay Round.[56] At the previous Quad ministerial in September 1994, the United States had called for multilateral negotiations to complete unfinished areas of the Uruguay Round such as services and agriculture, and to deal with new issues involving investment, labour, and the environment. At the Whistler Quad, Canada joined the United States in supporting new trade talks, but the Quad did not reach a consensus on which issues should receive priority in the negotiations. For example, the United States and Canada sought quick action to accelerate tariff cuts, but the EC and Japan were reluctant to support a new tariff initiative. The Chair's Statement therefore simply indicated that Quad ministers "will actively pursue elimination of remaining barriers and senior officials of the Quad will *study* how this can best be done"[57] (italics added). In the view of one Quad official, "when ministers say that officials will study something, it usually means it's not on a fast-track."[58]

Ministers at the Whistler Quad also disagreed on the role and nature of the WTO. First, the USTR wanted to increase transparency through more rapid derestriction of WTO documents including dispute settlement panel reports, but some Quad members warned that this would eliminate the opportunity for disputing parties to reach a negotiated settlement. A second area of disagreement related to the commitment of resources to the WTO secretariat. Although the WTO director-general had requested increased funding because of the organisation's new responsibilities, the Quad reached no decision to take action on this issue. A third contentious issue related to a USTR proposal that the WTO establish a branch office in Washington, D.C. The stated rationale was to improve WTO coordination with the Washington-based IMF and World Bank, but U.S. Congressional pressure was also a factor. Some Congressional members maintained that a WTO office in Washington would demystify the organisation and contribute to U.S. public support for the WTO. Whereas Canada and the EU supported the U.S. proposal in principle, Japan believed a Washington office would create an image that the United States was dominating the WTO. Thus, a consensus on this proposal was also elusive.[59]

Despite these ministerial differences, the Whistler Quad began the process of building a consensus on key issues needed to maintain the momentum of trade liberalisation at the OECD, the G7 summit in Halifax, and the first WTO ministerial in Singapore. For example, there was some unity in the Quad on WTO accession issues. Although Quad ministers supported the accession of emerging economies to the WTO, they wanted these economies to bring their policies into line with the rules-based global trade regime. Negotiations on China's entry into the WTO had broken down in December 1994, and the Quad agreed to offer China a more flexible timetable for reforming its trade policies. In return, the Quad indicated that China should improve its trade liberalisation offer which was below the minimal requirements needed to join the WTO. The Whistler Quad also endorsed the OECD's work in a number of areas, including trade-related labour standards, competition principles, regulatory reform, and the decision to begin negotiations on a multilateral agreement on investment (MAI). Finally, the ministers agreed that the Quad should continue to serve as a forum for informal discussions in the post-Uruguay Round era.[60]

The twenty-seventh Quad ministerial in Yorkshire, Britain on 20-21 October 1995 devoted considerable attention to preparations for the 1996 WTO ministerial in Singapore, and the WTO director-general strongly supported the Quad's leadership role in these preparations:

> I very much welcome the reconfirmed commitment by the Ministers of the world's four largest trading entitities to the World Trade Organization. I especially appreciate

the forward-looking nature of the concluding statement. Not only did it provide support for current negotiations, ... but [it] looked ahead to an ambitious first WTO Ministerial Meeting next year in Singapore.[61]

Some issues discussed at the Whistler Quad such as China's accession to the WTO re-emerged at the Yorkshire Quad. To avoid a stalemate the EU suggested that China be offered special arrangements in its accession negotiations, but the United States argued that giving China special arrangements would set a bad precedent for other WTO accession cases. Despite these differences, the Quad members agreed that China would have to offer major concessions in return for WTO membership. The Yorkshire Quad also discussed regional initiatives, with the EU arguing that the WTO rules for regional trade agreements should be more flexible than those under GATT Article XXIV. Although the other Quad ministers opposed a relaxation of the rules for RTAs, they agreed that a WTO committee should be formed to assess Article XXIV and ensure that RTAs are consistent with the multilateral trade regime. The WTO director-general welcomed the Quad's suggestion for "a new WTO body to help ensure that regional trade initiatives contribute to, rather than detract from, efforts at the multilateral level."[62] Subsequently, the WTO established a Committee on Regional Trade Agreements.

The Yorkshire Quad also addressed the contentious matter of the best venue for negotiating rules on foreign investment. The EU wanted the investment talks moved from the OECD to the wider forum of the WTO, because developing countries were the recipients of over half of new foreign investment flows. In the EU's view, "developing countries have never been as receptive as they are today to the message that foreign direct investment is not a threat but a positive tool for economic growth, bringing capital, technology, and management expertise."[63] The United States by contrast argued the OECD's MAI talks should be completed before the process was moved to the WTO, because the OECD was more hospitable to capital exporters and would develop strict limits on foreign investment controls. Although Japan and Canada generally supported the EU's position, the OECD continued to oversee the MAI negotiations.[64] Another sensitive issue at the Yorkshire Quad related to labour, because the developing countries strongly opposed any linkage of trade with labour standards. Although the Quad agreed that the WTO should discuss the relationship between trade and labour standards, Japan was reluctant to pursue this issue. The Japanese minister opposed the use of trade sanctions to enforce labour standards, and warned that labour standards could be used as an excuse for adopting protectionist trade policies.[65]

The twenty-eighth Quad ministerial in Kobe, Japan on 19-21 April 1996 had an important role in the lead-up to the Singapore WTO ministerial. Quad ministers agreed that the WTO had to be perceived as a dynamic organisation, and Canada's Minister for International Trade indicated that the Quad "can play a vital part and lead by example in setting the pace for a successful meeting in Singapore."[66] Nevertheless, discussion of specific trade issues demonstrated both divisions within the Quad, and between the Quad and developing countries. The United States wanted the Singapore ministerial to expand and strengthen the government procurement agreement, develop agreements to deal with labour standards and information technology, and pressure China to follow intellectual property regulations. Although developing countries are not members of the Quad, their policies inevitably have an effect on Quad discussions. For example, the Quad agreed to renew its "efforts to expand membership" in the GPA "and to improve its disciplines."[67] Most developing countries, however, continued to refuse to join the GPA.

Labour standards was a far more contentious issue than government procurement at the Kobe Quad (and also in U.S. and EU domestic politics). In response to domestic pressures, the United States wanted the Singapore ministerial to establish a working party on labour standards. However, Democrats and Republicans were at loggerheads on this issue, with the pressure for trade-labour linkages coming from Democrats in the U.S. Congress and President Bill Clinton's administration. U.S. pressure for a labour standards agreement posed a threat to the success of the WTO Singapore ministerial, because many developing countries believed such an agreement would hinder their access to developed country markets. In the developing country view, the ILO (which is less authoritative than the WTO) was already dealing with labour standards, and there was no reason to involve the WTO. Within the Quad, Japan expressed unease over linking trade with labour standards, and the EU expressed ambivalent views on the issue (stemming from divisions within the EU). The Chair's Statement on the Kobe Quad therefore took an extremely cautious approach, indicating that "the relation between trade and labour standards should be discussed at the Singapore Ministerial Conference, with a view to determining how to proceed."[68]

The United States gained the support of the EU, Japan, and Canada at Kobe for informally linking intellectual property rights with China's accession to the WTO. Although the Chair's Statement indicated that WTO membership should be expanded "as rapidly as possible," it added that "effective enforcement of intellectual property rights protection is necessary for confidence building among the members needed for accession."[69] Whereas the main divisions over the

U.S. proposals for government procurement, labour standards, and intellectual property rights were between North and South, the main division on the U.S. information technology initiative was within the Quad. Domestic interests were a major factor in U.S. support for an Information Technology Agreement (ITA). Indeed, the U.S. computer industry had proposed that the Quad and other interested countries should phase out tariffs on computers, computer parts, semiconductors and software, because the GATT Uruguay Round had failed to eliminate tariffs on information technology products. Although the Kobe Quad agreed to "strongly support the negotiation of an Information Technology Agreement," the EU added a number of conditions to its support.[70] Several European semiconductor manufacturers wanted the EU to maintain high tariffs on computer chips, and the European Commission did not initially have the mandate to negotiate an ITA.[71]

The EU had its own priorities for the Singapore WTO Ministerial, in the areas of investment and competition policy. As in the Yorkshire Quad, the EU argued at Kobe that the WTO should have an active role in investment talks, because the North could not "expect the rest of the world to accept an OECD agreement without being involved in the discussions on this issue."[72] However, the United States continued to argue that the investment talks should be limited to the OECD. The Chair's Statement at Kobe was vaguely worded to give recognition to both the U.S. and EU positions: "Without in any way detracting from our determination to reach the OECD agreement [on investment], we agreed that an informal WTO Working Group should now be set up in Geneva with a view to establishing a formal WTO Working Group at the Singapore Ministerial Conference."[73] The EU with Canada's support also wanted to establish a WTO working group on competition policy, but the United States opposed this proposal. The Chair's Statement was therefore noncommittal, indicating that "we agreed on the importance of enhancing the coherence between trade and competition policy, and agreed that this issue should be discussed at the Singapore Ministerial Conference with a view to determining how to proceed."[74]

Despite their differences over specific issues, the ministers at Kobe all wanted to reinforce the credibility of the WTO as a new organisation. Thus, the Kobe Quad emphasised the need to fully implement WTO agreements, and to review any measures that violated WTO obligations. The Quad also affirmed its commitment to the work of the WTO Committee on Trade and Environment, and supported its establishment as a permanent committee. Despite the U.S.-EU differences over WTO involvement in an investment agreement, the Quad expressed a strong commitment to the successful completion of the OECD's

MAI negotiations by Spring 1997. Finally, Quad members were aware that they focused primarily on developed country priorities, and they recognised that the Singapore WTO agenda would also have to include issues of interest to developing countries.

The twenty-ninth Quad ministerial in Seattle, Washington on 26-28 September 1996 was held to "ensure that the outcome [of the Singapore meeting] reflects the Quad's positions and concerns."[75] However, the Seattle Quad came at a time of heightened tensions over the U.S. Helms-Burton Law, which was to go into effect in early 1997. This law would penalise foreign companies for doing business in Cuba if they used property or assets of U.S. multinationals or individuals that were nationalised after the 1959 Cuban Revolution. The other Quad members viewed Helms-Burton as a violation of international law, and the EU and Canada threatened retaliatory measures.[76] Despite these tensions, the Seattle Quad identified a number of areas where a common effort was needed. For example, the Quad recognised the special problems of the least-developed countries, and "agreed that preferential policies and liberalization efforts in their favour should continue to be the focus of international discussions and autonomous national decisions."[77] Many of the issues in the Seattle Quad such labour standards, the GPA, and a proposed ITA had been discussed in earlier Quads.

The results of the Singapore WTO ministerial in December 1996 demonstrated both the influence and limitations of the Quad. As discussed, some Quad ministers had proposed that the Singapore ministerial devote attention to investment and competition policy. Although major developing countries such as India, Pakistan, Bangladesh, and Egypt opposed any WTO action on investment, the ministers in Singapore agreed to establish working groups "to examine the relationship between trade and investment," and to study "the interaction between trade and competition policy."[78] The U.S.-led Quad initiative calling for increased membership and stronger discipline in the GPA also experienced some success in Singapore, despite developing country skepticism. Thus, the Singapore Declaration called for the creation of "a working group to conduct a study on transparency in government procurement practices … and based on this study, to develop elements for inclusion in an appropriate agreement."[79] Furthermore, the Singapore Declaration supported the Quad's regional initiatives, stating that "we welcome the establishment and endorse the work of the new Committee on Regional Trade Agreements."[80]

In contrast to the U.S. and Quad successes, the Singapore statements on labour fell far short of the U.S. proposal in the Quad to establish a WTO working group on labour standards. Instead, the Singapore Declaration emphasised that "the International Labour Organization (ILO) is the competent body to set and deal with these standards," rejected "the use of labour standards for protectionist purposes," and warned that "the comparative advantage of ... low-wage developing countries, must in no way be put into question."[81] Developing countries achieved their preferred outcome in this case because their strong opposition to labour standards threatened the success of the Singapore ministerial, and because the Quad itself was divided on this issue. Even within the United States many Republicans opposed the Democrats' emphasis on labour standards. The Quad statements calling for an ITA were also not fulfilled in Singapore, because of continuing U.S.-EU divisions, and opposition from developing countries. However, a number of WTO members including the Quad announced their intention at Singapore to conclude an ITA (the EU position on this issue was changing). On 26 March 1997, forty governments agreed to decrease customs duties on information technology products beginning in July 1997.

In summary, the Quad had a role of some importance in determining what agenda items would be discussed in Singapore. However, the Quad's degree of influence on particular issues depended on the relationship among Quad members, among developed countries, and between the North and the South. When differences among Quad ministers blocked a consensus on issues, the Quad was not in a position to seek a broader agreement at the Singapore ministerial. Labour standards was the area where the Quad had the least amount of influence, because of strong developing country opposition, significant divisions within the Quad, and divisions within the United States and the EU. The Quad had the most influence in Singapore on issues where they had common objectives, and where developing countries were either supportive of the Quad position or deeply divided. In some cases such as government procurement and information technology where most developing countries were not prepared to join in an agreement, developed countries established or strengthened plurilateral agreements, and opened them to any countries willing to meet the conditions of membership.

From the WTO Singapore Ministerial to the WTO Geneva Ministerial

The thirtieth Quad ministerial in Toronto, Ontario from 30 April to 2 May 1997 discussed the trade policy agenda endorsed by the WTO Singapore ministerial, and considered future directions for international trade.[82] The United States continued to emphasise the labour issue at the Toronto Quad, but other Quad members were sensitive to developing country opposition and the Quad Chair's statement did not endorse any linkage between trade and labour standards. The EU continued to pressure for a consensus on holding a new Millennium Round, but the United States, Japan, and Canada considered support for a new round to be premature. Whereas the EU believed that a new MTN would provide opportunities for tradeoffs among issues, the other Quad members first wanted assurances that the WTO was functioning well and that developing countries would support a new round.[83] Although the Quad ministers supported the Singapore decisions to establish working groups on competition and investment, they disagreed on the details. For example, the United States and the EU insisted that the competition group should not evaluate antidumping laws, but Japan felt that antidumping practices should be considered.

China's accession to the WTO was another issue that reappeared at the Toronto Quad. Although the Quad members agreed that China should be admitted to the WTO, they disagreed on the best approach to Chinese accession. The EU and Japan were willing to focus the accession negotiations on trade in goods, but the United States insisted that China should also promptly table an offer on services trade. The Quad ministers all predicted that Chinese membership would produce major changes, and one trade official warned that "the greatest challenge to the Quad-based system would be if China joins with India, currently the only developing country which consistently opposes the Quad countries."[84] The Quad ministers also shared a belief to varying degrees that the WTO had to respond to civil society demands for greater transparency. Thus, they invited the WTO director-general "to consult with members regarding appropriate means" to encourage informal dialogue between the WTO and "business, non-governmental organizations and other interested parties."[85] The Quad also agreed that the WTO should do more to "increase the capacity of … [the least developed countries] to enjoy the benefits that flow from increased trade and investment."[86] Furthermore, the Quad expressed a commitment to pressure for the completion of the MAI negotiations before the 1998 OECD ministerial.

The Toronto Quad was the only Quad ministerial held in 1997, largely because there was little momentum at that time for further trade liberalisation. Japan was reluctant to discuss liberalisation outside of the electronics and automotive sectors, the U.S. Congress had not granted President Clinton a renewal of fast-track authority, and the EU planned to wait for the next MTN round before considering any major new trade initiatives. Although the Toronto Quad was the thirtieth ministerial, the next ministerial held in Versailles, France is identified as the thirty-second Quad (see Table 5.1). The briefing material prepared by Canada's Department of Foreign Affairs and International Trade clearly described the Versailles Quad as the thirty-first meeting; but the Chair's statement incorrectly referred to Versailles as the thirty-second meeting! The error apparently resulted from the fact that a planned second Quad ministerial in 1997 was never held.[87]

A major purpose of the 29-30 April 1998 Versailles Quad was to determine "the contribution that the Quad could make to the success" of the May 1998 WTO ministerial in Geneva.[88] The EU again supported a new Millennium Round, and this time Japan largely endorsed the EU view. The United States by contrast indicated that it was too early to decide on a new round, and Canada favoured a smaller cluster of negotiations because it felt that a new comprehensive round was politically unfeasible. Nevertheless, the Quad agreed that "the 1998 WTO Ministerial should set in motion a process that would enable decisions to be taken in 1999 on the scope and modalities of ... further liberalization."[89] The Versailles Quad also addressed a range of "newer" issues, including the environment, WTO transparency, services trade, and electronic commerce. Regarding the environment, the Quad agreed to pressure for a high-level meeting of the long dormant WTO Committee on Trade and Environment. The Quad also revisited the WTO transparency issue and encouraged "the Director General to explore means within the WTO that would allow for enhanced consultations with representatives of civil society."[90] Furthermore, the Quad agreed that the services trade negotiations mandated by the Uruguay Round should "begin promptly and in earnest at the beginning of the year 2000," and decided to form a Quad working group to assess the technical work required for a new market access package on services.[91] Finally, the Versailles Quad addressed the issue of "electronic commerce," a complex mixture of technologies, processes and products that is rapidly evolving.[92]

The delegates to the second WTO ministerial in Geneva in May 1998 engaged in prenegotiations to determine what issues would be included in a new MTN round. Many of the same subjects discussed at the first WTO ministerial in Singapore and in the Quads again received attention in Geneva. Most importantly, the Geneva ministerial provided the WTO with a mandate to develop a work program with a view to launching a new round at the third WTO ministerial scheduled for 1999 in Seattle. A number of NGOs participated in street demonstrations in Geneva to protest what they viewed as their lack of access to the WTO, and a lack of WTO transparency. The Geneva delegates were of course unaware that this was merely a preview of much larger and more violent protests that would accompany the Seattle WTO ministerial.

From the Geneva WTO Ministerial to the Seattle WTO Ministerial

Although the Versailles Quad was the only Quad ministerial held in 1998, several Quad officials' meetings after the Geneva WTO ministerial focused on services trade, WTO accessions, and trade and the environment.[93] The thirty-third Quad ministerial in Tokyo, Japan on 11-12 May 1999 was held to prepare for launching a new trade round at the Seattle WTO ministerial; but continuing differences among the ministers precluded a consensus on many issues. For example, the Quad Chair's Statement walked a fine line between the EU preference for negotiations on investment and competition, and the U.S. preference simply for working groups; and the Chair's Statement did not refer to possible negotiations on antidumping rules because of strong U.S. opposition to any consideration of this issue.[94] The United States received some support from the EU and Canada for possible negotiations on labour and the environment, but Japan opposed addressing these issues in the WTO. The Quad ministers also supported different candidates for the next WTO director-general, but they wanted to avoid a vote and "agreed on the necessity of appointing the next Director-General on the basis of consensus."[95]

Despite their divergent positions, the Quad ministers did agree on certain issues. In addition to the agricultural and services negotiations mandated by the Uruguay Round, the Tokyo Quad agreed that negotiations should cover government procurement and intellectual property, and should take into account the special circumstances of developing countries. In addition, the Quad wanted to build the necessary momentum for a successful launch of a new MTN. The Quad also agreed that its next meeting should be held in the United States in September 1999. However, the ministers continued to have divergent preferences regarding the scope of new negotiations. While the EU and Japan (and to a lesser extent Canada) wanted comprehensive negotiations, the United States wanted to limit negotiations primarily to market access issues for agriculture, services, industrial tariffs, and non-tariff measures. The EU and Japan were also unwilling to move as fast as the United States and the Cairns Group wanted on liberalising agricultural trade. In view of these differences, the United States decided it would not be useful to hold another Quad ministerial in 1999.

The inability of the Quad to arrange another meeting was a clear indication of discord and a lack of political will at the highest political level. Indeed, "the failure of the G8 to show leadership negatively affected the ability of the Quad to present a united front in the months preceding the Seattle ministerial."[96] In the view of many analysts, the Seattle ministerial "failed because of the inability of the established players, principally the Quad group, to agree on an agenda between themselves."[97] Thus, the Chair of the U.S. House Ways and Means Trade Subcommittee charged that the Quad's "lack of proper preparation and organization to work out an agenda that was doable ... was one of the causes for failure" of the Seattle WTO Ministerial.[98] In addition to the Quad's shortcomings, divisions between the North and the South was another major factor interfering with progress at Seattle. Indeed, WTO members' views were so divergent that the WTO director-general was unable to develop a draft declaration for the Seattle ministerial. Some of the major disputes related to agricultural negotiations, labour standards, and benefits to be extended to developing countries. President Clinton's comments in Seattle favouring sanctions against countries that did not respect core labour rights made agreement with the developing countries virtually impossible.[99]

The Seattle ministerial also brought to the forefront the strong reaction by civil society groups to the WTO. Civil society refers to "a broad collectivity of non-governmental, non-commercial" organisations outside of official circles pursuing "objectives that relate explicitly to reinforcing or altering existing rules, norms and/or deeper social structures."[100] Of particular interest are environmental, labour, women's, development, and human rights groups. Although civil society pressures were already evident at the first two WTO ministerials, the pressures were far stronger and more visible in Seattle.[101] Whereas civil society protests were an inconvenience to the WTO delegates in Seattle, the main causes of the failure of the ministerial were the divisions among developed countries (as reflected in the G8 and the Quad), and the North-South differences.

From the Seattle WTO Ministerial to the Doha WTO Ministerial

In early 2000 Canada and Japan proposed that another Quad ministerial be held, but the United States was highly skeptical that the Quad ministerials continued to be a useful forum, and it preferred instead to meet individually with the Quad members.[102] Nevertheless, the USTR recognised that "obviously, some understanding within the Quad would be necessary in order to help rebuild consensus for a round."[103] Despite their differences, the Quad members had a sufficient degree of common interests to continue communications and meetings at the senior and junior official levels in preparation for a new round. For example, the Quad had a common commitment to liberalisation in trade in services, government procurement, and intellectual property. Although they disagreed on specifics, the Quad members also had a common interest in incorporating rules on investment into the global trade regime. Furthermore, the Quad was strongly committed to the success of the WTO, and it considered a new MTN round to be necessary to promote trade liberalisation and bolster the WTO.

Although no regular Quad ministerials were held after the May 1999 meeting in Tokyo, a number of Quad officials' meetings were held to prepare for launching a new round at the fourth WTO ministerial in Doha. For example, Quad officials met in June and September 1999 to develop a common position on the upcoming services trade negotiations, the Quad presented a proposal in April 2000 to extend more benefits to the least developed countries, Quad senior officials met in March 2001 to discuss prospects for a new round and to find ways to bridge the differences with developing countries, and the Quad trade ministers held an informal meeting on 16 May 2001 at the margins of the OECD ministerial.[104] In September 2001 the Quad produced an implementation paper, which along with a paper produced by the WTO director-general served as a basis for discussions in the lead-up to the fourth WTO ministerial in Doha, Qatar on 9-13 November 2001. As discussed, the WTO decided to launch a new round at Doha.

To summarise, the Quad ministerials had a role of some importance in determining the agenda items at the Singapore WTO ministerial in 1996. However, the Quad's influence in determining issue outcomes at Singapore was highly variable, and depended on the relationship among Quad members, among developed countries, and between the North and the South. After the Singapore ministerial, Quad meetings were held less frequently, and the last regular Quad ministerial was in Tokyo in May 1999. The failure of the Quad ministers to meet as planned in September before the Seattle WTO ministerial was a clear indication of the Quad's growing disarray and lack of purpose. Although there are a number of reasons for the changing position of the Quad, the G8's unwillingness to directly confront the difficult trade issues was a major factor. Quad ministers and senior officials continue to meet informally – often on the margins of other meetings, and the Quad continues to be an important informal institution. The Quad's importance stems from the fact that its members have a common commitment to trade liberalisation, account for a large percentage of international trade, and have the economic power necessary to provide leadership in the global trade regime. Nevertheless, regular Quad ministerials have not been held since the May 1999 meeting in Tokyo, and it remains to be seen when the Quad ministers will again be holding regular meetings.

Organisation for Economic Co-operation and Development

In the post-Uruguay Round period the OECD has continued to perform its roles as a purveyor of new ideas, and as a source of background studies and prenegotiation of issues of interest to the developed countries. For example, the OECD has been actively involved in research and discussion of competition policy, foreign investment, and environmental and labour standards. Nevertheless, the OECD encountered serious problems in the 1990s stemming from poor leadership and misguided efforts to become a forum for negotiating a multilateral agreement on investment.[105] In previous chapters, we discussed many of the OECD's strengths in dealing with export credit, government procurement, and trade in services and agriculture. This section focuses on the reasons for the failure of the MAI in efforts to identify some of the OECD's limitations as an international institution.

In 1995 the OECD became the venue for the MAI negotiations, and in some respects it seemed to be a highly suitable forum. The OECD had considerable experience in developing a framework for foreign investment issues. In 1961 the OECD had adopted two codes on the liberalisation of capital flows, and in 1976 it had endorsed a Declaration on International Investment and Multinational Enterprises. Furthermore, the OECD countries account for about 85 percent of foreign direct investment outflows and for 65 percent of FDI inflows. Despite these possible advantages, the selection of the OECD as a forum for negotiating an MAI was marked by controversy. The strongest proponent of the OECD as the proper forum was the United States. The United States wanted a comprehensive and binding MAI, and it had been frustrated by developing country opposition even to the limited TRIMs (Trade-Related Investment Measures) agreement negotiated in the GATT Uruguay Round. Since OECD members were mainly developed countries, the United States believed the OECD would be the best forum for negotiating a comprehensive and effective MAI.[106] The EU and Canada, by contrast, argued that their business communities had few complaints about the treatment of FDI in other OECD countries. The South posed the main obstacles to the liberalisation of FDI, and it was the practices of developing countries that required the most control. Thus, the EU and Canada believed that MAI negotiations would be more successful in the wider WTO forum, even if the negotiations were more protracted.

Despite the EU and Canadian arguments, the MAI negotiations were conducted in the OECD rather than the WTO for two major reasons. First, and most importantly, there was no consensus to even address the issue of negotiating an MAI in the WTO because of strong opposition from many developing countries. Second, the European Commission negotiates on behalf of all EU members in the WTO, but EU members negotiate for themselves in the OECD. Although the European Commission negotiates for the EU on trade issues, the Commission's role in regard to foreign investment issues is not as clearly defined. Some EU members were therefore reluctant to expand the Commission's mandate by holding the MAI negotiations in the WTO. To allay concerns about the exclusivity of the MAI negotiations, the OECD ministers indicated that non-OECD countries would be consulted. However, shifting the MAI negotiations from the OECD to the wider forum of the WTO was not a feasible alternative.[107]

In January 1997 the OECD secretariat produced the first draft text of an MAI which emphasised the protection of investors, the principle of national treatment, and plans for a dispute settlement process. A wide diversity of views was evident, however, within the OECD. For example, the EU and Canada resented the Helms-Burton law that the United States threatened to use to sanction foreign companies for investing in Cuba, France and Canada wanted to exempt culture from the MAI to protect their arts and media sectors, and OECD members had differing views regarding the inclusion of environmental and labour measures. The differences among OECD members prevented negotiators from reaching an agreement by the original deadline of May 1997, and the prolonged negotiations gave an opportunity to outside critics to organise opposition to an MAI. Among OECD non-member states, the harshest criticism came from the Third World. A number of developing countries led by India, Egypt, Pakistan, and Malaysia strongly opposed the negotiation of an MAI in the OECD without their participation. Although most developing countries had become far more open to foreign investment after the 1982 foreign debt crisis, they were concerned that the MAI would impose far more obligations on host governments than on MNCs. In the view of developing countries, the East Asian financial crisis demonstrated that capital and foreign investment should be regulated, and that an MAI would threaten their autonomous development.

Another major source of opposition to the MAI negotiations was a wide-ranging coalition of civil society NGOs. These NGOs argued that the MAI would threaten protection of human rights, labour and environmental standards, and developing countries. A particular concern was that the MAI would result in a race to the bottom among countries willing to lower their labour and environmental standards to attract foreign investment. A crucial turning point occurred when Ralph Nader acquired a copy of an OECD draft MAI agreement on behalf of the consumer advocacy group Global Trade Watch and put it on the Internet. (Global Trade Watch, which is headed by Lori Wallach, played a leading role not only in the anti-MAI campaign, but also in opposing the renewal of fast-track authority in the United States, and in the anti-WTO demonstrations in Seattle.[108]) By the time the OECD decided to suspend their negotiations in October 1998, about 600 groups in 70 countries had expressed opposition to the draft agreement, mainly through the Internet. The Internet helped to usher "civil society groups into the negotiating room, ending the days when negotiations were the province of expert officials working solely under political guidance from their governments."[109]

The unsuccessful efforts to negotiate an MAI demonstrate that the OECD is better placed to introduce new ideas, conduct background studies, provide policy advice and analysis, and engage in prenegotiations than to serve as a forum for negotiating agreements on sensitive issues that involve binding and enforceable commitments. In one area discussed in this book, export credits, the OECD has been the primary venue for negotiation. The OECD has served as a negotiating forum in this area because OECD states are the main providers of export credit, and because export credit is not viewed as a threat to a wide range of domestic groups. Although smaller groups such as the OECD, the Quad, and the G7/G8 have an important role in facilitating negotiations in sensitive areas, the OECD experience with the MAI demonstrates that there are definite limits to the role of minilateralism.

The Role of Developing Countries

Previous chapters of this book discussed the marked change from the GATT Tokyo Round to the Uruguay Round, when developing countries became more actively involved in global trade negotiations and accepted the idea of the Uruguay Round agreement as a single undertaking. Whereas special and differential treatment in earlier years focused on preferential market access and special rights for developing countries, in the Uruguay Round S&D treatment emphasised greater flexibility for developing countries in fulfilling their commitments, longer transition times for implementing agreements, and technical assistance from the advanced industrial states.[110] As the results of the Uruguay Round were implemented, the developing countries assumed new responsibilities in areas such as services trade and intellectual property. However, they did not receive as much access to developed country markets as they expected in agriculture and textiles/clothing. As discussed, the commitment of developed countries to open their textile/clothing markets to the South was largely "backloaded" toward the end of the transition period, and there was reason to question whether the North would fulfill its commitment in this area. The North also provided less technical assistance than expected to help the South implement its Uruguay Round commitments. The promise by the North to provide technical assistance was not legally binding, and in 1999 the WTO technical assistance budget was less than one million Swiss francs. In contrast to lowering tariffs, implementing Uruguay Round agreements in such areas as customs valuation, sanitary and phytosanitary standards, and TRIPs can be costly, especially for developing countries. For example, to implement agreements on sanitary and phytosanitary standards, a country must improve its food safety regulations, establish animal vaccination programs, and build inspection and quarantine facilities. Technical assistance to the South to implement these Uruguay Round agreements was simply inadequate.[111]

A number of developing countries led by India and Egypt were therefore reluctant to agree to a new WTO round until the promises developed countries made in the Uruguay Round were implemented. Thus, the G77 trade ministers met in late 1999 and indicated that the implementation of past agreements was an essential prerequisite for the launching of a new round. The South also wanted assurances that the North would devote more attention to Southern views and interests before it would agree to launching a new round. For example, the South wanted the North to focus the GATS and TRIPs agreements on sectors of interest to developing countries. Whereas post-Uruguay Round services negotiations focused on sectors of interest to the North such as financial services and telecommunications, the South wanted talks to also focus on sectors where it has a comparative advantage such as construction, shipping, and tourism. Whereas the TRIPs tended to redistribute income from consumers in poor countries to patent-holders in rich countries, developing countries wanted the TRIPs to focus more on technology transfer to the South and on providing technical assistance to help the South implement the intellectual property rights regulations. Furthermore, the South wanted a new WTO round to reopen the textile/clothing agreement to renegotiation, to reform the system of anti-dumping rules that was often used against Southern exports, and to provide further commitments for S&D treatment especially for the least-developed countries. The South also strongly opposed the linking of labour and environmental issues with trade, and it generally opposed NGO proposals for increased WTO transparency and for the involvement of NGOs in dispute settlement cases.[112]

Despite the nearly unified position of the South on some issues such as labour and environmental standards, divisions within the South of course continued to exist after the Uruguay Round, and so did North-South coalition behaviour. As was the case during the Uruguay Round, the most important

North-South coalition after the Uruguay Round was the Cairns Group. In the post-Uruguay Round period, the Cairns Group called for a phasing out of U.S. and EU agricultural export subsidies, but it continued to be more closely aligned with the United States, and to be highly critical of the EU. The Cairns Group also pressured for the full implementation of the Uruguay Round agreement on agriculture, and for further agricultural reform.[113] For example, the eighteenth Cairns Group ministerial in Sydney, Australia on 1-3 April 1998 issued a "vision statement" outlining its requirements for "completing the task" of agricultural trade liberalisation in the new WTO round. Focusing on the issues of export subsidies, market access, and domestic support, the vision statement indicated that

> The Cairns Group is united in its resolve to ensure that the next WTO agriculture negotiations achieve fundamental reform which will put trade in agricultural goods on the same basis as trade in other goods. All trade distorting subsidies must be eliminated and market access must be substantially improved so that agricultural trade can proceed on the basis of market forces.[114]

The Cairns Group also acted as an important bridge-builder between North and South in the post-Uruguay Round period. Some leading members of the Cairns Group such as Australia, Canada, and South Africa are Commonwealth members and have followed Commonwealth traditions of promoting North-South linkages and of engaging in persuasive diplomacy.[115] Thus, the April 1998 Cairns Group vision statement indicated that

> The principle of special and differential treatment for developing countries, including least developed countries and small states, must ... remain an integral part of the next WTO agriculture negotiations. The framework for liberalisation must continue to support the economic development needs, including technical assistance requirements, of these WTO members.[116]

On the eve of the Doha WTO ministerial, the twenty-second Cairns Group ministerial in Punta del Este, Uruguay on 3-5 September 2001 outlined its demands for agriculture and signalled that it would continue to pressure for agricultural trade liberalisation in the Doha Round.

The determination of the South to be a more significant actor in a new WTO round was evident both to the North and to the GATT secretariat. When the WTO Director-General Michael Moore took office in September 1999, he stated that his top priority for the next three years would be to increase the opportunities for developing countries in the global trade regime. Some developing country demands were not met at Doha. For example, the United States refused to renegotiate the Uruguay Round agreement on textiles and clothing, and at EU insistence the Doha ministerial declaration devoted considerable space to negotiations on trade and environment. However, the United States and the EU did agree to some key developing country demands for negotiation of issues such as anti-dumping actions and agriculture. Furthermore, the North took the issue of technical assistance to the South in implementing its agreements more seriously at Doha than it had in the GATT Uruguay Round. As a result of the Doha ministerial, the WTO established a new Global Trust Fund to help developing countries build their capacity and participate more fully in the new WTO round.[117] In addition, the North agreed to review the WTO provisions on S&D treatment, "with a view to strengthening them and making them more precise, effective, and operational."[118]

The Doha Round is scheduled for completion in the very short period of only three years, and its success will depend largely on the formation of a consensus on key issues among the major traders in the G7 and the Quad – especially the United States and the EU. However, a degree of North-South consensus will also be essential, and the leadership of the major traders will be important in achieving this consensus. For example, U.S. willingness to make concessions on anti-dumping actions, and EU and Japanese willingness to provide concessions on agriculture could be key factors in the success or failure of the round. The G7/G8 and the Quad also have potentially important leadership roles. The Quad in particular has intervened in several North-South issues both before and after the Uruguay Round, and its interactions with the South can have a significant effect on the outcome of the Doha Round. For example, on 31 March 2000 the Quad put forward a "confidence-building package" in which it suggested that technical assistance to developing countries be increased to meet WTO obligations.[119] Although the Quad offered no funding to pay for the technical assistance at the time, the Global Trust Fund for the South was established after the Doha ministerial.

The Quad also has some major differences with the South. For example, a dispute broke out between the Quad and developing countries at the first meeting of the Committee on Trade and Development's Special Session on S&D treatment. The developing countries wanted the review of WTO rules on S&D treatment to be made part of the single undertaking launched at Doha, but the Quad members wanted the review to be part of the WTO work program. If the review were part of the single undertaking, the South could use a failure to obtain WTO concessions as a basis for not agreeing to the negotiating priorities of the Quad.[120] The importance of North-South relations in this round will become increasingly evident as of 1 September 2002, when Supachai Panitchpakdi of Thailand will become the first individual from a developing country to hold the post of WTO director-general.

Conclusion

The Uruguay Round was the most ambitious round of GATT negotiations, resulting in the formation of the WTO and in the extension of the regime principles, norms and rules to trade in services and intellectual property as well as trade in goods. After the Uruguay Round, however, there was a notable lack of leadership in the global trade regime. Although the United States had exerted a leadership role for over 50 years of GATT negotiations, its leadership waned as it adopted a more protectionist stance in the latter half of the Uruguay Round. After the Uruguay Round, U.S. leadership continued to lag as it wanted to limit negotiations largely to areas where it had a comparative advantage such as agriculture and services rather than seeking a new comprehensive WTO round. The EU and the GATT director-general helped to fill the leadership gap in the latter part of the Uruguay Round, and after the round the EU was the main proponent of a comprehensive new WTO round. However, the EU's economic power and unity of purpose were insufficient to substitute for U.S. global leadership. Furthermore, persistent U.S.-EU trade conflicts and U.S. and EU intransigence on issues such as anti-dumping actions and agriculture raised questions about the ability and willingness of the two largest trading entities to provide leadership.

The G7/G8, the Quad, and the OECD all encountered new problems in exerting leadership in the post-Uruguay Round period, that stemmed from a combination of U.S.-EU leadership problems, North-South differences, and negative reactions from civil society groups. As always, trade had to compete with a wide range of other issues in the G7/G8's overloaded summit agenda. However, the G7/G8's tendency to neglect international trade issues was far more noticeable after the Uruguay Round. A number of factors accounted for the G7/G8's inattention to trade including a more evident lack of consensus on trade within the G7/G8, and among developed countries in general; and less acceptance of G7/G8 leadership on trade issues by developing countries and a wide range of civil society groups. Whereas the internal developed country divisions made the G7/G8 less able to act forthrightly, the divisions with developing countries and civil society groups made the G7/G8 less willing to act because of concerns that it might appear to be dictating the agenda on trade issues.

The G7/G8's lack of leadership inevitably had a negative effect on the Quad. One indication of the Quad's declining role after the Uruguay Round was the decreasing number of Quad ministerials. Whereas Quad ministerials were normally held twice a year from 1982 to 1996, they were held only once a year from 1997 to 1999; and in 2000 and 2001 there were no regular Quad ministerials. From the end of the GATT Uruguay Round to the WTO Singapore ministerial in 1996, the Quad ministers held their regular biannual meetings, and they had a major role in setting the agenda items at the Singapore ministerial. However, the Quad's influence in determining issue outcomes at Singapore was highly variable, and depended on the relationship among Quad members, among developed countries in general, and between the North and the South. After the Singapore ministerial, Quad ministers held fewer meetings and exerted less leadership for a number of reasons: the Quad ministers had serious disagreements over a wide range of issues, personal relationships among Quad ministers were less close, the United States was more skeptical that the Quad was an effective institution, there was a proliferation of other fora in which Quad members could discuss trade issues, and the South was expressing more hostility to Northern dominance of the trade agenda. The Quad members continue to be important because they are the major actors in the global trade regime, and Quad officials below the ministerial level continue to communicate with each other and to meet regularly. Nevertheless, the Quad ministerial's visibility as an institution clearly declined in the post-Uruguay Round period.

As was the case for the G7/G8 and the Quad, the OECD encountered new challenges in pursuing its trade agenda after the Uruguay Round. The OECD continues to be actively involved in research, discussion, and prenegotiation of older issues such as agriculture and newer issues such as trade in services, competition policy, foreign investment, and environmental and labour standards. Nevertheless, the OECD encountered serious problems in the 1990s stemming from poor leadership and misguided efforts to become the forum for negotiating an MAI. The OECD has been able to serve as the negotiating forum for export credit because OECD states are the main providers of export credit, and because export credit is not viewed as a threat to a wide range of domestic groups. However, divisions among OECD members combined with a strong reaction of developing countries and civil society groups to the OECD's MAI negotiations indicates that it is not the proper forum for negotiating highly sensitive issues. The suspension of the MAI negotiations demonstrates that in most cases (export credit is an exception) the OECD is better placed to engage in research, the generation of new ideas, policy advice, and prenegotiation than to serve as the primary forum for negotiation.

The U.S.-EU divisions and resultant lack of leadership by the G7/G8 and the Quad were the main factors explaining the failure of the 1999 WTO ministerial in Seattle to result in the launching of a new trade round. Another major factor explaining the failure in Seattle was the differences between the North and the South. The developing countries had been more actively involved in the Uruguay Round than in any previous GATT round, and they continued to be involved after the Uruguay Round because of their dependence on exports to developed country markets. Nevertheless, the developing countries were highly disillusioned with the results of the Uruguay Round. As the results of the Uruguay Round were implemented, the developing countries assumed new responsibilities in areas such as services trade and intellectual property. However, they did not receive as much access to developed country markets as they expected in agriculture and textiles/clothing. The North also provided less technical assistance then expected to help the South implement its Uruguay Round commitments.

A number of developing countries were therefore reluctant to agree to a new WTO round until the promises developed countries made in the Uruguay Round were implemented. The South also wanted assurances that the North would devote more attention to Southern views and interests before it would agree to launching a new round. For example, the South wanted a new WTO round to focus on sectors of interest to developing as well as developed countries in the GATS and TRIPs agreements, to reopen the textile/clothing agreement to renegotiation, to reform the system of anti-dumping rules that was often used against Southern exports, and to provide further commitments for S&D treatment especially for the least-developed countries. The South also insisted that more technical assistance from the North was essential to enable them to implement trade liberalisation agreements. Divisions within the South of course continued to exist after the Uruguay Round, and North-South coalitions such as the Cairns Group continued to have a significant role. Nevertheless, it was evident that the North would have to meet some of the South's general demands if developing countries were to support the launching of a new round.

Despite the obstacles to North-North and North-South cooperation at the Seattle ministerial, the major developed countries had become more dependent on trade and they shared an interest in launching a new round. In efforts to convince the developing countries to join in a new round, the developed countries devoted more attention to their interests and concerns. For example, the United States and the EU agreed to developing country demands for negotiation of anti-dumping actions and agriculture, and the North took the issue of technical assistance to the South in implementing its agreements more seriously at the

Doha WTO ministerial than it had in the GATT Uruguay Round. As a result of concessions on all sides, a new MTN round was finally launched at the Doha ministerial in November, 2001. Nevertheless, the Doha Round is to be concluded in a three-year period, and the United States, the EU, the G7/G8, the Quad, and the OECD must provide forthright leadership if the round is to succeed. Although these developed country-led institutions continue to be necessary for exerting leadership near the top of the global trade regime pyramid, their leadership in the WTO round will not succeed if they do not respond more effectively to the needs, interests, and demands of the developing countries. The North-South interdependent linkages in trade have greatly increased, and cooperation within the North is no longer sufficient for successfully concluding multilateral trade agreements.

Notes

1   Klaus Günter Deutsch, "The EU: Contending for Leadership," in Klaus Günter Deutsch and Bernhard Speyer, eds., *The World Trade Organization Millennium Round: Freer Trade in the Twenty-first Century* (London: Routledge, 2001), p. 34.

2   Jeffrey J. Schott, "The WTO After Seattle," in Jeffrey J. Schott, ed., *The WTO After Seattle* (Washington, D.C.: Institute for International Economics, July 2000), p. 7.

3   Andreas Falke, "The USA: Why Fundamentals Do Not Always Matter, or: It's Politics, Stupid!," in Deutsch and Speyer, eds., *The World Trade Organization Millennium Round*, pp. 18-33.

4   Falke, "The USA: Why Fundamentals Do Not Always Matter," p. 22.

5   Joseph Kahn, "House Supports Trading Powers Sought by Bush," *New York Times*, December 7, 2001, pp. A1 and A20.

6   Hugo Paemen, "The EU Approach to a New Round," in Schott, ed., *The WTO After Seattle*, pp. 53-54.

7   Deutsch, "The EU: Contending for Leadership," pp. 34-47.

8   J. Michael Finger and Philip Schuler, "Developing Countries and the Millennium Round," in Deutsch and Speyer, eds., *The World Trade Organization Millennium Round*, pp. 58-71.

9   "Marrakesh Agreement Establishing the World Trade Organization," Article IV.1 in World Trade Organization, *The Results of the Uruguay Round of Multilateral Trade Negotiations: The Legal Texts* (Geneva: WTO, 1994), p. 8. See also Bernard M. Hoekman and Michel M. Kostecki, *The Political Economy of the World Trading System: The WTO and Beyond* (Oxford: Oxford University Press, 2nd edition, 2001), ch. 2; WTO Secretariat, *Guide to the Uruguay Round Agreements* (The Hague: Kluwer Law International, 1999), p. 6; and Jeffrey S. Thomas and Michael A. Meyer, *The New Rules of Global Trade: A Guide to the World Trade Organization* (Scarborough: Carswell, 1997), pp. 337-338.

10 Hoekman and Kostecki, *The Political Economy of the World Trading System*, pp. 105-106; World Trade Organization, "Singapore Ministerial Declaration," Adopted on 13 December 1996, WT.MIN(96)/DEC, 18 December 1996.

11   See World Trade Organization, "Ministerial Declaration on Trade in Information Technology Products," Singapore, 13 December 1996, ST/MIN(96)/16, 13 December 1996. The signatories of this declaration were Australia, Canada, the EU, Hong Kong, Iceland, Indonesia, Japan, Korea, Norway, Singapore, Switzerland, Taiwan, Turkey, and the United States.

12   See World Trade Organization, "Geneva Ministerial Declaration," Adopted on 20 May 1998, WT/MIN(98)/DEC/1, 25 May 1998.

13   It is important to note that WTO officials were attuned to the need to increase interaction with civil society groups well before the Seattle ministerial. For example, Article V.2 of the Marrakesh agreement states that "The General Council shall make appropriate arrangements for consultation and cooperation with non-governmental organizations." See also Gabrielle Marceau and Peter N. Pedersen, "Is the WTO Open and Transparent? A Discussion of the Relationship of the WTO with Non-governmental Organisations and Civil Society's Claims for More Transparency and Public Participation," *Journal of World Trade* 33-1 (1999), pp. 5-49. Although the authors emphasise that their views in this article are strictly personal, they are both members of the WTO secretariat.

14   Falke, "The USA: Why Fundamentals Do Not Always Matter," p. 28.

15   Henry R. Nau, "Clinton's Legacy: US Trade Leadership Languishes," in Deutsch and Speyer, eds., *The World Trade Organization Millennium Round*, p. 245.

16   Nau, "Clinton's Legacy," p. 246.

17   The Doha work program for 2002 includes meetings of the Working Group on the relationship between Trade and Investment, the Working Group on the Interaction between Trade and Competition Policy, and the Committee on Trade and Environment.

18   "Beyond Doha," *The Economist*, November 17, 2001, p. 11.

19   World Trade Organization, "Ministerial Declaration," Ministerial Conference in Doha, Fourth Session, WT/MIN(01)/DEC/W/1, November 14, 2001; "The Doha Round: Seeds Sown for Future Growth," *The Economist*, November 17, 2001, pp. 65-67; "Chairman's Statement Casts Doubt on Final WTO Declaration," *Inside U.S. Trade*, November 15, 2001, pp. 1 and 15-16; Falke, "The USA: Why Fundamentals Do Not Always Matter," p. 19.

20   World Trade Organization, "Ministerial Declaration," Ministerial Conference, Fourth Session, Doha, 9-14 November 2001, WT/MIN(01)/DEC/W/1, 14 November 2001, paragraph 45.

21   Heidi Ullrich, "Trade Liberalization and Leadership: Challenges for the Doha Development Agends and Lessons Learned from the Uruguay Round," paper presented at German Council on Foreign Relations Conference, Berlin, 28 January 2002, p. 2.

22   Nicholas Bayne, *Hanging In There: The G7 and G8 Summit in Maturity and Renewal* (Aldershot: Ashgate, 2000), p. 114.

23   Nicholas Bayne, "The G7 and Multilateral Trade Liberalisation: Past Performance, Future Challenges," in John J. Kirton and George M. von Furstenberg, *New Directions in Global Economic Governance: Managing Globalisation in the Twenty-first Century* (Aldershot: Ashgate, 2001), pp. 178-179; Bayne, *Hanging In There*, pp. 120-121.

24   Nicholas Bayne, quoted in Ullrich, "Stimulating Trade Liberalisation after Seattle," p. 228.

25   "Statement of the Group of Seven Leaders," Genoa, Italy, 20 July 2001.

26   Bayne, *Hanging In There*, p. 115.

27   Peter I. Hajnal, *The G7/G8 System: Evolution, Role and Documentation* (Aldershot: Ashgate, 1999), pp. 60-61; Bayne, *Hanging In There*, p. 121.

28   JayEtta Z. Hecker, "Observations on the Ministerial Meeting in Singapore," Statement before the U.S. House of Representatives Subcommittee on Trade, Committee on Ways and Means, U.S. General Accounting Office, GAO/T-NSIAD-97-92, p. 11.

29   G7 Economic Summit Communiqué, Halifax, Nova Scotia, 15-17 June 1995, paragraphs 42 to 44; "U.S. Waters Down G-7 Statement on Global Competition Rules," *Inside U.S. Trade*, 23 June 1995, pp. 1-2.

30   All the quotations in this paragraph and the next are taken from G7 Summit Economic Communiqué, "Making a Success of Globalization for the Benefit of All," Lyon, France, 27-27 June 1996, paragraphs 19 to 24.

31   Bayne, *Hanging In There*, p. 117; Hajnal, *The G7/G8 System*, p. 62.

32   "ICC Calls on G-7 Leaders to Expand Trade Agenda to New Issues," *Inside U.S. Trade*, 20 June 1997; "Union Presidents Vow to Fight Fast-Track Bill without Labor Rules," *Inside U.S. Trade*, 13 June 1997.

33   See Nicholas Bayne, "Impressions of the Denver Summit." http://www.g7.utoronto.ca/g7/evaluations/1997denver/impression/agenda.html.

34   Bayne, *Hanging In There*, pp. 152-153; Hajnal, *The G7/G8 System*, p. 62.

35   Ullrich, "Stimulating Trade Liberalisation after Seattle," p. 224.

36   See Martin Dent and Bill Peters, *The Crisis of Poverty and Debt in the Third World* (Aldershot: Ashgate, 1999); Iain Guest, "Debt – The Next Cause Celebre?," *Christian Science Monitor*, May 27, 1998, p. 20; and John Davies and Mariette Maillet, "The Debt Crisis: Perspectives of a Bilateral Donor," *International Journal* 55-2 (Spring 2000), pp. 270-280.

37   G8 Communiqué, Cologne, Germany, 18-20 1999.

38   Ullrich, "Trade Liberalization and Leadership," p. 2; Ullrich, "Stimulating Trade Liberalisation after Seattle," p. 224. See also Bayne, *Hanging In There*, 154-158.

39   G8 Communiqué, Cologne, Germany, 18-20 June 1999, paragraph 10.

40   G8 Communiqué, Cologne, Germany, 18-20 June 1999, paragraphs 11 and 43.

41   Schott, "The WTO After Seattle," p. 5.

42   John Kirton, "Prospects for the Year 2000 Okinawa G7/G8 Summit," http://www.g7.utoronto.ca/g7/evaluations/2000okinawa/prospects.html; Ella Kokotsis, John Kirton, and Diana Juricevic, "Commitments from the G7 Statement, Okinawa, July 21, 2000: The G7/G8 Commitments Report 2000," http://www.g7.utoronto.ca/g7/conferences/2001/rome/conflictPrevention.pdf, p. 12.

43   The quotations in this paragraph are from G8 Communiqué Okinawa 2000, Okinawa, Japan, 21-23 July 2000. See also Nicholas Bayne, "First Thoughts on the Okinawa Summit, 21-23 July 2000," http://www.g7.utoronto.ca/g7/evaluations/2000okinawa/bayne.html.

44   Communiqué of the G8 Summit, Genoa, Italy, 22 July 2001, paragraph 10; Falke, "The USA: Why Fundamentals Do Not Always Matter," p. 19.

45   "Statement of the Group of Seven Leaders," Genoa, Italy, 20 July 2001, paragraph 6.

46   "Statement of the Group of Seven Leaders," Genoa, Italy, 20 July 2001, paragraph 9.

47   Heidi Ullrich and Michael Malleson, "Issue Performance Assessment – Trade" for the G8 2001 Genoa Summit, http://www.g7.utoronto.ca/g7/evaluations/2001genoa/assessment_trade.html; Sir Nicholas Bayne, "Impressions of the Genoa Summit, 20-22 July 2001 (Final Version, 28 July)," http://www.g7.utoronto.ca/g7/evaluations/2001genoa/assess_summit_bayne.html; "Statement of the Group of Seven Leaders," U.S. Department of State, International Information Programs website.

48   For an in-depth discussion of the civil society protests in Genoa see Peter I. Hajnal, "Personal Assessment of the Role of Civil Society at the 2001 Genoa G8 Summit," http://www.g7.utoronto.ca/g7/evaluations/2001genoa/assess_summit_hajnal.html.

49   Michael Daly and Hiroaki Kuwahara, "The Impact of the Uruguay Round on Tariff and Non-Tariff Barriers to Trade in the 'Quad'," *World Economy* 21-2 (March 1998), 208.

50   Before 1997 Quad ministerials had been held only once in 1987 and in 1991. In 1983 there were four Quad ministerials. In all other years from 1982 to 1996, there were two Quad ministerials each year. See Table 5.1.

51   Communications from Canada's Department of Foreign Affairs and International Trade, 7 February 2002 and 21 February 2002.

52   Heidi K. Ullrich, "Stimulating Trade Liberalisation after Seattle: G7/G8 Leadership in Global Governance," in John J. Kirton and George M. von Furstenberg, eds., *New Directions in Global Economic Governance: Managing Globalisation in the Twenty-first Century* (Aldershot: Ashgate, 2001), p. 229.

53   "Quad Trade Ministers to Meet on WTO Ministerial, New Negotiations,' *Inside U.S. Trade*, 23 April 1999, pp. 3-4; "WTO Director General Race Tightens between Supachai, Moore," *Inside U.S. Trade*, 19 March 1999; "U.S., Japan Launch Senior Dialogue on Short-term, Broad WTO Issues," *Inside U.S. Trade*, 10 March 2000, p. 8; communications from Canada's Department of Foreign Affairs and International Trade.

54   Quoted in Ullrich, "Stimulating Trade Liberalisation after Seattle," p. 227.

55   Communication from Canada's Department of Foreign Affairs and International Trade, 21 February 2002.

56   Cynthia Osterman, "Trade Ministers Meet under Cloud of Disputes," Vancouver, Reuter News Service, 3 May 1995; "EU-U.S. Meeting Fails to Break Deadlock in Banana Import Dispute," *Inside U.S. Trade*, 14 April 1995, p. 21; "U.S. Frustration Growing on Autos as Japanese Proposals Fall Short," *Inside U.S. Trade*, 14 April 1995, pp. 1 and 18-19.

57   Chairman's Statement, 26th Quadrilateral Trade Ministers Meeting, Whistler, B.C., 3-5 May 1995.

58   "Quad Ministers Dampen U.S., Canadian Hopes for New Tariff Cuts," *Inside U.S. Trade*, 12 May 1995, pp. 7-8.

59   "Kantor Proposes Establishment of WTO Office in Washington," *Inside U.S. Trade*, 12 May 1995, p. 10.

60   "Quad Trade Ministers Adopt Common Line on China WTO Negotiations," *Inside U.S. Trade*, 12 May 1995, pp. 1 and 19-20; Chairman's Statement, 26th Quadrilateral Trade Ministers Meeting, Whistler, B.C., 3-5 May 1995.

61   "Statement by Renato Ruggiero on the 'Quad' Meeting," *World Trade Organization Press Release* 27, 23 October 1995.

62   "Statement by Renato Ruggiero on the 'Quad' Meeting," *World Trade Organization Press Release* 27, 23 October 1995.

63   "Quad Launches New WTO Agenda with Work on Labor, Regionalism," *Inside U.S. Trade*, 27 October 1995, p. 6.

64   Elizabeth Smythe, "The Multilateral Agreement on Investment: A Charter of Rights for Global Investors or Just Another Agreement?," in Fen Osler Hampson and Maureen Appel Molot, eds., *Canada Among Nations 1998 – Leadership and Dialogue* (Toronto: Oxford University Press, 1998), pp. 241-245.

65   Canada Department of Foreign Affairs and International Trade, "27th Quadrilateral Trade Ministers' Meeting, 20-21 October 1995," Press Release no. 195, 23 October 1995; "Official Outlines Agendas for Quad, U.S.-EU and Singapore Summits," *Inside U.S. Trade*, 13 October 1995, pp. 20-21; Patrick Chalmers, "Quad Ministers Discuss China and Investment Rules," Reuters News Service, Harrogate, England, 20 October 1995; "Kantor Rejects EU Proposals for Special Treatment of China in WTO," *Inside U.S. Trade*, 27 October 1995, pp. 1 and 21-22.

66 "Eggleton to Visit Japan and Meet 'Quad' Trade Ministers," Canada's Department of Foreign Affairs and International Trade, *International Trade News Release* no. 69, 16 April 1996.

67 28th Quadrilateral Trade Ministers' Meeting, April 19-21, 1996, Chairman's Statement.

68 28th Quadrilateral Trade Ministers' Meeting, April 19-21, 1996, Chairman's Statement.

69 28th Quadrilateral Trade Ministers' Meeting, April 19-21, 1996, Chairman's Statement.

70 Canada Department of Foreign Affairs and International Trade, "28th Quadrilateral Trade Ministers' Meeting, April 19-21, 1996, Chairman's Statement," *News Release* no. 76.

71 "U.S. Proposes Interim WTO Procurement Deal to Combat Corruption," *Inside U.S. Trade*, 22 March 1996, pp. 1 and 29-31; "Computer Industry Proposing Sweeping Tariff Elimination by 2000," *Inside U.S. Trade*, 17 February 1995, pp. 1 and 16-17.

72 EU Commissioner Leon Brittan quoted in "Quad Ministers Approve Informal WTO Investment Work Program," *Inside U.S. Trade*, 26 April 1996, p. 2.

73 28th Quadrilateral Trade Ministers' Meeting, April 19-21, 1996, Chairman's Statement.

74 28th Quadrilateral Trade Ministers' Meeting, April 19-21, 1996, Chairman's Statement.

75 Charlene Barshefsky quoted in Imbert Mathee, "Trade Routes Lead to Summit Here: Actions of 'Quad' Watched Closely," *Seattle Post Intelligencer*, 23 September 1996, p. A5.

76 Paul Lewis, "Cuba Trade Law: Export of U.S. Ire and Politics," *New York Times*, 15 March 1996, pp. C1 and C3; "Biter Bitten: The Helms-Burton Law," *The Economist*, 8 June 1996, p. 45.

77 Quadrilateral Trade Ministers Meeting, Seattle, Washington, 27-28 September 1996 – Chairperson's Summary.

78 World Trade Organization, "Singapore Ministerial Declaration" adopted on 13 December 1996, WT/MIN(96)/DEC., 18 December 1996, paragraph 20.

79 World Trade Organization, "Singapore Ministerial Declaration," paragraph 21.

80 World Trade Organization, "Singapore Ministerial Declaration," paragraph 7.

81 World Trade Organization, "Singapore Ministerial Declaration," paragraph 4.

82 "'Quad' Trade Ministers to Meet in Toronto," International Trade *News Release* no. 74, 21 April 1997.

83 "Quad Countries Fail to Agree on New Sectoral Tariff Initiatives," *Inside U.S. Trade*, 2 May 1997.

84 "WTO Members Cautiously Optimistic China WTO Entry will be a Plus," *Inside U.S. Trade*, 26 December 1997.

85 30th Quadrilateral Trade Ministers' Meeting, "Chair's Statement," p. 2.

86 30th Quadrilateral Trade Ministers' Meeting, "Chair's Statement," p. 4.

87 Communication from an official at Canada's Department of Foreign Affairs and International Trade, 11 June 2001.

88 Quadrilateral Ministerial Meeting, Versailles, France, 29 to 30 April 1998, "Chairman's Statement."

89 Quadrilateral Ministerial Meeting, Versailles, France, 29 to 30 April 1998, "Chairman's Statement."

90 Quadrilateral Ministerial Meeting, Versailles, France, 29 to 30 April 1998, "Chairman's Statement."

91 Quadrilateral Ministerial Meeting, Versailles, France, 29 to 30 April 1998, "Chairman's Statement," "Quad Ministers Reveal Competing Visions for New WTO Negotiations," *Inside U.S. Trade*, 1 May 1998.

92 Catherine L. Mann and Sarah Cleeland Knight, "Electronic Commerce in the WTO," in Schott, ed., *The WTO After Seattle*, pp. 253-266.

93   "Quad Negotiators to Lobby for High-Level WTO Environment Meeting," *Inside U.S. Trade*, 31 July 1998; "WTO Members Clash in Preparatory Talks on WTO Negotiations," *Inside U.S. Trade*, 2 October 1998.

94   The 33rd Quadrilateral Trade Ministers Meeting, Tokyo, 11-12 May, 1999, "Chair's Statement."

95   The 33rd Quadrilateral Trade Ministers Meeting, Tokyo, 11-12 May, 1999, "Chair's Statement."

96   Ullrich, "Stimulating Trade Liberalisation after Seattle," p. 228.

97   Falke, "The USA: Why Fundamentals Do Not Always Matter," p. 28.

98   Phil Crane, quoted in "Donahue Says Seattle Failure due to U.S., EU Domestic Pressures," *Inside U.S. Trade*, 17 December 1999, p. 13.

99   "Geneva Process Ends without Draft Declaration, Moore Presses On," *Inside U.S. Trade*, special report, 24 November 1999.

100 Jan Aart Scholte with Robert O'Brien and Marc Williams, "The WTO and Civil Society," *Journal of World Trade* 33-1 (February 1999), p. 109.

101 Robert O'Brien, Anne Marie Goetz, Jan Aart Scholte, and Marc Williams, *Contesting Global Governance: Multilateral Economic Institutions and Global Social Movements* (Cambridge: Cambridge University Press, 2000), pp. 85-97; David Robertson, "Civil Society and the WTO," *World Economy* 23-9 (September 2000), pp. 1121-1123.

102 "WTO Members Press for Early Action on Draft Ministerial Declaration," *Inside U.S Trade*, 24 September 1999, p. 17; "WTO at Most to Relaunch Work with Modest Program, Consultations," *Inside U.S. Trade*, 21 January 2000, p. 11; "U.S., Japan Launce Senior Dialogue on Short-term, Broad WTO Issues," *Inside U.S. Trade*, 10 March 2000, p. 8.

103 USTR Charlene Barshefsky quoted in "U.S., EU Efforts to Build New Round Consensus Stall at Summit," *Inside U.S. Trade*, 16 June 2000, p. 14.

104 "Quad to Meet on Services Next Week as WTO Talks Falter," *Inside U.S. Trade*, 2 March 2001, p. 28; "U.S. Support for New Round Contrasts with Hardline on LDCs," *Inside U.S. Trade*, 18 May 2001, pp. 1-2; Communication from official at Canada's Department of Foreign Affairs and International Trade, 11 June 2001.

105 Razeen Sally, "Looking Askance at Global Governance," in John J. Kirton, Joseph P. Daniels, and Andreas Freytag, eds., *Guiding Global Order: G8 Governance in the Twenty-first Century* (Aldershot: Ashgate, 2001), p. 64.

106 For a discussion of the various fora over time for negotiating foreign investment issues see Theodore H. Cohn, *Global Political Economy: Theory and Practice* (New York: Addison Wesley Longman, 2000), pp. 300-308.

107 Elizabeth Smythe, "The Multilateral Agreement on Investment: A Charter of Rights for Global Investors or Just Another Agreement?," in Fen Osler Hampson and Maureen Appel Molot, eds., *Canada Among Nations 1998: Leadership and Dialogue* (Toronto: Oxford University Press, 1998), pp. 241-245; William A. Dymond, "The MAI: A Sad and Melancholy Tale," in *Canada Among Nations 1999: A Big League Player?* (Toronto: Oxford University Press, 1999), p. 26.

108 See "Lori's War," *Foreign Policy* no. 118 (Spring 2000), pp. 28-55.

109 Dymond, "The MAI," p. 50.

110 John Whalley, "Special and Differential Treatment in the Millennium Round," *World Economy* 22 (November 1999), pp. 1065-1093; Mari Pangestu, "Special and Differential Treatment in the Millennium: Special for Whom and How Different?," *World Economy* 23-9 (September 2000), pp. 1285-1302.

111 Finger and Schuler, "Developing Countries and the Millennium Round," pp. 61-62.
112 Finger and Schuler, "Developing Countries and the Millennium Round," pp. 64-68; "Beyond Doha," *The Economist*, November 17, 2001, p. 11.
113 For a discussion of Cairns Group positions and strategies in the post-Uruguay Round period see Kym Anderson and Paul Morris, "The Elusive Goal of Agricultural Trade Reform," *Cato Journal* 19-3 (Winter 2000), pp. 385-396.
114 Eighteenth Cairns Group Ministerial Meeting, Sydney, Australia, 3 April 1998, *Communiqué*.
115 See Ian Taylor, "The Cairns Group and the Commonwealth: Bridge-Building for International Trade," *Round Table* 355-1 (2000), pp. 375-386.
116 Eighteenth Cairns Group Ministerial Meeting, Sydney, Australia, 3 April 1998, *Communiqué*.
117 See, for example, World Trade Organization, "Governments Pledge CHF 30 Million to Doha Development Agenda Global Trust Fund," Doha Development Agenda Press Release 279, 11 March 2002.
118 World Trade Organization, "Ministerial Declaration," Ministerial Conference, Fourth Session, Doha, paragraph 44.
119 Finger and Schuler, "Developing Countries and the Millennium Round," p. 62.
120 "Quad, Developing Members Face Off on Special & Differential Treatment," *Inside U.S. Trade*, 8 March 2002, pp. 5-6.

9 Conclusion

International relations theorists explicitly differentiate international regimes from international organisations. International regimes are most commonly defined as "principles, norms, rules, and decision-making procedures around which actors' expectations converge in a given area of international relations."[1] International organisations are physical entities with personnel, offices, and budgets that are embedded in international regimes; that is, they provide a platform or physical setting in which international regimes can operate.[2] For example, the GATT/WTO is an international organisation embedded in the global trade regime. Although international relations specialists distinguish between regimes and organisations in theory, *in reality* they often consider them to be virtually identical. In sectoral areas such as trade where there is a predominant international organisation, Robert Keohane maintains that in practice "organization and regime ... may seem almost coterminous."[3] Thus, most regime theorists describe the GATT/WTO as being "virtually coterminous" with the global trade regime;[4] and some studies specifically refer to the "GATT/WTO regime."[5]

Regime theorists often equate the GATT/WTO with the global trade regime, because the GATT/WTO has been the international organisation with primary legal responsibility for upholding the principles, norms, and rules of the global trade regime. However, it is *not* sufficient to limit one's study to the GATT/WTO when examining the decision-making procedures of the global trade regime. Decision-making procedures are "prevailing practices for making and implementing collective choice," and collective choice in the global trade regime develops as a multi-layered process through discussion and negotiation in a wide array of formal and informal institutions.[6] It is important to direct more attention to regime decision-making procedures, because these procedures can have a significant effect on the development and evolution of regime principles, norms and rules. Thus, the predominant role of advanced industrial states in trade decision-making has insured that the trade regime principles, norms and rules most closely reflect their views and concerns. When one focuses on decision-making procedures, John Jackson's statement in 1969 that the "regulation of international trade is ... an extraordinarily complex and muddled affair, involving a wide variety of organizations and institutions," continues to be true today.[7]

This book examines the role of three formal and informal institutions in the global trade regime, and their relationship to the GATT/WTO: the Group of 7/ Group of 8, the Quadrilateral group, and the Organisation for Economic Co-operation and Development. Of these institutions, the Quadrilateral group of trade ministers from the United States, the EU, Japan, and Canada has received the least amount of attention in the literature. These three institutions are plurilateral, with their membership limited mainly to the developed countries. Figure 1.1 (in Chapter 1) shows that the decision-making procedures of the global trade regime are in many respects pyramidal, with developed country institutions near the top of the pyramid, and developing country institutions near the bottom. Thus, the G7/G8, the Quad, and the OECD have occupied important positions at the upper levels of the trade decision-making pyramid. The most important members of the Quad are the United States and the EU, the world's largest trading entities. Thus, the United States and the EU are at the top of the global trade regime pyramid (see Figure 1.1). Gilbert Winham described the GATT Tokyo Round as a pyramidal process, where agreements were "initiated by the major powers at the top and then gradually multilateralized through the inclusion of other parties in the discussions."[8] However, Winham's description of a pyramidal structure referred to GATT/WTO negotiations, whereas this book broadens the discussion of pyramidal structure to examine the relationship among several formal and informal institutions in the global trade regime. The G7/G8 and the Quad are placed above the OECD in the global trade regime pyramid because only the most economically important of the OECD members are included in these more select institutions. Furthermore, the G7/G8 which meets at the heads of government and state level is higher on the pyramid than the Quad which meets at the trade ministers level.

This book devotes a smaller amount of space to institutions representing developing country interests such as the Group of 77 and the United Nations Conference on Trade and Development, because they have been far less influential in the global trade regime. However, the South has had a more active and important role in trading relationships in recent years, and this book examines changes in the involvement and influence of developing countries in the global trade regime over time. The latter part of the book discusses the role of North-South coalitions such as the Cairns Group during and after the GATT Uruguay Round.

Although we refer to other institutions throughout the book, they are discussed only for illustrative purposes. Other plurilateral institutions in addition to the G7/G8, the Quad, and the OECD of course have had an important effect on decision-making in the global trade regime. For example, regional trade agreements have had a significant impact from the time the EC began functioning in January 1958, and the effect of RTAs increased considerably in the 1980s and 1990s with the deepening of integration in the EU, and the formation of the CUSFTA, the NAFTA, and Mercosur. Nevertheless, this book focuses on the governing of global trade, and the G7/G8, the Quad, and the OECD have been much more *directly* involved with global trade issues than the RTAs. The only RTA this book devotes significant attention to is the EC/EU, because the European Commission is the "negotiator for the European Union ... on trade issues, but always operating under the watchful eyes of the member governments."[9] As discussed in this book, the EU has a unique role among RTAs in the G7/G8, the Quad, and the OECD.

We also devote less attention to private groupings in this book, even though such groupings have had a significant role in the global trade regime. Regime analysis has generally been state-centric, and has underestimated the role of MNCs, NGOs, epistemic communities of experts such as scientists and economists, and other private groups. In recent years, a growing body of literature has begun to appear on the role of non-state actors in international regimes.[10] This book contains some discussion of the role of epistemic communities in legitimising the international regulation of services and agricultural trade, and of the role of NGO civil society groups in challenging trade regime principles, norms, and rules. However, a more detailed examination of private groups in trade decision-making must await another study.

The Role of the G7/G8, the Quad, and the OECD

This book examines three major questions regarding the role of the G7/G8, the Quad, and the OECD: Why have these institutions been influential in the global trade regime, what is the nature of their influence, and how has their influence changed over time? Beginning with the "why" question, the book hypothesises that the influence of institutions other than the GATT/WTO in the global trade regime stems from four major factors: the dominance of developed countries in the North over developing countries in the South, the decline of U.S. economic hegemony, the growing interaction of trade with other issues as a result of globalisation, and the unique characteristics of the GATT/WTO as an international organisation. The first factor, the North's dominance over the South, has contributed to the pyramidal structure of institutions in the global trade regime. Thus, the major developed countries often confer among themselves in smaller "like-minded" groups such as the G7/G8, the Quad, and the OECD before seeking endorsement of their policies by the GATT/WTO. The second factor, the decline of U.S. economic hegemony, has increased the need for plurilateral institutions to provide collective management and to resolve disputes among the major traders. As this book discusses, the change from the OEEC to the OECD in the 1960s, the formation of the G7 in the 1970s, and the creation of the Quad in the 1980s all resulted in part from the need for collective decision-making as U.S. economic hegemony declined. The third factor, the growing interaction of trade with other issues as a result of globalisation, has resulted in an increased blurring of the divisions between the GATT/WTO's functions and the functions of other formal and informal institutions. The G7/G8 and the OECD are especially well-suited to addressing trade issues in the context of other issues, because these two institutions deal with a wide range of issue areas.

The fourth factor, the nature of the GATT/WTO as an international organisation, has encouraged developed country members to turn to other institutions to supplement their influence over trade issues. The GATT/WTO is a pyramidal organisation, in which the largest developed country traders have the most influence in multilateral trade negotiations. In addition, the GATT/WTO has had various informal groupings ranging from the Consultative Group of 18 to the green room sessions, in which the major developed country traders have had a central role. Nevertheless, the developed countries have no *formal* minilateral prerogatives in the GATT/WTO. The GATT/WTO has nothing comparable to the smaller executive boards of the IMF and World Bank, and the GATT/WTO's one-nation, one-vote system contrasts with the weighted voting systems of the IMF and World Bank. The developed countries' lack of formal minilateral prerogatives is one factor explaining their unwillingness to provide more funding to the GATT/WTO secretariat, and their tendency to rely on plurilateral institutions such as the G7/G8, the Quad, and the OECD as a means of increasing their influence in the global trade regime. The GATT/WTO's legalistic, rules-bound nature is another reason that developed countries have preferred to deal with certain sensitive trade issues in less legalistic, more flexible institutions such as the OECD.

Most of this book addresses the second and third questions mentioned above, in regard to all the actors/institutions listed on the global trade regime pyramid in Figure 1.1 – the United States, the EU, the G7/G8, the Quad, the OECD, and the developing countries (the G77 and UNCTAD). For each of these actors/ institutions, we ask what is the nature of their influence in the global trade regime, and how has their influence changed over time? The global trade regime pyramid is not static, and the influence of these actors/institutions *has* changed over time. The remaining part of this chapter discusses the main findings of this study for each of these actors/institutions, moving from the top to the bottom of the pyramid.

The United States and the EC/EU

Beginning in 1943, the United States took the primary initiative, often along with Britain, in discussions that resulted in the creation of the GATT, and "almost all the clauses in GATT can be traced to one or another of the clauses" in the 1934 U.S. Reciprocal Trade Agreements Act.[11] The United States dominated the first GATT conference in 1947, and the first four rounds of GATT negotiations were subject to prevailing American influence. The 1960-61 GATT Dillon Round, however, witnessed a new array of relationships that became much more evident during the 1964-67 Kennedy Round. The EC formed by six Western European countries was an important new regional actor in the Dillon Round, and by the time of the Kennedy Round the EC had become a major trader along with the United States. As Ernest Preeg noted about the Kennedy Round, if the United States and the EC "could agree, the negotiations would move forward; if they should fail to reach an accord, a serious and perhaps fatal crisis would undoubtedly follow."[12] Nevertheless, EC membership did not increase during the 1960s because of two French vetoes of British applications to join the Community, and the United States continued to remain above the EC on the global trade regime pyramid.

The 1970s was a period marked by significant change in the American, European, and Japanese positions in the global trade regime. In 1971, the United States had a balance of trade deficit for the first time in the twentieth century, and on 15 August 1971 President Richard Nixon suspended the convertibility of the U.S. dollar into gold and imposed a ten percent tariff surcharge on all dutiable imports. The U.S. position as global economic hegemon deteriorated further in January 1973, when Britain, Denmark, and Ireland joined the EC, making it the world's largest trading entity. Thus, during the 1973-79 GATT Tokyo Round the EC began to occupy a place alongside the United States at the top of the global trade regime pyramid. Japan like the EC was a far more prominent trader by the 1970s, and the EC and Japan were less willing to defer to American leadership on trade issues. The United States continued to have a great deal of influence in the Tokyo Round, and some of the early initiatives leading to the Tokyo Round came from U.S. committees such as the Williams Commission. However, the United States and the EC held informal discussions on contentious issues throughout the Tokyo Round to avoid the risk of a major confrontation, and U.S.-EC cooperation in fact directed the negotiation. When the United States and the EC did not cooperate, the negotiation became deadlocked because they had effective veto power. When the United States and the EC adopted a unified position, only the combined efforts of others had any chance of changing the outcome.[13]

Despite the relative decline of U.S. economic hegemony, the United States continued to play a critical role in pressuring others to move toward a new GATT round in the 1980s. Indeed, "had it not been for the tenacity of the Americans, the [Uruguay Round] negotiations would never have taken place."[14] The United States was also the most important actor pushing for a broadening of the Uruguay Round to include such issues as services, intellectual property, investment, and agriculture. Moreso than in the past, however, American pressure to broaden the negotiating agenda stemmed from U.S. weakness as well as strength. Although the United States had the strength to exert pressure on others to move the prenegotiations forward, its choice of issues for inclusion stemmed largely from efforts to alleviate its growing balance of trade and payments deficits. In view of its trade deficit, the United States pressed aggressively for negotiations in areas where it still had a comparative advantage such as services and agriculture. The 12-member EC of 1986 was the largest trading power in the world. However, like the United States, the EC demonstrated some significant weaknesses. Although the European Commission has the power to initiate and execute decisions for its member countries in global trade negotiations, its proposals must first be approved by the Council of Ministers; that is, the Commission can only act on trade policy issues when it receives the support of the majority of member states. As a result of divisions within the EC, it did not assume a leadership role in the leadup to the Uruguay Round negotiations.

The United States and the EC both showed a lack of leadership in the early stages of the Uruguay Round, and major disputes between them – particularly in agriculture – posed a serious threat to the success of the round. Although U.S. initiative and tenacity was primarily responsible for the launching of the Uruguay Round, in the early stages of the round the United States demonstrated less willingness and ability to lead. The United States was less committed to nondiscrimination in trade as it showed an interest in concluding regional FTAs, and the United States also resorted more often to unilateral actions such as Section 301 cases outside the GATT. Despite the American shortcomings, alternatives to U.S. leadership were not readily apparent. The EC was unable to make specific offers in agriculture in the early stages of the Uruguay Round, and its preoccupation with deepening and broadening the regional integration process raised doubts about its commitment to the GATT negotiations. Although

Japan's economic status had increased greatly in the 1980s, it was on the defensive because of charges that it was following mercantilist trade policies, and it was not prepared to assume a leadership role in trade.[15]

There was a notable weakening of the U.S. leadership role during the latter stages of the Uruguay Round. Growing U.S. protectionist pressures and initial reluctance by the new U.S. President Bill Clinton to provide forceful direction for trade policy slowed the moves toward an Uruguay Round agreement. The EU Commissioner Leon Brittan by contrast began to adopt a more assertive role, and leadership in the latter stages of the Uruguay Round therefore shifted to a more balanced position between the United States and the EU. Indeed, in the latter stages of the negotiation the EU was sometimes pressuring more forcefully for a completion of the Uruguay Round than the United States. The GATT secretariat also supplemented U.S. leadership, and the assertive role of Peter Sutherland as GATT director-general was of critical importance. As we discuss in this book, the developing countries were more involved in the Uruguay Round than in any previous round. Whereas a degree of consensus between the United States and the EU was *necessary* for the successful conclusion of the Uruguay Round, it was no longer *sufficient*. A degree of approval from the developing countries was more essential for the completion of the Uruguay Round than for previous rounds.

In the post-Uruguay Round period, the United States shifted from its traditional position of favouring deeper integration, and instead wanted "to have a short negotiation, necessitating a limited agenda," and "to have concrete results in priority areas for US interests."[16] The change in the U.S. position resulted from several factors. First, despite U.S. economic prosperity, the late 1990s was a period of rapidly growing U.S. trade deficits. The U.S. interest in trade liberalisation was therefore largely limited to areas where it had a comparative advantage. Second, there was a substantial "domestication" of U.S. trade politics in the 1990s as a result of conflict over the NAFTA and the GATT Uruguay Round agreement. Environmental, labour, and other NGO civil society groups added greatly to the ranks of interest groups actively involved with trade policy during this period. Whereas some of these groups opposed only certain trade liberalisation agreements, others began to oppose trade liberalisation in general as a symbol of the threat globalisation posed to social welfare and national autonomy. The domestication of U.S. trade policy has interfered with the Congress's ability to take action to promote trade liberalisation.[17] For example, the divided Congress has been unwilling to this point to renew the U.S. president's fast-track (or trade-promotion) authority which is necessary to conclude major trade agreements.

In contrast to the United States, the EU devoted considerable effort in the late 1990s to encouraging others to launch a comprehensive WTO round. One reason the EU favoured a comprehensive round was that it did not expect the scheduled negotiations on agriculture and services to provide it with sufficient benefits. By broadening the agenda, EU officials believed there would be more opportunities for cross-cutting agreements among sectors. A more comprehensive agenda would also facilitate progress in the negotiations in general. Despite the EU's more proactive stance in favour of a new comprehensive round, the EU had neither the economic power nor the unity of purpose to substitute for U.S. leadership in the global trade regime. The EU's reluctance to fully commit to trade liberalisation in agriculture also limited its ability to adopt a leadership position. It was therefore evident that a degree of consensus was necessary between the United States and the EU if a new WTO round was to be possible. Despite their differences, the U.S. and the EU have both become highly dependent on trade, and they had a shared interest in launching the new WTO round at Doha. Whether they will cooperate sufficiently to help ensure that the Doha Round is a success remains to be seen.

Group of Seven/Group of Eight

The G7/G8 is the institution near the top of the global trade regime pyramid (see Figure 1.1), because the heads of government and state of the most powerful developed economies attend the summits. The G7 summits were established in 1975, partly to replace U.S. unilateral management of the global economy with collective management by the major economic powers (see Chapter 4 for a detailed discussion of reasons the summits were established). International trade has regularly been a topic of summit discussions, and one of the founders of the G7 summits – Helmut Schmidt – "saw the main rationale of the summits as deterring the leaders from protectionist policies."[18] Nevertheless, in the economic sphere the summits have historically given priority to financial and macroeconomic issues over trade. The summits have also had an expanding agenda dealing with political, security, and social as well as economic matters. Russia was gradually integrated into the summit process beginning in 1994, and Birmingham 1998 was the first G8 summit. The integration of Russia added to the pressures to focus the summits more on political and security matters. Thus, the G7/G8 has had an overloaded agenda, which has prevented it from devoting sufficient attention to global trade issues. Although this book refers to the G8 as well as the G7, Russia is not yet a member of the WTO. Thus, the G7 with the participation of the EU continues to hold most of the trade policy discussions at the annual summits.[19]

The G7 was established during the GATT Tokyo Round, and the efforts of the summits to advance the round demonstrated both the shortcomings and the strengths of the summit process. After summarising the shortcomings, we then turn to the strengths. First, in the middle phase of the Tokyo Round the G7 had less influence over the negotiations, because unlike the negotiators and technical experts, the G7 did not deal in detail with the work to be accomplished. In this phase the G7 was often stymied by divisions among the major economic powers, and its role was limited to persuading and cajoling rather than negotiating. Not surprisingly, the G7 had to revise deadlines that proved to be unrealistic for completion of the Tokyo Round on several occasions. It was only after the negotiations had proceeded to a final, breakthrough phase that the G7 leaders could exert more influence. A second shortcoming stemmed from the fact that the G7 was already beginning to develop a more crowded agenda. At the crucial 1978 Bonn I summit, for example, trade had to compete for attention with macroeconomic policy and energy problems. A third shortcoming resulted from the fact that the G7 summits were devoted primarily to resolving differences and reaching a consensus among the major developed countries. Because the G7 did not adequately address the interests of the South, the Tokyo Round could not be completed until more attention was given to developing country concerns.

Despite the G7's shortcomings, the summits encouraged actions to stem the rise of protectionism during the Tokyo Round, and had a significant influence on the trade negotiations in the latter stages of the round. Most importantly, the 1977 London I summit gave the USTR the mandate to pursue the negotiations more vigorously, and the 1978 Bonn I summit provided an interim deadline that served as a major impetus to concluding the round. In referring to the Bonn summit's impact on the GATT negotiators, a U.S. Under Secretary for Economic Affairs commented that "you can't judge summits just by what happens at the summit itself. Summit meetings also serve as an important focal point for other negotiations."[20] Thus, the G7's role near the top of the global trade regime pyramid was not evident until the final breakthrough stage of the Tokyo Round.[21]

The G7 found it more difficult to influence the Uruguay Round than the Tokyo Round, because there were many more key players in the Uruguay Round, and the round's agenda included a much broader range of highly sensitive issues such as agriculture, services, and intellectual property rights. As was the case for the Tokyo Round, the G7 demonstrated its limitations in the early to middle phases of the Uruguay Round. The G7's impact is normally greatest when it can muster the political will to launch a negotiation, help set the agenda for negotiations, and bring about the conclusion of an MTN. From 1986 to 1990, the U.S.-EC differences on agriculture were too extensive to bridge, and the Uruguay Round negotiations were in the technical, policy-making phase. The G7's influence was limited in this phase, because "the gap between the high-level strategic exchanges at the summit and the complex, detailed and technical discussions in Geneva often proved too wide to bridge."[22] Thus, the G7 summits could not avert major conflicts at the 1988 Montreal mid-term review and the 1990 Brussels ministerial.

At each summit from 1990 to 1992 the G7 pledged to take actions to help conclude the Uruguay Round, but continuing differences precluded the completion of the round until December 1993. Although the summits lost a good deal of credibility because of the repeated re-setting of deadlines, this re-scheduling may have served a useful purpose in pressuring for eventual results. During the later stages of the Uruguay Round the G7 summits helped limit protectionism and keep the negotiations going despite a recession, pressured for a stronger dispute settlement mechanism, supported the idea of the WTO, and exerted pressure that resulted in a crucial Quad agreement on market access. The market access accord demonstrated the G7's ability to act as a catalyst in the Uruguay Round, just as the G7's interim deadline for the 1978 Bonn I summit had served as a catalyst in the Tokyo Round. The conclusion of the Uruguay Round in December 1993 "restored the summit's morale" and some of its prestige as a meeting place for the leading industrial states.[23]

After the Uruguay Round, trade as usual had to compete with other issues in the G7/G8's overloaded summit agenda. However, the G7/G8's tendency to neglect trade issues was far more noticeable after the Uruguay Round. A number of factors accounted for this inattention to trade, including a lack of leadership by the United States and to a lesser extent the EU, a more evident lack of consensus on trade within the G7/G8, and less acceptance of G7/G8 leadership on trade issues by developing countries and a wide range of civil society groups. Of crucial importance was the G7/G8 leaders' failure to give their trade ministers "shared political direction in the critical period before the [WTO] Seattle ministerial," and to specify which sectors should be included in the negotiations beyond the WTO's built-in agenda for agriculture and services.[24] This was one factor explaining the Seattle ministerial's unsuccessful effort to launch a new WTO round in 1999. Despite the problems at Seattle, there was a consensus in the G7/G8 that a new MTN round was necessary to maintain the momentum of trade liberalisation and to strengthen the newly-formed WTO. Thus, at the July 2001 Genoa summit the G7 pledged "to engage personally and jointly in the launch of a new ambitious Round of global trade negotiations at the Fourth WTO Ministerial Conference in Doha, Qatar."[25] Although the new WTO round was launched in Doha, it is uncertain whether the G7/G8 will assume an active role to ensure that the negotiations are completed successfully in the scheduled three year time period.

Quadrilateral Group

The Quadrilateral group of trade ministers from the United States, the EU, Japan, and Canada is immediately below the G7/G8 on the global trade regime pyramid (see Figure 1.1). The Quad's importance stems from the fact that its members generally have been strong advocates of trade liberalisation, and account for a substantial share of world trade. The Quad's most significant functions are to resolve differences and form a consensus among the major traders, and to provide leadership in thought, policy direction, and political momentum in multilateral trade negotiations. Despite their differences, the Quad members can normally reach a consensus more easily than much larger institutions such as the GATT/WTO and even the OECD. Most importantly, the Quad enables the two largest traders – the United States and the EU – to discuss trade issues in a small, informal setting. The Quad has also prepared, managed, and followed up trade issues discussed at the G7/G8 Summits, OECD ministerials, UNCTAD conferences, and GATT/WTO ministerials. Although the Quad devotes most of its attention to issues of interest to the developed countries, it has attempted to respond to concerns and demands of developing countries and civil society groups. The Quad meets not only at the ministerial and senior officials levels, but also at lower levels to discuss issues and strategies. Indeed, there is Quad group of working level officials for every significant trade-related issue, agreement, and committee. Quad ambassadors and officials also hold regular meetings in Geneva.[26]

As was the case for the G7, the Quad was created to facilitate collective decision-making in view of declining U.S. economic hegemony. At the time the Quad was formed, the major traders wanted to fully implement the Tokyo Round and to consider launching a new MTN round. However, the proliferation of trade disputes among the United States, the EC, and Japan threatened to interfere with this process. The G7 could not address trade to the extent required, because it had to deal with an increasing array of political-security, economic, and social issues. As a result, various G7 ministerial groups began to emerge in the 1980s. After the Quad was formed in 1981-82, the G7 finance ministers emerged publicly at the 1986 G7 summit in Tokyo, and in more recent years ministers dealing with employment, the environment, and other areas have held periodic meetings. The Quad was the first of the G7 ministerial groups to be formed, because of the importance of trade and its lower ranking in the list of G7 priorities. Whereas the G7 finance ministries have always been part of the inner circle involved in summit preparations, the trade ministries "are rarely involved in broader discussions of summit strategy and tactics."[27]

The Quad ministerials resulted in some important accomplishments in the period leading up to the 1986 Punta del Este meeting launching the Uruguay Round. From 1982 to 1986, the Quads helped resolve disputes and develop a consensus among the major traders, moved the debate forward on issues of interest to the developed countries such as trade in services and intellectual property, and emphasised the importance of including areas of interest to developing countries to gain their approval for a new MTN round. Despite its important role in the preparatory period, the Quad had a lower profile in the early stages of the Uruguay Round. The Quad did serve as a venue in 1989 and 1990 for discussions on the need to establish a new global trade organisation. Although the Quad members were initially split on this issue (the EC and Canada were more supportive of a new organisation than the United States and Japan), the Quad discussions helped legitimise the idea that the WTO should replace the GATT. However, the Quad did not prevent unsuccessful outcomes at the 1988 Montreal mid-term review or the 1990 Brussels ministerial, and the Uruguay Round had to be extended. The Quad ministers also adhered to the initial December 1990 deadline for the Uruguay Round even after it had become unrealistic (perhaps to put pressure on the negotiators). As was the case for the G7, the Quad had less influence when the negotiations were still at the technical stage, and when key countries continued to have serious disagreements. Most importantly, the Quad could not reach a consensus on the critical issue of agriculture, because the United States and the EC remained far apart on this issue.

After the disappointing December 1990 GATT ministerial in Brussels, the Quad re-emerged as a prominent grouping. Quad ministerials supported by additional meetings at the senior officials level became more numerous, and at times had a pivotal role in the successful completion of the Uruguay Round. Although the Quad's main function was to produce understanding among the major traders, the Quad ministerial and officials meetings sometimes explored possible solutions to specific problems in the negotiations. On one occasion, the Quad served as a forum for negotiation of a key market access agreement in preparation for the 1993 Tokyo III G7 summit. Although the Quad benefited from its small size and importance, divisions among its members at times interfered with its ability to reach a consensus. The Quad's focus on developed country interests also sometimes antagonised developing countries that were excluded from the deliberations. Despite these shortcomings, the Quad had a significant role in helping to conclude the Uruguay Round.

Although the Quad continued to be important in the post-Uruguay Round period, its visibility began to decrease. Whereas Quad ministerials were normally held twice a year from 1982 to 1996, they were held only once a year from 1997 to 1999; and in 2000 and 2001 there were no regular ministerials. Quad ministers met informally on the margins of other meetings, and Quad officials below the ministerial level continued to meet. Nevertheless, the decreased visibility of Quad ministerials after the 1996 Singapore WTO ministerial was a significant development that stemmed from several changes. First, the Quad had serious disagreements over some key issues, particularly between the United States and the EU. Some of these differences could not be bridged at the Quad ministerials, and the major traders hoped they could be resolved at the GATT ministerials in Seattle and Doha. A second reason why Quad ministerials were held less often was that personal relationships among Quad ministers were more distant after the Uruguay Round. Third, although the Quad had been an important forum during the Uruguay Round, after the round the United States questioned the Quad's effectiveness and often preferred to meet with other Quad members individually. A fourth reason for the Quad's lower visibility stemmed from the proliferation of other fora in which members could discuss trade issues. For example, the United States and the EU discussed trade issues in their Transatlantic Business Dialogue, and the EU and Japan instituted a ministerial level exchange. Fifth, the WTO unlike the GATT had regular ministerials, and the major traders may have felt there was less necessity for holding Quad ministerials. Sixth, developing countries argued that the Uruguay Round agreements should be fully implemented before new negotiations were held, and their hostility to developed country dominance of the trade agenda may have contributed to a lower profile for the Quad ministerials.[28]

The Quad continues to be important, because its members are committed to trade liberalisation, account for a large percentage of international trade, and have the economic power to provide leadership in the global trade regime. Nevertheless, regular Quad ministerials have not been held since the May 1999 Tokyo meeting, and it remains to be seen when the Quad will again be holding regular ministerials. A reactivation of the Quad ministerials would seem to be essential if the Doha Round is to be successfully completed in three years.

Organisation for Economic Co-operation and Development

The OECD is a plurilateral organisation with 30 members which is placed beneath the Quad on the global trade regime pyramid in Figure 1.1. The OECD is primarily limited to the developed countries, even though six countries outside the industrial core group became members from 1994 to 2000. The OECD's predecessor, the OEEC, had been closely linked with U.S. Marshall Plan aid to Western Europe. Although the United States was clearly the global economic hegemon in 1961, the creation of the OECD symbolised the move towards a more egalitarian relationship between the United States and Western Europe. Western Europe had experienced a remarkable economic recovery from World War II, and "the Americans wanted a forum where they, the Europeans and other 'industrial democracies' could sit down together on equal terms."[29]

The OECD has been an important venue for promoting trade liberalisation for several reasons. First, it is easier to reach a consensus in the OECD with its smaller, relatively homogeneous membership than in the larger, heterogeneous GATT/WTO. Second, because of the OECD's more homogeneous membership it is able to deal with sensitive issues such as government procurement, agriculture, and services before they are dealt with by the GATT/WTO. Third, the OECD normally establishes non-binding agreements, and it is able to agree on constraints on state behaviour in areas where developed countries are reluctant to bind themselves legally in the GATT/WTO. Fourth, the OECD's research and investigatory capacities have been important in the trade area, because of the GATT/WTO's limited budget for these activities. Finally, the OECD's long-term experience with harmonising domestic policies has given it a special role in dealing with trade-related issues such as agriculture, services, and intellectual property, that blur the division between domestic and international policy-making. The OECD also has experience in dealing with NTBs, because they are "behind the border" measures that are closely linked with a country's domestic policies.

This book examines five trade-related areas where the OECD has been involved in research, prenegotiations, and/or negotiations: export credit, government procurement, services, agriculture, and a multilateral agreement on investment. OECD involvement with government procurement, services trade, and agricultural trade played an important role in the eventual inclusion of these areas in the GATT/WTO negotiations. The OECD first became involved in discussions on government procurement because the North was more interested than the South in reaching an agreement in this area. Developing countries view discriminatory government procurement as essential to their competitiveness as late industrialisers, and they therefore do not want to subject government procurement to multilateral discipline. The OECD's discussions and development of a draft agreement in the 1960s and 1970s were a major contribution to the negotiation of the government procurement agreement (GPA) in the GATT Tokyo Round. However, the OECD was far more successful in inducing the GATT to conclude the GPA than it was in including the developing countries. The membership in the Tokyo Round GPA consisted mainly of developed countries, and subsequent efforts to include developing countries in a strengthened GPA during the Uruguay Round were unsuccessful.

Multilateral discipline of services trade like government procurement was of interest primarily to the developed countries. The OECD's involvement with services trade in the 1970s and 1980s demonstrated that it was an important purveyor of new ideas. In conducting its research and policy development on services trade, the OECD relied on assistance from an epistemic community.[30] In 1972 an OECD-appointed High Level Group coined the term "trade in services," and from 1982 to 1986 the OECD helped to develop a conceptual framework for services trade. Thus, the OECD had a significant role in ensuring that services trade would be included in the Uruguay Round negotiations. As was the case for services trade, an agricultural epistemic community helped the OECD contribute to the "ideas" that domestic agricultural policies of developed countries were costly and ineffective, that domestic agricultural policies had a highly detrimental effect on agricultural trade, and that agricultural trade should be subject to multilateral discipline.[31] After legitimising the idea of agricultural trade negotiations, the OECD then helped develop a conceptual framework for negotiating agricultural issues in the Uruguay Round.

Although the OECD ensured that government procurement, services, and agriculture would be included in the GATT negotiations, there is a significant distance between the 30 OECD countries and the 144 developed, developing, and emerging countries in the GATT/WTO. Thus, the OECD was more successful in including these areas in the GATT negotiations than it was in ensuring that the GATT would develop strong, effective agreements. Agriculture and services were part of the "built-in agenda" for further negotiations after the Uruguay Round, because the agreements in these areas (although an important beginning) were clearly incomplete. As discussed, the GPA was also incomplete, because almost all developing countries refused to sign it.

The OECD adopted an uncharacteristic role for export credit, since it served as the main negotiating forum for an export credit agreement. Whereas the OECD members are almost all providers of export credit, the GATT/WTO also includes many developing countries and transition economies that are net consumers of export credit. These credit consumers would not support multilateral discipline that limits the softening of credit terms, because they benefit from the relaxation of developed country credit conditions. As a result, the OECD rather than the GATT/WTO has been the primary forum for negotiating export credit agreements. In 1978, the OECD countries approved the Arrangement on Guidelines for Officially Supported Export Credits, and they have gradually expanded its coverage for over twenty years. Although the 1978 Arrangement was not formally an OECD agreement, it was negotiated in the OECD, and the OECD Secretariat is responsible for servicing it. The OECD has been quite successful in extending discipline over export credit terms, because there is no need for developing countries to join export credit agreements.

The OECD was far less successful, however, in its attempt to negotiate a Multilateral Agreement on Investment. In 1995 the OECD became the venue for the MAI negotiations, and in some respects it seemed to be a suitable forum because it had considerable experience in dealing with foreign investment issues. However, disagreements among OECD members prevented negotiators from concluding an MAI by the original deadline of May 1997, and the prolonged negotiations gave an opportunity to outside critics to organise opposition to an MAI. Most developing countries strongly opposed the negotiation of an MAI in the OECD without their participation. Although developing countries had become more open to foreign investment after the 1982 foreign debt crisis, they were concerned that an MAI would impose more obligations on host governments than on MNCs. A number of civil society groups also launched a campaign against an MAI that was remarkably effective through the use of the Internet. In the end, the OECD was forced to suspend the MAI negotiations. Although the OECD was "reasonably well suited to its core task of policy surveillance through research and the regular exchange of information and ideas," it was "ill suited to house international negotiations" for an MAI.[32] Thus, the export credit case in which the OECD served as a substitute for the GATT/WTO as the forum for negotiations has proved to be the exception rather than the rule.

Developing Countries

Most of this book focuses on the Quad, the G7/G8, and the OECD, because of the prominent role of these institutions in the global trade regime. However, each chapter also discusses the changing role of developing countries, which have greatly outnumbered the developed countries in the GATT/WTO. As more developing countries joined the GATT in the 1960s they became increasingly disturbed about the GATT's inattention to their concerns, and in 1964 the G77 was successful in forming the UNCTAD over the initial objections of the industrial states. The developing countries wanted the UNCTAD to eventually replace the GATT as the main global trade organisation. However, the UNCTAD's influence is limited, and it has instead served largely as a pressure group on the GATT/WTO. For much of the postwar period, developing countries adopted two strategies toward international trade negotiations that were somewhat contradictory. First, they exerted pressure as a unified bloc in the G77 and UNCTAD for changes in the global trade regime; most importantly, they demanded special and differential treatment. Second, developing countries were largely passive participants, or non-participants, in the GATT MTNs.

In the 1970s, developing country demands for S&D treatment reached a peak, when the South tried to alter the Northern-dominated economic regimes by establishing a New International Economic Order. The South was able to exert more influence in the 1970s because of OPEC's success in drastically raising oil prices. The NIEO demands in trade were mainly concerned with improving markets for developing country exports, creating institutions that would favour Southern trade interests, and providing S&D treatment for the South in international markets. Despite the initial willingness of the North to confer with the South, the North became less amenable to the NIEO negotiations as they realised that developing country producers of other commodities would not be able to emulate the success of OPEC. In the early 1980s the ability of the South to influence the North declined sharply with the emergence of the Third World foreign debt crisis.

In view of their traditional attitude towards the GATT, many developing countries were initially either ambivalent or opposed to a new round of GATT negotiations in the 1980s. However, the South gradually adopted trade liberalisation strategies and became far more involved in the Uruguay Round than in previous rounds for several reasons. First, the foreign debt crisis induced the South to become more involved in the GATT negotiations, because it demonstrated the problems with inward-looking import substitution policies. Developing country debtors were also pressured to alter their policies because the IMF and World Bank linked their structural adjustment loans to the implementation of orthodox liberal reforms such as deregulation, privatisation, and greater openness to trade and foreign investment. A second factor explaining the South's interest in the Uruguay Round related to the disappointment of developing countries with the benefits they had received from S&D treatment.

Because of this special treatment, developed countries viewed developing countries as "free riders," and tended to marginalise them in trade negotiations. The South was therefore more willing to engage in a reciprocal exchange of concessions and less inclined to demand S&D treatment in the Uruguay Round. Thus, developing countries agreed to treat the Uruguay Round as a "single undertaking," in which they had to accept all of the agreements. The single undertaking was a marked contrast to the Tokyo Round's NTB codes, in which most developing countries did not participate. Although the single-undertaking weakened the concept of S&D treatment, the South continued to have S&D treatment in different forms. Whereas S&D treatment before the Uruguay Round focused on preferential market access and special rights for the South, in the Uruguay Round S&D treatment emphasised greater flexibility for the South in fulfilling commitments, longer transition times for implementing agreements, and technical assistance from the North. A third factor explaining the more active participation of developing countries in the Uruguay Round was a greater divergence in their interests. Thus, a number of North-South coalitions were formed during the Uruguay Round, the most important of which was the Cairns Group of so-called fair agricultural traders.

As discussed in Chapters 7 and 8, the South gained less in the Uruguay Round than it originally had thought. For example, developing countries were encouraged by the Agreement on Textiles and Clothing that provided a 10-year transition period for phasing out quantitative restrictions on imports. However, liberalisation was "back-loaded" toward the end of the 10-year period, and there were fears that restrictions on textile and clothing imports would in fact continue because of the misuse of protectionist measures by developed country importers. In addition, the developing countries maintained that it is difficult for them to implement some measures in the Uruguay Round agreement, and that developed countries did not provide as much technical assistance as expected to help them meet the agreed time periods.[33] A number of developing countries were therefore reluctant to agree to a new WTO round until the promises the developed countries had made in the Uruguay Round were implemented. The South also wanted assurances that the North would devote more attention to Southern views and interests before it would agree to launching a new round. Although there were notable divisions within the South and some North-South coalitions such as the Cairns Group continued to function, it was evident that some concessions to the South as a group were essential if there was to be a new round. Thus, the North agreed to some (but not all) of the South's demands in return for Southern agreement to a new WTO round. Although the success of the Doha Round will depend largely on the formation of a consensus on key issues among the major developed countries, a degree of North-South consensus will also be essential. As a result of the South's growing participation in global trade negotiations, it has become a more important actor in the global trade regime pyramid.

Concluding Comments on Theory and Policy Implications

This book has demonstrated that decision-making in the global trade regime is a pyramidal process, with developed country actors and institutions near the top of the pyramid. Historical developments also show that there have been changes in the hierarchy of actors and institutions over time. Whereas the United States was initially the hegemonic power in the global trade regime, the EU has now attained a position on a par with the United States. Furthermore, several important developed country-led institutions were added to the global trade regime hierarchy including the OECD in the 1960s, the G7 in the 1970s, and the Quad in the 1980s. Although developing country-oriented institutions such as UNCTAD remain near the bottom of the trade regime hierarchy, the South has gained some influence, particularly since the 1980s when it became more involved in the GATT. In addition to these long-term changes, there are also short-term changes in the global trade regime hierarchy. For example, the G7/G8 and the Quad are more influential in the initial agenda setting phase and the final breakthrough phase of MTNs than they are in the technical phase of negotiations. The OECD has also been particularly influential in introducing new ideas and in engaging in prenegotiations before a new MTN round is launched.

Despite the launching of a new WTO round in November 2001, divisions among the major developed country traders and dissatisfaction of developing countries and civil society groups presents a major challenge to the successful completion of the round in the scheduled 3-year period. The question arises as to what should be done about the current decision-making process in the global trade regime to facilitate the success of the Doha Round. The WTO had 144 members as of January 2002, and all WTO councils and committees are plenary bodies that are open to every member. Realistically, it is impossible to conduct all prenegotiations and negotiations in such a large, diverse body, because higher transaction and information costs interfere with the ability to resolve differences and identify common interests. Furthermore, multilateral trade agreements will not be effective without the participation of the major developed country traders, and smaller fora are necessary where they can discuss their differences and form a consensus on critical issues.

As discussed in Chapter 1, a number of scholars and practitioners have suggested that a smaller executive body be established in the WTO in which all the major traders would be represented. Some analysts have suggested that a group within the WTO would be preferable to the Quad, which they describe as divisive, elitist, and non-transparent.[34] The GATT/WTO has experimented with various smaller groups over the years ranging from the CG.18 to the green room sessions. However, these groups within the WTO have also been under attack in recent years. For example, the green room sessions to which developed and developing country principal traders were normally invited (see Chapter 1) were one of the sources of strife at the 1999 WTO Seattle ministerial. The discomfort of developing country nonparticipants with the Green Room process

> knew no bounds on the third day of the Ministerial when Ministers of African countries, the Caribbean Community, and some Latin American economies complained about the lack of transparency in the negotiations. They felt that they were excluded from deliberations on issues vital to their future growth, therefore they did not feel obliged to support a Ministerial text produced without consensus.[35]

Those proposing the creation of a smaller executive body in the WTO have argued that the group would be more acceptable than the green room sessions if it was more representative of the WTO membership, more transparent in its proceedings, and more willing to communicate with the broader membership. For example, one analyst indicates that it should be possible "to establish a committee of reasonable size and rotating membership, which would ensure that all countries and regions would be represented within a given time frame."[36] Another analyst indicates that the WTO members would not be willing to establish an executive board that would take decisions binding the membership, and he opts instead for a WTO consultative board similar to the old CG.18.[37] Certainly there would be advantages to establishing a smaller executive or consultative group within the WTO. However, to this point the WTO members have not agreed to establish such a group. Even if the group was more representative and more transparent than the green room sessions, the major developed countries would be better represented in this new group than the developing and emerging countries. Thus, it remains to be seen whether the developing and emerging countries will agree to establish such a group.

Even if such a group within the WTO were to be established, the question arises as to whether the major developed country traders would continue to confer with each other in plurilateral groupings outside the WTO. This author believes that it is perfectly legitimate for developed and developing countries to meet in their own smaller plurilateral groups to resolve their differences and form a consensus on major trade issues. Thus, the G7/G8, the Quad, the OECD, the G77, and UNCTAD continue to serve legitimate functions in the global trade regime for both developed and developing countries. North-South coalition groups such as the Cairns Group also have important functions to perform. The simple fact is that a degree of consensus among the United States and the EU as the largest trading entities is essential if trade liberalisation is to proceed, and it is more likely that they will reach a consensus in a small grouping of like-minded states such as the Quad.

However, along with the greater influence of developed country-led institutions such as the G7/G8, the Quad, and the OECD must come greater responsibilities. This book has cited numerous instances where the G7/G8, the Quad, and the OECD focused almost exclusively on furthering developed country interests, and largely ignored the interests and concerns of developing countries and civil society groups. In some cases, such as the WTO Seattle ministerial and the OECD negotiations for an MAI, this inattention contributed to spectacular failures. The members of the G7/G8, the Quad, and the OECD have been among the strongest supporters of trade liberalisation in the postwar period. To retain their legitimacy and influence, these institutions must be more willing to incorporate the views, concerns, and interests of developing countries and responsible civil society groups into their deliberations. One of the greatest concerns of both developing countries and civil society groups is that WTO liberalisation is extending to new areas that impinge on what was formerly considered to be domestic policy, and thus is threatening the social safety net. In their deliberations, the G7/G8, the Quad, and the OECD must be sufficiently sensitive to these legitimate social concerns.

Notes

1   Stephen D. Krasner, "Structural Causes and Regime Consequences: Regimes as Intervening Variables," in Stephen D. Krasner, ed., *International Regimes* (Ithaca: Cornell University Press, 1983), p. 1.

2   Oran R. Young, "International Regimes: Toward a New Theory of Institutions," *World Politics* 39 (October 1986), p. 108. See also Carsten Otto, "'International Regimes' in the Asia-Pacific? The Case of APEC," in Jörn Dosch and Manfred Mols, eds., *International Relations in the Asia-Pacific: New Patterns of Power, Interest, and Cooperation* (New York: St. Martin's Press, 2000), pp. 45-46.

3   Robert O. Keohane, *International Institutions and State Power: Essays in International Relations Theory* (Boulder: Westview Press, 1989), p. 5.

4   Jock A. Finlayson and Mark W. Zacher, "The GATT and the Regulation of Trade Barriers: Regime Dynamic and Functions," in Krasner, ed., *International Regimes*, p. 274.

5   See, for example, Yoshi Kodama, *Asia Pacific Economic Integration in the GATT/WTO Regime* (The Hague: Kluwer Law International, 2000).

6   Krasner, "Structural Causes and Regime Consequences," p. 2.

7   John H. Jackson, *World Trade and the Law of GATT* (Indianapolis: Bobbs-Merrill, 1969), p. 11.

8   Gilbert R. Winham, *International Trade and the Tokyo Round Negotiation* (Princeton, NJ: Princeton University Press, 1986), p. 376. See also Gilbert R. Winham, "The Prenegotiation Phase of the Uruguay Round," *International Journal* 44-2 (Spring 1989), pp. 289-290.

9   Stephen Woolcock, "European Trade Policy: Global Pressures and Domestic Constraints," in Helen Wallace and William Wallace, eds., *Policy-Making in the European Union* (Oxford: Oxford University Press, 4th ed., 2000), p. 373.

10 See Peter M. Haas, "Do Regimes Matter? Epistemic Communities and Mediterranean Pollution Control," *International Organization* 43-3 (Summer 1989), pp. 377-403; Peter M. Haas, "Introduction: Epistemic Communities and International Policy Coordination," *International Organization* 46-1 (Winter 1992), pp. 1-35; Virginia Haufler, "Crossing the Boundary between Public and Private: International Regimes and Non-State Actors," in Volker Rittberger with the assistance of Peter Mayer, ed., *Regime Theory and International Relations* (Oxford: Clarendon Press, 1995), pp. 94-111; Robert Wolfe, "Rendering unto Caesar: How Legal Pluralism and Regime Theory Help in Understanding 'Multiple Centres of Power'," in Gordon Smith and Daniel Wolfish, eds., *Who is Afraid of the State? Canada in a World of Multiple Centres of Power* (Toronto: University of Toronto Press, forthcoming).

11 Jackson, *World Trade and the Law of GATT*, p. 37.

12 Ernest H. Preeg, *Traders and Diplomats: An Analysis of the Kennedy Round of Negotiations under the General Agreement on Tariffs and Trade* (Washington, D.C.: The Brookings Institution, 1970), p. 5.

13 Sidney Golt, *The GATT Negotiations 1973-1979: The Closing Stage*, (London: British-North American Committee, May 1978), p. 1; Winham, "The Prenegotiation Phase of the Uruguay Round," pp. 289-290; D.M. McRae and J.C. Thomas, "The GATT and Multilateral Treaty Making: The Tokyo Round," *American Journal of International Law* 77 (1983), pp. 70-71.

14 Hugo Paemen and Alexandra Bensch, *From the GATT to the WTO: The European Community in the Uruguay Round* (Leuven: Leuven University Press, 1995), p. 91.

15 Paemen and Bensch, *From the GATT to the WTO*, pp. 93-98; Ernest H. Preeg, *Traders in a Brave New World: The Uruguay Round and the Future of the International Trading System* (Chicago: University of Chicago Press, 1995), pp. 110-113.

16 Jeffrey J. Schott, "The WTO After Seattle," in Jeffrey J. Schott, ed., *The WTO After Seattle* (Washington, D.C.: Institute for International Economics, July 2000), p. 7.

17 Andreas Falke, "The USA: Why Fundamentals Do Not Always Matter, or: It's Politics, Stupid!," in Klaus Günter Deutsch and Bernhard Speyer, eds., *The World Trade Organization Millennium Round: Freer Trade in the Twenty-first Century* (London: Routledge, 2001), p. 22.

18 Nicholas Bayne, *Hanging In There: The G7 and G8 Summit in Maturity and Renewal* (Aldershot: Ashgate, 2000), p. 62.

19 Heidi Ullrich, "Trade Liberalization and Leadership: Challenges for the Doha Development Agends and Lessons Learned from the Uruguay Round," paper presented at German Council on Foreign Relations Conference, Berlin, 28 January 2002, p. 2.

20 Richard Cooper, quoted in George de Menil, "From Rambouillet to Versailles," in George de Menil and Anthony M. Solomon, *Economic Summitry* (New York: Council on Foreign Relations, 1983), p. 26.

21 Theodore H. Cohn, "Securing Multilateral Trade Liberalisation: International Institutions in Conflict and Convergence," in John J. Kirton and George M. von Furstenberg, eds., *New Directions in Global Economic Governance: Managing Globalisation in the Twenty-first Century* (Aldershot: Ashgate, 2001), pp. 198-199.

22 Bayne, *Hanging In There*, p. 62.

23 Bayne, *Hanging In There*, pp. 63-64.

24 Heidi K. Ullrich, "Stimulating Trade Liberalisation after Seattle: G7/G8 Leadership in Global Governance," in Kirton and von Furstenberg, eds., *New Directions in Global Economic Governance*, p. 224.

25 "Statement of the Group of Seven Leaders," Genoa, Italy, 20 July 2001, paragraph 6.

26 Communication from Canada's Department of Foreign Affairs and International Trade, 21 February 2002.

27 Robert D. Putnam and Nicholas Bayne, *Hanging Together: Cooperation and Conflict in the Seven-Power Summits,* revised ed. (London: SAGE, 1987), p. 56. Putnam and Bayne refer to some exceptions where trade ministries have played a greater role.

28 "Quad Trade Ministers to Meet on WTO Ministerial, New Negotiations,' *Inside U.S. Trade*, 23 April 1999, pp. 3-4; "WTO Director General Race Tightens between Supachai, Moore," *Inside U.S. Trade*, 19 March 1999; "U.S., Japan Launch Senior Dialogue on Short-term, Broad WTO Issues," *Inside U.S. Trade*, 10 March 2000, p. 8; communications from Canada's Department of Foreign Affairs and International Trade.

29 Nicholas Bayne, "Making Sense of Western Economic Policies: The Role of the OECD," *The World Today* 43-2 (February 1987), p. 27.

30 See William J. Drake and Kalypso Nicolaïdis, "Ideas, Interests and Institutionalization: 'Trade in Services' and the Uruguay Round," *International Organization* 46-1 (Winter 1992), pp. 37-100.

31 See Robert Wolfe, *Farm Wars: The Political Economy of Agriculture and the International Trade Regime* (London: Macmillan, 1998); and Heidi Ullrich, "The Impact of Policy Networks in the GATT Uruguay Round: The Case of the US-EC Agricultural Negotiations," unpublished Ph.D. thesis, London School of Economics, London, 2002.

32 Razeen Sally, "Looking Askance at Global Governance," in John J. Kirton, Joseph P. Daniels, and Andreas Freytag, eds., *Guiding Global Order: G8 Governance in the Twenty-first Century* (Aldershot: Ashgate, 2001), p. 64.

33 Marcelo de Paiva Abreu, "Trade in Manufactures: The Outcome of the Uruguay Round and Developing Country Interests," in Martin and Winters, eds., *The Uruguay Round and the Developing Countries*, p. 72; Joseph E. Stiglitz, "Two Principles for the Next Round or, How to Bring Developing Countries in from the Cold," *World Economy* 23-4 (April 2000), pp. 437-454.

34 See, for example, see Sylvia Ostry, "The WTO and International Governance," in Deutsch and Speyer, eds., *The World Trade Organization Millennium Round*, p. 292; Jeffrey J. Schott and Jayashree Watal, "Decision Making in the WTO," Schott, ed., *The WTO After Seattle*, p. 286; and Dilip K. Das, *Global Trading System at the Crossroads: A Post-Seattle Perspective* (London: Routledge, 2001), p. 39.

35 Das, *Global Trading System at the Crossroads*, pp. 40-41.

36 Ostry, "The WTO and International Governance," p. 292.

37 Richard Blackhurst, "Reforming WTO Decision Making: Lessons from Singapore and Seattle," in Deutsch and Speyer, eds., *The World Trade Organization Millennium Round*, p. 303.

Bibliography

Books and Shorter Monographs

Aaronson, Susan Ariel. *Trade and the American Dream: A Social History of Postwar Trade Policy*. Lexington: University Press of Kentucky, 1996.

Aggarwal, Vinod K. *Liberal Protectionism: The International Politics of Organized Textile Trade*. Berkeley: University of California Press, 1985.

Ansari, Javed A. *The Political Economy of International Economic Organization*. Boulder: Lynne Rienner, 1986.

Archer, Clive. *Organizing Western Europe*. London: Edward Arnold, 1990.

Arter, David. *The Politics of European Integration in the Twentieth Century*. Aldershot: Dartmouth, 1993.

Aubrey, Henry G. *Atlantic Economic Cooperation: The Case of the OECD*. New York: Praeger, 1967.

Bard, Robert. *Food Aid and International Agricultural Trade*. Lexington: D.C. Heath, 1972.

Bayne, Nicholas. *Hanging In There: The G7 and G8 Summit in Maturity and Renewal*. Aldershot: Ashgate, 2000.

Bergsten, Fred C., and C. Randall Henning. *Global Economic Leadership and the Group of Seven*. Washington: Institute for International Economics, 1996.

Blair, David J. *Trade Negotiations in the OECD: Structures, Institutions and States*. London: Kegan Paul International, 1993.

Brown, William Adams, Jr. *The United States and the Restoration of World Trade: An Analysis and Appraisal of the ITO Charter and the General Agreement on Tariffs and Trade*. Washington: Brookings Institution, 1950.

Calleo, David P. *Beyond American Hegemony: The Future of the Western Alliance*. New York: Basic Books, 1987.

Camps, Miriam. *"First World" Relationships: The Role of the OECD*. New York: Council on Foreign Relations, 1975.

Clarkson, Stephen. *Canada and the Reagan Challenge: Crisis and Adjustment, 1981-85*. Toronto: Lorimer, 1985.

Cohen, Stephen D, and Ronald I. Meltzer. *United States International Economic Policy in Action: Diversity of Decision Making*. New York: Praeger, 1982.

Cohn, Theodore H. *The International Politics of Agricultural Trade: Canadian-American Relations in a Global Agricultural Context*. Vancouver: University of British Columbia Press, 1990.

Cohn, Theodore H. *Global Political Economy: Theory and Practice*. 2nd edition. New York: Addison Wesley Longman, forthcoming, 2002.

Cooper, Andrew F. *In Between Countries: Australia, Canada, and the Search for Order in Agricultural Trade*. Montreal: McGill-Queen's University Press, 1997.

Cooper, Andrew F., Richard A. Higgott, and Kim Richard Nossal. *Relocating Middle Powers: Australia and Canada in a Changing World Order*. Vancouver: University of British Columbia Press, 1993.

Cortney, Philip. *The Economic Munich: I.T.O. Charter, Inflation or Liberty, The 1929 Lesson*. New York: Philosophical Library, 1949.

Croome, John. *Reshaping the World Trading System: A History of the Uruguay Round*. Geneva: World Trade Organization, 1995.

Curzon, Gerard. *Multilateral Commercial Diplomacy*. London: Michael Joseph, 1965.

Cutajar, Michael Zammit, ed. *UNCTAD and the North-South Dialogue: The First Twenty Years*. Oxford: Pergamon Press, 1985.

Dam, Kenneth W. *The GATT: Law and International Economic Organization*. Chicago: University of Chicago Press, 1970.

Das, Dilip K. *Global Trading System at the Crossroads: A Post-Seattle Perspective*. London: Routledge, 2001.

Dent, Martin, and Bill Peters. *The Crisis of Poverty and Debt in the Third World*. Aldershot: Ashgate, 1999.

Destler, I.M. *American Trade Politics*. 2nd edition. Washington: Institute for International Economics, 1992.

Diebold, William, Jr. *The End of the I.T.O., Essays In International Finance* 16. Princeton: Princeton University, October 1952.

Dinan, Desmond. *Ever Closer Union: An Introduction to European Integration*. 2nd edition. Boulder: Lynne Rienner, 1999.

Esty, Daniel C. *Greening the GATT: Trade, Environment, and the Future*. Washington: Institute for International Economics, 1994.

Evans, John W. *The Kennedy Round in American Trade Policy: the Twilight of the GATT?* Cambridge: Harvard University Press, 1971.

Feketekuty, Geza. *International Trade in Services: An Overview and Blueprint for Negotiations*. Cambridge: Ballinger, 1988.

Finlayson, Jock A., and Mark W. Zacher. *Managing International Markets: Developing Countries and the Commodity Trade Regime*. New York: Columbia University Press, 1988.

Gardner, Richard N. *Sterling-Dollar Diplomacy in Current Perspective*. New York: Columbia University Press, 1980.

Gerschenkron, Alexander. *Economic Backwardness in Historical Perspective*. Cambridge: Harvard University Press, 1962.

Golt, Sidney. *The GATT Negotiations 1973-1979*. London: British-North American Committee, 1978.

Griffiths, Brian. *Invisible Barriers to Invisible Trade*. London: Macmillan, 1975.

Grilli, Enzo R. *The European Community and the Developing Countries*. Cambridge: Cambridge University Press, 1993.

Hajnal, Peter I. *The G7/G8 System: Evolution, Role and Documentation.* Aldershot: Ashgate, 1999.

Hart, Jeffrey A. *The New International Economic Order: Conflict and Cooperation in North-South Economic Relations, 1974-77.* New York: St. Martin's Press, 1983.

Hoekman, Bernard M., and Michel M. Kostecki. *The Political Economy of the World Trading System.* 2nd edition. Oxford: Oxford University Press, 2001.

Hudec, Robert E. *The GATT Legal System and the World Trade Diplomacy.* New York: Praeger, 1975.

Hudec, Robert E. *Developing Countries in the GATT Legal System.* Aldershot, UK: Gower, for the Trade Policy Research Centre, 1987.

Iklé, Fred Charles. *How Nations Negotiate.* New York: Harper and Row, 1964.

Jackson, John H. *World Trade and the Law of GATT.* Indianapolis: Bobbs-Merrill, 1969.

Jackson, John H. *Restructuring the GATT System.* Pinter, 1990.

Jackson, John H. *The World Trading System: Law and Policy of International Economic Relations.* 2nd edition, Cambridge: MIT Press, 1997.

Jacob, Philip E., Alexine L. Atherton, and Arthur M. Wallenstein. *The Dynamic of International Organization.* Homewook: Dorsey, 1972.

Jacobson, Harold. *Networks of Interdependence: International Organizations and the Global Political System.* New York: Alfred A. Knopf, 1979.

Jacobson, Harold, and Michel Oksenberg. *China's Participation in the IMF, the World Bank, and GATT.* Ann Arbor: University of Michigan Press, 1990.

Jones, Joseph M., Jr. *Tariff Retaliation: Repercussions of the Hawley-Smoot Bill.* Philadelphia: University of Pennsylvania Press, 1934.

Kennedy, Paul. *The Rise and Fall of the Great Powers: Economic Change and Military Conflict from 1500 to 2000.* New York: Random House, 1987.

Keohane, Robert O. *After Hegemony: Cooperation and Discord in the World Political Economy.* Princeton: Princeton University Press, 1984.

Keohane, Robert O. *International Institutions and State Power.* Boulder: Westview Press, 1989.

Kissinger, Henry. *White House Years.* Boston: Little, Brown & Co., 1979.

Kock, Karin. *International Trade Policy and the GATT 1947-1967.* Stockholm: Almqvist & Wiksell, 1969.

Kodama, Yoshi. *Asia Pacific Economic Integration and the GATT/WTO Regime.* The Hague: Kluwer, 2000.

Krueger, Anne O. *Trade Policies and Developing Nations.* Washington: Brookings Institution, 1995.

Kuhn, Michael G., Balazs Horvath, and Christopher J. Jarvis. *Officially Supported Export Credits: Recent Developments and Prospects.* Washington: 1995.

List, Friedrich. *The National System of Political Economy.* London: Longmans, Green, 1916.

Long, Olivier. *Law and Its Limitations in the GATT Multilateral Trade System.* Dordrecht: Martinus Nijhoff, 1985.

Low, Patrick. *Trading Free: The GATT and U.S. Trade Policy*. New York: Twentieth Century Fund, 1993.

McFadzean, Frank. *Towards an Open World Economy*. London: Macmillan, 1972.

Nye, Joseph S. *Bound to Lead: The Changing Nature of American Power*. New York: Basic Books, 1990.

O'Brien, Robert, Anne Marie Goetz, Jan Aart Scholte, and Marc Williams. *Contesting Global Governance: Multilateral Economic Institutions and Global Social Movements*. Cambridge: Cambridge University Press, 2000.

Olson, Mancur. *The Logic of Collective Action: Public Goods and the Theory of Groups*. Cambridge: Harvard University Press, 1965.

Paarlberg, Robert L. *Fixing Farm Trade: Policy Options for the United States*. Cambridge: Ballinger, 1988.

Paemen, Hugo and Alexandra Bensch. *From GATT to the WTO: The European Community in the Uruguay Round*. Belgium: Leuven University Press, 1995.

Palmer, Michael, and John Lambert, et al. *European Unity: A Survey of European Organizations*. London: Allen & Unwin, 1968.

Pastor, Robert A. *Congress and the Politics of U.S. Foreign Economic Policy, 1929-1976*. Berkeley: University of California Press, 1980.

Patterson, Gardner. *Discrimination in International Trade, The Policy Issues: 1945-1965*. Princeton: Princeton University Press, 1966.

Pearce, Joan. *Subsidized Export Credit*. London: Royal Institute of International Affairs, 1980.

Pentland, Charles. *International Theory and European Integration*. London: Faber and Faber, 1973.

Peterson, John, and Elizabeth Bomberg. *Decision-Making in the European Union*. London: Macmillan, 1999.

Prebisch, Raúl. *The Economic Development of Latin America and Its Principal Problems*. New York: United Nations Commission for Latin America, 1950.

Prebisch, Raúl. *Towards a Dynamic Development Policy for Latin America*. New York: United Nations, 1963.

Preeg, Ernest H. *Traders and Diplomats: An Analysis of the Kennedy Round of Negotiations Under the General Agreement on Tariffs and Trade*. Washington: Brookings Institution, 1970.

Preeg, Ernest H. *Traders in a Brave New World: The Uruguay Round and the Future of the International Trading System*. Chicago: University of Chicago Press, 1995.

Putnam, Robert D. and Nicholas Bayne. *Hanging Together: Cooperation and Conflict in Seven-Power Summits*. London: SAGE, 1987.

Schattschneider, E.E. *Politics, Pressures and the Tariff*. Hamden: Archon Books, 1963.

Schott, Jeffrey J., with Johanna W. Buurman. *The Uruguay Round: An Assessment*. Washington: Institute for International Economics, 1994.

Shelp, Ronald Kent. *Beyond Industrialization: Ascendancy of the Global Service Economy*. New York: Praeger, 1981.

Srinivasan, T.N. *Developing Countries and the Multilateral Trading System*. Boulder: Westview, 2000.

Stone, Frank. *Canada, the GATT and the International Trade System*. 2nd edition. Montreal: Institute for Research on Public Policy, 1992.

Thomas, Jeffrey S. and Michael A. Meyer. *The New Rules of Global Trade: A Guide to the World Trade Organization*. Scarborough: Carswell, 1997.

Trade Policies for a Better Future: The 'Leutwiler Report', the GATT and the Uruguay Round. Dordrecht: Martinus Nijhoff, 1987.

Twiggs, Joan E. *The Tokyo Round of Multilateral Trade Negotiations*. Lanham: University Press of America, 1987.

Urwin, Derek W. *The Community of Europe*. 2nd edition. New York: Longman, 1995.

Whalley, John and Colleen Hamilton. *The Trading System After the Uruguay Round*. Washington, D.C.: Institute for International Economics, 1996.

Wilcox, Clair. *A Charter for World Trade*. New York: Macmillan, 1949.

Williams, Gwyneth. *Third-World Political Organizations*. London: Macmillan, 1987.

Williams, Marc. *Third World Cooperation: The Group of 77 in UNCTAD*. London: Pinter, 1991.

Williams, Marc. *International Economic Organizations and the Third World*. New York: Harvester Wheatsheaf, 1994.

Winham, Gilbert R. *International Trade and the Tokyo Round Negotiation*. Princeton: Princeton University Press, 1986.

Wolfe, Robert. *Farm Wars: The Political Economy of Agriculture and the International Trade Regime*. London: Macmillan, 1998.

Wood, David M., and Birol A. Yeşilada. *The Emerging European Union*. 2nd edition. New York: Longman, 2002.

Yusuf, Abdulqawi. *Legal Aspects of Trade Preferences for Developing States*. The Hague: Martinus Nijhoff, 1982.

Articles in Books

Abreu, Marcelo de Paiva. "Trade In Manufactures: The Outcome of the Uruguay Round and Developing Country Interests." In *The Uruguay Round and the Developing Countries*. Edited by Will Martin and L. Alan Winters. Cambridge: Cambridge University Press, 1996, 59-87.

Bayne, Nicholas. "The G7 and Multilateral Trade Liberalisation: Past Performance, Future Challenges." In *New Directions in Global Economic Governance: Managing Globalisation in the Twenty-first Century*. Edited by John Kirton and George M. von Furstenberg. Aldershot: Ashgate, 2001, 171-187.

Behrman, Jere R. "Rethinking Global Negotiations: Trade." In *Power, Passions, and Purpose: Prospects for North-South Negotiations*. Edited by Jagdish N. Bhagwati and John Gerard Ruggie. Cambridge: MIT Press, 1984, 231-258.

Berthoud, Paul. "UNCTAD and the Emergence of International Development Law." In *UNCTAD and the South-North Dialogue: The First Twenty Years*. Edited by Michael Zammit Cutajar. Oxford: Pergamon Press, 1988, 101-121.

Blackhurst, Richard. "The Capacity of the WTO to Fulfill Its Mandate." In *The WTO as an International Organization*. Edited by Anne O. Krueger, with Chonira Aturupane. Chicago: University of Chicago Press, 1998, 31-58.

Blackhurst, Richard. "Reforming WTO Decision Making." In *The World Trade Organization Millennium Round*. Edited by Klaus Günter Deutsch and Bernhard Speyer. New York: Routledge, 2001, 295-310.

Cohn, Theodore H. "Canada and the Ongoing Impasse over Agricultural Protectionism." In *Canadian Foreign Policy and International Economic Regimes*. Edited by A. Claire Cutler and Mark W. Zacher. Vancouver: University of British Columbia Press, 1992, 62-88.

Cohn, Theodore H. "The Changing Role of the United States in the Global Agricultural Trade Regime." In *World Agriculture and the GATT*. Edited by William P. Avery. Boulder: Lynne Rienner, 1993, 17-38.

Cohn, Theodore H. "Securing Multilateral Trade Liberalisation: International Institutions in Conflict and Convergence." In *New Directions in Global Economic Governance*. Edited by John J. Kirton and George M. von Furstenberg. Aldershot: Ashgate, 2001: 189-217.

Curzon, Gerard and Victoria. "The Management of Trade Relations in the GATT." In *International Economic Relations of the Western World 1959-1971*. Edited by Andrew Shonfield. London: Oxford University Press, 1976, 141-283.

De Menil, George. "From Rambouillet to Versailles." In *Economic Summitry*. Edited by George de Menil and Anthony M. Solomon. New York: Council on Foreign Relations, 1983, 9-41.

Deutsch, Klaus Günther. "The EU: Contending for Leadership." In *The World Trade Organization Millennium Round*. Edited by Klaus Günther Deutsch and Bernhard Speyer. London: Routledge, 2001, 34-47

De Vries, Margaret Garritsen. "Bretton Woods Fifty Years Later: A View from the International Monetary Fund." In *The Bretton Woods – GATT System: Retrospect and Prospect after Fifty Years*. Edited by Orin Kirshner. Armonk: M.E. Sharpe, 1996, 3-18.

Dymond, William A. "The MAI: A Sad and Melancholy Tale." In *Canada Among Nations 1999: A Big League Player?* Edited by Fen Osler Hampson, Martin Rudner, and Michael Hart. Toronto: Oxford University Press, 1999, 25-53.

Evans, Peter C. and Kenneth A. Oye. "International Competition: Conflict and Cooperation in Government Export Financing." In *The Ex-Im Bank in the 21st Century: A New Approach?* Edited by Gary Clyde Hufbauer and Rita M. Rodriguez. Washington: Institute of International Economics, 2001, 113-158.

Falke, Andreas. "The USA: Why Fundamentals Do Not Always Matter, or: It's Politics, Stupid!" In *The World Trade Organization Millenium Round*. Edited by Klaus Günther Deutsch and Bernhard Speyer. London: Routledge, 2001, 18-33.

Finger, J. Michael, and Philip Schuler. "Developing countries and the Millennium Round." In *The World Trade Organization Millenium Round*. Edited by Klaus Günther Deutsch and Bernhard Speyer. London: Routledge, 2001, 58-71.

Finlayson, Jock A. and Mark W. Zacher. "The GATT and the Regulation of Trade Barriers: Regime Dynamics and Functions." In *International Regimes*. Edited by Stephen D. Krasner. Ithaca: Cornell University Press, 1983, 273-314.

Fratianni, Michel, Paolo Savona, and John J. Kirton. "Introduction, Summary, and Conclusions." In *Governing Global Finance: New Challenges, G7 and IMF Contributions*. Edited by Michel Fratianni, Paolo Savona, and John J. Kirton. Aldershot: Ashgate, forthcoming.

Garavoglia, Guido. "From Rambouillet to Williamsburg: A Historical Assessment." In *Economic Summits and Western Decision-Making*. Edited by Cesare Merlini. London: Croome Helm, 1984, 1-42.

Gilpin, Robert. "The Politics of Transnational Economic Relations." In *Transnational Relations and World Politics*. Edited by Robert O. Keohane and Joseph S. Nye, Jr. Cambridge: Harvard University Press, 1972, 48-69.

Griffiths, Richard T. "'An Act of Creative Leadership': The End of the OEEC and the Birth of the OECD." In *Explorations in OEEC History*. Edited by Richard T. Griffiths. Paris: OECD, 1997, 235-256.

Haufler, Virginia. "Crossing the Boundary between Public and Private: International Regimes and Non-State Actors." In *Regime Theory and International Relations*. Edited by Volker Rittberger with Peter Mayer. Oxford: Clarendon, 1995, 94-111.

Henderson, David. "International Agencies and Cross-Border Liberalization." In *The WTO as an International Organization*. Edited by Anne O. Krueger with Chonira Aturupane. Chicago: University of Chicago Press, 1998, 97-132.

Hoekman, Bernard. "Assessing the General Agreement on Trade in Services." In *The Uruguay Round and the Developing Countries*. Edited by Will Martin and L. Alan Winters. Cambridge: Cambridge University Press, 1996, 88-124.

Hoekman, Bernard M. and Petros C Mavroidis. "The WTO's Agreement on Government Procurement: Expanding Disciplines, Declining Membership?" In *Public Procurement Law Review 1995*. Edited by Sue Arrowsmith. London: Sweet & Maxwell, 1995, 63-79.

Hopkins, Raymond F. "Developing Countries in the Uruguay Round: Bargaining under Uncertainty and Inequality." In *World Agriculture and the GATT*. Edited by William P. Avery. Boulder: Lynne Rienner, 1993, 143-163.

Hufbauer, Gary Clyde. "Background Paper." In *The Free Trade Debate*. New York: Priority Press, 1989, 37-232.

Josling, Timothy E. "Agriculture and the Next WTO Round." In *The WTO After Seattle*. Edited by Jeffrey J. Schott. Washington: Institute for International Economics, 2000: 91-117.

Josling, Timothy E., Fred H. Sanderson, and T.K. Warley. "The Future of International Agricultural Relations: Issues in the GATT Negotiations." In *Agricultural*

Protectionism in the Industrialized World. Edited by Fred H. Sanderson. Washington: Resources for the Future, 1990, 433-464.

Kahler, Miles. "Multilateralism with Small and Large Numbers." In *Multilateralism Matters: The Theory and Praxis of and Institutional Form*. Edited John Gerard Ruggie. New York: Columbia University Press, 1993, 295-326.

Kahler, Miles and John Odell. "Developing Country Coalition-Building and International Trade Negotiations." In *Developing Countries and the Global Trading System, vol. 1*. Edited by John Whalley. Ann Arbor: University of Michigan Press, 1989, 149-167.

Kelly, William B., Jr. "Nontariff Barriers." In *Studies in Trade Liberalization*. Edited by Bela Balassa. Baltimore: John Hopkins Press, 1967, 278-284.

Keohane, Robert O. "The Demand for International Regimes." In *International Regimes*. Edited by Stephen D. Krasner. Ithaca: Cornell University Press, 1983, 141-171.

Krasner, Stephen D. "Structural Causes and Regime Consequences: Regimes as Intervening Variables." In *International Regimes*. Edited by Stephen D. Krasner. Ithaca: Cornell University Press, 1983, 1-21.

Lipson, Charles. "The Transformation of Trade: The Sources and Effects of Regime Change." In *International Regimes*. Edited by Stephen D. Krasner. Ithaca: Cornell University Press, 1983, 258-262.

Maizels, Alfred. "Reforming the World Commodity Economy." In *UNCTAD and the South-North Dialogue: The First Twenty Years*. Edited by Michael Zammit Cutajar. Oxford: Pergamon Press, 1988, 101-121.

Mann, Catherine L. and Sarah Cleeland Knight. "Electronic Commerce in the WTO." In *The WTO After Seattle*. Edited by Jeffrey J. Schott. Washington, D.C.: Institute for International Economics, 2000: 253-266.

Moore, John L. "Export Credit Arrangements." In *Emerging Standards of International Trade and Investment*. Edited by Seymour J. Rubin and Gary Clyde Hufbauer. Totowa: Rowman & Allanheld, 1984, 139-173.

Nau, Henry R. "Clinton's Legacy: US Trade Leadership Languishes." In *The World Trade Organization Millenium Round*. Edited by Klaus Günther Deutsch and Bernhard Speyer. London: Routledge, 2001, 245-261.

Nogués, Julio J. "Comment: The Linkages of the World Bank and the GATT/WTO." In *The WTO as an International Organization*. Edited by Anne O. Krueger with Chonira Aturupane. Chicago: University of Chicago Press, 1998, 82-95.

Odell, John and Barry Eichengreen, "The United States, the ITO, and the WTO." In *The WTO as an International Organization*. Edited by Anne O. Krueger with Chonira Aturupane. Chicago: University of Chicago Press, 1998, 181-209.

Ostry, Sylvia. "The WTO and International Governance." In *The World Trade Organization Millenium Round*. Edited by Klaus Günther Deutsch and Bernhard Speyer. London: Routledge, 2001, 285-294.

Otto, Carsten, "'International Regimes' in the Asia-Pacific? The Case of APEC." In *International Relations in the Asia-Pacific*. Edited by Jörn Dosch and Manfred Mols. New York: St. Martin's Press, 2000, 39-66.

Oye, Kenneth A. "Explaining Cooperation Under Anarchy: Hypotheses and Strategies." In *Cooperation Under Anarchy*. Edited by Kenneth A. Oye. Princeton: Princeton University Press, 1986, 1-24.

Paarlberg, Robert L. "Why Agriculture Blocked the Uruguay: Evolving Strategies in a Two-Level Game." In *World Agriculture and the GATT*. Boulder: Lynne Rienner, 1993, 39-54.

Pelkmans, Jacques. "Collective Management and Economic Cooperation." In *Economic Summits and Western Decision-Making*. Edited by Cesare Merlini. London: Croom Helm, 1984, 89-136.

Putnam, Robert. "The Western Economic Summits: A Political Interpretation." In *Economic Summits and Western Decision-Making*. Edited by Cesare Merlini. London: Croom Helm, 1984, 43-88.

Ricupero, Rubens. "Integration of Developing Countries into the Multilateral Trading System." In *The Uruguay Round and Beyond*. Edited by Jagdish Bhagwati and Mathias Hirsch. Ann Arbor: University of Michigan Press, 1998, 9-36.

Sally, Razeen. "Looking Askance at Global Governance." In *Guiding Global Order: G8 Governance in the Twenty-first Century*. Edited by John J. Kirton, Joseph P. Daniels, and Andreas Freytag. Aldershot: Ashgate, 2001, 55-76.

Schnittker, John A. "Reflections on Trade and Agriculture." In *Essays in Honour of Thorkil Kristensen*. Paris: OECD, 1970, 255-274.

Schott, Jeffrey J. "The WTO After Seattle." In *The WTO After Seattle*. Edited by Jeffrey J. Schott. Washington, D.C.: Institute for International Economics, 2000: 3-40.

Schott, Jeffrey J. and Jayashree Watal. "Decision Making in the WTO." In *The WTO After Seattle*. Edited by Jeffrey J. Schott. Washington, D.C.: Institute for International Economics, 2000: 283-292.

Sewell, John W. and I. William Zartman. "Global Negotiations: Path to the Future or Dead-End Street?" In *Power, Passions and Purpose*. Edited by Jagdish N. Bhagwati and John Gerard Ruggie. Cambridge: MIT Press, 1984, 87-124.

Smythe, Elizabeth. "The Multilateral Agreement on Investment: A Charter of Rights for Global Investors or Just Another Agreement?" In *Canada Among Nations 1998 – Leadership and Dialogue*. Edited by Fen Osler Hampson and Maureen Appel Molot. Toronto: Oxford University Press, 1998, 239-266.

Solomon, Anthony M. "A Personal Evaluation." In *Economic Summitry*. Edited by George de Menil and Anthony M. Solomon. New York: Council on Foreign Relations, 1983, 42-54.

Stafford, David. "Wallén, Helsincki, Schaerer et al.: "Some Major Achievements, Some Challenges to Meet." In *The Export Credit Arrangement: Achievements and Challenges 1978-1998*. Paris: OECD, 1998, 45-50.

Ullrich, Heidi K. "Stimulating Trade Liberalisation after Seattle: G7/G8 Leadership in Global Governance." In *New Directions in Global Economic Governance*. Edited by John J. and George M. von Furstenberg. London: Ashgate, 2001, 219-240.

Vernon, Raymond. "The U.S. Government at Bretton Woods and After." In *Bretton Woods – GATT System: Retrospect and Prospect after Fifty Years*. Edited by Orin Kirshner. Armonk: M.E. Sharpe, 1996, 52-69.

Warley, T.K. "Western Trade in Agricultural Products." In *International Economic Relations of the Western World 1959-1971, Vol. 1: Politics and Trade*. Edited by Andrew Shonfield. London: Oxford University Press, 1976, 285-402.

Warley, T.K. "Agriculture in the GATT: A Historical Perspective." In *Agriculture in the Uruguay Round of GATT Negotiations: Implications for Canada's and Ontario's Agrifood Systems*. Guelph: University of Guelph, Department of Agricultural Economics and Business, 1989, 8-13.

Watal, Jayashree. "Developing Countries' Interests in a 'Development Round'." In *The WTO After Seattle*. Edited by Jeffrey Schott. Washington, D.C.: Institute for International Economics, 2000, 71-83.

Whalley, John. "Recent Trade Liberalisation in the Developing World." In *Global Protectionism*. Edited by David Greenaway, Robert C. Hine, Anthony P. O'Brien, and Robert J. Thornton. London: Macmillan, 1991, 225-253.

Wolfe, Robert. "Rendering unto Caesar: How Legal Pluralism and Regime Theory Help in Understanding 'Multiple Centres of Power'." In *Who is Afraid of the State? Canada in a World of Multiple Centres of Power.* Edited by Gordon Smith and Daniel Wolfish. Toronto: University of Toronto Press, forthcoming.

Woolcock, Stephen. "European Trade Policy: Global Pressures and Domestic Constraints." In *Policy-Making in the European Union*. 4th ed. Edited by Helen Wallace and William Wallace. Oxford: Oxford University Press, 2000, 373-400.

Wyndham-White, Eric. "Negotiations in Prospect." In *Toward a New World Trade Policy: The Maidenhead Papers*. Edited in C. Fred Bergsten. Lexington: Heath, 1975, 321-340.

Articles in Journals

Ahn, Dukgeun. "Linkages between International Financial and Trade Institutions: IMF, World Bank and WTO." *Journal of World Trade* 34-4 (2000): 1-35.

Ahnlid, Anders. "Comparing GATT and GATS: Regime Creation under and after Hegemony." *Review of International Political Economy* 3-1 (Spring 1996): 65-94.

Amuzegar, Jahangir. "A Requiem for the North-South Conference." *Foreign Affairs* 56-1 (October 1977): 136-159

Anderson, Kym and Timothy Josling. "The Challenge to Economists of Multilateral Trade Negotiations on Agricultural Protection." *Food Research Institute Studies* 22-3 (1993): 275-303.

Anderson, Kym and Paul Morris. "The Elusive Goal of Agricultural Trade Reform." *Cato Journal* 19-3 (Winter 2000): 385-396.

Bayne, Nicholas. "Making Sense of Western Economic Policies: The Role of the OECD." *The World Today* 43-2 (February 1987): 27-30.

Bhattacharya, Anindya K. "The Influence of the International Secretariat: UNCTAD and Generalized Tariff Preferences." *International Organization* 30-1 (Winter 1976): 75-90.

Bourgeois, J.H.J. "The Tokyo Round Agreements on Technical Barriers and on Government Procurement in International and EEC Perspective." *Common Market Law Review* 19-1 (1982): 5-33.

Burgess, Randolph W. "Problems of Managing in International Institutions." *California Management Review* 5-3 (Spring 1983): 3-12.

Chenery, Hollis. "The Structuralist Approach to Development Policy." *American Economic Review* 65-2 (May, 1975): 310-316.

Cheney, David M. "The OECD Export Credits Agreement." *Finance and Development* 22-3 (September 1985): 35-38.

Cohen, Michael and Thomas Morante. "Elimination of Nontariff Barriers to Trade in Services: Recommendation for Future Negotiations." *Law and Policy in International Business* 13-2 (1981): 495-519.

Colas, Bernard. "The OECD's Legal Influence in a Global Economy." *World Economic Affairs* 1-3 (Spring/Summer 1997): 66-67.

Cooper, Richard N. "Economic Interdependence and Foreign Policy in the Seventies." *World Politics* 24 (January 1972): 159-181.

Corbett, Hugh. "Prospect of Negotiations on International Trade in Services." *Pacific Community* (April 1977): 454-469.

Cowhey, Peter F. and Edward Long. "Testing Theories of Regime Change: Hegemonic Decline or Surplus Capacity?" *International Organization* 37-2 (Spring 1983): 157-188.

Daly, Michael and Hiroaki Kuwahara. "The Impact of the Uruguay Round on Tariff and Non-Tariff Barriers to Trade in the 'Quad'." *World Economy* 21-2 (March 1998): 207-234.

Davies, John and Mariette Maillet. "The Debt Crisis: Perspectives of a Bilateral Donor." *International Journal* 55-2 (Spring 2000): 270-280.

Devos, Serge A. "Service Trade and the OECD." *Journal of Japanese Trade &Industry*, 4 (1984): 16-19.

Drake, William J. and Kalypso Nicolaïdis. "Ideas, Interests and Institutionalization: 'Trade in Services' and the Uruguay Round." *International Organization* 46-1 (Winter 1992): 37-100.

Duff, John M. Jr. "The Outlook for Official Export Credits." *Law and Policy in International Business* 13-4 (1981): 891-959.

Fiaschetti, Joanne. "Technical Analysis of the Government Procurement Agreement." *Law and Policy in International Business* 11 (1979): 1345-1358.

Fitzgerald, Bruce and Terry Monson. "Export Credit and Insurance for Export Promotion." *Finance and Development* 25-4 (December 1988): 53-55.

Frenkel, Orit and Claude G.B. Fontheim. "Export Credits: An International Domestic Legal Analysis." *Law and Policy in International Business* 13-4 (1981): 1069-1088.

Gerster, Richard. "Proposals for Voting Reform within the International Monetary Fund." *Journal of World Trade* 27-3 (June 1993): 121-136.

Goldstein, Judith. "Ideas, Institutions, and American Trade Policy." *International Organization* 42-1 (Winter 1988): 179-217.

Graz, Jean-Christophe. "The Political Economy of International Trade: The Relevance of the International Trade Organization Project." *Journal of International Relations and Development* 2-3 (September 1999): 288-306.

Green, Randy. "The Uruguay Round Agreement on Agriculture." *Law and Policy in International Business* 31-3 (Spring 2000): 819-839.

Gross Stein, Janice. "Getting to the Table: Processes of International Prenegotiation." *International Journal* 44-2 (Spring 1989): 231-236.

Grunberg, Isabelle. "Exploring the 'Myth' of Hegemonic Stability." *International Organization* 44-4 (Autumn 1990): 431-477.

Haas, Peter M. "Do Regimes Matter? Epistemic Communities and Mediterranean Pollution Control." *International Organization* 43-3 (Summer 1989): 377-403.

Haas, Peter M. "Introduction: Epistemic Communities and International Policy Coordination." *International Organization* 46-1 (Winter 1992): 1-35.

Hamilton, Colleen and John Whalley. "Coalitions in the Uruguay Round." *Weltwirtschaftliches* 125-3 (1989): 547-561.

Higgott, Richard A. and Andrew Fenton Cooper. "Middle Power Leadership and Coalition Building: Australia, the Cairns Group, and the Uruguay Round of Trade Negotiations." *International Organization* 44-4 (Autumn 1990): 589-632.

Hirschman, Albert O. "The Political Economy of Import-Substituting Industrialization in Latin America." *Quarterly Journal of Economics* 82-1 (February 1968): 1-32.

Houck, James P. "U.S. Agricultural Trade and the Tokyo Round." *Law and Policy in International Business* 12-1 (1980): 265-295.

Huntington, Samuel. "The U.S. – Decline or Renewal?" *Foreign Affairs* 67-2 (Winter 1988-89): 76-96.

Kessie, Edwini Kwame. "Developing Countries and the World Trade Organization: What Has Changed?" *World Competition* 22-2 (June 1999): 83-110.

Kirton, John. "The Diplomacy of Concert: Canada, the G7 and the Halifax Summit." *Canadian Foreign Policy* 3-1 (Spring 1995): 63-80.

Knapp, Lawrence A. "The Buy American Act: A Review and Assessment." *Columbia Law Review* 61 (1961): 430-462.

Krasner, Stephen D. "The Tokyo Round: Particularistic Interests and Prospects for Stability in the Global Trading System." *International Studies Quarterly* 23-4 (December 1979): 491-531.

Lavelle, Kathryn C. "Ideas within a Context of Power: The African Group in an Evolving UNCTAD." *Journal of Modern African Studies* 39-1 (2001): 25-50.

"Lori's War." *Foreign Policy* no. 118 (Spring 2000): 28-55.

Macdonald, Donald S, The Honourable. "The Multilateral Trade Negotiations – A Lawyer's Perspective." *Canadian Business Journal* 4 (1979-80): 139-162.

Marceau, Gabrielle, and Peter N. Pedersen. "Is the WTO Open and Transparent? A Discussion of the Relationship of the WTO with Non-governmental Organisations and Civil Society's Claims for More Transparency and Public Participation." *Journal of World Trade* 33-1 (1999): 5-49.

Marshall, Peter. "Whatever Happened to the NIEO?" *The Round Table* Issue 331 (July 1994): 331-339.

McRae, D.M. and J.C. Thomas. "The GATT and Multilateral Treaty Making: The Tokyo Round." *American Journal of International Law* 77 (January 1983): 51-83.

Meier, Gerald M. "The Tokyo Round of Multilateral Trade Negotiations and the Developing Countries." *Cornell International Law Journal* 13-2 (Summer 1980): 239-256.

Meyer, John W., David John Frank, Ann Hironaka, Evan Schofer, and Nancy Brandon Tuma. "The Structuring of a World Environmental Regime, 1870-1990." *International Organization* 51-4 (Autumn 1997): 623-651.

Moravcsik, Andrew M. "Disciplining Trade Finance: The OECD Export Credit Arrangement." *International Organization* 43-1 (Winter 1989): 173-205.

Owada, Hisashi. "A Japanese Perspective on the Role and Future of the G-7." *International Spectator* 29-2 (April-June 1994): 95-112.

Pangestu, Mari. "Special and Differential Treatment in the Millennium: Special for Whom and How Different?" *World Economy* 23-9 (September 2000): 1285-1302.

Pomeranz, Morton. Toward a New International Order in Government Procurement." *Law and Policy in International Business* 11 (1979): 1263-1300.

Putnam, Robert D. "Diplomacy and Domestic Politics: The Logic of Two-Level Games." *International Organization* 42 (Summer 1998): 427-460.

Ray, John E. "The OECD 'Consensus' on Export Credits." *The World Economy* 9-3 (September 1986): 295-309.

Reforming World Agricultural Trade. A Policy Statement by Twenty-Nine Professionals from Seventeen Countries. Washington, D.C.: Institute for International Economics, and Canada: Institute for Research on Public Policy, May 1988.

Robertson, David. "Civil Society and the WTO." *World Economy* 23-9 (September 2000): 1119-1134.

Russett, Bruce. "The Mysterious Case of Vanishing Hegemony: or Is Mark Twain Really Dead?" *International Organization* 41-4 (Autumn 1987): 207-231.

Sapir, André. "The General Agreement on Trade in Services: From 1994 to the Year 2000." *Journal of World Trade* 33-1 (1999): 51-66.

Scholte, Jan Aart with Robert O'Brien and Marc Williams. "The WTO and Civil Society." *Journal of World Trade* 33-1 (February 1999): 107-123.

Shelp, Ronald K. "Trade in Services." *Foreign Policy* 65 (Winter 1986): 64-84.

Shonfield, Andrew. "Can The Western Economic System Stand The Strain?" *The World Today* 32-5 (May 1976): 164-172.

Singer, Hans W. "The Distribution of Gains Between Investing and Borrowing Countries." *American Economic Review* 4-2 (May 1950): 473-485.

Snidal, Duncan. "The Limits of Hegemonic Stability Theory." *International Organization* 39-4 (Autumn 1985): 579-614.

Steinberg, Richard H. "Great Power Management of the World Trading System: A Transatlantic Strategy for Liberal Multilateralism." *Law and Policy in International Business* 29-2 (1998): 205-256.

Stiglitz, Joseph E. "Two Principles for the Next Round or, How to Bring Developing Countries in from the Cold." *World Economy* 23-4 (April 2000): 437-454.

Strange, Susan. "The Persistent Myth of Lost Hegemony." *International Organization* 41-4 (Autumn 1987): 551-574.

Tangerman, Stefan, T.E. Josling and Scott Pearson. "Multilateral Negotiations on Farm-Support Levels." *World Economy* 10-3 (September 1987): 265-281.

Taylor, Ian. "The Cairns Group and the Commonwealth: Bridge-Building for International Trade." *Round Table* 355-1 (2000): 375-386.

Trionfetti, Federico. "Discriminatory Public Procurement and International Trade." *World Economy* 23-1 (January 2000): 57-76.

Tyers, Rod. "The Cairns Group and the Uruguay Round of International Trade Negotiations." *Australian Economic Review* 93-101 (1993): 49-60.

VanGrasstek, Craig. "Is the Fast Track Really Necessary." *Journal of World Trade* 31-2 (April 1997): 97-123.

Vernon, Raymond. "Organizing for World Trade." *International Conciliation* 505 (November 1955): 163-222.

Walters, Robert S. "UNCTAD: Intervener Between Poor and Rich States." *Journal of World Trade Law* 7-5 (September/ October 1973): 527-554.

Warley, T.K. "Issues Facing Agriculture in the GATT Negotiations." *Canadian Journal of Agricultural Economics* 35 (1987): 515-534.

Wellenstein, E.P. "Unity, Community, Union – What's in a Name?" *Common Market Law Review* 29-2 (1992): 205-212.

Whalley, John, "Special and Differential Treatment in the Millennium Round." *World Economy* 22-8 (November 1999): 1065-1093.

Whyman, William E. "We Can't Go On Meeting Like This: Revitalizing the G-7 Process." *Washington Quarterly* 18-3 (Summer 1995): 139-165.

Winham, Gilbert R. "The Prenegotiation Phase of the Uruguay Round." *International Journal* 44-2 (Spring 1989): 280-303.

Winham, Gilbert R. "The World Trade Organization: Institution-Building in the Multilateral Trade System." *The World Economy* 21-3 (May 1998): 349-368.

Wolfe, Robert. "Global Trade as a Single Undertaking: The Role of Ministers in the WTO." *International Journal* 51-4 (Autumn 1996): 690-709.

Wolff, Alan W, Ambassador. "The Larger Political and Economic Role of the Tokyo Round." *Law and Policy in International Business* 12-1 (1980): 1-19.

Young, Oran R. "International Regimes: Toward a New Theory of Institutions," *World Politics* 39 (October 1986): 104-122.

Zamora, Stephen. "Voting in International Economic Organizations." *American Journal of International Law* 74-3 (July 1980): 566-608.

Zartman, William I. "Prenegotiation: Phases and Functions." *International Journal* 44-2 (Spring 1989): 237-253.

Unpublished Works

Ullrich, Heidi. *The Impact of Policy Networks in the GATT Uruguay Round: The Case of the US-EC Agricultural Negotiations.* Unpublished thesis. London School of Economics. London, UK, 2002.

Ullrich, Heidi. *Trade Liberalization and Leadership: Challenges for the Doha Development Agenda and Lessons Learned from the Uruguay Round.* Paper presented at German Council on Foreign Relations Conference. Berlin, 28 January 2002.

Wolfe, Robert. *The Making of the Peace, 1993. The OECD in Canadian Economic Diplomacy.* International Economic Relations Division. External Affairs and International Trade Canada. Centre for International Relations: Queen's University, October 1993.

Government Publications

Atlantic Council of the United States. *GATT Plus – A Proposal for Trade Reform.* Report of the Special Advisory Panel to the Trade Committee of the Atlantic Council. New York: Praeger, 1975.

Commission on International Trade and Investment. *United States International Economic Policy in an Interdependent World.* Report Submitted to the President. Washington, D.C.: July 1971.

Hecker, JayEtta Z. *Observations on the Ministerial Meeting in Singapore.* Statement before the U.S. House of Representatives Subcommittee on Trade, Committee on Ways and Means. U.S. General Accounting Office, GAO/T-NSIAD-97-92.

Kohler, Daniel F. and Peter H. Reuter. *Honor Among Nations: Enforcing the 'Gentlemen's Agreement' on Export Credits.* RAND Note N-2536-USDP prepared for the Office of the Under Secretary of Defense for Policy, December 1986.

United States. Senate Committee on Finance. *MTN and the Legal Institutions of International Trade.* Report Prepared at the Request of the Subcommittee on International Trade. Washington, D.C.: Government Printing Office, June 1979.

International Organisation Publications

Food and Agriculture Organization. *FAO Principles of Surplus Disposal and Consultative Obligations of Member Nations.* 2nd edition. Rome: FAO, 1980.

General Agreement on Tariffs and Trade. *Trends in International Trade.* Report by a Panel of Experts. Geneva: GATT, 1958.

General Agreement on Tariffs and Trade. *Differential and More Favourable Treatment*

Reciprocity and Fuller Participation of Developing Countries. Decision of 28 November 1979, GATT document L/4903.

General Agreement on Tariffs and Trade. *The Tokyo Round of Multilateral Trade Negotiations.* Report by the Director-General of GATT. Geneva: GATT, 1979.

General Agreement on Tariffs and Trade. *Trade Policies for a Better Future: Proposals for Action.* Geneva: GATT, March 1985.

General Agreement on Tariffs and Trade. *Text of the General Agreement.* Geneva: GATT, 1986.

General Agreement on Tariffs and Trade. *The Texts of the Tokyo Round Agreements.* Geneva: GATT, 1986.

General Agreement on Tariffs and Trade. *Report on the Uruguay Round.* Trade Negotiations Committee. MTN.TNC/W.113, 13 July 1993.

International Bank for Reconstruction and Development. *Articles of Agreement,* as amended effective February 16, 1989. Washington, D.C.: IBRD, 1991.

International Monetary Fund. *Articles of Agreement.* Washington, D.C.: IMF, 1993.

Organisation for Economic Co-operation and Development. *Convention on the Organisation for Economic Co-operation and Development.* Paris: OECD, 14 December 1960.

Organisation for Economic Co-operation and Development. *Government Purchasing in Europe, North America and Japan: Regulations and Procedures.* Paris: OECD, 1966.

Organisation for Economic Co-operation and Development. *Policy Perspectives for International Trade and Economic Relations.* Report by the High Level Group on Trade and Related Problems to the Secretary-General of OECD. Paris: OECD, 1972.

Organisation for Economic Co-operation and Development. *Government Purchasing: Regulations and Procedures of OECD Member Countries.* Paris: OECD, 1976.

Organisation for Economic Co-operation and Development. *Problems of Agricultural Trade.* Paris: OECD, 1982.

Organisation for Economic Co-operation and Development. *Elements of a Conceptual Framework for Trade in Services.* Paris: OECD, 1987.

Organisation for Economic Co-operation and Development. *National Policies and Agricultural Trade.* Paris: OECD, 1987.

Organisation for Economic Co-operation and Development. *The OECD and Agricultural Trade Analysis: Recent History, Possible Future Directions.* OECD Workshop on Emerging Trade Issues in Agriculture, COM/AGR/CA/TD/TC/WS(98)109,16 October 1998.

Organisation for European Economic Co-operation. *A Decade of Co-operation: Achievements and Perspectives.* 9th Report of the OEEC. Paris: OEEC, 1958.

United Nations Conference on Trade and Development. *Services and the Development Process.* Study by the UNCTAD Secretariat. New York: United Nations, 1985.

United Nations Conference on Trade and Development. *Towards a New Trade Policy for Development.* Report by the Secretary-General of the UNCTAD. New York: United Nations, 1964.

World Bank. *Global Economic Prospects and the Developing Countries – 2001.* World Bank Report no. 21596, 31 December 2000.

World Trade Organization. *The Results of the Uruguay Round of Multilateral Trade Negotiations: The Legal Texts.* Geneva: WTO, 1995.

World Trade Organization Secretariat. *Guide to Uruguay Round Agreements.* The Hague: Kluwer Law International, 1999.

Internet Sources

Bayne, Nicholas. "First Thoughts on the Okinawa Summit, 21-23 July 2000." http://www.g7.utoronto.ca/g7/evaluations/2000okinawa/bayne.html

Bayne, Nicholas. "Impressions of the Denver Summit." http://www.g7.utoronto.ca/g7/evaluations/1997denver/impression/agenda.html

Bayne, Nicholas. "Impressions of the Genoa Summit, 20-22 July 2001." (Final Version, 28 July) http://www.g7.utoronto.ca/g7/evaluations/2001genoa/assess_summit_bayne.html

Hainsworth, Susan. "The Coming of Age: The European Community and the Economic Summit." http://www.g7.utoronto.ca/g7/scholar/hainsworth1990/bispre.html

Hajnal, Peter I. "Personal Assessment of the Role of Civil Society at the 2001 Genoa G8 Summit." http://www.g7.utoronto.ca/g7/evaluations/2001genoa/assess_summit_hajnal.html

Kirton, John. "Prospects for the Year 2000 Okinawa G7/G8 Summit." http://www.g7.utoronto.ca/g7/evaluations/2000okinawa/prospects.html

Kokotsis, Ella, John Kirton, and Diana Juricevic. "Commitments from the G7 Statement, Okinawa, July 21, 2000: The G7/G8 Commitments Report." http://www.g7.utoronto.ca/g7/conferences/2001/rome/conflictPrevention.pdf

Ullrich, Heidi and Michael Malleson. "Issue Performance Assessment – Trade" for the G8 2001 Genoa Summit? http://www.g7.utoronto.ca/g7/evaluations/2001genoa/assessment_trade.html

Index

1974 U.S. Trade Act – See United States
1978 Arrangement – See export credit
1982 GATT ministerial – See General
    Agreement on Tariffs and Trade
    (GATT)

additionality 45
Aggregate Measurement of Support – See
    agriculture
Agreement on Agriculture – See GATT
    Uruguay Round
Agreement on Government Procurement or
    Government Procurement Agreement
    (GPA) – See government procurement
Agricultural Trade Development Assistance
    Act or Public Law 480 (PL 480) – See
    United States
agriculture
    Aggregate Measurement of Support
      184
    agricultural export subsidies 138, 147,
      177, 178, 189, 190, 221, 226, 234,
      264
    agricultural products 45, 58, 60, 61,
      103, 105, 112, 148, 152, 189, 224
    agricultural trade 7, 21, 39, 40, 45, 59,
      64, 131, 141, 147, 148, 149, 150,
      151, 152, 153, 159, 171, 173, 174,
      177, 178, 179, 181, 183, 184, 185,
      187, 189, 191, 192, 203, 219, 221,
      224, 226, 257, 264, 279, 290, 291,
      294
    Blair House Accord 172, 203, 204, 208
    consumer subsidy equivalents (CSEs)
      152, 159, 184
    producer subsidy equivalents (PSEs)
      152, 159, 184
aid credits – See export credit
Andreissen, Frans 181

Anti-Dumping Code 86
anti-dumping duties 245
Arrangement on Guidelines for Officially
    Supported Export Credits (1978) – See
    export credit
Articles of Agreement – See International
    Monetary Fund; World Bank
Associated African States and Madagascar
    (AASM) 50
Association of Southeast Asian Nations
    (ASEAN) 213, 216
Atlantic Council 18, 19
Australia 13, 19, 24, 42, 45, 62, 68, 102,
    137, 168, 169, 171, 184, 189, 219, 264

balance of payments 10, 13, 37, 38, 41, 43,
    48, 59, 69, 72, 77, 91, 100, 104, 190
balance of trade 68, 83, 94, 158, 282
    balance of trade deficit 9, 76, 83, 130,
      140, 144, 149, 215, 281
    balance of trade surplus 83
Barshefsky, Charlene 247
Bayne, Nicholas 24, 88, 130
Bensch, Alexandra 155, 199
Berne Union – See export credit
Blair House Accord – See agriculture
Brazil 76, 105, 141, 153, 154, 169, 171,
    172, 188, 189, 201, 206, 212, 213, 216
Bretton Woods system 93
Britain 9, 12, 14, 15, 35, 41, 47, 57, 58, 61,
    65, 70, 83, 88, 91, 92, 93, 95, 96, 98,
    100, 113, 127, 130, 131, 132, 173, 206,
    208, 249, 281
Brittan, Leon 200, 212, 215, 231, 247, 283
Brock, William 125, 135
Brussels ministerial (1990) – See GATT
    Uruguay Round
Bush, George 168, 180, 206, 233, 247
Buy American Act – See United States